Crystal Reports .NET Programming

Brian Bischof

D1565580

Crystal Reports .NET Programming

Copyright © 2004 Brian Bischof

ISBN (pbk):0-9749536-5-2

First Edition: February, 2004

2nd Printing: August, 2004

Printed in the United States of America

Resellers and distributors can contact Brian Bischof directly. Contact information is at www.CrystalReportsBook.com.

The source code for this book is available at www.CrystalReportsBook.com.

Dedicated to my nephews and nieces Jason Luker, Jessica Luker, Brittani Loeser and Bradley Loeser. You guys are my first priority when I come home to visit. Its always fun spending time with you and you are the highlight of my trips. I love you all.

Table of Contents

Acknowledgements

Thanks to my best friend John McHugh for his support when I was working on this book. He graciously let me spend months working on his backyard deck enjoying the canyon view while I wrote the book. We've also taken many trips together while I was writing the book (diving in Malaysia and the Caribbean, skiing in California, and partying in Cancun). Even though I took my laptop everywhere, he never complained.

Jackie Zhang and Amy Kelly were incredibly helpful. They edited some of the chapters in the book and found a lot of corrections that I missed. I really appreciate all the time they took to help me out.

Mike Curtis again came to my rescue and took care of all client emergencies while I was working on the book. His diligence let me focus on finishing the book and not stress over any problems that had cropped up.

Brian Madden is a best-selling self-publisher of Citrix books (see www.BrianMadden.com). He gave me a lot of advice about the self-publishing process and got me over the hurdles.

Lastly, I want to thank Gary Cornell and Karen Watterson of Apress for supporting this book during its early stages. Unfortunately, the economy's downturn caused Apress to cancel my contract. But it was great that they got me started. They also connected me with Ryan Marples and Mandeep Jassal at Crystal Decisions. Prior to the book contract being cancelled, Ryan was the technical reviewer on the book and gave me insight on how to present information to the reader. Mandeep provided daily technical support and came to my rescue many times with his advice and in-depth knowledge. He is a true Crystal Reports .NET guru.

About the Author

Brian Bischof, CPA, MCSD is the author of, "The .NET Languages: A Quick Translation Guide" (Apress, ISBN 1-893115-48-8) and the President of DotNet Tech, Inc.

Brian discovered a marketing niche early in his career; many software consultants were adequate working with software applications but did not understand or know the corporate language to discover a company's true needs. Contrarily, business managers knew that they wanted to improve their business processes but did not know how to communicate this information to a computer "tech". After spending years developing software and working as an auditor and consultant at Arthur Andersen, Brian created a software development and training firm that provides a unique merger of business expertise and technical knowledge using Microsoft's .NET technologies.

DotNet Tech, Inc. provides custom software solutions and corporate training in a continually fluctuating industry. Brian understands that the end product is not the software provided, but a level of commitment to its customers to support the ongoing technical changes a company experiences. He has trained programmers from many Fortune 500 companies including Intel, Hewlett-Packard, and Toshiba.

You can learn more about the author and DotNet Tech, Inc. by visiting the company's website at www.DotNetTech.com.

PREFACE

With the release of Visual Studio .NET, Microsoft gave programmers the first powerful report writing tool that is completely integrated into the development environment. Crystal Reports has been included with previous versions of Visual Studio in the past, but never with this degree of integration. Programmers can now build a powerful reporting solution using the standard Visual Studio installation.

The one piece of the puzzle that is still missing is a solid set of documentation on how to use Crystal Reports .NET to create a sophisticated reporting solution. The help files are great, but they don't hold your hand and walk you through the various steps to be productive. Prior to this book being printed, all the Crystal Reports books available have focused their attention on the end user and treated programmers as they were an after-thought. Finding useful code is like looking for a needle in a haystack. This is the first and only book on the market written by a professional software developer for other software developers. Within these pages you will find countless code listings to make every code-junkie happy. Beginning programmers and advanced programmers alike will find that this book meets their needs.

Who this Book Is For

This book is for programmers that are new to Crystal Reports as well as programmers that are experienced with Crystal Reports. If you are new to Crystal Reports, you will be shown how easy it is to quickly create your first report and add it to your project. As you want to learn more reporting features you can turn to the appropriate chapter and see how easy it is to make your reports more professional. If you are experienced with Crystal Reports, you will be interested in learning what the .NET version of Crystal Reports lets you do as well as what its limitations are. Learning how to perform runtime report customization will let you take your reporting solution to the next level.

How the Book is Organized

This book is divided into two parts: Part I - Designing Reports and Part II - Programming Reports. Each part is designed for two different types of report development.

Part I - Designing Reports is for the user who has either never used Crystal Reports before or has used a previous version and wants to get up to speed on the .NET version. It walks you through the steps of creating reports using the report designer. You are also shown how to add sophistication to your reports by learning how to program with Crystal Syntax and Basic Syntax.

Part II - Programming Reports is for the advanced programmer who has mastered the art of designing reports and wants to take their reports to the next level by customizing them during runtime. You will learn the intricacies of how the Crystal Reports object model is designed. This lets you take control of the report during runtime. Unlike Part I which is focused on using the Report Designer, Part II focuses on writing code with either VB.NET or C#.

Which Language: VB.NET or C#?

One thing that makes .NET so interesting is the fact that VB.NET and C# are almost equal. Choosing the programming language used on a project becomes more of personal decision rather than a technological decision. However, this really complicates things for the authors of .NET books. When planning a new book, it seems that one of the biggest decisions a publishing company makes is deciding which language to focus on.[1] From the many book reviews I've read, no one is ever happy with the decision. In this book, I've decided to use both languages, but do it in a way that hasn't been done yet.

I decided not to put the different languages side by side within the chapter like other publishers are doing because I feel this makes a chapter hard to read and requires your eyes to jump around too much.

The last option I considered was to create a separate edition of the book for each language. Unfortunately, this isn't practical because I'm self-publishing and printing one version of the book is very expensive. Printing two editions is not an option. Of course, if you tell all your colleagues to buy this book and tell the company you work for to buy everyone a copy, then I'll see sales skyrocket and I won't hesitate to create a seperate edition for each language.[2] ☺

The body of each chapter shows sample code written in VB.NET. I feel that VB.NET is easy enough to read that C# programmers will quickly understand the code and the chapter is still effective. If I wrote the sample code in C#, I worry that a lot of VB.NET programmers will get stuck trying to understand the syntax. This misses the point of learning how to use Crystal Reports.

---

[1] I worked on a book for Wrox where halfway through the project they decided that everyone should switch the examples from C# to VB.NET. Arghh!

[2] I can always dream… Seriously, if I can just sell enough copies to break even on this project then I'll be delighted.

However, I certainly don't want the C# programmers to think that they were forgotten. In fact, when I had this book available online as a free ebook I didn't have any C# code listed because I didn't have time to finish it. I got many(!) emails from C# programmers saying that they really needed the C# code to implement the examples. To make sure everyone is happy, the C# code is listed at the end of each chapter. The listing numbers match the VB.NET listings so that it is easy to find the one you need.

Part I of the book focuses on designing reports and doesn't have any C# code listed. The few examples in VB.NET are very trivial and easy to understand. Part II of the book focuses on advanced runtime report customization and every chapter has C# code listed at the end.

> Shameless Plug: If you are looking for a book that shows
> you how to convert code between VB.NET and C#, my first
> book, "The .NET Languages" gives you tables of side-by-
> side syntax comparisons. It's easy to take code written in
> either language and convert it to the other language.
> (Apress, ISBN 1893115488)

All the examples in this book declare object variables using the fully qualified class name. This lets you see the namespaces that are used to reference a class. When learning a new object model, it's easy to get confused as to which namespace a class belongs to. The downside of doing this is that it can make the variable declarations very long and harder to understand. It is often hard to fit the entire namespace on a single line in the book. This requires putting the remainder of the namespace on the next line. In VB.NET this isn't syntactically correct. In your own applications I suggest that you either use the VB.NET Imports statement or the C# using statement to reference the namespaces directly. This will make your code easier to write.

Installing Crystal Reports

Crystal Reports for .NET is included with Visual Studio .NET. When you install Visual Studio .NET it is one of the tools installed by default. After installation, Crystal Reports is listed as one of the components that can be added to a project.

Crystal Reports for .NET is not included in the VB.NET or C# Standard versions. You need to purchase one of the Visual Studio .NET packages to get Crystal Reports.

Installing Service Packs

If you look at the Crystal Decisions support site for .NET, you'll see that there are dozens of known bugs with the product. As a result, Crystal Decisions is always making corrections and improvements to the product. It is critical that you go to their website on a regular basis to check for new downloads. In fact, you should put down the book right now and install the lastest service packs.

There are two types of downloads available: Service Packs and Hot Fixes. Service packs are released every six months. They include comprehensive bug fixes and additional features. Service packs have also been regression tested. Hot fixes are released at the beginning of each month. They include minor bug fixes and have not been as thoroughly tested as service packs.

Make sure you download the proper service pack for your version of Visual Studio. Service packs with a prefix of "CR10" are for Visual Studio 2002. Service packs with a prefix of "CR11" are for Visual Studio 2003.

Service Packs: http://support.CrystalDecisions.com/ServicePacks

Hot Fixes: http://support.CrystalDecisions.com/hot_fix_application_guide/

Grammatical Errors

In the first printing of this book, I made a comment that the book was completely self-edited and I apologized for any grammatical errors that I may have overlooked. Consequently, I got some bad reviews on Amazon.com that the book had too many grammatical errors. After reading these bad reviews, my mom took a copy of the book and started making it up. Even though she didn't understand any of what I wrote, she meticulously read every single page and found every typo in the book. Because of her, this second printing is as perfect as it's going to get. Thanks, Mom! You're the best.

Download the Sample Code

The sample code for this book can be found at www.CrystalReportsBook.com.

Questions and Comments

Please email me your questions and comments to Comments@CrystalReportsBook.com. I can't respond to every email individually, but I will post new information on the book's website. Any comments about the book will be used to improve the 2nd edition that will come out for the next version of .NET.

PART I
Designing Reports

Learn how easy it is to design your first report and integrate it into a .NET application. After designing a couple sample reports for both Windows and ASP.NET, you begin to understand report layouts and adding new report objects. You'll quickly move beyond the report wizards and create reports using grouping and sorting, running totals, and subreports. If you want to perform dynamic formatting of report objects, learn how to program in Basic syntax or Crystal syntax. This chapter takes you from being a novice to intermediate report designer.

The code samples in Part I are deliberately kept simple so you can focus on learning how to design professional looking reports. When you're ready to tackle .NET runtime customization with VB.NET or C#, move to Part II of the book.

This page intentionally left blank

Introducing Crystal Reports

Visual Studio .NET is the first Windows development environment that gives developers a fully integrated and robust reporting solution. Crystal Reports is now installed with Visual Studio so developers can write applications that have reports seamlessly integrated into them. Starting with Visual Basic 3.0, Crystal Reports was included with the language, but not part of the default installation. It was also a stand-alone product that was independent of the programming language.

Over the years Microsoft has been including Crystal Reports with each version of Visual Basic. With version 6 they even wrote a Data Report component that was supposed to be a replacement for Crystal Reports. But it failed miserably.

With the release of Visual Studio.NET, Microsoft finally woke up to the needs of developers. They licensed Crystal Decisions to write a version of Crystal Reports to be the default reporting solution installed with .NET.[3] Built into the IDE, Windows developers now have the tools to write presentation-quality interactive reports.

Creating Your First Report

Before you learn about all the features of Crystal Reports, it is best to start by creating a quick report. Open Visual Studio and create a new project. This can be either VB.NET or C#, and it can be either a Windows Application or ASP.NET. Designing reports with Crystal Reports is independent of the application type. The following steps are the same for both types of applications.

Once the project is open, select Project | Add New Item. This displays the list of available templates. Scroll down near the bottom and select the Crystal Report template. Enter the name "Employee List". Figure 1-1 shows this dialog box for a Windows Application. Click Open to create the report.

---

[3] Crystal Reports for .NET is a set of Runtime Callable Wrappers (RCW) around modified Crystal Reports 8.5 DLLs. They have been modified to support the Crystal Reports 9/10 file formats.

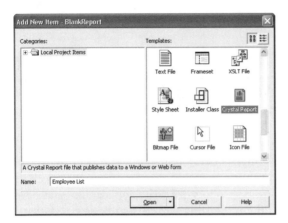

Figure 1-1. The Add New Item dialog box.

When the Crystal Report Gallery dialog box appears, accept the defaults of "Use Report Expert" and "Standard Report". This opens the Standard Report Expert shown in Figure 1-2.

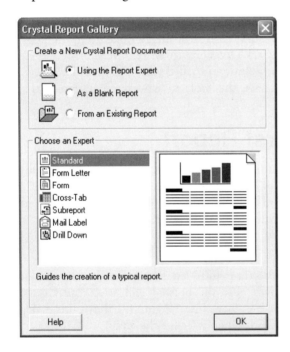

Figure 1-2. The Standard Report Expert dialog box.

The first tab shown is the Data tab. Select the Xtreme Sample Database (it comes with Crystal Reports) by clicking on the OLE DB(ADO) option in the Available Data Sources list. This brings up a new dialog box. Select Microsoft Jet 4.0 OLE DB Provider. On the next dialog box enter the database name (database name is the fully qualified file path). By default it is located at C:\Program Files\Microsoft Visual Studio .NET\Crystal Reports\Samples\Database. Select Finish.

You are back at the Data tab of the expert. Click on the Tables node to expand and double-click on the Employee table name (or drag and drop it) to move it to the window titled Tables In Report. Click Next.

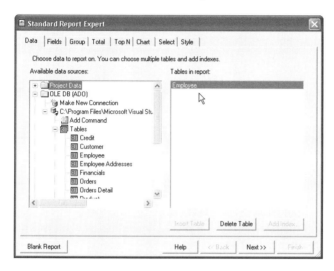

Figure 1-3. The Data tab of the report expert.

To display fields on the report, you have to select them at the Fields tab. Double click on the following fields to add them to the right window: Employee ID, Last Name, and Hire Date. This is shown in Figure 1-4.

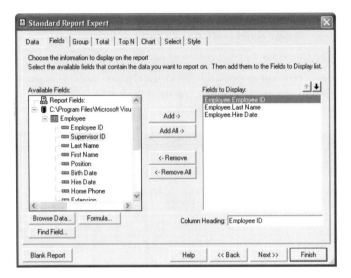

Figure 1-4. The Fields tab of the report expert.

At this point you could continue with the report expert to do things such as grouping and selecting which records to print. But for this simple example, ignore those tabs and click on the Style tab. Enter the title Employee List and keep the default style of Standard. Click Finish.

The report expert closes and builds a fully functioning report that is ready to run (Figure 1-5). If this report were to be used in a real application, the next step would be to modify the form so that it can preview and print the report.

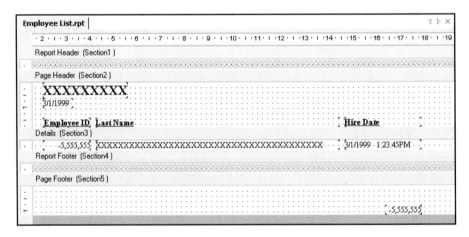

Figure 1-5. Employee List report file.

Previewing with a Windows Form

After creating the Employee List report in the previous section, you can preview it using either a Windows Form or an ASP.NET application. This section shows you how to preview it from a Windows Form. ASP.NET is covered in the next section.

Previewing the report requires modifying the form. When you created the new project, Form1 should have been automatically added to the project for you. Open Form1 in design mode and add a CrystalReportViewer control to it. This is normally listed as the last component in the Windows Forms section of the Toolbox. Resize the viewer so that it fills up the entire form. Do this by finding its Dock property and clicking on the drop-down box. Click on the middle square so that the property is set to Fill.

The viewer control has many ways to preview reports.[4] This example uses the ReportDocument component because it is the easiest of the choices. Add the ReportDocument component to the form by double-clicking on it from the Componets section of the Toolbox. A Choose a ReportDocument dialog box automatically appears, allowing you to select which report to display. The dropdown control lists all the reports that are part of your project. For this example, it only shows the Employee List report.

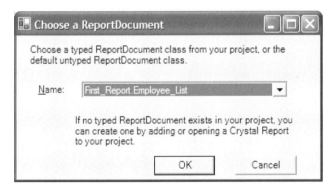

Figure 1-6. The ReportDocument dialog box.

Select the Employee List report and click the OK button. This adds the ReportDocument component to your form.

You have to tell the viewer that the report it is going to preview is in the ReportDocument component. Look at the Properties Window and find the ReportSource property. It has a dropdown control which lists the

---

[4] Chapter 3 gives a complete explanation of using the viewer control.

ReportDocument components on the form. In this example, the Employee List will be the only one listed. Click on the Employee_List component to select it.

Run the application. When the form loads it automatically instantiates the Employee List report object and displays it using the viewer. Print it by clicking on the printer button in the menu bar. The preview of the Employee List report is shown in Figure 1-6.

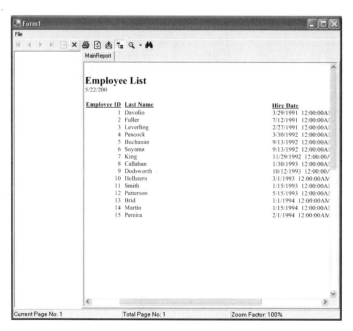

Figure 1-6. Employee List report output in preview mode.

You can see that this quick report isn't perfect. The Hire Date column shows times as always being 12:00:00 AM and the Group Tree is visible even though there aren't any groups in the report. As is usually the case, the report expert gives you a good basis for writing a report, but you still need to make some changes to clean it up.

Previewing with ASP.NET

Previewing a report with ASP.NET requires adding a CrystalReportViewer control to the web page and setting its data bindings. Open the default web page in design mode and add a viewer control to it. The viewer is located near the end of the Toolbox under the Web Forms tab. Once you add it to the form you will see a medium sized rectangle on the web page.

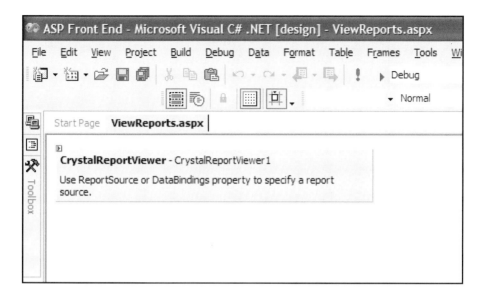

Figure 1-7. The ASP.NET report viewer control.

Notice that the web viewer control looks totally different than the Windows viewer control. The web viewer is simply a placeholder for where the report will be displayed.

Add a ReportDocument component to the web page by double-clicking on the ReportDocument component. The ReportDocument component is listed in the Components section of the Toolbox. As mention in the previous section, when you add a ReportDocument component to your form, it automatically displays the Choose a ReportDocument dialog box. This lets you select which report will be displayed. The dropdown control lists all the reports that are part of your project. For this example, it will only show the Employee List report.

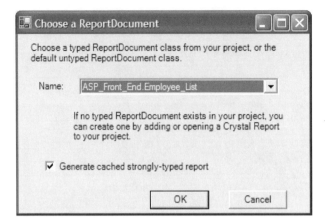

Figure 1-8. The ReportDocument dialog box.

Select the Employee List report and click the OK button. This adds the ReportDocument component to your form.

You have to associate the ReportDocument component with the viewer control so that the viewer knows which report to display. Look at the viewer's properties and at the very top is the DataBindings property. Click on it and then click on the ellipses button to open the DataBindings dialog box.

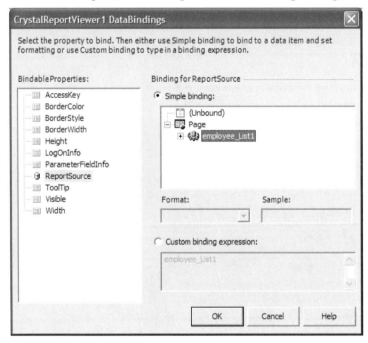

Click on the ReportSource property listed on the left. Expand the Page item in the Simple Binding window. It shows you the reports that were added to the page using the ReportDocument components. In this example, only the Employee List report is shown.

Click on the Employee List report item and click the OK button. A preview of the report is immediately displayed. Unlike Windows development, the viewer control shows you what the report looks like while you are in design mode. This is a great feature for web developers!

At this point, you've performed all the same steps that were shown during the previous example for previewing with a Windows application. However, if you ran your ASP.NET application now, the report wouldn't be shown. To make the report display on the web page you have to call its DataBind() method. Do this in the Page_Load() event.

```
Private Sub Page_Load(ByVal sender As System.Object, ByVal e As System.EventArgs) Handles
MyBase.Load
   'Put user code to initialize the page here
   CrystalReportViewer1.DataBind()
End Sub
```

After typing in this code, run the web application and you'll see the Employee List report automatically previewed when the page opens.

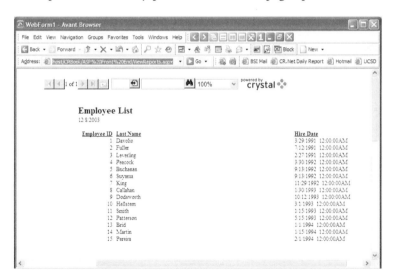

Figure 1-9. The Employee List report shown in an ASP.NET application.

Examining the Report Designer

Each report within your application is just like any other component that your application uses. It is listed in the Solution Explorer window as a class in your project. When you double-click it, it opens the report in design mode and you can make changes to it.

Each report starts with five sections: Report Header, Page Header, Detail, Page Footer, and Report Footer. These sections are described in Table 1-1.

Table 1-1. Report sections.

Section	Description
Report Header	Appears at the top of the first page of the report.
Page Header	Appears after the Report Header on the first page. On all the remaining pages it appears at the top of the page.
Group Header	Appears at the beginning of each new group.
Details	The row that displays the record information. There is usually one detail row for every record in the table.
Group Footer	Appears after all records of a group have been printed.
Page Footer	Appears at the bottom of each page.
Report Footer	Appears as the bottom of the page for the last page in the report.

To the left of the report layout is the Toolbox as shown in Figure 1-10. When you have the report designer open, there are only a few controls available in the Toolbox. They are the Text Object, Line Object, and Box Object. These are the most basic of the controls available.

Figure 1-10. Crystal Report's toolbox.

Oddly enough, there are more controls that can be used on a report, but they aren't listed in the toolbox. You have to right-click on the report and select the Insert menu option. This menu is shown in Figure 1-11. There are ten controls on it that can be added to a report as well as a lot of special fields that display report specific information (e.g. page number, print date, etc.). These controls are described in Chapter 2.

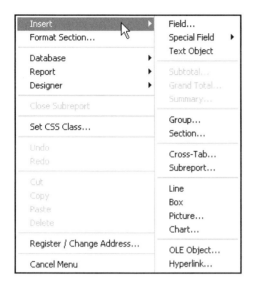

Figure 1-11. Crystal Report's Insert menu.

In the bottom right hand corner of the IDE is the Properties window. As expected, these properties are only applicable for the control that has the focus.

The CrystalReportViewer Control

The CrystalReportViewer control is used on a form to display a report. You have to use this control when you want to preview and print a report.[5] It is found in the form's Toolbox as the last control listed. To access it, you have to use the down arrow to scroll down to it.

The CrystalReportViewer control is fully customizable. Since it is the only way to display a report in your application, you may need to customize it for some applications. You don't want a user to feel like they are looking at a third-party control when using your application. Each of the buttons can turned on or off in design mode or during runtime. You can also add your own buttons to a form and have them manipulate the report layout and respond to user events. This is described in Chapter 2.

---

[5] You can print a report without previewing it in the viewer. This is discussed in Chapter 2.

Two-Pass Report Processing

Crystal Reports processes reports in two stages. This is called the Two-Pass Report Processing Model. The first pass creates the primary data to be printed. During the second pass this data is further processed to finalize it for printing.

The first pass reads individual records one at a time and calculates all formulas. This pass only calculates the formulas that are based on raw data within a record or that perform simple calculations. As each record is read and the formulas are calculated, the results are stored in a temporary file to be used during the second pass.

After the first pass is finished, Crystal Reports performs a second pass where it evaluates all summary functions on the data. This wasn't possible during the first pass because all the data had not been read yet. During the second pass all of the raw data has already been read into the temporary file and it can be evaluated and summarized as a whole.

After the second pass is finished, the report engine calculates the total number of pages if the report needs it or if the special field Page N of M is used.

Understanding the type of data that is processed during the Two-Pass Processing Model is essential to being able to write formulas and summarize data. Different chapters throughout this book reference this model for explaining when you can and can't use certain reporting functionality.

2
Creating Reports

Since Crystal Reports is fully integrated with Visual Studio .NET, you may be tempted to think that creating a new report is a simple matter that only takes a minute or two. While this is true after you have a little experience, creating a report the first time can be confusing if you don't follow the proper steps. This chapter shows you what steps are required and how to do them, providing you with a foundation for all chapters to follow. After writing a couple of reports, these steps become second nature. There are two parts to learn: creating a report and printing a report.

Creating a Report

Reports are files that must be created with the Visual Studio IDE. This requires opening a project and building the files within it. Adding a report to a project involves 5 steps. Each step has different options that you need to consider before implementing it.

Table 2-1. Steps for writing a report.

Step	Description
1. Creating a new report file	From the menu, select Project/Add New Item. Follow the prompts to select the report type.
2. Running the report experts	Use the different report experts to identify the tables and fields to print and get a good start in the right direction. This is optional.
3. Setting the designer's defaults	Make sure your development environment is the way you want it before working on your report.
4. Adding report objects to the report	Add the different objects that your report needs. These objects consist of textboxes, fields, etc.
5. Formatting the objects	Set the properties of the objects so that they are formatted properly. These properties consists of fonts, sizes, etc.

Before you add a report to your project, you need to know what your reporting goals are, and how the report will help fulfill these goals for your application. None of the options presented here are complex, you just need to be aware of what they are in advance. The following sections explain each step in detail and tell you what you need to consider when doing each one. The last section of the chapter, Coding Samples, pulls together everything you learned in this chapter and shows sample code of how to print and preview reports.

Creating a New Report Class

To create and print a report, you need to create a new report class for your project. Once the class is created, you can modify it using the report designer and then call it from your application.

Creating a new report class is done two different ways. The first is to select the menu options Project | Add New Component. The other way is to right-click on your project name in the Solutions Explorer window and select Add | Add New Component. Both of these methods open the Add New Item dialog. Scroll down near the bottom to select Crystal Report, type in a report name, and click Open.

The Crystal Report Gallery dialog box opens (see Figure 2-1). You are given the option of using the report expert, creating a blank report, or creating a report using an existing report. If you choose the Report expert option, you can tell it the type of report expert to use in the list box below the options. If you choose to start with a blank report, the gallery goes away and a new report is created. This report gives you the five basic report sections and each is empty. Add report objects to the proper sections and format them to build your report.

You can also create a new report based off an existing report by selecting Project | Add Existing Item. This skips the Gallery dialog box and immediately shows you the Open File dialog box. A copy of the report is saved in the same folder as your application. All changes are made to the local copy and do not effect the original report.

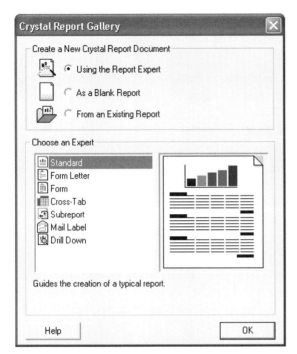

Figure 2-1. The Report Gallery dialog box.

Using the Report Experts

Depending upon your needs, creating reports can be a simple or complicated process. For example, it is very easy to print mailing labels from an address database or a form letter to a list of subscribers. On the other hand, it can be very complicated to write a report that uses multiple sub-reports which are based off of user entered parameters. Fortunately, the report experts that come with Crystal Reports, often referred to as "Wizards" in other applications, make it easy to quickly produce a variety of reports. The experts are useful for writing complex reports because they give you a way to quickly make a professional looking report template that you can customize for your specific needs.

Crystal Reports uses different experts to create seven types of reports: Standard, Form Letter, Form, Cross-tab, Sub-report, Mailing Label, and Drill-Down.

Since experts are designed to be easy to use, you might be wondering why this chapter needs to explain them. The problem with experts is that they are supposed to be simple to use, but often a tool that is simple is generally not very useful. As a result, today's applications are designed so that not only can you quickly answer the questions presented and create the final product, but you can also click on various buttons and checkboxes to add advanced functionality. This gives you the best of both worlds: a simple to use interface with extra features for advanced users.

Each expert consists of a multi-tabbed dialog box. Many of the tabs on each expert are used elsewhere within the main functionality of Crystal Reports. This chapter summarizes each tab and the details are covered in later chapters.

Using the Tabbed Dialog Boxes

Each report expert uses a combination of different tabbed dialog boxes to question you about how to build your report. Each expert presents a slightly different combination of these tabs. This section describes how to use each tab and explains any aspects of it that may not be obvious. The report expert tabs are called Data, Links, Fields, Group, Total, TopN, Chart, and Select.

The Data Tab

The Data tab is the first dialog box presented after you select which type of report you want. It lets you select the database and tables that store your data. The database can be a standard data source such as SQL Server or a non-standard data source such as an Excel spreadsheet.

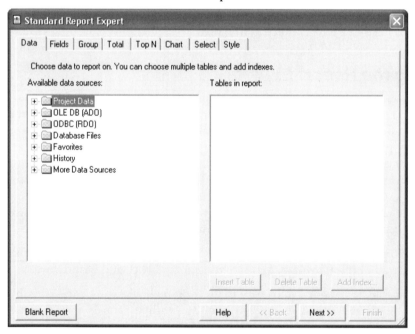

Figure 2-2. The Data tab of the report experts.

The Links Tab

Reports that use two or more tables need to have the tables linked so that data can be pulled from both of them. The Links tab lets you set the fields for creating relationships between the tables. Crystal Reports automatically attempts to link the tables together by using common field names. If two tables have a field with the same name and the data types are compatible, then Crystal will link them using this field.

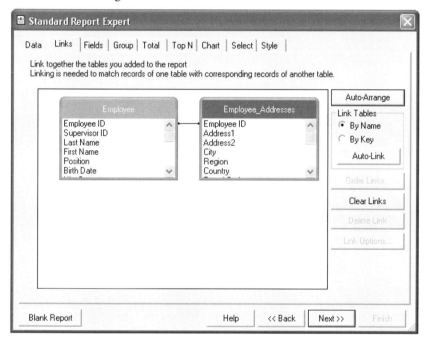

Figure 2-3. The Links tab of the report experts.

The Fields Tab

After selecting which tables you want to use for your report, the Fields tab allows you to select which fields will be shown. Adding and deleting fields is done in the standard manner of dragging and dropping them between windows or selecting a field and clicking on the appropriate arrow button.

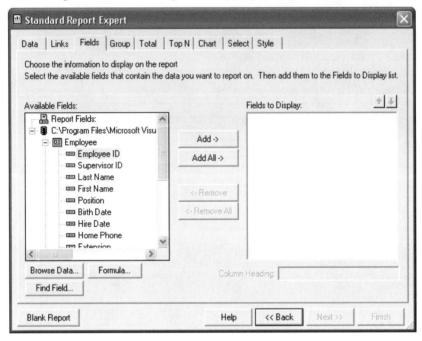

Figure 2-4. The Fields tab of the report experts.

After you add all the necessary fields to your report, you are free to reorder them by using the arrow buttons above the window. Select the field to move and click the up or down arrow to reposition it.

The Group Tab

Some reports have so much data on them that they can be a little hard to understand. When reports are dozens or even hundreds of pages long, you need to organize the information in a way that makes it easier to absorb the data in smaller pieces. You do this by creating groups within the report. Groups can be based on many things. Some examples are grouping on months of the year or the names of the different branch offices for a company.

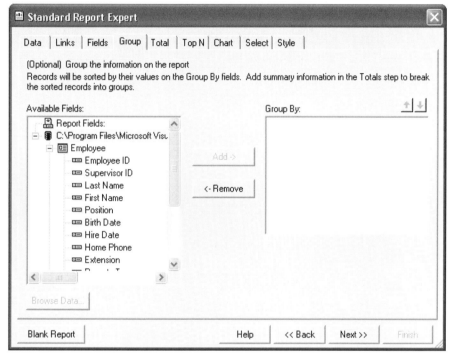

Figure 2-5. The Groups tab of the Report Expert.

The Total Tab

It is very common for reports to calculate sub-totals and other summary calculations on the numeric fields. The Total tab, shown in Figure 2-6, is where you define the summary calculations for the different fields. The left listbox shows all the available fields. The right listbox shows the fields that will have summary functions calculated for them.

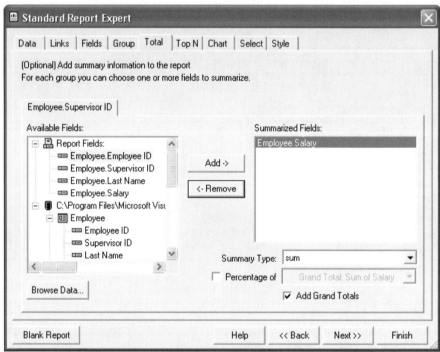

Figure 2-6. The Total tab of the Report Expert.

The Top N Tab

When adding a group to a report, you probably assume that every record within the group will be displayed. In most circumstances this is the case. However, you can tell Crystal Reports to only display a certain number of records based upon their rank. For example, you could have a top salesperson report where you show the top 10 salespeople in your office. You could also have another report that shows the worst 10 salespeople. The Top N tab lets you do this by sorting the groups based on a summary field.

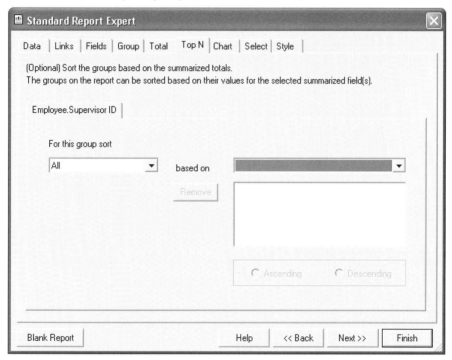

Figure 2-7. The Top N tab from the Report Expert.

The Chart Tab

This tab lets you add a chart to your report. You can also set a variety of options for what type of chart to display and how to display it.

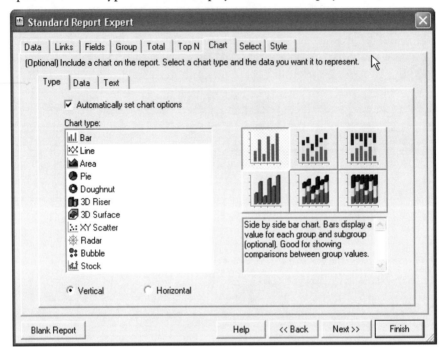

Figure 2-8. The Chart tab from the Report Expert.

The Select Tab

Some reports need to only show a sub-set of all the data that is in a recordset. For example, a financial report may only show the corporate data for a single quarter or a range of quarters. To filter out certain data so that you limit how much information is shown on a report, use the Select tab shown in Figure 2-9.

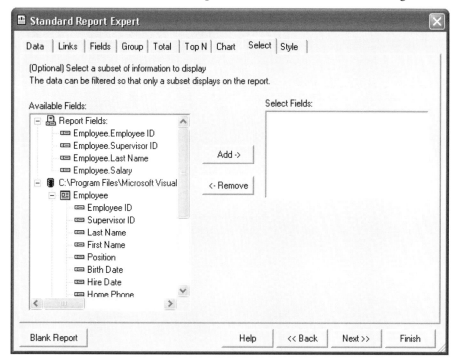

Figure 2-9. The Select tab from the Report Expert.

The Style Tab

After specifying the report details, use the Style tab to format everything so that the report has a professional look to it. This tab, shown in Figure 2-10, lists 10 different pre-determined formats that can be applied to your report. These styles make it easy for you to take some raw data and spice it up enough to make everyone think you worked really hard on this report!

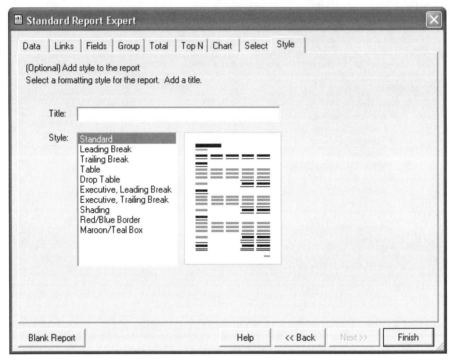

Figure 2-10. The Style tab from the Report Expert..

The Form Letter Tab

This tab is only available when using the Form Letter Expert. It lets you write the entire form letter within this tab. See Figure 2-11. At the top is a drop-down box that lists the different sections of the report. For example, it lists the Report Header, Page Header, any group header sections and the Detail section. Select the section you want to write and type the text in the scrollable textbox below it. You can also insert formulas or fields from the data sources in this textbox and the expert keeps track of it all. When you are finished and you close the expert, it adds a large text box to your report for each section and fills in the information you entered.

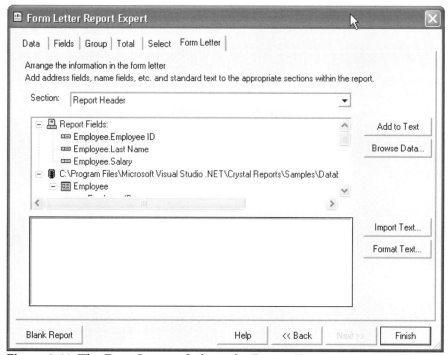

Figure 2-11. The Form Letter tab from the Report Expert.

The Form Tab

The Form tab, shown in Figure 2-12, is only available when using the Form Expert. It gives you a way to easily add a picture or logo to the sections of a report. Often when you add a picture using the expert, it might not be sized properly and could look distorted. Don't worry about that because it will look fine on the report and if you need to, you can always change its properties in design mode.

The Form tab also makes it easy to write reports that print onto standardized forms. Scan in the form that you want to print onto. Then use an image editor to crop it into the appropriate sections: Header, Detail, Footer, etc. Insert each section into the proper section of your report. Add the fields so that they line up exactly with the scanned image. When you are finished adding all the fields, delete the images. This leaves you with only the fields to print and they are lined up perfectly.

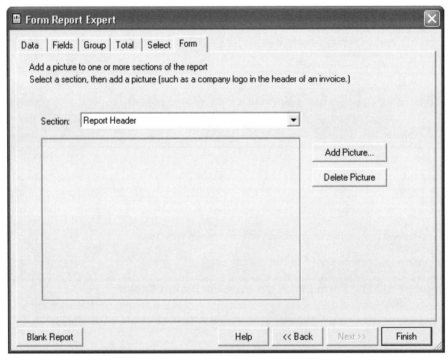

Figure 2-12. The Form tab from the Report Expert..

The Cross-Tab and Customize Style Tabs

These tabs are only available when using the Cross-Tab Expert. They let you modify the cross-tab data for what appears in the rows and columns. Modifying these tabs is very involved and is explained in detail in Chapter 11.

The Drill Tab

The Drill tab is only available when using the Drill-Down Expert. When creating drill-down reports, you allow the user to see a summarized view of their data. If they want to examine the data in more detail, they can expand a record to see more detail relating to the summarized information. The summarized fields are listed on this tab. When you click on the field's name, it will toggle it back and forth between "Show" and "Hide". This will alternate the default of whether it gets displayed or not.

Setting the Designer's Defaults

The report designer is where you will spend all your time creating reports and modifying them. There are many different default settings that you can set that control how you interact with the report designer as well as controlling how you access and display data on a report. Knowing what the different options are will not only make you more efficient, but it can also save you a lot of headaches. It is very likely that once you set these default values you will not come back to this step. However, when starting a new application, it would be beneficial to set the default values for how different report objects are displayed. For example, if you decide to always make group headers a certain font, then you can set that to be the default and you won't have to modify it every time.

To modify the default settings, right-click anywhere on the report and select Designer/Default Settings. The Default Settings dialog box appears. There are seven different tabs that control the default settings. Each tab affects different parts of the designer and report output.

Figure 2-13. The Default Settings dialog box.

The Layout Tab

The Layout tab effects your interaction with the report designer. The Field Options frame sets how fields are shown on the designer. You have the option of showing the names of the fields that are being displayed, the names that were assigned to each object, or format symbols. Showing the format symbols is useful for seeing how the different numbers will be formatted and seeing the maximum width that a string can use.

The Grid Options frame will be discussed in the Adding, Resizing and Moving Controls section. It lets you turn the grid markers on and off and set whether objects must align with them. The View Options frame sets what is shown in design mode.

The Database Tab

The Database tab effects how items are displayed in the Field Explorer and it has settings for tweaking performance. See Figure 2-14. The settings for changing the Field Explorer are many. They consist of deciding what types of objects are to be displayed and how the items will be sorted.

Figure 2-14. The Database tab.

Performance related settings are listed in the Advanced Options frame. The setting to use indexes on the server is set by default. Using indexes on the server gives you better performance because the server is optimized for doing this. The other performance related setting is to perform grouping on the server. Just like performing indexes on the server is faster, so is having the server do the grouping. Unfortunately, you can only use this option for accessing SQL tables directly. It isn't available when reporting off queries.

The Editors Tab

The Editors tab modifies those fonts that the Formula Editor and SQL Expression Editor use to display the programming code. You are free to customize the different programming elements to your heart's content.

The Data Source Defaults Tab

The Data Source tab lets you specify a default folder for where the database files are located. This is used with the Data tab of the Report Expert. When selecting Database Files it will display the Open dialog box and default to the folder you specified.

The Reporting Tab

The Reporting tab affects the output of your reports. See Figure 2-15. The top frame lets you set how data is read from the data source. You can automatically convert DateTime data to a String, a Date, or keep it as a DateTime data type. See Chapter 8 for a discussion of the date data types. Within this frame you can also convert NULL fields to their default value. This is very useful for ensuring that numeric fields are printed as a zero and not an empty field.

Figure 2-15. The Reporting tab.

The bottom frame contains miscellaneous options. Reports can save their data so that they don't have to reload and process the records every time (this really improves printing speed). If you want your reports to discard the old data and always re-query the data source for the latest data, then turn the option on. You can also tell it to re-import subreports so that they are always refreshed when printing a report.

You can set whether drill-down reports will show the column names for the drill-down data. A preview picture (thumbnail) can be saved every time you run a report. The last option lets you set the default formula language as discussed in Chapter 8.

The Fields Tab

Every data type that can be displayed on a report has a default display format. For example, the default for displaying a number is to use two decimal places. The Fields tab lets you set the default formats for all the available data types (see Chapter 8 for a list of data types). By changing the default here, every new object that is added to your report after changing the default will use this setting. Any objects that were added before you made the change will not reflect the new format.

The Font Tab

Just as the Fields tab sets the default format for the different data types, the Font tab sets the default font for the different fields on a report. For example, you can make field titles appear in italics while group names appear in bold. Once again, these changes will only affect objects that are added after you make your changes.

Using the Report Objects

A report is very similar to a Windows form. Just like a form, the report is listed as a separate object under your project in the Solution Explorer window, there are various controls that can be added, and it is a class that has to be instantiated before using it. The objects that are added to a report are also similar to the ones you use when building forms. This section describes the different objects and how they are used. It also gives you a reference for the properties of each object. Every property isn't listed because that would require reprinting the MSDN documentation.[6] But the properties you'll need to use on a regular basis are highlighted here.

There are three controls in the report toolbox (see Figure 2-16). You can access these and many others by right-clicking on the report and selecting the Insert menu option (see Figure 2-17).

Figure 2-16. The control Toolbox.

---

[6] There are already too many .NET books that consider printing out the MSDN tables to be quality writing. I don't want this book to be put in that category.

Figure 2-17. The Insert menu option.

Adding, Resizing and Moving Report Objects

The objects on a report work the same as the controls on a form. The objects that are listed in the toolbox can be added to the report by dragging and dropping them onto the proper section of the report. You can also double-click on them and they will be automatically added to the section that has the focus (its header bar will be blue while the other header bars will be gray). If you have an existing control that you want to reuse and it has already been formatted, then you can highlight it and copy and paste it. This creates a copy that is attached to your pointer and will move around as you move your mouse. When you have it positioned properly, click the mouse button to drop it there. You can also select multiple objects for copy and paste.

Selecting multiple objects is done by holding down the control or shift key and clicking on the individual controls. You can also draw a temporary window on the report and any controls that are included in the window get selected. Do this by holding down the mouse button and moving the mouse to enlarge the box. Let go of the mouse when the box is complete and the objects will be selected.

There is a strange behavior to be aware of when selecting multiple objects using the window technique. You can't draw a window if another object is already selected. You have to first click anywhere on the report to unselect the current object and then you can draw the box. For example, assume that you selected a textbox object. You then decide that you really wanted to select multiple textboxes so you click elsewhere on the report and attempt to draw a window.

Unfortunately, nothing will happen. It only results in the textbox getting unselected. You need to click the mouse again to start drawing the window.

You can only select multiple objects when they are compatible. For example, the box and line objects can be selected together, but the box object can't be selected with the text object.

Resizing a control is done by selecting it to give it the focus. Position the mouse over the sizing handles on any side and drag them. When resizing multiple objects, the sizing handle will only appear on the last control selected. As you resize the last control, its new size changes as you move your mouse. The other controls will not change until you release the mouse button. An option for resizing objects is to let Crystal adjust their size to be the same for each one. After selecting all the objects, right-click on one and select the Size menu option. From there you can choose Same Width, Same Height, or Same Size.

When moving objects on the report, it can be helpful to display the grid lines. This makes it easier to line up objects with each other. You have the option of making the objects snap to the grid lines. This means that when you move a control, its edge must be placed on a grid line. It can't be placed between grid lines. When you release the mouse, the object will automatically snap to the nearest grid line. Turning grid lines feature and the snap-to feature on and off is controlled by changing the designer properties. Right click on the report and select Designer/Default Settings.

Turning on the snap-to grid lines option can be a blessing or a curse. There are two problems that can occur when this option is turned on, and they both seem to occur most frequently with reports that have been created with the report experts. The first problem is that when the report expert creates a report, it doesn't always place the controls on the grid lines. When you later want to rearrange the controls on the report, or add more controls, you can't get the new objects to line up because they are snapping to the grid lines. Since the wizard placed the objects between grid lines, they won't line up properly when they are on the grid lines. The second problem with using the snap-to grid lines option is that it can be impossible to move multiple objects and keep their spacing consistent. I call this the "rubber band effect". As you drag the objects across the report, some will move and others won't. But as you move your mouse further, the ones that haven't moved will now seem to snap into place and catch up with the other objects. If you move your mouse fairly quickly across the page they will appear to bounce around like they are being pulled by rubber bands. Unfortunately, you have no control over this and sometimes it can be impossible to make all the objects line up as you expected.

An easy way to align multiple objects is to use the Align menu option. After selecting the objects, right-click on one of them and select Align. The options to choose from are Tops, Middles, Bottoms, Baseline, Lefts, Centers, Rights, and ToGrid. Each of these options aligns multiple objects to a single object.

The object that is used as the basis for alignment is the last object selected. You can identify the last object selected by seeing which one has the sizing handles on it.

Formatting Strings

String output can be formatted in a way similar to formatting a cell in a spreadsheet. You can modify its font and border. There are also formatting options that are specific to Crystal Reports. These options consist of suppressing the field, letting the width grow, rotating the text, paragraph specific formatting and hyperlinks. Almost every option on this dialog box can be set using formulas. This is discussed in more detail in Chapter 7. The formatting options are available for textbox objects, formulas, report fields, and special fields. Access the formatting dialog box by right-clicking on the field and selecting Format.

The first tab of the Format Editor dialog box is the Common tab (see Figure 2-18). The properties shown on this tab are common to most of the report objects available. These properties are described in Table 2-2.

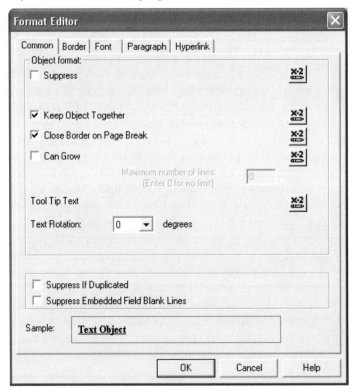

Figure 2-18. The Common tab.

Table 2-2. Properties of the Common Tab

Property	Description
Can Grow	Allow the field to expand if the object isn't big enough to hold the data. The field will only expand vertically and result in the height increasing. The width does not expand.
Close Border on Page Break	If a field has a border, and the field extends to another page, then this will close the border on the first page.
Horizontal Alignment	Sets the alignment to Left, Right, Center or Justified.
Keep Object Together	Do not let the object cross over into another page.
Suppress	Hides the object.
Suppress If Duplicated	Hide the object if it had the same value in the prior record.
Text Rotation	Rotate the text to a specified angle. A value of 0 is the default and the text displays horizontally. A value of 90 rotates it vertically upward. A value of 270 rotates it vertically downward.
Tool Tip Text	Use the formula editor to set a string that is displayed when the mouse hovers above the field.

The next two tabs on the Format dialog box are the Border tab and the Font tab. Both of these tabs are simplistic and don't have anything unusual in them. The Border tab lets you specify which sides should have a border and it also lets you can change the shading around the object. The Font tab has properties to change the font and use different effects such as strikethrough and underline.

The third tab of the dialog box is the Paragraph tab. This is useful when using multi-line objects and you want it to be formatted like a standard paragraph (see Figure 2-19). It lets you customize the indentation on the left and right sides. You can also specify a different indentation for the first line so that it is inset from the rest of the lines. You can also set the line spacing, the reading order (left to right or vice-versa), and specify if it uses plain text or text formatted as RTF.

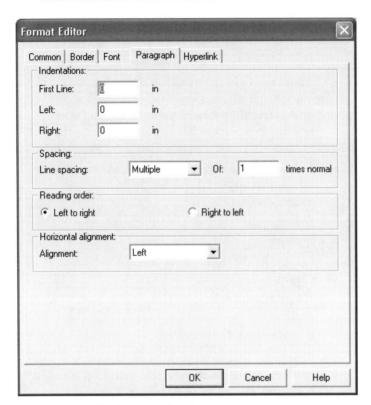

Figure 2-19. The Paragraph tab.

The last tab is the Hyperlink tab. This is used for fields that store text to be used as a hyperlink to a website, an email address, a file, or another report. When you select what type of hyperlink it is, the middle frame changes so that you can enter the appropriate type of link. You can either hardcode the hyperlink or use the formula editor to make it dynamic depending upon what is in the field. Depending on the type of object, the hyperlink tab might be unavailable.

The Text Object

The text object is used to display text, database fields, and special report fields. Each text object can display one of these or a combination of all three. After adding a text object to the report, click on it to edit it.

When writing form letters, using the textbox object with a combination of text and database fields is very helpful. Text in form letters is different than standard reports because it doesn't follow the standard format of showing individual rows and columns. It is displayed in paragraph format with a single space between each word/number. The textbox makes this possible by automatically trimming the spaces around each word and number. Thus, you can insert database fields in with standard text. Any extra spaces around the database fields are not shown. If you have ever programmed in HTML, then you are familiar with this concept. Within HTML, no matter how many spaces you put between words, they will be separated by only one space.

The properties that apply to the Textbox object are covered in the section Formatting Text Objects.

The Field Object

The standard field object displays data from a table or a formula. The field object is added to your report by dragging and dropping it from the Field Explorer window onto your report. The Field Explorer window is normally docked on the toolbar to the left side of the screen. If you don't have it there, you can pull it up by clicking on the menu items and selecting View/Other Windows/Document Outline. The properties that apply to the field object are covered in the Formatting Text Objects section.

The Line Object

The line object does exactly what you expect. It draws a line. There isn't a whole lot you can do with this except change its color, the width and its style (single line, dashed line, etc.) It does have one interesting feature that solves a common problem with line objects. The problem occurs when you draw a vertical line on a detail section. There are times when the detail section has a field that can grow down the report and make the section longer than expected. You expected the line to be unbroken down the report and now that isn't the case because the line is too short. To fix this, set the property ExtendToBottomOfSection to True. This insures that no matter how short your line is, the end point will be the bottom of the section. If it is a horizontal line, this always moves it to the bottom of the section.

The Box Object

Like the Line object, the Box object isn't too exciting. You can change its color, width and style. One nice feature about it is that you can change its properties to round the edges. Depending on how you set the properties, you can make it elliptical or even turn it into a circle. The properties that affect this are CornerEllipseHeight and CornerEllipseWidth. Rather than modify these directly using the Properties window at the bottom right hand corner of the screen, it is much easier to use the Format dialog box. The second tab is the Rounding tab. It has a picture of what the box looks like and below it is a slider. As you move the slider from the left to the right, it increases the curvature of the edges. When the slider is at the far right, the box has turned into a circle. Once you click OK, the dialog box modifies the corner ellipse properties for you.

The Picture Object

The picture object is used for displaying the following image file formats: BMP, JPG, TIFF, and PNG. It doesn't display GIF files. The formatting options are similar to the other controls in that it has the tabs Common, Border, and Hyperlink with similar functionality. There is a Picture tab, shown in Figure 2-20, that lets you resize, scale and crop the image. If at any point you feel that you resized or scaled it improperly and you want to restore it to its original size, click the Reset button.

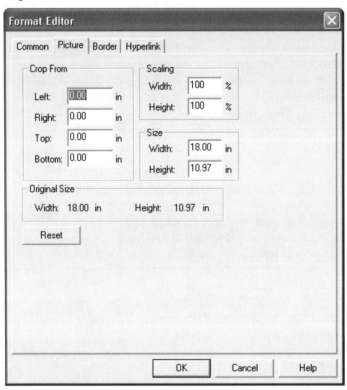

Figure 2-20. The Picture tab of the Picture object's dialog box.

The Chart Object

The Chart object lets you add a chart to your report. There are a variety of options to choose from so that you can customize the chart however you need to. There is so much to cover with this object that it was given a separate chapter. See Chapter 10 for more information.

The OLE Object

The OLE object lets you embed objects inside of your report. Some examples are embedding Word documents or Excel spreadsheets. This is a feature that was brought forward from previous versions of Crystal Reports it isn't used much anymore.

The Hyperlink Object

The Hyperlink object is used for giving your report the ability to show a hyperlink to an on-demand subreport. When a user clicks on the hyperlink, the subreport opens in the viewer and gets its own tab. This creates an on-demand subreport. The user can toggle back and forth between the two tabs to see both reports.

The Special Field Object

The Special Field object is used for printing all report-related information. For example, it can print the current page number or the total number of pages. This field was created as a catch-all for all the miscellaneous types of report information that you need. Table 2-3 lists the available fields and what they mean. These fields are treated the same as a database field object. They can be added to the report by themselves, or included in a textbox object. They also have the same formatting options described in the Formatting Strings section.

Table 2-3. Special Fields.

Special Field	Description
DataDate	The date when the report was last refreshed.
DataTime	The time when the report was last refreshed.
FileAuthor	The file author that is stored with the report.
FileCreationDate	The date when the report was created.
Filename	The report's file name.
GroupNumber	The current group number.
GroupSelection	The group selection formula.
ModificationDate	The date the report was last modified.
ModificationTime	The time the report was last modified.
PageNofM	Prints "Page X of Y".
PageNumber	The current page number.
PrintDate	The date the report was printed.
PrintTime	The time the report was printed.
RecordNumber	The current record number.
RecordSelection	The record selection formula.
ReportComments	The report comments that are stored with the report.
ReportTitle	The report title.
TotalPageCount	The total number of pages.

3
Integrating Reports

After creating a report and formatting it to your satisfaction, the report needs to be integrated into the application. There are many ways to do this which makes chapter 3 one of the more complicated to understand, and yet one of the most important in the book. Understanding the best way to integrate reports into your application is essential for designing the best reporting solution.

There are a lot of different ways to integrate a report into an application, and some of the ways can be combined. The different combinations create an interesting matrix of possibilities for you to choose from. If this is your first experience to writing reports with .NET, it may seem a little overwhelming. To try to make this as easy as possible to understand, I first give you an overview of each option and show its benefits and drawbacks. This lets you see the big picture and learn which options work for which types of applications. Afterwards, I break down each option and show the steps and programming code to integrate it into your application. This is done for Windows applications as well as ASP.NET applications. If you get to the examples and something doesn't make sense, just refer back to the beginning of the chapter for an explanation.

Sound good? Now let's get started!

The first reporting related decision is whether the report will be previewed before it gets printed. Many users like to see the report prior to printing it so that they can verify that it will print the information they are looking for. This is especially true for reports that let the user choose how to filter and display the data. For other reports you may not want to give the user the option to preview the report. An example is a reporting application that runs a batch print job at a scheduled time during the night. Requiring user intervention would cause the program to hang indefinitely until someone arrives to push the right button. Another example is a group of standardized reports that get printed every month. It is quicker for the user to select the reports to be printed by clicking on checkboxes and printing them all at once. Since the format and filters never change, making the user preview each report is unnecessary.

Previewing reports can be done in a Windows application as well as an ASP.NET application by adding a CrystalReportViewer control to the form/web page. Using the viewer control gives you many benefits. The first is obviously that the user can see what is going to be printed prior to printing it.

If it isn't exactly what they want, they can close the preview window and repeatedly modify the report parameters until the report delivers the necessary information. No waste and another tree gets to live. Another benefit is that the viewer control has numerous built-in reporting functions that save you a lot of work. Rather than writing the code to export reports in different formats, the viewer has a button on the toolbar that does it for you. In fact, the viewer is so useful that I would guess that most of the applications you write are going to use it.

Of course, the viewer isn't ideal for every situation. It requires user intervention for it to be useful. Another downfall of the viewer is that it can only view one report at a time. You can't pass multiple reports to it. Displaying multiple reports simultaneously requires using multiple viewers.

If you decide to send reports directly to the printer and not use the viewer control, you are going to have to write the programming code to implement the functionality that you need. This could include writing code for printing the report, selecting the page range, and exporting the report to other formats. That's a lot of work! Of course, Part II of this book shows you all the programming code to do this, but it's still your responsibility to implement it in the application and test it.

If you don't use the viewer control, there will be a certain amount of code you always have to write. This code serves as the foundation adding more reporting functionality later. Part II of this book builds upon this code for advanced runtime customization.

To start coding, declare and instantiate an object variable from the ReportDocument class. The ReportDocument class has all the properties and methods necessary for loading and printing a report.

Note
Although I didn't mention it before, if you use the viewer control to preview a report, the ReportDocument class is still used to load and print the report. The viewer control does all the work for you behind the scenes and you don't have to be aware of it.

```
Dim MyReport As New CrystalDecisions.CrystalReports.Engine.ReportDocument
MyReport.Load("C:\Report1.rpt")
MyReport.PrintToPrinter(1, False, 0, 0)
```

The first line of code declares an object variable MyReport and instantiates a new instance of the ReportDocument class. As I said earlier, this ReportDocument class is responsible for managing all report related functions.

The second line of code calls the Load() method to load an Untyped report into memory. The last line of code calls the PrintToPrinter() method to send the report to the printer.

Note

Once you get into advanced programming techniques, you'll learn that there are times when you will use the viewer control and still create a ReportDocument object variable. This is when you want to perform runtime customization. See Part II of the book for more information.

The PrintToPrinter() method needs to be explained in more detail because the parameters passed to this method aren't intuitive. The parameters of the PrintToPrinter() method are listed in Table 3-1.

Table 3-1. PrintToPrinter() parameters.

Parameter	Description
nCopies	The number of copies to print.
Collated	Set to True to collate the pages.
startPageN	The first page to print. Set to 0 to print all pages.
endPageN	The last page to print. Set to 0 to print all pages.

The first parameter, nCopies, sets how many copies of the report to print. If more than one copy of the report is being printed, the second property tells whether to collate the copies or not. Passing False tells it to print each full report prior to printing the next copy. If nCopies is set to 1, then the collated parameter is ignored. The last two parameters, startPageN and endPageN, set the page range. Pass it the first page to print and the last page to print. To print the entire report, pass 0 to both parameters.

When using the viewer control, you also have the option of using a ReportDocument component (see the example in Chapter 1). The ReportDocument component gives you a visual way of telling the viewer which report you want to print. If you are writing a Windows application, adding the ReportDocument component lets you preview a report without writing any code whatsoever. The ReportDocument component also gives you the benefit of being in design mode and letting you see the name of the report that is going to be printed without having to read the programming code.

At this point in the chapter, you've had the chance to examine when you should use the viewer or when to send reports directly to the printer. If you use the viewer control, you have the option to add a ReportDocument component.

The next major decision to make is how you want to instantiate the report object.

.NET applications are fully object oriented and thus everything is considered an object. Reports are no different. Crystal Reports .NET uses the ReportDocument class to manage all report functionality. Before a report can be printed, you must instantiate a new ReportDocument object variable and load the report into it. The steps for instantiating the object and loading the report are dependent on the report type and classification. A report can be classified as either Strongly-Typed or Untyped.

Strongly-Typed

When you create a report, .NET automatically creates a report class within the current project. Just like all the other classes in a project, the report is instantiated by its class name. Reports that are referenced by their class name are called Strongly-Typed reports. These reports are compiled into the applications executable file.

Untyped

When you save a .NET project, each report in the project is saved as a separate ".rpt" file. Although these files are saved in the same folder in your .NET application, they are independent of the project. In other words, you can copy these .rpt files to another folder and use them in another project. You could also copy them to a reporting library to be shared among many applications. Report files that are separate from the current project and are referenced by their filename and path. Reports that are referenced by their filename, rather than their class name, are called Untyped Reports. When you build your application, these reports will not be part of the application.

Each report type has its own benefits and drawbacks. Untyped reports are useful for applications that let the user choose from a dynamic list of reports. An example of this is when the user browses to a directory location and selects which report to print. You can also use Untyped reports to share reports between different applications. This lets you create a reporting library that is shared on the network. Another benefit is that if you distribute an application and later find that you have to modify a report, you can change the report without rebuilding the application. A drawback of using Untyped reports is that when deploying your application you have to remember to include each report file in the deployment project (unless it's stored on the network). If you are writing an ASP.NET application, you also have to make sure that the security settings let you access the report.

Strongly-Typed reports are the easiest to work with in your application. Since the class is already part of your project, it is pretty simple to reference it by name. You also get the benefit of having the report compiled within the application's executable and you don't have to distribute the report file. There are two limitations however to using Strongly-Typed reports. First is that you can't reference reports designed by other applications or by the Crystal Reports stand-alone application. Second is that if you modify a report, you have to recompile and redistribute the application's executable.

> **Note**
>
> Report types are not mutually exclusive within an application. For example, choosing to open a report as a Strongly-Typed report doesn't mean you can't open other reports as Untyped reports. The purpose of classifying reports into types is for determining the best way to write your application. Each report can be opened in the way that is best suited for it.

That's it! Now that you've read about the various options available for integrating reports into your application, look at table 3-2 for a summary of each option.

Table 3-2. Summary of report integration options.

Integration Option	Key Points
CrystalReportViewer	Lets the user visually verify. Saves you programming effort.
Printing to the printer	Print report without user intervention. You have to instantiate a ReportDocument object variable. Could require a lot of programming. Useful for printing batch reports or printing standard reports.
Adding the ReportDocument component	Must be used with the viewer control. Gives you a visual way of specifying which report to print.
Untyped reports	Used when you have to specify the report by its filename. Allows you to share reports between applications. Report changes don't require recompiling and redistributing the application. Can be added to reporting library.
Strongly-Typed reports	Used when the report was created within the same application that is using it. Coding is easier than using Untyped reports because the report is a class within the project. Modifying a report requires recompiling and redistributing the application.

The next two sections take each option and show you the exact steps for implementing each one in your application. The first section is specific to Windows applications and the second section is for writing ASP.NET applications.

Windows Development

Each of the integration options presented in the previous section have a specific way that they must be implemented to work properly. This section discusses the details of each option and walks you through the steps to implement them in a Windows application.

Previewing Reports with the CrystalReportViewer

Most applications give the user the ability to preview a report before printing it. With Crystal Reports, this is controlled by the CrystalReportViewer control. In fact, using the viewer is the only way to preview a report in your application. The viewer is found in the Toolbox at the bottom of the other components. Double-click on it to add it to your form.

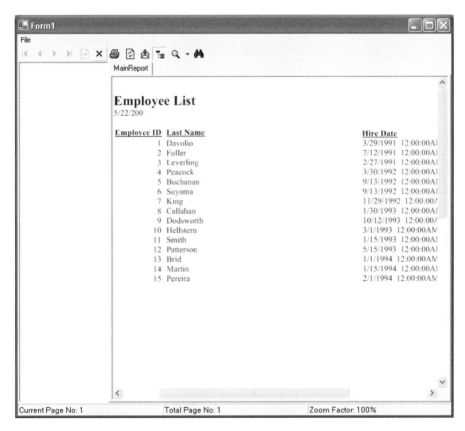

Figure 3-1. The CrystalReportViewer previewing a report.

Figure 3-1 shows the viewer previewing a report. Along the top of the viewer is a toolbar with a variety of navigational buttons. In the center is the report preview window with a Group Tree window to the left of it. Along the bottom is a status bar that shows the page number information and the current zoom factor.

By default, the toolbar buttons and Group Tree window are all enabled. Each of these features has a corresponding property that can be set in design mode and during runtime so that can turn them on or off. For example, a report that doesn't have any groups certainly doesn't need to show the Grouping Tree

---

window. You may also want to turn off all these features so that you can create a customized preview form using your own buttons. Having a customized preview form lets you control the user interface by using your own style of buttons. This insures that your application has a consistent look and feel across all forms.

Tip

The status bar can't be modified. There are no properties to turn it on or off. Nor are there any properties to control what it displays. You can work around this limitation by extending the bottom of the viewer below the edge of the form or panel it is located in. This results in hiding the status bar.

Table 3-3 lists the properties of the CrystalReportViewer. The properties let you enable or disable the features of the viewer. Table 3-4 lists its methods. The methods let you implement the viewer's functionality by calling them from your own buttons. Most of these are self-explanatory, but the tables make good reference material.

Table 3-3. CrystalReportViewer Properties

Property	Description
DisplayBackgroundEdge	A background edge creates a border around the edge of the report page in preview mode. Setting this to False makes the edge of the page flush against the viewer's window.
DisplayGroupTree	Toggles the Group Tree window on and off.
DisplayToolbar	Toggles the toolbar on and off.
EnableDrillDown	Sets whether the user can drill down on reports.
ShowCloseButton	Sets whether the Close button is available.
ShowExportButton	Sets whether the Export button is available.
ShowGotoPageButton	Sets whether the GotoPage button is available.
ShowGroupTreeButton	Sets whether the GroupTree button is available.
ShowPrintButton	Sets whether the Print button is available.
ShowRefreshButton	Sets whether the Refresh button is available.
ShowTextSearchButton	Sets whether the Search button is available.
ShowZoomButton	Sets whether the Zoom button is available.

Table 3-4 CrystalReportViewer Methods

Method	Description
CloseView()	Pass a null value to close the current view. Pass a view name to close a specific view.
DrillDownOnGroup()	Drill down on a specific group. See Chapter 12 for details on implementing this method.
ExportReport()	Show the Export dialog box.
PrintReport()	Show the Print dialog box.
RefreshReport()	Refresh the report view. The user will be prompted for the parameters and logon information again.
SearchForText()	Pass a string to search for. If found, it returns True and moves to the page that has the string.
ShowFirstPage()	Move to the first page of the report.
ShowGroupTree()	Shows the Group Tree window. It doesn't take any parameters. There is no corresponding method to hide it.
ShowLastPage()	Move to the last page of the report.
ShowNextPage()	Move to the next page of the report.
ShowNthPage()	Pass an integer to move to that page number.
ShowPreviousPage()	Move to the previous page of the report.
Zoom()	Pass an integer to set the zoom level.

Binding Reports to the Viewer

The viewer needs to be told which report to display. This is called binding the report to the viewer. The property used for binding is the ReportSource property. There are three ways to set the ReportSource property: using the ReportDocument component, passing it an Untyped report filename, and passing it a Strongly-Type report class name. Each method is covered in the next three sections.

Using the ReportDocument Component on the Viewer

Adding a ReportDocument component to the form is the easiest way to specify which report to print. Everything about it is visual and there is no code to write. Add it to your form by going to the Components section of the Toolbox and double-clicking on it. It will automatically display the Choose a ReportDocument dialog box. This lets you select which report to display. The dropdown control lists all the reports that are part of your project. Once you select which report to use, the dialog box closes and it the component gets added to your form.

After the component is added to the form, tell the viewer to use it by clicking on the viewer's ReportSource property and selecting the ReportDocument's name from the dropdown list.

When you run the application and open the form, the viewer automatically displays the report to the user. You don't have to write any code.

Using Untyped Reports with the Viewer

Untyped reports are, by definition, referenced by their filename. The viewer loads the report into memory and displays it to the user. The viewer's ReportSource property has to be passed the report's filename.

Setting the ReportSource property can be done anywhere within your form. For example, you could call it in response to the user clicking on a button or a menu item. In this example (and almost all the examples in this book), I put the code in the form's Load() event. I do this because it is easy to understand and it makes the form preview the report immediately. In this example the report used is the Employee List report created in Chapter 1. You should replace the report filename with your own report.

```
Private Sub Form1_Load(ByVal sender As System.Object, ByVal e As System.EventArgs) Handles yBase.Load
    CrystalReportViewer1.ReportSource = "Employee List.rpt"
End Sub
```

Using Stongly-Typed Reports with the Viewer

Strongly-Typed reports are referenced by their class name. Create a new instance of the report class and pass it to the viewer's ReportSource property. As mentioned in the last section, the code in this example is called within the form's Load() event so that the report is displayed immediately upon opening the form. The Employee_List class name is from the example report in Chapter 1. Replace it with the class name of the report in your own application.

```
Private Sub Form1_Load(ByVal sender As System.Object, _
ByVal e As System.EventArgs) Handles MyBase.Load
    CrystalReportViewer1.ReportSource = New Employee_List
End Sub
```

Notice that the report's class name is "Employee_List" and the actual report name is "Employee List". When there are spaces in the report name, the class name that .NET creates will use underscores instead of spaces.

Printing Reports Directly to the Printer

If you decide not to user the viewer control for previewing reports, you will have to write all the code for loading and printing reports. The following sections show you examples of how to instantiate report objects and send their output to the printer.

At this point in the book, the amount of code you need to write is still very limited and it is easy to understand. Once you get into Part II of this book, you'll see that this code serves as the foundation for performing advanced runtime customization of your reports.

Printing Untyped Reports Directly

Printing Untyped reports without using the viewer requires a bit more coding than the examples you've seen so far. First you must declare and instantiate a ReportDocument object. The ReportDocument object has methods for loading the report into memory and printing it. Call the Load() method and pass it the report's filename. Call PrintToPrinter() to send the report to the printer.

```
Private Sub Form1_Load(ByVal sender As System.Object, _
    ByVal e As System.EventArgs) Handles MyBase.Load
    Dim MyReport As New CrystalDecisions.CrystalReports.Engine.ReportDocument
    MyReport.Load("Employee List.rpt")
    MyReport.PrintToPrinter(1, False, 0, 0)
End Sub
```

This example loads the Employee List report in the MyReport object variable. Then it calls the PrintToPrinter() method to print a single copy of the report, including all pages.

Printing Strongly-Typed Reports Directly

Printing Strongly-Typed reports is a little easier than printing Untyped reports. With Strongly-Typed reports, the report's class name is part of the project and can be instantiate directly. Unlike Untyped reports, you don't have to use the generic ReportDocument class and you don't have to worry about loading the report from a file. After instantiating the report object, call the PrintToPrinter() method to send it to the printer.

```
Private Sub Form1_Load(ByVal sender As System.Object, _
    ByVal e As System.EventArgs) Handles MyBase.Load
    Dim MyReport As New Employee_List
    MyReport.PrintToPrinter(1, False, 0, 0)
End Sub
```

This declares the object variable MyReport to be of type Employee_List and instantiates it. For your application, use the class name of the report that you want to print. The PrintToPrinter() method prints a single copy of the report.

ASP.NET Development

The CrystalReportViewer control is the interface for previewing reports in an ASP.NET application. Adding a viewer control to a web page is as simple as dragging the control from the Toolbox onto the web page. After it is added to an ASP.NET page, it is represented by a simple rectangle.

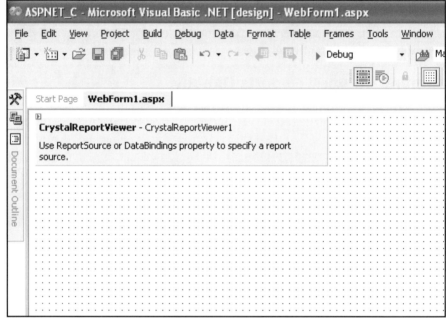

Figure 3-2. The viewer control as positioned on an ASP.NET page.

If you worked through the Windows example where you added the viewer control to a form, you will immediately notice that the ASP.NET viewer looks different than the Windows viewer. When you add the viewer to an ASP.NET page, it only displays a simple rectangle. It doesn't show you a template of what the viewer looks like.

Although the viewer control is very small when you add it to the web page, when you run the application it automatically grows to fill the remainder of the web page. It expands horizontally across the page as well as vertically down the page. This ensures that the report is readable when the page is displayed.

The viewer has a BestFitPage property (default value of True) that controls whether it fills the page or not. If you set this property to False, the viewer control will not resize itself and the report will be displayed within the bounds of the viewer. Setting it to False is useful when you want to limit the amount of space on the web page that is allocated to viewing reports. Obviously, if you decide to set BestFitPage to False, you should resize the viewer to make it large enough to comfortably display your report.

When BestFitPage property is True, the control does not expand upward. It only expands downward and across. Any information above the viewer control remains intact and properly formatted.

Note

If the Page Layout is set to FlowLayout, all information below the viewer will be pushed down the page so that it appears after the viewer control. If the Page Layout is set to GridLayout, the information after the viewer control will not be pushed down. The ASP.NET controls will overlap the viewer control. This could either make for a very messy report or you could get creative and implement some interesting formatting effects.

As you can see in Figure 3-3, when the viewer is displayed in an ASP.NET page, it looks very similar to the report preview that you've seen with Windows applications.

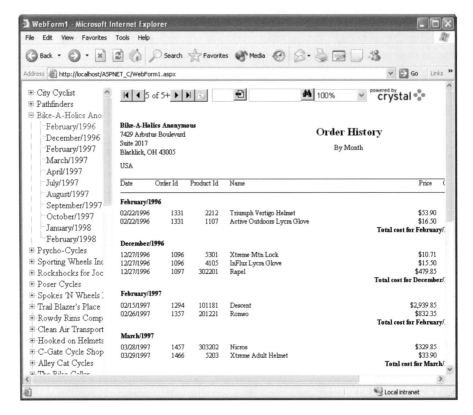

Figure 3-3. The report preview in an Internet Explorer browser.

The ASP.NET viewer control has some interesting differences between it and the Windows viewer.

There are no tabs shown along the top of the ASP.NET viewer. When you drill down on reports in a web viewer, it opens a new page rather than showing all the tabs on a single page. There is also no Print button. A very disappointing aspect of the viewer is that it can't send a report to the printer. You have to use the browser's built-in print functionality to print the web page. This has the adverse effect of printing non-professional reports because it prints everything in the browser window. This includes the toolbar, the group tree and the web page information. Printing professional reports requires advanced programming techniques which are discussed in Chapter 19.

The last thing you might notice is the "Powered by Crystal" icon at the top of the toolbar. Although this is totally harmless, many people don't like it appearing on their reports.[7] You can get rid of this logo, or even replace it with your own, by deleting or overwriting the GIF file on your computer. You can find it within the Visual Studio .NET installation folder under "..\crystal reports\viewers\images\toolbar\logo.gif"

The properties of the Web viewer control are similar to that of the Windows viewer control. It has properties for changing the look of the viewer by hiding the toolbar, hiding the toolbar buttons and hiding the Group Tree window.

Although the Windows and Web viewer controls have properties that perform the same functionality, they often have different names. There are also certain properties that are unique to each control. Table 3-5 compares the common properties of each control so you can see the similarities and differences.

Table 3-5. Comparing the property names of the two viewer controls.

Windows Viewer	Web Viewer
DisplayGroupTree	DisplayGroupTree
N/A	DisplayPage
DisplayToolbar	DisplayToolbar
Dock	BestFitPage
EnableDrillDown	EnableDrillDown
N/A	DrilldownTarget
N/A	HasDrillUpButton
ReportSource	(DataBindings) | ReportSource
SelectionFormula	SelectionFormula
ShowCloseButton	N/A
ShowExportButton	N/A
ShowGotoPageButton	HasGotoPageButton
ShowGroupTreeButton	N/A
ShowPageNavigationButtons	HasPageNavigationButtons
ShowPrintButton	N/A
ShowRefreshButton	HasRefreshButton
ShowTextSearchButton	HasSearchButton
ShowZoomButton	HasZoomFactorList
N/A	HyperlinkTarget
N/A	PageToTreeRatio
N/A	SeparatePages

---

[7] Later in the book you'll see more examples of where Crystal Decisions has decided to stamp their logo within your report output. I'm sure their marketing department loves this, but I consider it unprofessional. With a little work all these logos can be removed.

Both controls have properties for hiding the different buttons, but they use different names for them. For example, the properties of the Windows viewer that hides the toolbar buttons are prefixed with "Show", but the web viewer properties are prefixed with "Has". The Dock property of the Windows viewer is similar to the BestFitPage property in the Web viewer.

There are certain properties that only belong to the Windows viewer and not the web viewer. For example, there are more buttons in the Windows toolbar than the web toolbar. As a result, the properties to hide these buttons aren't in the web viewer. The web toolbar is missing the buttons for Close, Export, GroupTree, and Print. The Close button is missing because there are no tabs displayed for drilling down into the report detail. The Export and Print button are missing because the web viewer can't perform either function. The GroupTree button is missing because the user isn't allowed to directly turn this off. If you want to give the user this ability, add a button to the web page that toggles the value of the DisplayGroupTree property.

The web viewer also has properties that aren't in the Windows viewer. The DisplayPage property hides the report preview when it is set to False. The web viewer also has properties that are HTML target values. When initially opening the report's web page or opening a sub-report, you can set whether the new page opens in the same browser window or in a new window. Table 3-6 shows the possible values. These values can be assigned to the HyperlinkTarget and DrilldownTarget properties.

Table 3-6. Hyperlink target values.[8]

Target String Value	Description
_blank	Opens the page in a new, unframed window.
_parent	Opens the page in the immediate frameset parent.
_self	Opens the page in the current frame.
_top	Opens the page in a full, unframed window.

The Windows viewer uses tabs along the top of the form to display different pages of data as the user drills down into the report for more information. As mentioned earlier, there are no tabs in the web viewer control. When a user drills down into group details and sub-reports, a new web page is generated to display the information. Rather than using tabs to look at the different pages, the user has to click on the Back and Forward buttons. To make this a little easier to navigate, the web viewer control has a button for moving up to the

---

[8] These are the standard target values used with HTML hyperlinks.

parent level. This is called the DrillUp button. When report is at the top-most level, this button is disabled.

The PageToTreeRatio property sets how wide the Group Tree control is. It represents the relationship between how wide the viewer is compared to how wide the Group Tree is. The number entered for this property tells how many units the report page is compared to one unit of the Group Tree control. For example, if the number is 1, then the two areas have a 1:1 ratio and they are equal sizes. Thus, the page is split in half. If the number is 4, the two areas will have a 4:1 ratio, which makes the width of the Group Tree control use 20% of the total browser width. A good number to start with is 4 or 5.

The SeparatePages property determines whether the report uses different pages or not. If the property is set to True, each web page displays a single report page. If the property is False, the entire report is displayed on a single web page and the user has to scroll up and down.

Caution

Setting the SeparatePages property to True is the most efficient because Crystal Reports only has to process enough information to display one page at a time. Setting the SeparatePages property to False can cause a long delay to rendering the page. Crystal Reports has to process the entire report before it can display it.

Binding Reports to the Web Viewer

After adding a viewer to the web page and setting its properties, the report needs to be bound to the viewer. This can be done with any of the three options listed earlier in the chapter: using the ReportDocument component, using Untyped reports, and using Strongly-Typed reports.

Using the ReportDocument Component on the Viewer

The ReportDocument component makes it easy to specify which report the viewer is supposed to display. Add a ReportDocument component to the web page by double-clicking on the ReportDocument component. The ReportDocument component is listed in the Components section of the Toolbox. When you add a ReportDocument component to your form, it automatically displays the Choose a ReportDocument dialog box. This lets you select which report will be displayed. The dropdown control lists all the reports that are part of your project. For this example, it will only show the Employee List report.

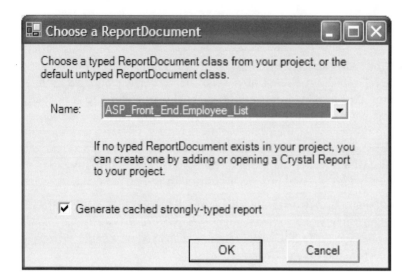

Figure 3-4. The ReportDocument dialog box.

Select the Employee List report and click the OK button. This adds the ReportDocument component to your form.

You have to associate the ReportDocument component with the viewer control so that the viewer knows which report to display. Look at the viewer's properties and at the very top is the DataBindings property. Click on it and then click on the ellipses button to open the DataBindings dialog box.

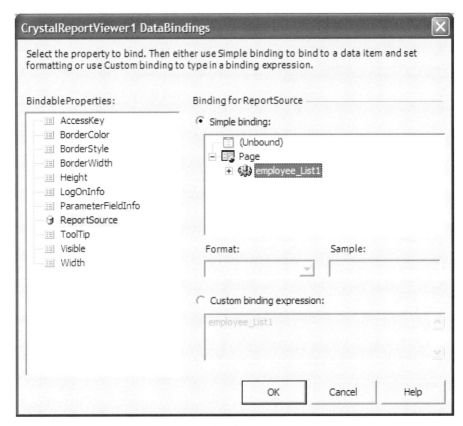

Figure 3-5. The DataBindings dialog box.

Click on the ReportSource property listed on the left. Then expand the Page item in the Simple Binding window. It shows you the reports that were added to the page using ReportDocument component.

Select the report name and click the OK button. Once the dialog box closes, a preview of the report is immediately displayed. Unlike Windows development, the viewer component shows you what the report looks like while you are in design mode.

When the application runs, you have to tell the viewer to use the DataBindings property. This is done by calling the DataBind() method. Put this code in the Page_Load() event.

```
Private Sub Page_Load(ByVal sender As System.Object, ByVal e As System.EventArgs) _
Handles MyBase.Load
    'Put user code to initialize the page here
    CrystalReportViewer1.DataBind()
End Sub
```

Run the web application and you'll see the Employee List report automatically previewed when the page opens.

Using Untyped Reports with the Viewer

Untyped reports are referenced by their filename and they are external to the application's executable code. Open an Untyped report by passing the filename to the ReportSource property of the viewer. In this example, I set the ReportSource property in the Load() event of the page. I also pass it the name of the Employee List report that I created in Chapter 1. For your application you should pass the filename of the report you want to display.

```
Private Sub Page_Load(ByVal sender As System.Object, ByVal e As System.EventArgs)
Handles MyBase.Load
    CrystalReportViewer1.ReportSource = Server.MapPath("Employee List.rpt")
End Sub
```

A second way to bind an Untyped report to the viewer is to set the ReportSource property in the DataBindings dialog box. Look at the Property Window for the viewer and at the very top is the DataBindings property. Click on it and then click on the ellipses button to open the DataBindings dialog box.

When the dialog box opens, click on the ReportSource property and then click on the Custom Bindings Expression option. Within the text area enter the report's full path name and enclose it in quotes. You should also be aware that there is no Browse button for this property. You have to type in the file path exactly.

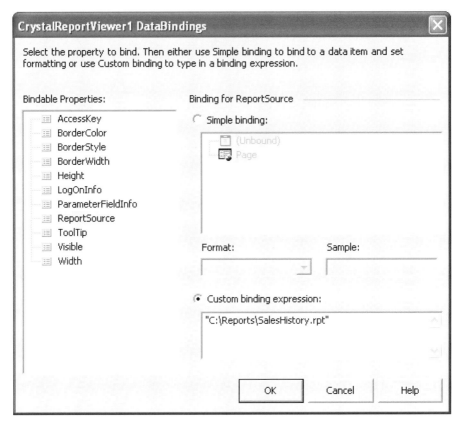

Figure 3-6. Setting the custom binding expression.

Caution

Be careful when entering the report filename in this dialog box. It is a common source of problems. First of all, the file path must be accessible by the report server and you must have permission to access it. Secondly, always put quotes around the file path string. Otherwise you will get an error when the viewer attempts to open the report.

Using Strongly-Typed Reports with the Viewer

Strongly-Typed reports are referenced by passing an instance of the report class to ReportSource property of the viewer. In this example I pass a new instance of the Employee_List class to the ReportSource property. For your application you would pass the class name of the report you want to display.

```
Private Sub Page_Load(ByVal sender As System.Object, ByVal e As System.EventArgs) _
Handles MyBase.Load
  CrystalReportViewer1.ReportSource = New Employee_List
```

Caution

When using Untyped or Strongly-Typed reports, don't call the viewer's DataBind() method. If you call DataBind() after setting the ReportSource property, the ReportSource value is reset and the report won't display. I see this mistake a lot because people assume that calling the DataBind() method is a requirement for using the viewer. This isn't the case at all. It's only necessary if you set properties within the DataBindings dialog box. If you do need to call the DataBind() method, call it prior to setting the ReportSource property in code

4

Sorting and Grouping

In Chapter 2 you saw how to build a report using the different report objects and tie it into a database. For creating simple reports this is all you need to know. But you will quickly find yourself developing reports that require more effort than listing records one by one. For reports that consist of dozens, if not hundreds, of pages, providing a meaningful format that groups the data into logical units will go a long way towards making your reports easier to read. Crystal Reports .NET makes this possible by giving you the ability to sort and group data. Grouping reports also gives you the ability to create drill-down reports and summarize data. All of these features are covered in this chapter.

Sorting Records

Being able to sort records in either ascending or descending order is a reporting fundamental. Sorting makes it easy for a user to quickly find a particular piece of data buried inside many pages of data.

Reports can be sorted on a single field or on multiple fields. When sorting on multiple fields, you have to specify which field gets sorted first. When there are duplicate values for the first field, then the next field is used to resolve which record gets listed first. An example of this type of report is an employee report that sorts by name. The primary sort field is the last name. When there are duplicate last names, the secondary sort field, the first name, is used.

Using the Record Sort Order dialog box makes sorting records easy (shown in Figure 4-1). To use this dialog box, right-click on the report and select Report | Sort Records. On the left is the standard tree-view control listing the available fields. You can sort on fields from the report's data sources or your own custom formulas.

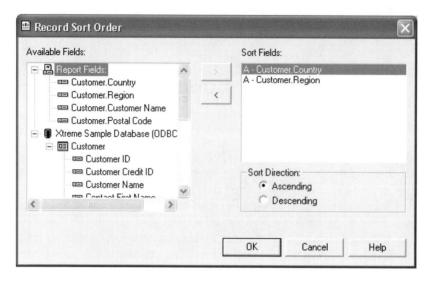

Figure 4-1. The sort order dialog box.

To select a field, either drag and drop it to the Sort Fields window on the right or click on the arrow buttons to move it over. The order in which you add the fields determines which one gets priority in the sort order. The first field listed becomes the primary sort field. The next field is the secondary field, and so on. When there are duplicate values in one of the fields, then the next field on the list is used to resolve the conflict. This continues through all the sort fields as long as there are duplicates at each level.

Caution
Once you add a field to the Sort Fields window, you can't change its ranking among the other fields. There are no up/down arrows that make it easy to reorder the list. You need to remove the fields that are out of order and then add them back in the proper order.

At the bottom of the dialog box is where you set whether the field is sorted in ascending or descending order. Each field is treated individually. First click on the field name and then click on the sort order.

As an example, let's look at the example sort order shown in Figure 4-2. The primary sort field is the country. The secondary field is the region and this is followed by the customer name. This report produced by this dialog box is shown in Figure 4-2.

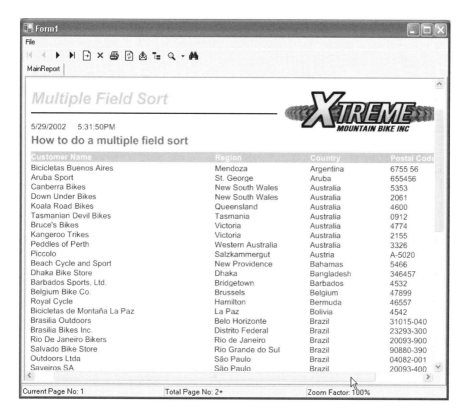

Figure 4-2. The multiple field sort report.

The report first lists all the countries that start with the letter "A". The country Australia has multiple records, so the report performs a secondary sort on the Region field.

If you later determine that you need to change the sorting order, you can modify it using the same steps mentioned earlier. Just right-click on the report and select Report | Sort Records.

Grouping Records

When a report has a lot of pages, it is hard to quickly find information as well as get a general idea of what the report is telling you. Sorting the data helps you find a specific record, but it doesn't give you high-level summary of what the data means. Grouping records lets you summarize data in a way that the reader can quickly grasp what the report is trying to say.

Grouping records is an advanced form of sorting. It lets you create categories to visually organize the records. You can summarize the data on critical fields and perform summing operations on the data within each group. If you need to see more information you can explore the detail records that make up the group.

Sorting records in a report results in the records being ordered differently than their natural order, but it doesn't have any effect on how the report is structured. Grouping is different because it creates new sections in the report's design. For every group added to a report there is a corresponding group header and group footer added. This lets you add formatting to designate when a new group starts and when the group ends. Within each section you can show report fields, formula fields or summary fields. It's common to make fields in the group header to be a different font (possibly bold) and in the footer it's common to show sub-totals. The footer gives you a summary of the data within a group without having to read every line. If you don't need to display the group header or footer, each can be hidden.

Adding and Customizing Groups

Adding and customizing groups is very similar to working with the other sections of a report. Add a new group by right-clicking on the report and selecting Insert | Group. This displays the dialog box shown in Figure 4-3.

Figure 4-3. The Insert Group dialog box.

The Common tab has two frames for changing how the group is displayed and changing the sort order of the values within the group. The top frame sets which field the group is based on and the sorting order of the group values.

The lower frame, titled Group Options, only lets you make a few changes to how the group is formatted.

Selecting the Grouping Field

The first dropdown box at the top of the dialog box selects the field that the group is based on. You can choose from a current field on the report, any fields in the current data source, or a formula field. When selecting a group field that is a data type of Date, Time or DateTime, you have more options for how to group. A new dropdown box appears that lets you group on the specific part of the date or time (e.g. month, quarter, hour, etc.)

Sorting In a Specified Order

The second dropdown box at the top selects the sorting order of how the groups are listed. With one exception, the sorting options are what you would expect and don't need any explanation. You can choose a sort order that is Ascending, Descending, Original Order (no sorting) or Specified Order.

Specified Order is the option that is not completely intuitive. Specified Order means that you specify the exact order to display every possible data value in that field. Once you select this option two new tabs appear in the dialog box: Specified Order and Others. This is shown in Figure 4-4.

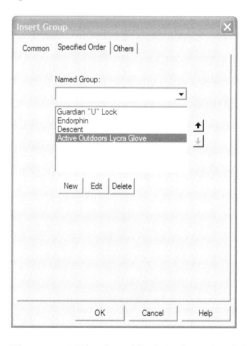

Figure 4-4. The Specified Order tab of the Insert Group dialog box.

The Specified Order tab is where you build the list of how the values are to be sorted. There are two controls in this dialog box. To top control is a dropdown box that lists all the possible values for the group field. The lower control is a listbox which shows the order that each value is to be listed in. Take values from the dropdown box and add them to the listbox in the appropriate order.

The order of the items in the listbox can be changed. Select the item to move and click on either the up or down arrows located to the right of the listbox.

There are two ways of adding items to the list box: adding individual items or adding named groups (a sub-group). Adding individual items is the easiest method because you simply click on one of the values from the dropdown box and it gets added to the list. Unfortunately, if you have a lot of possible values, this could be very time consuming. To make this a little easier, there is a second way of adding items to the list.

The second way of adding items is by creating named groups that specify a range of values. Specifying a group is done in the typical fashion of specifying a lower and upper bounds for the range or building a formula using Boolean logic. It may be easier to think of this as a sub-group. Any value that falls within this range gets put into the named group. This is obviously a faster way of adding the items because you don't have to specify individual values. Named groups also give you a lot of flexibility because the formulas can be quite complex.

To create a named group, click on the New button located below the list. This brings up the dialog box called Define Named Group. You can see in Figure 4-5 that this is a fairly simple dialog box.

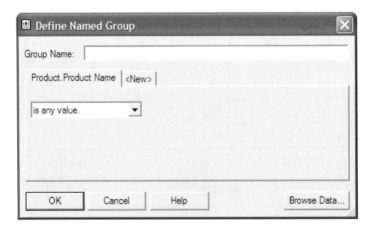

Figure 4-5. The Define Named Group dialog box.

Assign a name to the group in the top textbox. In the left dropdown you specify how to filter the range of values. The dropdown box shows numerous ways to select a range of values. A few of these are: Is Equal To, Is Not One Of, and Is Between. When you select one of these operators, the proper input controls automatically appear to the right of the dropdown box. The input controls change depending upon the information needed to complete the filter. There are so many different variations of filtering options and their associated input controls, that they won't be explained here. They are all very intuitive and you shouldn't have any problem entering the proper data.

Within a named group, you have the option of using more than one filter. By clicking on the <New> tab, you are shown the same filtering options as on the first tab. But now you can make new selections and the resulting values are also associated with the current named group. From a Boolean logic standpoint, these filters are linked together using an OR operand. Thus, any of them can be true and the record will be included in the named group.

The last tab in the Change Group Options dialog box is the Others tab. Since it is very possible that some reports won't need to specify how every value will be grouped, this tab is used to accumulate all the remaining values that didn't get included in one of the named groups.

This is also useful for reports that group on fields where the data is dynamic and new values are being added. If the new values don't fall within the current named groups, they get associated with the group called Other.

Values in the Other group can either be excluded from the report or included in the report. If they are included in the report then they are always listed as the last group.

Customizing the Group Name

In most circumstances, the group name that is displayed on the report is the current value. For example, if you are grouping by country, then the group name is the country name. If you don't want to display the current value as the group name, you have the option of displaying another value instead. For example, a report group that lists how many products were sold for each day of the month is typically based on the inventory number. If the report is intended for users who recognize a product's name, but not its inventory number, then the group header won't mean anything to the reader. You want the group header to show the product's common name.

Within the Group Options frame you can set another value to be displayed for a group's name. Click the option button Choose From Existing Field to use another field for the group name. Then select that field from the dropdown box below it. When the group name is displayed, the value from the other field is displayed instead.

There are times when the group name you want to display isn't a field in the table. It could be a custom formatting field that is derived from a formula. To make the group name display a formula instead, click the option button Use a Formula as Group Name and then click the formula button.

Organizing the Group

The remaining two checkboxes effect how the group data is displayed on the report. The first checkbox controls whether the report should try to keep the entire group on the same page. The second checkbox controls whether the group header should be repeated on each page.

Setting the Keep Group Together checkbox is important if you want to prevent having only a few records of a group appearing at the bottom of a page. When this option is on, the entire group is analyzed before it is printed. If it can't fit on the rest of the page, then the remainder of the page is left blank and the group is started at the top of the next page.

The second checkbox, Repeat Group Header on Each Page, forces the group header to print at the top of every page. This is important for groups that can span multiple pages. By default, if a group extends to a second page then its header is not printed at the top of the second page. It might not be obvious how the detail records are related to each other. If you feel that showing the group header at the top of the page makes your report easier to read, then you should click this checkbox.

Sorting the Group Data

After creating the groups and running a test report, you may notice that although your groups are fine, the individual rows within the group are out of order. If this happens, it is because you still need to add sort fields to your report. Telling the report how to group data doesn't imply that it knows which fields to use for sorting the detail records with. When using groups, the data within the group gets sorted according to how you set up the sort fields. If no sort fields are used, then the records appear in their natural order (which still may not be what you expect because the grouping process reorders the records as well). Look at the earlier section Sorting In a Specified Order for instructions on adding sort fields.

Changing the Field to Group On

Once the report is finished you might decide that the records need to be grouped differently or create a new report that looks the same but has different groups. For example, the original design of the sales report groups by region and it works fine. But you also need a similar report that groups by salesperson. Rather than redo the report from scratch, you can make a copy of the report and modify the group fields that need to change. Changing the group field is done via the Change Group dialog box.

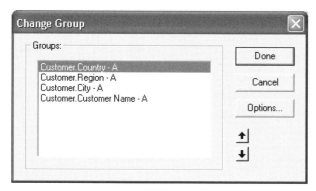

Figure 4-6. The Change Group dialog box.

This dialog box can be accessed in two ways. The first way is to right-click on the group header bar and select Change Group. The other way is to click anywhere else on the report and select Report | Change Group Expert.

The groups are listed in their current order. You can use the arrow buttons to the right to rearrange their order. To modify a group field, click on the group and then click on the Options button. This brings up the Change Group Options dialog box mentioned earlier. Since this is the same dialog box you used to create the group, then you can also change any of the other group properties as well.

Note

The Change Group dialog box lets you modify the existing groups, but you can't add new groups with it. To do that, you have to right click on the report and select Insert | Group (as mentioned at the beginning of this section).

Displaying Top N Reports

An alternative to the standard grouping is to create reports that show the first or last set of records in a certain group. For example, rather than showing all the sales people for the company, you could show the 5 sales people that have the best sales for the month. Or you can do the opposite and show the 5 sales people with the lowest sales for the month. The first report shows who deserves a bonus and the second report shows who should be talked to about improving their performance.

Generating a Top N report has a couple of requirements. The first is that your report must have at least one group in it. The second requirement is that the group must have a summary field in it (a sub-total, average, etc). The summary field is required because a Top N report needs a numeric value to calculate how to rank the groups.

To create a Top N report, right-click on the report and select Report | Top N/Sort Group Expert. If it is grayed out, then that means that you either don't have a group section or you don't have a summary field within the group. Correct this and it won't be grayed out any more.

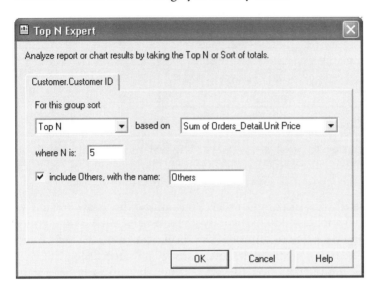

Figure 4-7. The Top N Expert dialog box.

When the Top N Expert dialog box opens, it defaults to a setting of All, for displaying all values. By clicking on this dropdown box, you can choose from a Top N or Bottom N selection basing it on a certain quantity or as percentage of the total records. It lets you select which field to base the comparison on (this must be a summary field), how many groups to show and whether all the remaining groups should be lumped into a final group called Others (or another name that you specify). If you want to select the number of groups based on the percentage of the total groups, then select that in the dropdown box and the dialog box will stay the same with the exception that the number now represents a percentage.

The Top N Expert dialog box shows a separate tab for every group on your report that uses a summary field. This lets you create different Top N selections for each group.

This dialog box actually has a dual purpose. I quickly skimmed over the fact that the dropdown box defaults to All because it isn't relevant to printing a Top N report. However, it is useful for creating new ways of sorting your groups. Normally, the group sorting is set via the Change Group dialog box. In this circumstance, you can override that by sorting on the value of a group's summary field. Select the summary fields with the right-most dropdown box. Each summary field you select gets added to the listbox below it. You can change whether the field is sorted in ascending or descending order by clicking on it in the listbox and then selecting the sort order. By using summary fields to sort your groups, you get a lot more flexibility with how the groups get displayed.

Displaying Hierarchical Reports

A hierarchical report displays data to show relationships between records in the same table using a tree format. This is similar to having a self-join SQL statement that needs to join a table to itself using a common field. For example, this can be used to show employees that are subordinate to another employee. When printing a supervisor list, you will show which employee reports to which supervisor. Ideally, you would link the Supervisor table to the Employee table. But in this circumstance, a supervisor is an employee as well. So you have to link the Employee table to the Employee table, thus creating a self-join SQL statement. Rather than do this work, open the Hierarchical Options dialog box. In this dialog box specify which field is the parent and it will do all the linking for you. In this case, the Supervisor ID field is the parent of the Employee ID field. This is shown in Figure 4-8.

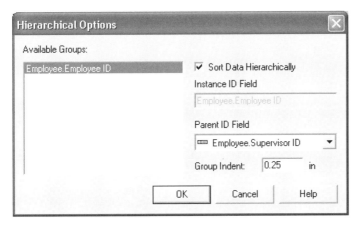

Figure 4-8. The Hierarchical Options dialog box.

The Available Groups listbox shows the current groups in your report. To use it for hierarchical grouping, click on it and then check the Sort Data Hierarchically checkbox. The field for that group will be the subordinate field. In the dropdown box below the checkbox, select the field that will be the parent field. Since the parent field and employee field are going to be linked together, and the parent field will be listed in the group header field, both of these fields must be the same data type. The default indentation is 0.25 inches. You can change that if you wish.

Figure 4-9 shows what the supervisor report looks like. This is the Hierarchical Grouping report that is installed in the Samples directory with Crystal Reports.

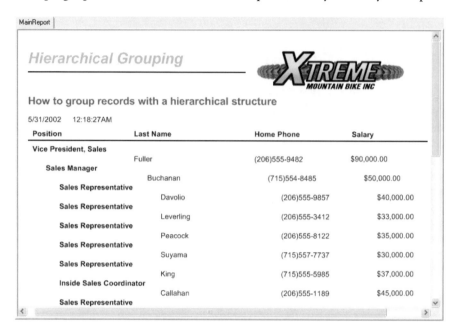

Figure 4-9. The Hierarchical Grouping report.

You might notice one small problem with hierarchical reports: when the rows are shifted to the right to represent a subordinate level, the columns no longer line up with the column header. Unfortunately, this can't be prevented and you must compensate for it with wider than normal column header widths.

Drilling Down on Data

Grouping data on a report gives you the added feature of letting you create drill-down reports. A drill-down report lets the user look at the detail records that make up a summary value. It takes a snapshot of the detail records that make up the summary and displays that snapshot on a separate tab. This lets the user look at the detail data without being distracted by the rest of the report.

Drill-down reports never change their original format. As you double-click on the group data to drill down into the detail data, new tabs are created to show you that detail. But the original report format never changes. If the original report is already showing the group's detail, you can still double-click on it to open the detail in another tab on the viewer.

Since drill-down reports are designed with the purpose of having a user navigate through the data, they can only be used with the CrystalReportViewer control. Obviously, this wouldn't work on a report that has been printed because paper doesn't have a user interface.

The viewer shows you which groups can be drilled down into by changing the cursor into a magnifying glass as it passes over the group data. Perform the drill-down by double-clicking on the field.

By default, the group details are shown on a report and the drill-down feature is also turned on for every group. This just means that the details will be shown on the report and the user can click on the group header to display the details in a separate tab. If you want to hide the details, but still allow someone to drill-down into the details, right-click on the report and select Hide. If you don't want the details viewed at all, select Suppress.

An advanced example is a report that has secure data that can only be viewed by the appropriate level of personnel (e.g. an employee payroll report), but you want all other users to be able to view the group summary data. To implement this behavior, modify the group's object during runtime to either turn Suppress on or off depending upon the user. Modifying the group objects during runtime is covered in Part II of this book.

Summarizing Data

The purpose of grouping data is to make the report easier to read by creating categories that the detail records fit into. Within these categories you perform various summary functions on fields so that the user can get an overview of the information within the group without having to read all the data. Crystal Reports has a large variety of summary functions to display for a group. Examples of these summary functions are sub-totals, averages, and maximum values. Table 4-1 shows a complete list of the summary functions available.

Table 4-1. Summary functions for groups.

Function	Description
Average	Calculates the average value. (2)
Correlation	Calculates the correlation of two fields. (1) (2)
Count	Counts the number of detail records. Fields with NULL values are not included in the calculation. (3)
Covariance	Calculates the measure of the linear relation between paired variables. (1)
DisctinctCount	Calculates the number of unique values for that field.
Maximimum	Finds the maximum value of all the fields.
Median	Returns the middle value if all the fields were sorted. (1)
Minimum	Finds the minimum value of all the fields.
Mode	Returns the value with the most duplicates.
NthLargest	Finds the largest value of all the fields with a ranking of N. For example, if N were 6, it would return the sixth largest value.
NthMostFrequent	Finds the Nth ranking field with the most duplicate values. For example, if N were 6, it would return the value with the 6th most duplicates.
NthSmallest	Finds the smallest value of all the fields with a ranking of N. For example, if N were 6, it would return the sixth smallest value.
Percentage	Returns a percentage of the grand-total for the selected field. (2)
Percentile	Returns the value for the specified percentile of the field. (2)
PopStandard Deviation	Calculates how much a field deviates from the mean value. (1) (2)
SampleStanadard Deviation	Returns the sample standard deviation for the field. (1) (2)
SampleVariance	Returns the sample variance for the field. (1) (2)
Sum	Returns the total of all the detail fields.(2)
WeightedAverage	Returns the weighted average of all the detail fields. (2)

Chart Notes:

1) See a statistics book for more information.

2) Can only be used for numeric data.

3) NULL values can be included if you set them to return their default values. To do this, right-click on the report and select Report | Report Options. Then check the box for converting NULL field values to their default.

To summarize a field within the groups, right-click on the field that you want to summarize. The pop-up menu gives you the option of inserting a subtotal, a grand total or a summary. Each of these menu options gives you a different dialog box.

Inserting a subtotal brings up the dialog box in Figure 4-10. The top textbox shows the field you clicked on. Below that is a dropdown box that shows the current groups on your report as well as all the other report fields. Normally, you will select one of the existing groups. However, if there are no groups based upon the field you want to associate this summary field with, then click on that field and after you close the dialog box a new group will be created. Ideally, this won't be necessary because you will plan out your report so that it already has all the necessary groups created.

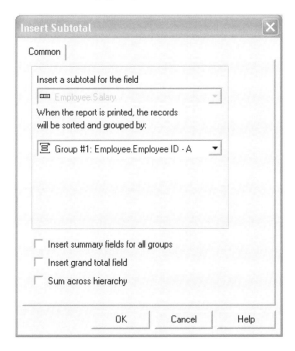

Figure 4-10. The Insert Subtotal dialog box.

Inserting a Grand Total displays a dialog box that lets you choose which function should be performed on the field. As the report is run, this function is calculated for each field and its total is displayed. After selecting the OK button, the grand total field is added in the Report Footer section and aligned directly below the original field.

Inserting a summary field brings up the dialog box in Figure 4-11. The top dropdown box lets you select which function to perform on the field. The field that you are summarizing is listed below that dropdown box. After that you can select which group to put this summary into. Again, if you pick a field that doesn't already have a group for it, a new group will be added to your report. At the bottom of the dialog box you can tell it to insert the summary for every group, insert a grand total as well, or sum across a hierarchy. The summary field is placed in the group footer aligned directly below the original field.

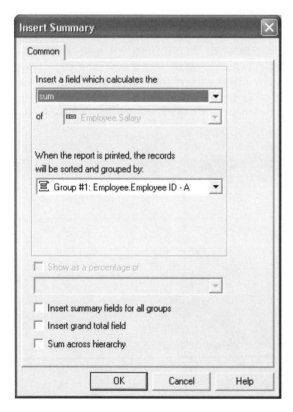

Figure 4-11. The Insert Summary dialog box.

By default, the summary field is automatically placed in the group footer. You can move this field to the group header if you want to keep all the summary information in the same section and printed before the detail rows.

To change the summary function after it has been created, right-click on the summary field and select Change Summary Operation. That brings up a dialog box with a dropdown box of all the available summary functions. Select the one you want to change it to and click on the OK button.

This page intentionally left blank

5
Using Parameters and Formulas

As Crystal Reports has become increasingly advanced over the years, the number of ways to customize reports has also increased. However, passing data to a report hasn't changed much. Parameters are still the preferred method of passing data to a report. This chapter explores how to create parameters, query the user for input, and use parameters to customize a report. Parameters have been a very effective way to getting user input, but parameters are showing their age and are ripe for improvement now that Crystal Reports has been integrated into .NET. Formulas address some of the parameters' weaknesses. They are easier to work with during runtime and are less complex to set up. This is discussed in more detail in Chapter 16.

Inputting Parameters

Crystal Reports considers parameters to be the programming language equivalent of a constant data type. The parameter is assigned a value when the report loads and that value never changes. A parameter is like any other field on the report: It can be displayed on the report, used in filters, and used to change the formatting of report objects.

In their simplest form, parameters are used as an easy way to let the user enter a value. At another level, they can be thought of as a way of creating advanced input boxes. Parameters can have default values defined in such a way that the user is able to enter the value by selecting it from a predefined list in the combobox. The programmer controls how many options a user has in the combobox. The section on default values details the setting up of parameters in this way. When a report loads, parameters get their values by displaying a dialog box to the user. This dialog box prompts the user for information and it has input fields for the user to enter one or more values. Once the user closes the dialog box, the report uses the user input to generate the report. An example of this is a report that prints records between a valid data range. Parameters confine the beginning and ending date ranges.

Adding Parameters

Parameters are another type of report object. The steps to add and modify them are similar to what you've already been doing. Add a parameter by clicking on the Field Explorer tab (on the left side of the IDE by default) and right-clicking on Parameter Fields. Then, select the New menu option. Clicking on an existing item allows the option to edit, delete or rename the item. Figure 5-1 shows this menu.

Figure 5-1. Menu option for adding a new parameter.

Once you select New, the Create Parameter Field dialog box appears, shown in Figure 5-2.

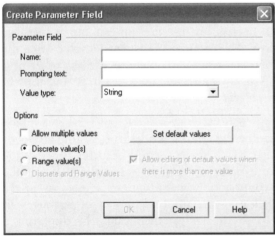

Figure 5-2. The Create Parameter Field dialog box.

This dialog box has three textboxes at the top, for entering the necessary properties: the parameter's name, the prompting text and the value type. The Name property is how the parameter is referenced in the report. Running the report triggers the display of the Prompting Text, which should describe what the user is asked to enter. The Value Type property selects the data type for the parameter field. All the available data types are listed in this dropdown box.

The lower half of the dialog box lets you set the options for the data that the parameter can store. Table 5-1 describes four options.

Table 5-1. Options for parameter fields

Option	Description
Discrete value(s)	The user must enter must a single value.
Range value(s)	The user enters two values that are the beginning and ending points of a range. The range includes the values entered. For example, if you entered a range of 1,000 and 1,999 then it would include all numbers from 1,000 up to and including 1,999.
Discrete and Range values	The user can enter both discrete and range values.
Allow multiple values	Allow a parameter to accept more than one value.

The option to allow multiple values is used with discrete values and range values. For discrete values, the user can enter multiple single values and they are each treated individually. For range values, the user can enter multiple sets of ranges and each range is treated separately from the other ranges entered. A parameter can also have a collection of both discrete values and range values.

Boolean parameters can be thought of as being similar to checkboxes or option buttons. With checkboxes, each value is independent of the other. That is, selecting or changing one checkbox has no effect on other checkboxes. This is the default behavior of Boolean parameters. Option buttons are used in groups and each is mutually exclusive of the other. Selecting one will automatically turn off all others in the same group. The Place in Parameter Group option lets you place a Boolean parameter in a parameter group. Give it a group number and set whether the parameters in that group are mutually exclusive to each other. If the parameters are mutually exclusive, only one Boolean parameter can be assigned to True at a time. If the user sets two or more parameters to True, only the most recent will keep its value; the others are reset to False.

The Create Parameter Field dialog box for Boolean data types has different options. When you change the Value Type property to Boolean, the lower half of the dialog box changes to reflect the new options (see Figure 5-3).

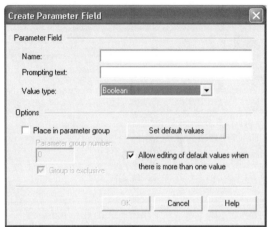

Figure 5-3. The Create Parameter Field dialog box for Boolean data.

Setting the Default Values

Default values give the user a list of values to choose from, which saves the user from the chore of memorizing all the available values that could be entered. Default values also restrict what can be entered. This prevents a user from making a typographical error.[9]

One drawback of using default values is that they create additional overhead and increase the risk of error because it goes against the methodology of Object Oriented Programming (OOP). The goal of writing applications using OOP techniques is to consolidate all the information about a business object within its respective classes. This gives you encapsulation and makes it easier to maintain your code. Setting default values within a report breaks this rule because you are storing information about an object outside of its classes. In fact, this data is being stored in a separate file entirely. This requires additional documentation stating that all rules regarding an object's default values must also be replicated to the related reports. If there is a bug in the report, both the report and the business objects would have to be debugged. This creates additional work during testing.

The best method is to not set default values within the report; instead use the .NET application to maintain this. Since the .NET front end is used to get input from the user before printing the report, logic can be added here to pre-populate the front end with the appropriate default values that are derived from the class.

---

[9] In CR.NET default values have numerous bugs and do not work as expected. Make sure you have the latest service pack if you plan on using default values in your reports.

Of course, not everyone is going to write fully compliant OOP applications, nor will every report warrant the extra time required to fully integrate it into the .NET application. That being the case, this chapter explains how to create and use default parameters within a report.

Note

Default values aren't used with ASP.NET applications. With an ASP.NET application, Crystal Reports isn't able to prompt the user to enter a value for each parameter. You are required to set each parameter during runtime prior to viewing the report. Thus, default values lose their significance with ASP.NET applications.

Default values are added by clicking on the Set Default Values button on the Create Parameter dialog box. This brings up the Set Default Values dialog box. As Figure 5-4 shows, this is a fairly complex dialog box. This is because it allows the entry of every possible combination of values for each parameter type. That's a lot of combinations!

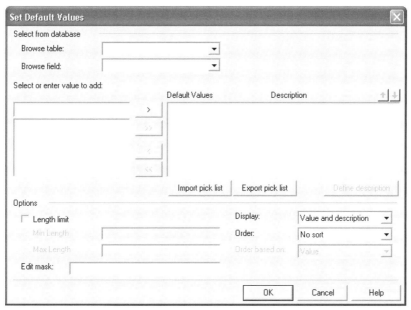

Figure 5-4. The Set Default Values dialog box for string data types.

It was mentioned earlier that default values can be designed so that the user is presented with a listbox showing all the possible values. The Set Default Values dialog box is where this is done. Within this dialog box, one can create either a single default value or a list of default values. If a single default value, the input box is pre-populated with that value.[10] If you create a list of default values, the user, when entering a value for the particular parameter, can select one of those values from a combobox.

The middle of the dialog box is the central part of setting default values. The left side is the place to enter a default value in the textbox. Click on the right arrow to move it to the list of possible default values. There is no limit to the number of values added to the right listbox.

An alternative to manually typing all the default values by hand, if entering a lot of default values, is to pull them from existing tables. This neat trick is performed by selecting from the top two dropdown boxes, a table and a field to get the values from. Once the two items are selected, the values are pulled from the field and put into the listbox on the left. Clicking on the arrow keys allows one to select and transfer to the default value list any number of these items. Alternately, to import a list of default values from a text file, click on the Import Pick List button.

Tip
The options to pull a list of values from a table or from a text file are better served by creating your own interface using .NET. Both of these options are just a mediocre attempt at creating a data-bound combobox. In Crystal Reports, there is no way to create a data-bound control for parameter values. This is just too complex for a reporting tool to implement. So presenting a static list of values from a table or text file is the next best option. Using this technique results in the problem that if your database were updated, you would have to come back to this report and update the list of possible values. But with .NET report integration, you can provide the user with a true data-bound combobox on a form in your application. This is a more practical solution to implement and it insures that the user always has a current list of values to choose from.

There are two options that are unique to string values. Refer again to Figure 5-4. You can limit the length of a string size and set the edit mask in the lower left corner of the Set Default Values dialog box. Limiting the length of the string allows you to set the minimum length and the maximum length.

---

[10] This requires installing the latest service pack.

However, these options do not exist if using parameters with a numeric data type. Instead, set a valid range by entering minimum and maximum values.

The bottom right corner of the dialog box is the place to go to for setting a description for each value, as well as the sorting order. This is similar to the functionality of a data-bound combobox because of the option to show a description rather the actual value.[11] This is useful for having the user select a table's primary key by clicking on the description rather than the numeric id. The values can be sorted in ascending, descending and natural order.

Closing the Set Default Value dialog box brings back the Create Parameter Field dialog box. Now that the parameter has a stored default value, the checkbox Allow Editing of Default Values is no longer grayed out (it is checked by default). When this is checked, the user can enter a new value in addition to selecting an item in the list of default values. Unchecking this option then requires the user to select an item from the list of values, which prevents him or her from entering an invalid value.

Entering Parameters when Running Reports

When a report has parameters, the user is prompted to enter values when the report is loaded, but before it is printed. After the user enters the values, the report is shown in the viewer or sent to the printer. Figure 5-5 is the Enter Parameter Values dialog box.

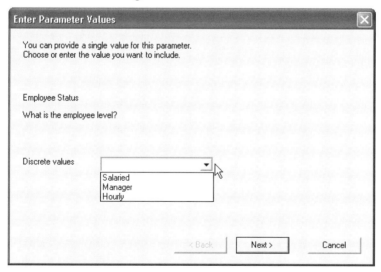

Figure 5-5. The Enter Parameter Values dialog box.

---

[11] This requires installing the latest service pack.

At the top is a description of what information can be entered. Below that is the prompt that is assigned to the parameter. The bottom of the dialog box is where the user enters the value(s) for the parameter field. Click on the Next button to go to the next field. Clicking on the Cancel button at any time cancels the report. Nor will it be displayed in the viewer. If the user refreshes the report, this dialog box gets displayed again.

If you have used Crystal Reports 8.5, then you might notice that .NET treats mutually exclusive Boolean parameters differently than 8.5 does. With 8.5, mutually exclusive Boolean parameters were grouped together as a single step on the dialog box and you selected which one should be set to True. The other parameters within that group remained False. With .NET, this is no longer the case. Each parameter is shown separate from the others. If you select True for more than one parameter, only the most recent one will be True. The others will be reset back to False. Unfortunately, .NET doesn't tell you that this is happening nor does it give any indication that the parameter is part of a mutually exclusive group. Once again, this is just another reason to manage default values within your .NET application and not rely upon the report.

Caution

If you run a report and get the error "Operation illegal on linked parameter" it is because a formula references a parameter, but that parameter isn't used on the report. To fix this error make sure that the parameter appears on the report.

Customizing Reports

You've had the opportunity to create basic report formats, including sorting, grouping and adding parameters. This chapter takes that knowledge a little further by showing you how to add more customization to your report. This customization consists of filtering records, using report sections for advanced formatting techniques, and creating running totals. Once you are finished with this chapter, you will have the foundation needed to generate the majority of reports you need on a daily basis.

Selecting Records

Up to this chapter all the reports have all selected records from a table without regard to filtering the data. It was assumed that you wanted to display every record in the table. While this is true some of the time, you frequently want to filter the data so that only a subset of records gets printed. This lets you customize a report to only show the information that pertains to the current user. For example, you can design a sales report so that it selects data based upon the region, the sales person, or even on a sales person for just the last month. Almost any way that you can imagine to filter data can be done for a report.

Crystal Reports makes selecting records easy. It provides a Select Expert dialog box that lets you pick one or more fields and set the selection formula. The Select Expert dialog box is similar to other Crystal Report experts and is easy to learn.

Using the Select Expert

To open the Select Expert, right click on the report and choose Report | Select Expert. If this is the first time the Select Expert has been run for the report, it shows the Choose Field dialog box. As you can see in Figure 6-1, it simply lists all the fields available, including report fields as well as database fields.

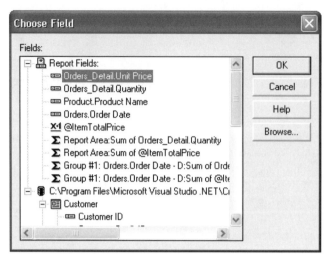

Figure 6-1. The Choose Field dialog box.

Once you select a field from this dialog box and click the Ok button, the dialog box is not shown again. Instead, you are always taken to the Select Expert dialog box shown in Figure 6-2.

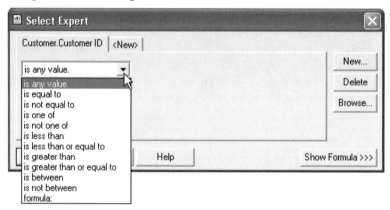

Figure 6-2. The Select Expert dialog box.

There are two tabs in this dialog box. The first is titled with the field that was selected in the Choose Field dialog box and the second is titled <New>. The tab with the field name has a combobox for selecting the filter criteria. By default this is set to is any value. By default, reports don't have any filters turned on and every record gets selected. Click the combobox to view available filtering options and select the one you want. The dialog box in Figure 6-2 shows all the options in this combobox. This list is the textual equivalent of the basic comparison operators that you would normally use in your programming code (e.g. =, >, <=, etc.). Except for the formula: option (discussed later), these are all standard comparisons and require no explanation.

Selecting a field that is of the DateTime data type give you additional options listed with the comparison operators. These options include selecting dates that are within a certain fiscal quarter, within the past month, or even aging dates according to how many days ago they occurred. These advanced filtering options demonstrate the power of Crystal Reports for working with dates. See Chapter 9 for more information on how these date functions work.

After selecting a comparison method, the right side of the dialog box changes so that you can enter the value to compare the field to. With the majority of the comparisons, only a single combobox is shown. A very helpful feature is that all the current values for the field are listed in the dropdown box. Crystal Reports populates the list with the current data for that field from all the records. In fact, you will probably notice a short delay as it opens and reads in the records from the table. You can either select one of these fields from the list or enter a new value that isn't in the list.

If the report uses a connection to the database on the server, make sure you have an active connection to it. Otherwise Crystal Reports temporarily freezes up while it pings the server waiting for a response.

Although most comparison operators only have a single dropdown box for entering values, there are a couple of exceptions. The is between and is not between comparisons give you two dropdown boxes. This lets you enter a beginning and ending range. The is between comparison is inclusive. The is not between comparison is exclusive. The other exception is when choosing a comparison of is one of or is not one of; then the dialog box looks like Figure 6-3. This lets you build a list of items where the field should either be in the list or not in the list. As you select items from the combobox, they are added to the listbox below it. If you type in a value manually, add it by clicking on the Add button. If you add an item by mistake, delete it from the list by clicking the Remove button.

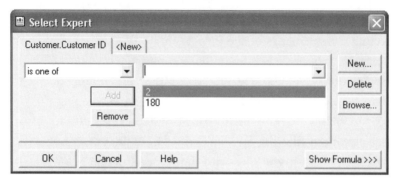

Figure 6-3. Building a list of items.

You are not limited to selecting records based on a single field. The <New> tab lets you select additional fields for record selection. Clicking on this tab shows the same Choose Field dialog box that you saw when you first opened the Select Expert. After selecting a field you are brought back to this tab and that field is now in the tab header. The rest of the selection process is the same as what was just discussed.

When selecting multiple fields, Crystal Reports treats each field as being part of a Boolean AND statement. For a record to be selected by the report, it must successfully meet the criteria specified for each field listed in the dialog box. If there were four fields listed, and a record only matched three of the fields, then the record won't be selected.

From what you have seen so far, the Select Expert is a very helpful tool for selecting one or more fields using the basic comparison operators. This is probably adequate for many of the reports you write. But what about the other reports, where you need to build more complex filtering criteria? For those reports, there is the Formula Editor. The Formula Editor is described in complete detail in Chapter 7, but here is a summary of how to use it.

The Formula Editor lets you use Crystal syntax, the built-in programming language, to create sophisticated selection formulas. There is a large library of functions to choose from for building a selection formula. A simple example is when you don't want to use the Select Expert's default of requiring a field to match all the criteria selected. You can change the formula so that rather than use the default Boolean AND to join the conditions, it uses Boolean OR. Another example is rather than selecting a range of records based upon customer name, select the records based upon the first character of the customer name. This would let you choose all the customers with names starting with the letter "B".

Caution

When opening the Formula Editor from within the Select Expert, you are only given the option of using Crystal syntax as the programming language. As you will see in Chapter 7, Crystal Reports also gives you the option of using Basic syntax, which is very similar to VB.NET. Unfortunately, the Formula Editor requires using Crystal syntax.

There are two ways to enter a custom formula. The first way is to click on the Show Formula button. This shows the existing formula built using the fields already selected. You can change this formula directly so that it matches the selection criteria you need. If you can't remember the different built-in functions well enough to type them in directly, click on the Formula Editor button. This brings up the Formula Editor dialog box (discussed in Chapter 7) and you can use it as a reference tool to build the formula. The second way to enter a formula is to click on the comparison list dropdown box and at the very bottom is an item called formula:. Clicking on this item changes the right side to a multi-line text box that lets you type a formula from scratch.

Caution

Crystal Reports raises the error "Failed to open rowset" when a record selection formula performs an empty string comparison on a field with a null value.

Formula = {table.field} <> ""

To correct this you also have to check for null values.

Formula = not(isnull({table.field})) AND {table.field} <> ""

Selecting Records for Grouping

Setting a filter on summary data isn't done with the regular selection formula. Selecting records has the limitation that you can only set filters for raw data or basic formulas. You can't set filters that operate on summary fields or on formulas built with summary fields. You also can't use any fields that use second-pass data. As mentioned in Chapter 1, second-pass data includes summaries and subtotals. The reason for these restrictions is that filtering is done during a report's first pass. Second-pass data hasn't been calculated yet and consequently you can't filter on something that doesn't exist.

To get around this problem, you have to perform a grouping selection. Crystal Reports performs grouping selections during the second-pass when summary data is available.

There are two ways to add a grouping selection. The first way to add a grouping selection is to right-click on the report designer and select Reports |

Edit Selection Formula | Group. This brings up the Formula Editor dialog box where you can enter the necessary formula.

The second way is using the standard Select Expert dialog box and entering the filter as you normally would. The expert automatically recognizes that the formula entered is only valid as a grouping filter and will flag it as such. You can see this by clicking on the Show Formula button and the Grouping option button will be selected.

Sections

Sections are used to determine where report objects will appear on a report. Each section has a different purpose and different rules that it follows to determine when and where it should appear on a report. For example, the Report Header section only appears at the top of the first page of a report. It does not appear on any other pages in the report. Although each section follows certain rules, there are many options available for customizing a section so that the report comes out just right. This section of the book shows you the different formatting options available as well as how to add sub-sections to a report for greater customization.

Formatting Sections

Report sections have many formatting options. You can hide a section, force it to print at the bottom of the page, force a page break afterwards and many other options. Creative use of these formatting options gives you control over how the report looks.

The formatting of each section is controlled by a single dialog box. The Section Expert, shown in Figure 6-4, is accessed by right-clicking on the report designer and selecting Format Section.

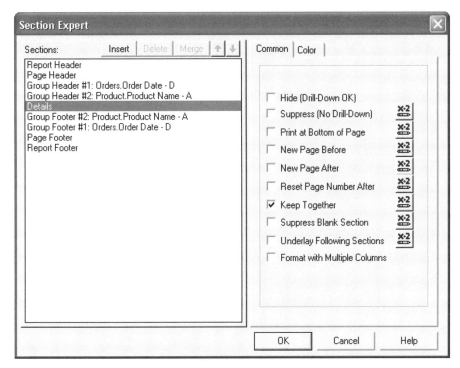

Figure 6-4. The Section Expert dialog box.

The Section Expert lists every section in the report and the formatting options available. The formatting options are represented by checkboxes because they are either enabled or disabled. Beside each option is a formula button that sets whether the option is enabled or disabled. This gives you flexibility for setting when a formatting option is turned on because the formula can use data from the currently printing record. Every time a section is printed, the formula is evaluated and its result determines whether the formatting option should be applied. This is described in more detail in Chapter 7.

When selecting the section from the list on the left, the formatting options on the right that are applicable to that section are enabled and the other options are grayed out. The list of formatting options doesn't change, but you are prevented from choosing the ones that don't apply.

With .NET, you can also access section properties via the Properties Window of the IDE. When you click on a section header, the properties in the window change to match the section selected. Each option shows whether it is enabled (True) or disabled (False). The drawback of using the Properties Window is that it has the limitation of not being able to use the advanced functionality of the Formula Editor.

Table 6-1 lists the different formatting options for sections.

Table 6-1. The formatting options for sections.

Formatting Option	Description
Hide (Drill-Down OK)	Don't show the section, but allow the user the drill-down into the data.
Suppress (No Drill-Down)	Don't show the section. Drill-down is not allowed.
Print at Bottom of Page	Force the section to always print at the bottom of the page.
New Page Before	Force a page break before the section prints.
New Page After	Force a page break after the section prints.
Reset Page Number After	Reset the page number counter back to 1 after the section prints.
Keep Together	Keep the section together on the same page.
Suppress Blank Section	If there is no data in the section, do not print it.
Underlay Following Sections	Print the current section on top of the following sections. Proper alignment is critical so that objects don't overlap each other.
Format with Multiple Columns	Creates mailing labels and newspaper column style reports. This is only listed for the Details section.

Hiding and Suppressing Sections

Hiding sections is used for drilling-down on detail records. As discussed in Chapter 4, you can design your report so that groups only display summary information. This presents the user with a much smaller report. If they are previewing the report with the CrystalReportViewer, then they can look at the detail information by double clicking on the group header. This creates a new tab in the viewer with the detail information being displayed inside.

Suppressing a section is done when you don't want the user to see the information in it. Of course, this leads to the question that if you don't want the user to see the information then why did you add the section? Suppressing sections is usually used in conjunction with conditional formatting. The Formula Editor is used to turn this option on or off depending upon other data that the report has access to. For example, if this is sensitive data then you would only let administrators see the detail information. All other users would have the detail section suppressed and they would only be able to see the summary information. This effectively lets you use one report for different users and different purposes.

Printing Sections at the Bottom of a Page

Printing sections at the bottom of the page is useful when printing reports that are one page long and have summary data listed at the bottom. Add a group to the report and set the group footer to print at the bottom of the page. An example is an invoice where the bottom of the page prints the total amount due. Invoices also print the aging schedule of past due balances at the bottom of the page. Another example is a form letter that requires authorized signatures of certain parties. Just put the signature lines in the group footer and set it to always print at the bottom of the page.

> **Note**
>
> Although you can set the Details section to print at the bottom of the page, this will have no effect. The detail records always print one after the other from top to bottom.

Forcing a Page Break

Page breaks are useful when you want groups to appear on their own pages. It is very common to want groups to appear by themselves so that data is listed separately from the other groups. An example is a report that has to be broken apart and distributed to multiple people. The group is used to identify where one report ends and the next one starts. Use the page breaks so that it is easy to separate the report pages and distribute them to the appropriate people.

Page breaks can be forced to occur either before or after a section. Unfortunately, each option has the problem of causing one blank page to be printed. If you force a page break before a group header, then the first page of the report will be blank. If you force a page break after the group footer, then the last page will be blank. The way around this is to use one of two built-in functions in the conditional formula: OnFirstRecord or OnLastRecord. By doing a Boolean Not in the formula, it temporarily turns suppression off for the section. For example, if you wanted to force a page break after the group footer, use the following formula (using Basic syntax) in the New Page After format option:

```
Formula = Not OnLastRecord
```

This formula returns True for every record leading up to the last record. Thus, there is always a page break after the group footer. Once the last record is printed, this formula returns False and the option to force a page break is turned off. The last page will not have a page break printed after it.

Resetting the Page Number

Resetting a page number back to Page 1 makes the page appear as if it is the first page in the report. This is good to use in combination with forcing a page

---

break after a section. When you distribute the pages of the report to different people, each person will have a report that starts on page 1.

Keeping Sections Together

Since it is very hard to control exactly where a section is printed on a page, it is common for sections to be split across pages. A report can start printing a section at the bottom of the page but not have enough room to print all of it and will print the remaining portion of the section on the next page. If it is important that all the information within a section be printed together, turn this option on. Before the section is printed, it is analyzed to see whether it fits on the page. If it doesn't fit then a page break is forced and the section prints on the next page.

As discussed in Chapter 4, when using this formatting option with groups, the report will try to fit the entire group (including the footer) onto the page. If the group is larger than one page, a page break is forced and the group gets printed on the next page.

Suppressing Blank Sections

Printing sections that don't have any data leaves blank rows in the report. This makes a report look unprofessional because of the gaps that seem to randomly occur. To fix this, set the option Suppress Blank Section. The report skips over any sections that don't have any data and goes to the next record. This option is used most frequently in conjunction with creating multiple report sections. This is covered in section Adding Multiple Sections.

Underlaying the Following Sections

When formatting a section so that it underlays the following sections, the following sections print on top of it. This has the effect of superimposing one or more sections on top of another section.

Underlaying sections is useful when working with images or charts and the related information is printed beside the image. This concept might be tough to grasp at first, so let's look at two examples. The first example is an employee report which shows the employee's picture on the left and the employee detail listed next to it. The example in Figure 6-5 is from the Xtreme database.

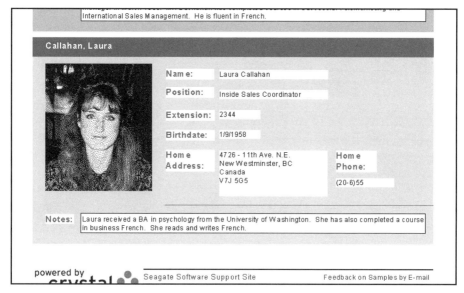

Figure 6-5. Employee Profile report with photo.

The data listed next to the employee picture is from the Employee table. It shows the different fields from a single employee record. There is a one-to-one relationship between the employee photo and the employee data.

This example is limited in that the photo can only be printed next to the data within a single employee record. If you wanted to print a photo with multiple detail records next to it, this approach won't work. The next example shows how to fix this problem by underlaying sections.

Let's look at an inventory report which lists how many products are on-hand for each inventory item. These items are grouped together by category and a generic picture of each category is displayed.

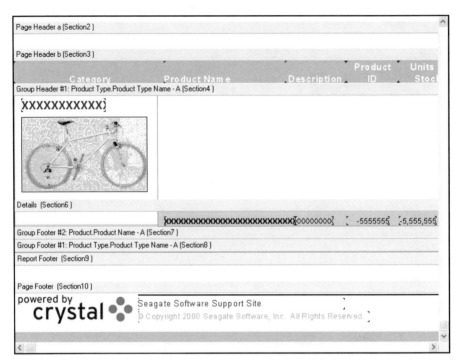

Figure 6-6. The Inventory report with pictures for each category.

To create this report, put the photo in the group header on the left most portion of the page. Put the detail fields in the detail section and make sure that all the fields are to the right of the picture. Lastly, turn on the Underlay format option for the group header.

Category	Product Name	Description	Product ID	Units Stock
Saddles	Roadster Jr BMX Saddle	youth	6401	75
	Roadster Micro Mtn Saddle	youth	6402	124
	Roadster Mini Mtn Saddle	youth	6403	165
	Vesper Comfort ATB Saddle	mens	7401	41
	Vesper Comfort Ladies Saddle	ladies	7402	69
	Vesper Gelflex ATB Saddle	mens	7403	88
	Vesper Gelflex Ladies Saddle	ladies	7404	97

Figure 6-7. Inventory report with Underlay turned on.

This causes all the group's detail records to be printed on top of the group header. Since the image and the records aren't on the same part of the page, this gives the effect of printing multiple details records beside a single image.

Printing a Watermark

Using the underlay feature is also useful when you want your report to have a watermark image on each page. Put the image in the page header and set the Underlay option on. Everything after the header is printed on top of it. Be sure to test the image to make sure it isn't too dark. A faint image works best as a watermark because it allows the rest of the report to be easily read.

Formatting with Multiple Columns

The default layout of a report is designed so that each detail record uses the entire width of the page and each row is printed below the one before it. Sections aren't designed to only use a partial page width. However, if you want to print mailing labels or a newspaper style report, then you need to use sections that are small enough that they can be repeated across the page. Setting the Format With Multiple Columns option lets you do that.

When selecting this option, a Layout tab appears in the dialog box. This tab lets you set the column width and spacing so that your information is put onto mailing labels. You can also set whether the records go down the page first and then to the next column, or go across the page first before going down to the next row. Figure 6-8 shows the options on the Layout tab.

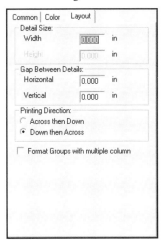

Figure 6-8. The Layout tab of the Section Editor.

The only problem with using the Layout tab is that it takes a little experimentation to get the formatting perfect. Precision is a necessity when printing labels and making a mailing list could take some work. You are much better off by using the Report Expert dialog box to create mailing labels. As Figure 6-9 shows, using the Report Expert lets you pick from a list of standard Avery numbers for the label format. Unless you are using a custom designed label, you can let Crystal Reports do all the work for formatting the label. This makes it easy to create mailing labels that print perfectly the first time!

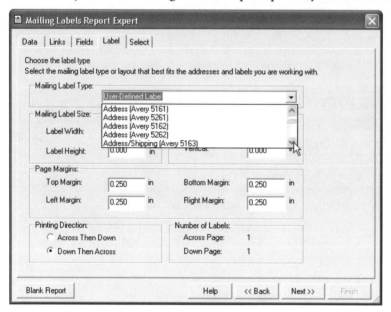

Figure 6-9. The Mailing Labels Report Expert.

Caution

Once you create a report using the Mailing Label Report Expert, you can always go back and change the Avery label number by right-clicking on the report and selecting Report | Report Expert. However, if you create a standard report and later turn the Multiple Column option on, you have to format the labels manually. You can't open the Mailing Label Report Expert.

Adding Multiple Sections

Throughout this book, when different parts of a report were discussed, they were referred to by their section name. For example, when adding an object displayed in the header of a group, the portion of the report would be called the Group Header section. However, reports also have Areas. By default, when you create a new report each area is composed of a single section, and every section is only in one area. In fact, an area is the container for a section. This gives you a one to one relationship between areas and sections. Thus, there is an area for the Report Header, Page Header, Details section, etc.

Crystal Reports lets you create dynamic reports by letting you add multiple sections to an area and format each section differently. This changes the relationship between Areas and Section to a one-to-many relationship. One area can have multiple sections within it. All sections can be displayed or formulas can be used to determine which section to show and which ones to suppress.

> **Note**
>
> An area can have more sections added to it, but the sections must be of the same type. For example, the Details area can have two Detail sections in it, but it can't have a Group Footer section in it.

An example of multiple sections is shown in Figure 6-10.

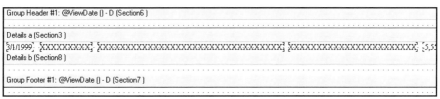

Figure 6-10. Multiple detail sections.

In this example, there are two sections between the group header and footer: Details a and Details b[12]. Each section is part of the Details area. The benefit of having two sections within the same area is that it gives you a lot of flexibility for formatting the report. Creative use of multiple sections solves many reporting problems.

You first have to understand a couple of rules for working with multiple sections. The first rule is that multiple sections are printed consecutively. The first section (labeled with the 'a') is printed first. The 'b' section is printed second, and so on. The second rule is that you can change the formatting of any section and it doesn't effect the formatting of the other sections. A section can be suppressed or have its background color changed and this has no effect on the other sections within that area.

Multiple sections can be inserted, deleted and merged with other sections. When you right-click on a section header, you get the menu shown in Figure 6-11.

---

[12] Adding additional sections automatically gets the next letter of the alphabet assigned to it.

Figure 6-11. Mulitple section menu.

When selecting Insert Section Below, it inserts a new section below the section that was clicked on. Select Merge Section Below to combine the current section with the one below it. Crystal Reports merges the two by taking all the objects in the lowest section and copying them to the section above it. All the new objects go underneath the existing objects. Select Delete Section to delete a section from the report.

If a section has too much white space underneath the report objects, make the space tighter by placing your cursor at the top of the section below it and dragging it higher. An easier, and more accurate, way of doing this is to select the Fit Section menu option. Crystal Reports adjusts the section height to fit the exact space needed for the report objects. No extra space is allocated.

Selecting Move Section brings up the Section Expert again. This dialog box displays all the report sections on the left-hand side. Now that you have multiple sections, the tabs along the top are no longer disabled. The dialog box with multiple sections is displayed in Figure 6-12. Use the arrow keys shown at the top to move the sections up or down.

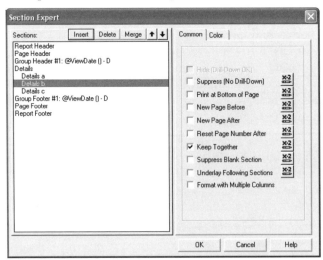

Figure 6-12. The Section Expert for multiple sections.

When looking at the menu options along the top of this dialog box, you see that it also has the options to Insert, Delete and Merge sections. If you are working in the designer, you can also go to this dialog box by right-clicking on a section header and selecting Format Section.

The key to making multiple sections work is to use formatting in combination with formulas. Although formulas are discussed in complete detail in Chapter 7, it is easy to understand the basic concepts before reading that chapter. Formulas are used to turn formatting options on and off using built-in functions with other data in the report. The best way to understand this is to see examples. Here are some common uses of formulas with multiple sections that you can start using right away.

Example 6-1. Eliminating blank address lines.

A common problem with printing addresses is that each one can have a different number of lines. Every address has a line allocated for the street address, but some addresses need a second line for other miscellaneous information. This could be an "Attention:" comment or the suite number. If an address doesn't use this second line, then it appears as a blank line and messes up the formatting of the address. An example of these labels is shown in Figure 6-13.

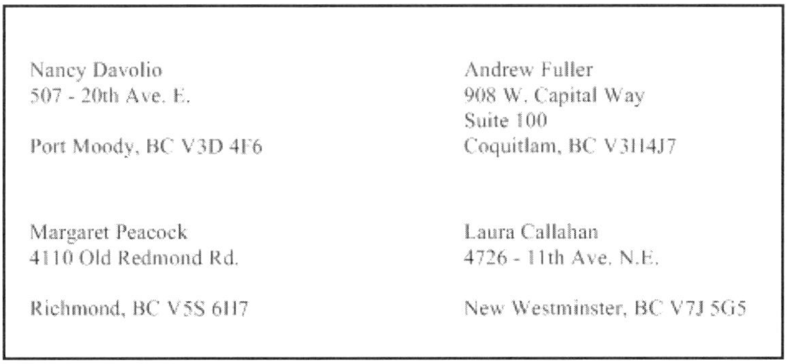

Nancy Davolio
507 - 20th Ave. E.

Port Moody, BC V3D 4F6

Margaret Peacock
4110 Old Redmond Rd.

Richmond, BC V5S 6H7

Andrew Fuller
908 W. Capital Way
Suite 100
Coquitlam, BC V3H4J7

Laura Callahan
4726 - 11th Ave. N.E.

New Westminster, BC V7J 5G5

Figure 6-13. Address labels with blank lines.

To fix this problem, create three sections. The first section has the addressee's name and street. The second section only has the second address line. The third section has the rest of the address fields. To make the second section only appear when there is data in the second address line, set the formatting options Suppress Blank Section. If the second address line doesn't have any information, then the section isn't printed and the blank line is eliminated. The labels in design mode are shown in Figure 6-14. The printed labels are shown in Figure 6-15.

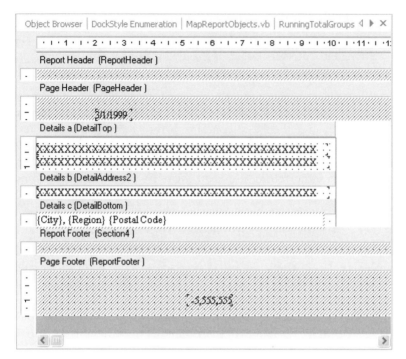

Figure 16-14. Address labels in design mode.

Nancy Davolio 507 - 20th Ave. E. Port Moody, BC V3D 4F6	Andrew Fuller 908 W. Capital Way Suite 100 Coquitlam, BC V3II4J7
Margaret Peacock 4110 Old Redmond Rd. Richmond, BC V5S 6II7	Laura Callahan 4726 - 11th Ave. N.E. New Westminster, BC V7J 5G5

Figure 6-15. Address labels that suppress blank sections.

Example 6-2. Adding non-blank sections.

If you can use sections to suppress blank lines, you can do just the opposite: use sections to show special information. For example, you may want a report to only print a section for unique circumstances. There are a multitude of examples on how to use this feature. An employee report could print a special note if an employee's birthday falls within the current month. Invoices can print reminders to late customers that they need to pay or else penalties will be incurred. A recipe listing can print additional notes for favorite recipes. Each example benefits from using multiple sections because if the section doesn't have any data to print, additional room isn't allocated on the report.

Example 6-3. Suppressing sections for repeated fields.

The Suppress If Duplicated format option suppresses a field if its data is duplicated, but this option isn't available for suppressing entire records. Instead, write your own formula for this. The formula uses the PreviousValue() function to compare the current value of a field to the value in the previous record. If it returns True, the entire section is suppressed.

This code tests if the Orders.CustomerID field has been repeated. Take the following Basic syntax code and use is as the formula for the Suppress option for the section.

```
Formula = ({Orders.Customer Id} = PreviousValue({Orders.Customer Id}))
```

Example 6-4. Swapping sections with each other.

Dynamic formatting is implemented using multiple sections. They can be used so that they both have similar information, but they are formatted completely different. Only one section is printed at any given time and the other section is hidden. Set each section to print using the opposite logic of the other. For example, a company could have a large client that gets the rules bent for them since they generate a large percentage of the revenue. This client requires their invoices to be in a certain format that simplifies their internal record keeping. Although the data is the same as all the other invoices being printed, the format is customized.

To solve this problem, create duplicate sections for each part of the invoice. In the Suppress formatting option set the formula to only display the special sections for that customer. The other sections will have the opposite logic so that they get printed when it isn't that customer.

Another example is when printing multi-national reports that are grouped by country. Countries have data that is unique and doesn't need to get printed for the other countries. People reading the report would get distracted if there were a lot of blank fields allocated for data that doesn't apply to the current country. To fix this, create a different section for each country. Set the formula in the Suppress format property to only display the section when the data relates to that country.

Example 6-5. Alternating the background color.

A common reason for alternating the background color of sections is to make the report easier to read. It can be hard to visually move your eyes across a report and stay on the same row. To make this easier to do, reports often alternate the background color of each row. This is similar to the green-bar report paper that was frequently used at corporations.

This is done by creating two detail sections with different background colors. The Suppress formatting formula for each section would be either

```
Formula = Remainder(RecordNumber, 2) = 0
```

Or

```
Formula = Remainder(RecordNumber, 2) = 1
```

Once you become familiar with all the different formatting options available within Crystal Reports, you will find that there are many ways to do the same thing. For example, if you want to change the background color of a section to red when a salesperson's quota isn't met, there are two ways you could do it. One solution would be to have two different sections as just discussed. Another solution would be to use only one section and put that same formula in the Background Color property. This will only turn the background color to red when the formula is true. Both solutions work equally well, although in this example using a single section would require less work. The more you work with Crystal Reports, the more you will learn different tricks. The ones you use will depend upon what you think best fits the situation at the time.

Running Totals

Running totals are built-in fields that accumulate the total of another field. These fields save you the trouble of creating and maintaining a set of formulas that do the same thing. Since they are part of Crystal Reports, you have to do very little effort to use them in a report.

A running total takes a field on a report, performs a calculation on it, and adds the result to a report-wide variable that keeps track of the total amount so far. There are various calculations that can be used with running totals so that they can be customized to your exact needs. For example, you can calculate a running total that sums all the amounts, calculates the current average of all the amounts, or calculates the maximum amount. You can also set the interval for when to perform the calculation. You can do it on every field or whenever the field changes values.

To add a running total field to your report, right click on a numeric field that you want to track and select Insert Running Total. This presents you with the dialog box in Figure 6-16.

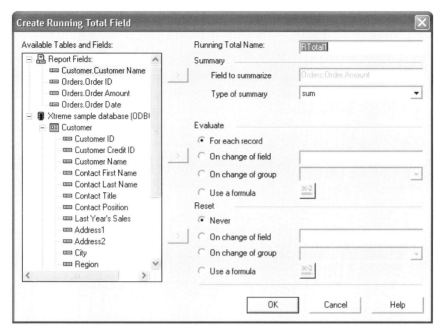

Figure 6-16. The Create Running Total dialog box.

When the dialog box opens, a default name and the field to summarize is already filled in. You should immediately change the name to something descriptive. There are also three options that can be set with a running total field: what type of calculation to perform, when to perform the calculation and when to reset the total back to zero.

Calling the field a running total is deceiving because the calculation doesn't have to calculate a running total. Don't think that just because the field is called Running Total that you are limited to calculations that only sum numbers. There are over a dozen different calculations available. It could calculate the average of all the numbers printed so far, or it can print the largest of all the numbers. The most simple, and the default, is the Sum operation. It sums a value as it is printed.

The value of the running total field is affected by when it is evaluated. You can have a value recalculated every time a detail record is printed, or if you have a group level field, then you can calculate it on every new group. You could also calculate it only when the summary field changes value.

Just as important as setting when to calculate the field is setting when to reset its value back to zero. If you want a running total to accumulate throughout the life of the report so that the last record shows the grand total, then you don't want the value to ever get reset. But if you are tracking the running total for individual groups, then you want it to reset every time the group changes. The dialog box also gives you the option to reset the running total when a field's value changes or by using a formula. Clicking the formula button brings up the Formula Editor dialog box so that you can write more advanced formulas for determining when the running total is reset.

Where you place the running total is very important. It is only as accurate as the most recent record printed. If you want to keep a running total of the detail records, then you would put the field in the detail section. If you put the field in the group summary section, then it will calculate the total as of the last record in the group.

You might recall from Chapter 4 that when printing a subtotal on a group, you can put that field in either the group footer or group header and it still prints the same result. The location of a subtotal doesn't affect its value. This isn't the case with running totals. If you put a running total in the group header, then it will only show the calculation for the first record. Since the other records haven't been printed yet, they aren't calculated. An example report showing this behavior is shown in Figure 6-17.

6/14/2002 3:17:33PM			MOUNTAIN BIKE INC
How to maintain running totals for a group			
Customer Name	Order ID	Order Amount	RunningTotal
Tienda de Bicicletas El Pardo			5,219.55
Tienda de Bicicletas El Pardo	1323	5,219.55	5,219.55
Tienda de Bicicletas El Pardo	1332	5,219.55	10,439.10
			10,439.10
Mad Mountain Bikes			8,897.31
Mad Mountain Bikes	1339	8,897.31	8,897.31
			8,897.31
Bikes, Bikes, and More Bikes			8,819.55
Bikes, Bikes, and More Bikes	1317	8,819.55	8,819.55
			8,819.55
Piccolo			5,895.20
Piccolo	1348	5,895.20	5,895.20
			5,895.20
Whistler Rentals			16.50
Whistler Rentals	1330	16.50	16.50
Whistler Rentals	1319	5,219.55	5,236.05
			5,236.05

Figure 6-17. The results of a running total field with a grouping report.

This is a Top N report that shows a running total column and there are three identical running totals fields. The running total field calculates the sum of each order amount, and it is reset when a group changes. There is a copy of it in the header, the detail, and the footer. You can see that the field in the detail section changes for every record and that the footer matches the value of the last record printed. But the header record doesn't match the footer value. Instead, it is equal to the first record printed in the group.

Running totals have similar functionality to summary fields, and they can also be duplicated with formula fields. This can cause some confusion as to when you should use a running total, a summary field, or a custom formula field. Each of these options has its unique characteristics.

Summary fields are useful for summarizing data outside of the detail section. For example, you can put subtotals in a group footer and put a grand total in the report footer. But you wouldn't want to put either of these fields in the Details section. Summary fields also have a limitation that if your report suppresses data, then the summary calculation will include the records that don't get printed. This is because the summary fields are calculated during the first-pass, and this occurs before the fields are suppressed. They can't take into account which fields don't get printed. But the running total fields are calculated as each record is printed. So if a record is suppressed, it doesn't get included in the calculation. As an example of this, the report in Figure 6-18 is the same Top-N report as the last example, but this report has two grand total fields added. The grand total in the right-most column is a running total field and it is a copy of the fields above it. The grand total field in the left column is a summary field that was added by right-clicking on the Order Amount field and selecting Insert Grand Total.

MOUNTAIN BIKE INC

How to maintain running totals for a group

Customer Name	Order ID	Order Amount	RunningTotal
Tienda de Bicicletas El Pardo			5,219.55
Tienda de Bicicletas El Pardo	1323	5,219.55	5,219.55
Tienda de Bicicletas El Pardo	1332	5,219.55	10,439.10
			10,439.10
Mad Mountain Bikes			8,897.31
Mad Mountain Bikes	1339	8,897.31	8,897.31
			8,897.31
Bikes, Bikes, and More Bikes			8,819.55
Bikes, Bikes, and More Bikes	1317	8,819.55	8,819.55
			8,819.55
Piccolo			5,895.20
Piccolo	1348	5,895.20	5,895.20
			5,895.20
Whistler Rentals			16.50
Whistler Rentals	1330	16.50	16.50
Whistler Rentals	1319	5,219.55	5,236.05
			5,236.05
		89,615.16	39,287.21

Figure 6-18. Summary field incorrectly calculates the grand total.

You can see that the grand total that is calculated with the summary field is much larger than it should be. It is including records that weren't printed on the report (they were filtered out). The running total field is correct because it only totals fields that were printed.

A formula should only be used when there isn't any other alternative. Not only does it incur more overhead when the report runs, but it requires more work on your part. If the previous two options are sufficient for your needs, then you should use them first. Having said that, there are times when a running total is limited and using a formula will give you the results you are looking for. An example is a report that tracks how many records are printed on each page. It shows the row number next to each record and it resets the counter to zero for every new page. Since there isn't an option with running totals to reset at the top of a page, a formula is required. To implement this report, you need two formulas. The first increments a global variable by 1 for each record. This formula is put in the detail section.

```
WhilePrintingRecords
Global LineNumber As Number
LineNumber = LineNumber + 1
Formula = LineNumber
```

The second formula resets the counter back to zero. It goes in the report footer so that it only gets called when a page is finished. It also has its Suppress format set so that the user can't see it on the report.

```
WhilePrintingRecords
Global LineNumber As Number
LineNumber = 0
Formula = LineNumber
```

When this report is run, the first record will always show a line number of 1 at the top of each page. The last record will show how many total records were printed on the page.

7

Using the Formula Editor

Formulas enable you to customize report output by analyzing the data in the report as it is being printed. There are two circumstances when you need to use formulas. The first is performing calculations based on the raw data. For example, when printing the monthly sales for a product you can calculate the percent of total sales. Storing this in the database isn't practical because it is more efficient to calculate that value on an as needed basis rather than waste space storing the number in the database. The second circumstance where formulas are needed is dynamically modifying the formatting of fields or sections on the report. For example, you can simulate a "green bar" report by using a formula that alternates the background color of every other row. The flexibility and power of formulas make them one of the most useful features of Crystal Reports.

This chapter is the first of three that show you how to use formulas to make reports vibrant. It shows you when and how to use the Formula Editor. The next chapter is a syntax primer for both Basic syntax and Crystal syntax. These are the two languages that Crystal Reports uses. Chapter 9 is a reference for the common functions that are built into Crystal Reports.

Throughout this chapter, the examples are written using Basic syntax. Although this language isn't covered in this chapter, it is very much like VB .NET and you shouldn't have any problem understanding the examples here. In fact, the two languages are so similar that you might be tempted to skip over the next two chapters if you already know how to program in VB .NET. I don't recommend this because Basic syntax has been designed to make reporting easier, and it adds a lot of new functionality not found in VB .NET. Learning about this new functionality can show you how to simplify some specific reporting tasks that would be more difficult than in VB .NET.

Writing Formulas in the Formula Editor

The Formula Editor shown in Figure 7-1 is where you create and edit formulas. It consists of four separate windows. The three windows along the top of the dialog box present the entire set of tools to write a formula. Within these three windows is every available field, syntax construct, and built-in formula. The bottom window is the formula window where you write and edit the formula.

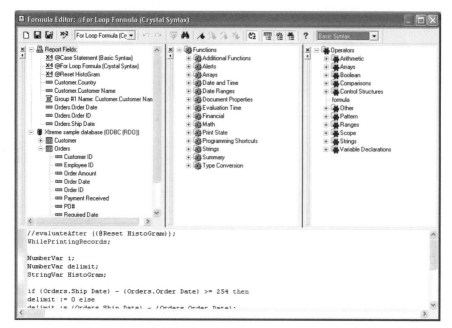

Figure 7-1. The Formula Editor window.

The top three windows assist you with writing formulas. Rather than having to use other tools to find out the names of the database fields and function names, they are listed in one of the windows at the top. When you double-click any of the items, that item appears in the code window at the current cursor position. You can also drag and drop the item into the code window. Effectively, you could write most of your formulas without doing any typing. Just double click the appropriate functions and insert the report fields and let the formula be built for you. Personally, as a programmer, I don't find this very practical. Scrolling through a hierarchy of syntax trees isn't nearly as efficient as just typing it in. However, it is very useful to have these trees available when you can't remember something because they are almost like having a mini-help file available. If there is a built-in function that you haven't used in a while, you can browse through the tree structure to look for it. You can also look at it just to find out all the parameters a function requires.

In the top right corner of this dialog box is the drop-down list for whether you want to use Crystal syntax or Basic syntax. The individual windows are discussed in more detail in the Chapter 5, but the following are brief descriptions.

The leftmost window is the Field Tree. It shows all the fields on the report. This consists of formulas, group fields, and data fields. Below that it shows every field in the current data source (whether they are in the report or not). You can use any report field in your formula as well as any database field. The database field doesn't need to be displayed on the report for it to be used in a formula.

The Function Tree is the middle window. It shows all the functions available. At first, this tree is a nice crutch to lean on as you learn the Basic syntax language. If you are a VB.NET programmer, you will find Basic syntax to be so similar that you will quickly learn the language and not rely on the Function Tree.

The Operator Tree shows the different operators grouped by category. Some of these categories are Arithmetic, Boolean, Comparisons, etc. It is similar to the Function Tree in that it is as a nice crutch when you are new to formulas, but you will quickly outgrow it.

The Formula window is where you write the formulas. The font is color-coded so that reserved words use a blue font. Comments are in green. Variables and value constants are in black.

As you write formulas, you need to save and check the syntax of the formula. The left most portion of the toolbar has buttons that provide this functionality. Figure 7-2 shows that portion of the toolbar.

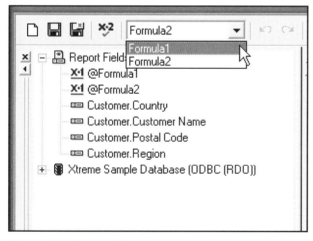

Figure 7-2. Formula buttons.

The buttons shown in Figure 7-2 are described here:

A blank sheet, the first button, creates a new formula. It first saves the current one and checks its syntax before creating a new formula.

A disk, the second button, saves the formula and checks the syntax. You can continue working on the existing formula.

The third button, a disk with an "x", checks the syntax, saves the formula and closes the Formula Editor. It returns you back to the report designer. You will probably use this one most of the time.

The fourth button, the formula icon with a checkmark, checks the syntax of the formula. It gives you a message box telling you whether the formula is okay and then lets you go back to working on the formula. Use this to verify the syntax with a function you aren't familiar with.

The dropdown list shows all the available formulas. Use this when you are done working on the current formula and you want to edit another formula. This can only be used with existing formulas, not creating new ones.

Whenever you save a formula, the syntax is always verified. This insures that if there is something wrong with the formula, it will be corrected right away. When a syntax error is found, a message box appears informing you of the problem. Unfortunately, the error messages that appear are usually not very helpful. You frequently have to decipher this yourself. If you find that there is a syntax error in your formula, you are not required to fix it right away. You can save it as is, and then come back later to fix the errors. Just don't forget to fix it or else your report won't run properly.

Using Formulas for Calculations

A report gets the majority of its data from a data source. This could be a table in a database, an XML data feed or a proprietary data source. Data usually consists of raw data that doesn't have extraneous information that can be derived by other means (e.g. calculations). It is more efficient to perform calculations on an as-needed basis than to save the results within the database. A formula can be calculated and displayed directly on the report or it can be used by other formulas.

Crystal Reports lets you add and edit formulas via the Field Explorer window in the report designer. Within the Field Explorer window, right click on any of the formula fields and select Edit or New to open the Formula Editor. You can also right click on the tree node Formula Fields. The Field Explorer window is shown in Figure 7-3.

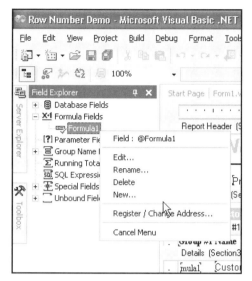

Figure 7-3. The field explorer window.

Once you've added a formula to the Field Explorer, you can display it on a report by dragging and dropping it to the report. You can tell the difference between database fields versus formulas because the formula fields are prefixed with a @. If you want to edit a formula field on the report, right click on it within the report layout and select Edit.

Dynamic Formatting with Formulas

Reports by their very nature are static. Although the printed data changes and the running totals are different every time, the report format stays the same. For example, if the first field in a column has a font of Arial and is black, every field in that column is also going to have a font of Arial and be black. After all, if every field in the same column had a different font, it would be very hard to read and people would question the abilities of the report designer. But wouldn't it be nice to use visual cues to highlight important data? For example, you could change the color of an inventory quantity to red when it is below the minimum. The reader immediately knows that the item needs to be reordered. There might even be a special note to the side of the report stating whom to notify. In this circumstance, making a report dynamic increases its usefulness to the reader without adding clutter.

Crystal Reports gives you the ability to use formulas that dynamically modify the visual properties of fields and sections on a report. For example, you can use a formula that returns either True or False with the Suppress property of a section to either show or hide a section. You could also use a formula that returns a string and this can be used to add a special message at the end of each row.

Adding Formulas

When modifying a property in the designer, the changes you make to that property stay the same as the report runs. Most properties, but not all, can have a formula attached to them so that their value can be modified based upon other fields in the report. Clicking on the formula button next to a property lets you add a formula to do this. The formula button is shown in Figure 7-4. It has a blue "X-2" and there is a horizontal pencil underneath it. Once you add a formula to a property the "X-2" turns red and the pencil is at an angle. This is shown in Figure 7-5. Only properties with a formula button next to them can use a formula to make the values dynamic.

Figure 7-4. A button with no formula associated with it.

Figure 7-5. A button with a formula associated with it.

When assigning a formula to a property, you have to determine the data type that the property uses. This can be anything from Boolean, string, number or Crystal pre-defined constants. The formula must return the proper data type to the property. If the formula returns the wrong data type, the Formula Editor returns an error when you try to save it.

As an example of using the proper data type, Figure 7-6 shows the Section Editor dialog box. All the properties displayed here use checkboxes. These properties are either on or off. Formulas that are associated with these properties have to return True or False. As expected, returning True is the same as a checked box, and returning False is the same as an unchecked box.

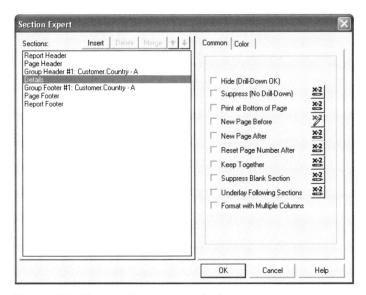

Figure 7-6. The section expert window.

As a more varied example, Figure 7-7 shows the Border tab of the Format Editor dialog box. This dialog box uses checkboxes, line styles and colors.

Figure 7-7. The Format Editor's border tab.

The values for the line style and color are predefined constants within Basic syntax. It can have values such as DashedLine, NoLine, etc. The color property can have values such as Aqua, Yellow, etc.

When you open the Formula Editor, the predefined constants for the current property are listed in the Function Tree. This list is dynamic and won't show predefined constants that don't apply to the current property. For example, if you are modifying a line style property, the Function Tree will show the different line styles, but won't list any colors. This is illustrated in Figure 7-8. If you are modifying a color property, then it will show the available colors, but no line styles. This is illustrated in Figure 7-9.

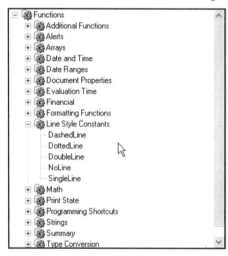

Figure 7-8. The Function Tree for line styles.

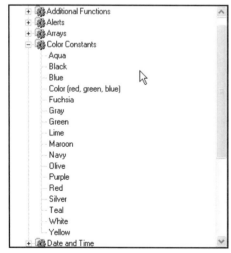

Figure 7-9. The Function Tree for colors.

Printing Checkboxes

There are many ways to display a Boolean constant. You can display the words Yes/No or True/False. Right-click on the field and select Format. The dialog box displays a drop-down box that lets you select how you want the data to be displayed (Yes/No, True/False, etc.).

You can also display Boolean values as a checkbox, but this requires a little more creativity. Crystal Reports doesn't have a built-in method for displaying checkboxes. You have to use the control characters in the Wingdings font. There are a variety of interesting characters in the Wingdings font. But five of them can be use for displaying checkboxes. Figure 7-10 shows some of the Wingdings characters available.

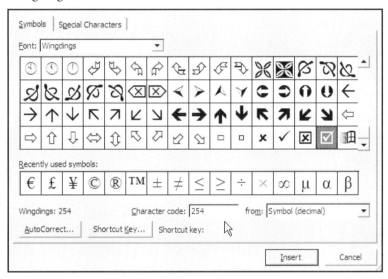

Figure 7-10. Wingdings control characters.

Find the character you want to display and click on it. At the bottom you will see the Character Code value that you need to print. Write down this number. The character that you may not find right away is the empty checkbox. If you scroll up you'll see that it is code 168.

To display a checkbox on the report, create a new formula field and insert the following formula.

```
If {Table.Field} = True Then
   'Display checked box
   Formula = Chr(254)
Else
   'Display empty box
   Formula = Chr(168)
End If
```

This formula tests a field to see if it is **True**. If so, it returns the control character 254 (a checked box). If it is false, it returns the control character 168 (an empty box). Save the formula and close the Formula Expert dialog box.

Drag this formula from the Field Explorer onto the report. Finally, change the font to be Wingdings by right-clicking on the field and selecting Format. Click on the Font tab and use the dropdown box to select the Wingdings font. Save the report and run it to see the checkbox displayed.

Using the Default Attribute and Current Field Value

The value assigned to a property in design mode is called the property's default attribute. When assigning a formula to that property, the default value is overridden by what is in the formula. There are many times when a formula is only used to specify what happens in a unique circumstance (e.g. an inventory item being out of stock) and you don't want the formula to override the default value every time. The rest of the time you want the default value to be left unchanged. There are two ways of doing this: not specifying a value in the formula or using the keyword DefaultAttribute.

When you don't specify a value, you are letting Crystal Reports use what was specified in the Format Editor. For example, you may want a field to be red if its value is less than the minimum quantity, otherwise use the attribute specified in the Format Editor. You can use a formula like the following:

```
If {Inventory.OnHand} < {InventoryItems.MinimumQty} Then
    Formula = crRed
End If
```

If the condition is true, then the color becomes red. If it is false, then the color is left unchanged.

Although this is acceptable, it isn't perfectly clear what the color will be if the condition isn't true. As a second alternative you can use an Else statement and specify the result to be DefaultAttribute. By doing this you are telling someone reading your code that the color will either be crRed or the attribute that is specified on the Format Editor. The new code would look like the following:

```
If {Inventory.OnHand} < {InventoryItems.MinimumQty} Then
    Formula = crRed
Else
    Formula = DefaultAttribute
End If
```

Formulas can be made generic so that they can be used on different fields. By replacing the field name with the keyword CurrentFieldValue, the formula can be called in various places on the report. This keyword returns the current value of the field that is being formatted. The CurrentFieldValue is seen in Chapter 11 which discusses Cross-Tab reports.

Use the Highlighting Expert?

The Highlighting Expert is a simplified version of the Format Editor. It gives you a wizard interface for creating rules that modify the font and border of a field. Figure 7-11 shows an example of using the Highlighting Expert for drawing a double box border around a field when its value is equal to "USA". The Sample column shows the result of what the field looks like after the rule has been applied. The Condition column shows the rule that is being applied. There can be multiple rules applied.

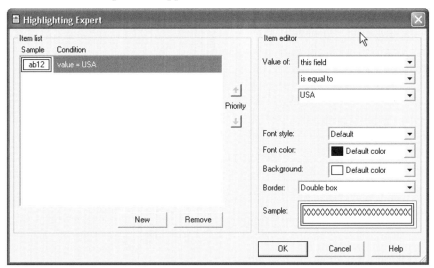

Figure 7-11. The Highlighting Expert window.

I don't recommend using the Highlighting Expert. There are two reasons for this. The primary reason is that it can create confusion when maintaining a report. There are now two places where the formatting of an object can be modified. If you inherited this report from another programmer and you want to determine if a field is going to have its format modified, you have to check the Format Editor and the Highlighting Expert. For a large report, this adds additional work. The second reason is that the rules in the Highlighting Expert always override the rules in the Format Editor. For example, if you create a formula in the Format Editor for the font and also use the Highlight Expert to modify the font, then the formula is ignored and only the Highlighting Expert is used. This is most likely to happen when inheriting a report from another programmer who used the Highlighting Expert. You might add a formula with the Format Editor and spend a lot of time trying to debug it. But you won't be able to fix it until you remember to check the Highlighting Expert. All in all, this tool has the potential to do more harm than good.

The Highlighting Expert was originally designed as an easy way for end users to modify the format of a field without having to know how to program. It let them create formulas by pointing and clicking. Once an end user felt comfortable with programming logic, then they would graduate to adding formulas with the Format Editor. As a .NET programmer, programming is what you do and you don't have to rely on a simplified tool for assistance. I recommend that you ignore it altogether and keep all the functionality within the Format Editor.

Evaluation Time Defaults

Chapter 1 discussed the Two-Pass Processing Model. Knowing how this model works is especially important when writing formulas. The type of formula determines when it is processed. Where you place a formula on a report and the functionality within that formula affects when the formula is evaluated and whether it returns the expected value or not. A formula can be placed on any section of your report, but you should plan this in advance so that you can guarantee the proper results. To determine where to place a formula, you need to know the rules that Crystal Reports uses to evaluate functions. The following list is the rules that are applied.

- A formula that only references variables (it doesn't use group/summary fields or database fields) is evaluated before any records are read.

- Formulas using database fields are evaluated while records are being read.

- Formulas using group fields, summary fields, or page related fields (e.g. the page number) are evaluated after the records are read and while the report is being printed.

- You can't determine which formula within a section will be called first. This is because formulas within the same section are not evaluated in any particular order.

There are times when the default rules listed above will not give you the results you desire. For example, there may be a situation where you have two formulas in the same section and one formula relies upon the other to be called first. According to the default rules listed above, you know that there is no way to determine which one will be called first. You need some way to force one formula to be called before the other. Fortunately, Crystal Reports lets you override the default rules to fit your particular situation. There are four keywords that let you set when a formula is evaluated: BeforePrintingRecords, WhileReadingRecords, WhilePrintingRecords, and EvaluateAfter. Each keyword is added to the beginning of a formula to set when it gets evaluated. These keywords are listed in Table 7-1.

Table 7-1. Evaluation Time Keywords

Evaluation Time Keyword	Description
BeforeReadingRecords	Evaluate the formula before any database records are read.
WhileReadingRecords	Evaluate the formula while reading the database records.
WhilePrintingRecords	Evaluate the formula while printing the database records.
EvaluateAfter(formula)	Evaluate after another formula has been evaluated.

If a formula isn't returning the expected results, there is a good chance it's because of when the formula is being evaluated. If you are trying to debug a formula, then you have to take many things into consideration: does the formula only use variables; should the formula be put in a different section; is the formula being evaluated while reading records or while printing records; does the report use a grouping section that may be effecting the order of evaluation. This is a lot to think about. You can cut down on the amount of time spent debugging formulas if you start out by following some general guidelines. The remainder of this section gives guidelines and examples for you to think about when writing your formulas.

Place formulas that reset variables to their default value in the Report Header or Group Header section. This insures that they are called before the formulas in the detail section are evaluated.

Be careful when using formulas that only have variables in them without any database fields. They will only get calculated one time prior to reading the records. If the formula is cumulative in nature, you need to force the evaluation time to be WhileReadingRecords. If the report uses groups then you should use the WhilePrintingRecords keyword.

The keyword BeforeReadingRecords can't be used with formulas that have database fields or grouping/summary fields in them.

When you place multiple formulas within the same section, you can't assume the order that they are executed in. If you need one formula to be evaluated before another formula (its result is used in other formulas) then put the EvaluateAfter keyword in the dependent formula. The following example shows how this is used. This formula relies upon the formula ParseName to take the {Customer.Name} field and parse the first name and last name out of it. The values are put into the global variables FirstName and LastName. This example formula returns the LastName variable so that it can be displayed on the report. The @ParseName formula isn't shown here.

```
EvaluateAfter({@ParseName})
Global LastName As String
Formula = LastName
```

Summary calculations are performed while printing records. They can only do calculations on formulas that were evaluated beforehand (i.e. while reading records). Thus, a formula that uses WhilePrintingRecords can't have summary functions performed on it.

Of course, these guidelines won't be able to prevent every problem from happening, but they are here to help give you a start in the right direction.

To illustrate the importance of using the proper keyword in a formula, let's look at a final example that shows you each stage of writing a formula and how the output is affected by the evaluation time keyword.

The example report is a customer report that uses the Xtreme.mdb database. The report has the first column as the row number. The row number is tracked using a variable called RowNumber. The formula is as follows:

```
Global RowNumber As Number   'Don't use Local b/c that resets the variable
RowNumber = RowNumber + 1
Formula = RowNumber
```

Figures 7-12 shows the output of this report.

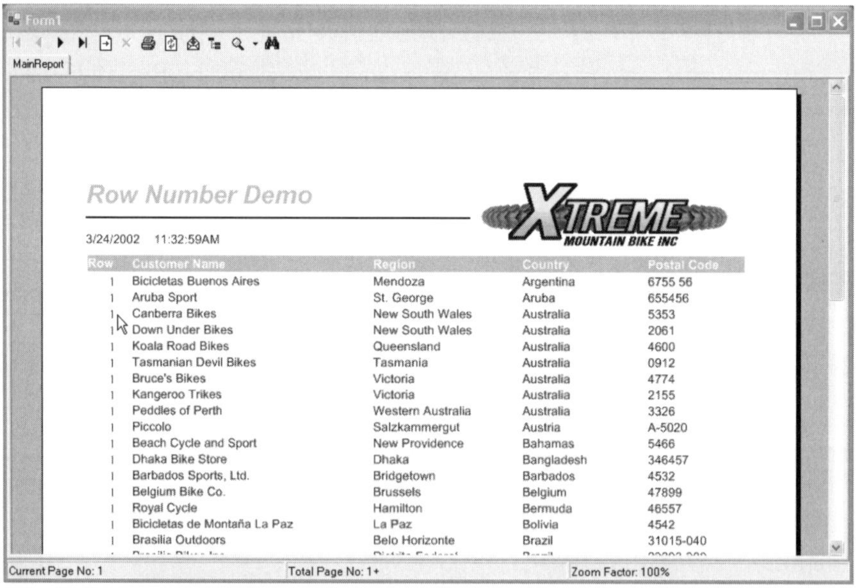

Row	Customer Name	Region	Country	Postal Code
1	Bicicletas Buenos Aires	Mendoza	Argentina	6755 56
1	Aruba Sport	St. George	Aruba	655456
1	Canberra Bikes	New South Wales	Australia	5353
1	Down Under Bikes	New South Wales	Australia	2061
1	Koala Road Bikes	Queensland	Australia	4600
1	Tasmanian Devil Bikes	Tasmania	Australia	0912
1	Bruce's Bikes	Victoria	Australia	4774
1	Kangeroo Trikes	Victoria	Australia	2155
1	Peddles of Perth	Western Australia	Australia	3326
1	Piccolo	Salzkammergut	Austria	A-5020
1	Beach Cycle and Sport	New Providence	Bahamas	5466
1	Dhaka Bike Store	Dhaka	Bangladesh	346457
1	Barbados Sports, Ltd.	Bridgetown	Barbados	4532
1	Belgium Bike Co.	Brussels	Belgium	47899
1	Royal Cycle	Hamilton	Bermuda	46557
1	Bicicletas de Montaña La Paz	La Paz	Bolivia	4542
1	Brasilia Outdoors	Belo Horizonte	Brazil	31015-040

Figure 7-12. Row Number example output with same row number.

Notice that all the row numbers are 1. This is because the default rule states if a formula only has variables in it, then it will be evaluated before any records are read. Even though this formula is placed in the detail section, it only gets evaluated once and the value variable never increases.

To fix this problem, use the keyword WhileReadingRecords in the formula.

```
WhileReadingRecords
Global RowNumber As Number   'Don't use Local b/c that resets the variable
RowNumber = RowNumber + 1
Formula = RowNumber
```

Figure 7-13 shows that the row number is now accurate because the formula is evaluated every time a record is read.

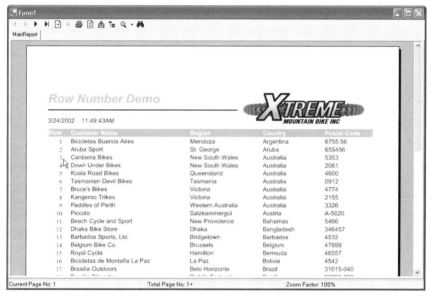

Figure 7-13. Row Number example output with correct row numbers.

Let's modify the example so that the report uses a grouping section based on the country name.

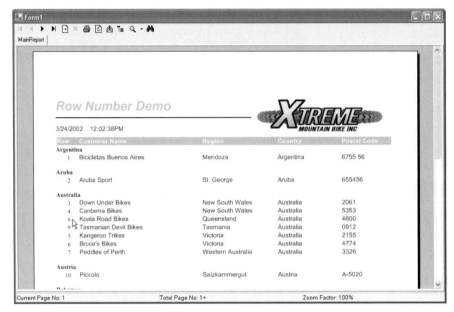

Figure 7-14. Row Number example output with grouping.

Figure 7-14 shows that the report now groups by country and uses a group header. Unfortunately, this change has introduced a bug in the report because the row numbers are now out of order (see the Australia group). This is because the row number is being calculated while the records are being read. After being read, the rows get resorted based upon their group. The row numbers get resorted as well. To fix this, change the formula so that the row number is being evaluated while the records are being printed and not while being read.

```
WhilePrintingRecords
Global RowNumber As Number    'Don't use Local b/c that resets the variable
RowNumber = RowNumber + 1
Formula = RowNumber
```

Figure 7-15 shows that the row number is now accurate.

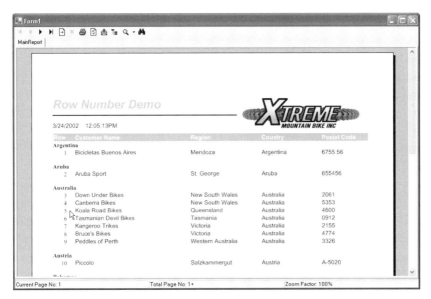

Figure 7-15. Row numbers are correct with grouping.

This series of examples shows that putting an Evaluation Time keyword at the beginning of a formula has a dramatic effect on the formula's value.

This page intentionally left blank

Programming with Basic Syntax

Formulas are used in Crystal Reports as a way to have enhanced control over a report as it prints. For example, if you want to have the rows on the report alternate colors then you can use a formula to change the background color of every other row. Another example would be using a field value in a row to determine when to hide a row.

Crystal Reports gives you the option to program formulas in either Crystal syntax or Basic syntax. This chapter teaches you how to program with Basic syntax. A reference for learning Crystal syntax is provided in Appendix A. You should read this chapter first before reading the Appendix.

Basic syntax is very similar (and in many ways identical) to the VB .NET syntax. Crystal syntax is similar to the C# syntax. If you are a C# programmer you will probably be more comfortable programming with Crystal syntax.

When creating formulas, Crystal Reports defaults to Crystal syntax so you need to select Basic syntax. It is very tedious to specify Basic syntax every time you create a new formula. To change the default language to Basic syntax, right click on the report in design mode and select Designer | Default Settings. Go to the Reporting tab and at the bottom you can specify Basic syntax as the default language.

After you switch to Basic syntax you'll notice that the syntax trees are refreshed so that they reflect the language you chose. Figure 8-1 shows how to choose Basic syntax from the Formula Editor.

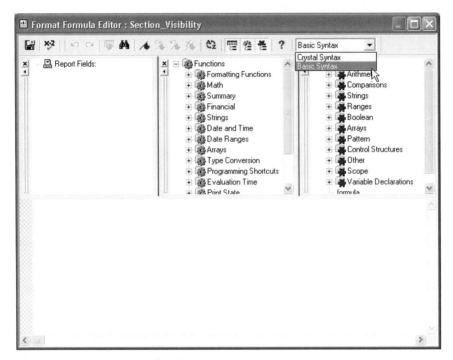

Figure 8-1. Language Selection

Since Basic syntax is so similar to VB .NET, this chapter gives an overview of the language and focuses on the areas where they are different. I assume that since you are already programming with Visual Studio .NET then you don't want to be bored with elementary programming concepts. Throughout this chapter, Basic syntax will be compared to VB .NET syntax to bring noteworthy differences to your attention. Detailed examples will be shown when it is deemed to be helpful.

Formula Fundamentals

This section on fundamentals of writing formulas covers Case Sensitivity, Writing Comments, Returning a Value, Using Data Fields, Declaring Variables, Simple Data Types, Array Data Types, and Range Data Types. Each topic has its own section.

Case Sensitivity

Basic syntax is not case sensitive. The variable FirstName is the same as the variable firstname. Although these two variables are syntactically equivalent, it is recommended that you keep the case consistent so that your program is easier to read. If you always capitalize the first letter of a word in a variable, you should do so for all variables.

Writing Comments

Comments are designated by using a single apostrophe. You can also use the familiar REM keyword

```
'This is a comment
REM This is also a comment
```

Line Terminators

Basic syntax assumes that each programming statement only takes a single line of text. The carriage return (hidden) marks the end of the line. If a statement needs more than one line, the line continuation character _ is used.

```
X = 5 'This is a single line
Y = "This takes " _
& "two lines"
```

Returning a Value

Formulas are always used to return a value. The data types of these return values can be Number, Currency, String, Boolean, Date, Time and DateTime. You cannot return data types of range and array.

Formulas return values by assigning the value to the Formula variable. Formulas have to always return a value. The following code simply returns the value True.

```
Formula = True
```

If a formula has multiple statements that return a value, all the assignments must be of the same data type. Although there is no way to specifically state what that data type is, the compiler will compare all the assignments and check them for consistency.

```
'The following IS NOT VALID due to the different data types returned
If Age > 65 Then
  Formula = "Retired"
Else
  Formula = Age
End If
```

Referencing Report Fields

Writing formulas requires referencing all types of data from your report and the databases that the report uses. The types of data that can be referenced consist of running total fields, the results of other formulas, and table fields. The syntax for referencing fields in a formula is to surround the field name with curly brackets. The syntax for referencing the field name is dependent upon the type of field it is.

Formulas are referenced by putting @ in front of the name.

{@Formula}

Parameters are referenced with a ? in front of the name.

{?Parameter}

Running total fields are referenced by putting # in front of the name.

{#RunningTotal}

Table fields are referenced by separating the table name and the field name with a period between the two. Spaces are allowed.

{Customer.First Name}

Group fields use the field name with the GroupName() formula.

GroupName({Table.GroupField})

Summary fields pass the field name and the group field to the summary function.

Sum({Table.FieldName}, {Table.GroupName})

Declaring Variables

Declaring a variable follows the standard format of declaring the variable using the As keyword and then its data type.

Dim var As dataype

Crystal doesn't reset its variables because of the way formulas and report sections work together. Formulas are usually added to sections of a report and a report section is repeatedly entered and exited as records are processed. If a variable lost its value every time a new record is processed, then you wouldn't be able to track what happened with the last record. Making it easy for variables to retain their values while different records are processed is one reason why Crystal Reports is so powerful. If you want to make sure that a variable is reset to its default value every time, then do so manually.

The first time a formula is called, all of the variables are automatically assigned their default values. See Table 8-1 for a list of the default values. Once you declare a variable and assign a value to it, that variable retains its value for the life of the report. Any future calls to that same formula will not initialize the variable back to its default value. This is the opposite of .NET. In .NET, a variable goes out of scope and its memory is released when the function exits. Every time the function is called, the variables are automatically reset to their default value.

Table 8-1. Data Type Default Values

Basic Data Type	Crystal Data Type	Default Value
Number	NumberVar	0
Currency	CurrencyVar	$0
Boolean	BooleanVar	False
String	StringVar	""
Date	DateVar	Date(0,0,0) – The Null Date value00/00/00
Time	TimeVar	No default valueNull
DateTime	DateTimeVar	No default valueNull

A variable's scope determines which formulas have access to that variable. There are three operators that you use to declare scope:

1. Local (Dim for Basic syntax): The variable can only be seen within the current formula. In a sense, a variable declared using the Dim keyword effectively defaults to Local scope.
2. Global: The variable can be seen within any formula inside the same report. Sub-reports do not have access to the variable.
3. Shared: Similar to Global, but the variable can also be seen within sub-reports.

```
Local HireDate As Date
Shared AffiliateCities() As String
```

An unusual aspect of the Global/Shared variables is that even though their scope says that they can be seen by other formulas, you still have to declare them in each formula that wants to use them. This is unique because in VB .NET if a variable is declared as Public, and another procedure re-declares that variable, then the new variable is created local to the procedure that declared it and the public variable is no longer accessible within the current procedure. When you re-declare the variable in Basic syntax, then that means you now have access to the Global/Shared variable's memory space. If you don't re-declare the variable, it will give you an error stating that the variable doesn't exist. So no matter what the scope of a variable is, every formula must declare every variable that it uses.

Variable Assignment

To assign a value constant to a variable use the equal sign.

```
X = 5
```

Simple Data Types

Basic syntax supports the standard simple data types that we expect in a language: Boolean, Number, Currency, String, DateTime, Date, and Time.

Notice that rather than have a large number of numeric data types such as integer, double, etc., there is simply a single data type called Number. There is no need to worry about whether the number will use a decimal point or what its largest value is.

The Currency data type is treated the same as a Number data type with a few exceptions. They are listed below:

- Currency can only have two decimal places. If assigned a number with more than two decimal places, it will round up to the nearest penny.

- Currency automatically gets formatted as a monetary value. This eliminates the overhead of you always having to format the variable whenever it gets printed.

- Since Currency is a different data type, it must be converted to a number to be used in mathematical assignments using non-currency variables. See the section "Converting Data Types" for more information.

Strings use the double quote, ", to specify a string literal. A character is represented by a string of length one. Referencing a position within a string is Base 1. Thus, if you want to refer to the first character in a string, you would use an index of 1. The maximum length of a string constant is 65,534 characters. Information on using the Basic syntax built-in string functions is in the next chapter.

```
'Demonstrate assigning a string constant to a variable
Dim Var As String
Var = "This is a string"
```

Dates are a little unusual in that there are three different data types available. The Date type can only store a date and the Time type can only store a time. It's preferable to use these data types if you don't need both values stored in a variable. If you do need both types in the same variable, use the DateTime type. Designate a DateTime constant by surrounding it with the # sign.

```
Dim MyBirthday As DateTime
MyBirthday = #5/23/1968#
```

Array Data Types

Arrays provide a means of storing a collection of data in a single variable and accessing each element of the array using an index. Unlike .NET arrays which are Base 0, an array in Basic syntax is Base 1. Thus, the first element is referenced using 1 as the index. The maximum size of an array is 1,000 elements.

Basic syntax uses rounded parentheses to specify the array bounds.

```
X(1) = 5
```

When you declare an array, specifying the number of elements is optional. If you don't specify the number of elements in the declaration, then before you use the array you have to either re-dimension it using the ReDim statement or assign an existing array to it.

```
Dim X() As Number 'Declare a non-dimensioned array
Dim Y(10) As Number  'Declare an array with 10 elements
```

The ReDim statement is the same as in VB.NET. It will change the number of elements in the array and reset their values. If you want to keep the existing values intact, then also use the Preserve keyword.

```
Redim var(number)              'Redminsion an array and reset all values
Redim Preserve var(number)     'Redime an array and preserve existing values
```

Assigning values to an array is done in different ways. If you know what the values of an array are during the development process, you can initialize the array with these values using the Array() function. Pass the Array() function all the elements as a comma delimited list and it returns an array that is fully populated with these elements. When using the Array() function you don't have to specify the array size. The compiler figures that out for you.

As expected, if you want to simply assign a value to an individual element in the array, then the index must be within the array's bounds. But if you are assigning an entire array to another array variable and they are different sizes, you do not have to redimension the target array. The target array will be overwritten and it will have the size of the existing array.

```
'Demonstrate initializing an array and then overwriting it
Dim MonthsInSeason() As String
MonthsInSeason = Array("May", "June")
If LongWinter = True Then
    MonthsInSeason = Array("June", "July", "August")
End If
```

If you don't know the array values during the development process, you will probably assign the initial values to the array by looping through it. A common way of doing this is using a For Next loop where the range of the loop is the lower and upper bounds of the array. Another common method of assigning values to each element is to do so as the report is looping through its detail records. For each pass through the detail section you assign one of the fields to the array.

```
'Sample code within the detail section to track customer sales
Dim RecordCounter As Number
Dim SalesDetail() As Number
RecordCounter = RecordCounter + 1
SalesDetail(RecordCounter) = {Customer.Sales}
```

Once the array is populated, you can test to see if a certain value already exists in the array by using the In operator. Using the In operator saves you the trouble of looping through the entire array searching for a particular value. If the value already exists, the In operator returns True.

```
'Sample code to fill an array with the unique zip codes for all customers being printed
Dim RecordCounter As Number
Dim ZipCodes(100) As Number
If Not {Customer.ZipCode} In ZipCodes Then
    RecordCounter = RecordCounter + 1
    ZipCodes(RecordCounter) = {Customer.ZipCodes}
End If
```

Basic syntax has many predefined functions for summarizing the values in an array. These functions range from summing the total of all the values in the array to getting the maximum value in the array. Table 8-2 lists the array functions.

Table 8-2. Array Summary Functions

Basic Function	Description
Average(array)	Calculate the average of all numbers.
Count(array)	Count how many numbers there are.
DistinctCount(array)	Count how many numbers there are without including duplicates.
Maximum(array)	Return the maximum number.
Minimum(array)	Return the minimum number.
PopulationStdDev(array)	Return the Population Standard Deviation calculation.
PopulationVariance(array)	Return the PopulationVariance calculation.
StdDev(array)	Return the Standard Deviation calculation.
Variance(array)	Return the Variance calculation.

Although the functions are designed to only work with arrays, you can use them with table fields as well. This is done by creating a new array with the Array() function and passing it the fields to work with.

```
'Sample code for getting the maximum value of three fields
Dim MaxSales1stQtr As Number
MaxSales1stQtr = Max(Array({Sales.Jan}, {Sales.Feb}, {Sales.Mar}))
```

Range Data Types

The Range data type is a very useful data type that doesn't exist in .NET. It allows you to store multiple values within a single variable. In .NET, if you want to be able to store a range of values that have a definite start and end, then you have to declare two variables where each variable represents an endpoint. If you want to see whether a field falls within this range, then you have to compare the field to both variables. Crystal Reports greatly simplifies this with the Range data type. It stores a range within one variable and performs tests to see if another variable falls within that range. However, you can't just store any values in this variable. It must be a group of values with a definite starting and ending. All values in between are included. Of course, it should go without saying that the starting point and end point must be of the same data type.

To declare a variable as a Range data type, declare it as one of the standard data types and put the Range keyword at the end. The data types that are allowed to have a related Range data type are Number, Currency, String, DateTime, Date, and Time.

```
Dim var As datatype Range
```

Defining a range uses a variety of different operators. These operators specify the beginning and end of the range. The most basic operator is the To operator. It is placed between the start and end values. Using the To operator means that you want the start and end values to be included as valid members of the range.

```
'Demonstrate creating a range of all the days in a year.
Dim DaysInYear as Date Range
DaysInYear = #1/1/2002# To #12/31/2002#
```

A variation of the To operator is to use it with the underscore character. Placing the underscore on one side of the To operator states that you want all values leading up to that constant to be included, but you don't want the constant specified to be included. The underscore can be placed on either side, or both sides.

The following example demonstrates creating a range with all the days in the month. However, we only want to do so using the first day of the months in our range. The date 2/1/2002 won't be included in our range. Instead, the last day of the month just prior to it will be included.

```
Dim DaysInMonth As Date Range
DaysInMonth = #1/1/2002# To_ #2/1/2002#
```

When you want to find out if a field or variable is included within a specified range, use the In operator. This is useful when writing If statement and Select Case statements.

```
'Demonstrate calculating a volume price discount
```

```
Select Case UnitsSold
Case In (1 To_ 1000)
   Formula = Price
Case In (1000 To_ 5000)
   Formula = Price * .95
Case >= 5000
   Formula = Price * .90
End Select
```

Basic syntax has many predefined date range constants that can be used in your report. These are commonly used to filter out records that have dates that don't fall within the specified range. Table 8-3 lists the predefined date ranges and specifies which dates are considered to be included. Many of these constants use today's date to determine one of the end points of the range. You can tell the report to use a date other than the system date by setting the PrintDate property. This is done by right clicking on the Field Explorer, selecting Report, and then selecting Set Print Date. This is saved with the report.

Table 8-3. Predefined Date Range Constants

Name	Description
AllDatesToToday	Includes any date prior to, and including, today.
AllDatesToYesterday	Includes any date prior to today. Today is not included.
AllDatesFromToday	Start: Today. End: Last date in field.
AllDatesFromTomorrow	Start: Tomorrow. End: Last date in field.
Aged0To30Days, Aged31To60Days, Aged61To90Days	Groups dates in 4 blocks of 30 days prior to today. Today's date is included in the Aged0To30Days range.
Calendar1stQtr, Calendar2ndQtr, Calendar3rdQtr, Calendar4thQtr	Groups dates in blocks of 3 months each. The first date is Jan 1 of the current year.
Calendar1stHalf, Calendar2ndHalf	Start: Jan 1 of the current year thru June 30. End: July 1 of the current year thru December 31.
Last7Days	Start: The six days prior to today. End: Today.
Last4WeeksToSun	Start: The first Monday of the four weeks prior to last Sunday. End: Last Sunday.

	Note: Does not include the days after the last Sunday thru today.
LastFullWeek	Start: The Sunday of the last full week.
	End: The Saturday of the last full week.
	Note: Does not include the days after Saturday thru today.
LastFullMonth	Start: The first day of last month.
	End: The last day of last month.
MonthToDate	Start: The first day of this month.
	End: Today.
Next30Days, Next31To60Days, Next61To90Days, Next91To365Days	Groups dates in 4 blocks of 30 days after today. Today's date is included in the Next30Days range.
Over90Days	Includes all days that come before 90 days prior to today.
WeekToDateFromSun	Start: Last Sunday.
	End: Today.
YearToDate	Start: Jan 1 of the current year.
	End: Today.

Conditional Structures

Conditional structures provide you with a way of testing one or more variables to see if they are equal to a value or are within a range of values. If the test succeeds, then a code block is executed. If the test fails, then a different code block is executed. Since there are many different circumstances where you will want to do this, Basic syntax provides you with a lot of options to match your circumstance. Each has its own benefits and drawbacks that you need to consider when deciding which to use. The conditional structures are: If, and Select Case.

The If statement uses the standard VB .NET syntax of testing a condition and performing one action if it's true and another action if it's false. The code in the Else block is executed if the test returns false. Basic syntax also supports the Else If statement. Finish an If block with End If.

```
If condition1 Then
    ...code...
ElseIf condition2 Then
    ...code...
Else
    ...code...
```

End If

The Select Case statement uses the standard VB .NET syntax of putting the variable to be tested at the end of the Select Case statement. After the Select Case statement, list the test conditions and the related code blocks using the Case statement. You can list multiple conditions for a single Case statement by separating the conditions with a comma. If none of the Case statements return True, then the code in the Case Else block is executed. Finish a Select Case block with End Select.

```
Select Case var
    Case condition1
        ...code...
    Case condition1, condition2
        ...code...
    Case Else
        ...code...
End Select
```

Conditional Functions

Conditional functions let you evaluate different conditions and return a value based upon the result. These are very similar to the conditional structures If Then and Case because both allow you to evaluate different conditions and perform some action. However, conditional functions are different in they can evaluate all the conditions in one line of code and they return a value when finished. Conditional structures require multiple lines of code. If a conditional structure needs to return a value, it must do so by storing it in a temporary variable for use after it finishes executing. Since conditional functions return the value themselves, and don't need a temporary variable, they can be used within another function! This gives you the ability to create a function that performs its operations using a number that changes depending upon certain conditions.

As an example, let's say you have an If statement that evaluates a condition and returns the result. This number is later used in another calculation. To make this work there would have to be a function just for the If statement and this function would be called elsewhere in the report. You can replace this code with a single IIF() function (discussed next) that evaluates those conditions within the function and returns the value for use in the function. Everything is cleanly written with one line of code. An example that demonstrates how this works is within the discussion of the IIF() function.

Although conditional functions sound pretty good, they do have a drawback. If you get carried away with their use, your code will be harder to read and maintain. For example, an IIF() function is good at replacing a single IF statement. But if you want to replace a nested If statement, you will have to write nested IIF() functions. Although this will compile and run, it can be pretty hard for you or another programmer to read and understand. Use caution when deciding what is appropriate for the task at hand.

Being able to test conditions and return a result within a single function is very powerful. This section describes three conditional functions: IIF(), Choose(), and Switch().

The IIF() Function

The IIF() function is unique to Crystal reports. It is a shortcut for the standard If statement. Its purpose is to put both the True and False actions on the same line. It consists of three parameters. The first parameter is the test condition. If the test condition is True, then the function returns whatever is in the second parameter. If the test condition is False, then the function returns whatever is in the third parameter. This function can return any data type except for an array.

Although this is convenient because you can condense a multi-line If statement into one line, there are two restrictions. The first is that the second and third parameters can only be a constant, variable or a function. You can't put a statement or code block within these parameters. The second restriction is that both parameters must be the same data type.

The syntax for the IIF() function is as follows:

```
var = IIF(condition, true_result, false_result)
```

I frequently use the IIF() function when concatenating strings together and a certain string may or may not be needed. Since it is a function, I make it return a string. The following example creates a person's full name. If the middle initial wasn't entered into the database then we want to make sure we don't insert a "." inappropriately. The IIF() function tests whether the middle name exists, and if it does it adds it to the string with the proper formatting.

```
'Demonstrate using the IIF() function to create a user's full name
Dim FullName As String
FullName = {Person.FirstName} & " " & IIF({Person.MI}<>"",  {Person.MI} & ". ", "") & {Person.LastName}
```

For purposes of comparing conditional functions with conditional structures, the following example is the same except that it uses an If Then statement.

```
'Demonstrate using the If Then statement to create a user's full name
Dim FullName As String
Dim MI As String
If {Person.MI}<>"" Then
    MI = {Person.MI} & ". "
End If
FullName = {Person.FirstName} & " " & MI & " " & {Person.LastName}
```

This example shows that using the If statement requires more coding. However, it does have the benefit of being easier to understand. It's a matter of personal preference as far as which one you choose to use. Personally, I always choose the IIF() function because it is an easy function to read. However, if the If statement were a lot more complicated, then using an IIF() function instead (or the other functions that are mentioned next) might make your code worse off.

The Choose() Function

The Choose() function returns a value chosen from a list of values. The value returned is determined by an index that is passed to the function. This function is like a shortcut for the If statement and the Select Case statement. You can use it when the range of possible values is relatively small and sequential.

The first parameter is an index representing which item to return. The remaining parameters are the items to choose from. The index range starts at 1 (it's not zero based). If the index is a value that is greater than the number of items passed, then the default value for the appropriate data type is returned (e.g. zero for numbers, "" for strings). This function can return any data type except for an array. As expected, each item in the list must be of the same data type.

The syntax for the Choose() function is as follows:

```
Var = Choose(index, value1, value2, value3, ...)
```

The Switch() Function

The Switch() function is also like a shortcut for the If statement and the Select Case statement. The parameters are grouped in pairs. The first parameter is an expression to test and the second parameter is a result value that is returned if the expression is true.

The syntax for the Switch() function is as follows:

```
Var = Switch(condition1, result1, condition2, result2, ....)
```

What makes this unique from the If and Select Case statements is that every parameter is evaluated before a result is returned from the function. This can have good or bad results depending upon your needs. The result can be bad because there could be a performance issue if you are passing time-intensive functions as parameters or it could result in an error being raised. It can be good if you want to force various functions to be called prior to returning a value. This function can return any data type except for an array. The data types of each result must be the same.

Looping Structures

Looping structures let you execute a block of code multiple times. The number of times this code block is executed depends upon the type of loop used and what happens within the code block. The looping structures covered are: For Next, While, and the various Do loops.

For Next Loop

The For Next loop uses the standard VB .NET syntax of using the For statement followed by a variable and the start and ending range. You have to decide in advance how many times the code block gets executed.

The default loop increment is 1. Use the Step keyword to define a new increment. Terminate the For block using the Next statement. Putting the variable name after the Next statement is optional. You can prematurely exit the loop by using the Exit For statement.

```
For var = start To end Step increment
    ...code...
    If condition Then
        Exit For
    End If
Next
```

While and Do Loops

The While and Do loops all follow the standard VB .NET syntax. The While block is terminated with a Wend statement. The Do loops are terminated with a Loop statement. The While keyword is used to continue looping as long as the condition evaluates to True. The Until keyword is used to continue looping when a condition evaluates to False. You can exit a Do loop with an Exit Do statement.

Code template for While … Wend:

```
While true_condition
    ...code...
Wend
```

Code template for Do While … Loop:

```
Do While true_condition
    ...code...
Loop
```

Code template for Do Until … Loop:

```
Do Until false_condition
    ...code...
Loop
```

Code template for Do … Loop While:

```
Do
   ...code...
Loop While true_condition
```

Code template for Do … Loop Until:

```
Do
   ...code...
Loop Until false_condition
```

Conditional Expressions

When performing actions based upon how a condition evaluates, there are numerous ways to build the condition. For example, when writing an If statement, you can compare a field to a constant using a variety of relational operators and you can join multiple conditions using Boolean operators. This section shows you all the ways you can evaluate fields and variables to see whether they match a certain value or a range of values.

You can test against a single constant or variable using the standard relational operators: <, >, <=, >=, =, <>.

You can also compare multiple expressions using the standard Boolean operators: And, Or, Not. A few operators that might be new to you are Xor, Eqv and Imp.

Eqv is for logical equivalence. It determines when the two expressions are the same. It returns True when both are true or both are false. If they are not the same, it returns Talse. The syntax is as follows:

```
exp1 Eqv exp2
```

Xor is for logical exclusion. It determines when the two expressions are different. It returns True if one is true and the other false. If both expressions are either true or false, then it returns False. The syntax is as follows:

```
exp1 Xor exp2
```

Imp is for logical implication. If the first expression is true, it implies that the second expression will also be true. If the second expression is also true, Imp returns True. If the second expression is False, Imp returns False because it didn't meet what was implied. On the other hand, if the *first* expression is False, nothing is implied and the result will be always be True. Thus, there is only one instance where Imp returns False: when the first expression is True and the second expression is False. The syntax is as follows:

```
exp1 Imp exp2
```

The Is operator is used with the Select Case statement when you want to use the relational operators (e.g. >, <, etc.). An example demonstrating this was already shown in the discussion on the Select Case statement.

The In operator is used for testing if a field or variable exists as an element in an array or if it falls within a range of values. For more information, see the previous sections Array Data Types and Range Data Types.

This page intentionally left blank

9
Using Built-In Functions

The Formula Editor in Crystal Reports gives you the ability to write very powerful functions. As you saw in Chapter 8, Crystal Reports lets you write functions to manipulate and analyze variables so that you can report on data specific to your business. In addition to writing your own formulas, Crystal Reports has dozens of built-in functions that decrease the amount of work you have to do. After all, why re-invent the wheel when you don't have too? This chapter shows you the different functions that come with Basic syntax. The functions are grouped by task so you can quickly find the ones you want. If you prefer to have an alphabetical list, then just reference the Index at the back of the book to see the page number of the one you are looking for. This chapter has a section for each of these categories: String Functions, Converting Data Types, Formatting Values for Output, Math Functions, Generating Random Numbers, and Date and Time Functions,

String Functions

The ability to modify and concatenate strings is a powerful feature of many programming languages, and Basic syntax doesn't disappoint. This section breaks out the different categories of string functions and summarizes how they work. The categories are: Analyzing a String, Parsing Strings, and Manipulating Strings.

Throughout this section, many functions are listed that use one or both of the parameters called compare and start. Rather than repeat a description of those parameters for each function, they are explained here for your reference.

The compare parameter determines when string comparisons are supposed to be case sensitive. If compare is 0, the search is case-sensitive. If it is 1, the search is not case-sensitive. This parameter is optional. If it is left out, the comparison defaults to 0, case sensitive.

The start parameter tells the function to process characters starting at the specified index.[13] Any characters that are prior to that index are ignored. This parameter is optional. If it is left out, then the function will be performed for the entire string.

---

[13] Remember from Chapter 8 that the first character of a string is at index 1.

Analyzing a String

Strings are used to store a variety of data that are displayed in a report. They can come from a variety of sources such as database tables, user input or even XML. Most of the time you will want to output the string directly to the report. But there are times when the information you want is stored as part of a larger string and you need to extract that data. To do this, it is necessary to analyze and parse a string's contents. Basic syntax gives you many functions for doing this. Table 9-1 shows the functions for analyzing a string's contents. Table 9-3 shows the functions for extracting sub-strings from a string. As a .NET programmer, you are already familiar with this functionality. Descriptions of each function are listed next to its name. Unless otherwise noted, the functions act the same as their .NET equivalents.

Table 9-1. String Analysis Functions

Function Name	Description
Asc(str)	Returns the ASCII value of a character.
Chr(val)	Returns a character equivalent of an ASCII value.
Len(str)	Gets the number of characters in the string.
IsNumeric(str)	Tells if it can be properly converted to a number.
InStr(start, str1, str2, compare)	Determines if str2 is a sub-string of str1. The start and compare parameters are both optional.
InStrRev(start, str1, str2, compare)	Same as InStr(), but it starts at the end of the string and searches towards the beginning.
StrCmp(str1, str2, compare)	Compares two strings to each other. The compare parameter is optional.
Val(str)	Returns the numeric equivalent

The StrCmp() function returns a value based upon how the two strings compare to each other. Table 9-2 summarizes what these results mean. Just like the Instr() functions, you can pass a compare parameter to set case sensitivity.

Table 9-2. StrCmp(str1, str2) Return Values

Return Value	Description
-1	str1 < str2
0	str1 = str2
1	str1 > str2

Table 9-3. String Parsing Functions

Function Name	Description
Trim(str)	Trim the spaces from both sides of a string.
LTrim(str)	Trim the spaces from the left side of a string.
RTrim(str)	Trim the spaces from the right side of a string.
Mid(str, start, length)	Return a given number of characters starting at a specified position. The start and length parameters are optional.
Left(str, length)	Return a given number of characters starting with the leftmost character.
Right(str, length)	Return a given number of characters starting with the rightmost character.

The Trim() functions will delete all extraneous spaces from either side of the string, depending on which function you call.

The Mid(), Left(), and Right() functions return a partial string whose size is based upon the number of characters you pass to the function. If you don't pass a length to the Mid() function then it returns all characters starting with the first one you specified.

Manipulating Strings

It is common for a string to be modified before it is displayed on a report. This can consist of simple reformatting or even joining the different elements of an array into a single string. Basic syntax has many functions for manipulating string data. Table 9-4 shows the functions for manipulating strings. Descriptions of each function are listed next to its name. The functions Filter(), Split(), and Picture() are different from .NET and are defined in more detail after the table.

Table 9-4. String Manipulation Functions

Function Name	Description
Filter(str, find, include, compare)	Search an array of strings for a sub-string and return an array matching the criteria.
Replace(str, find, replace, start, count, compare)	Find a string and replace it with another string. The parameters start, count and compare are all optional.
StrReverse(str)	Reverse the order of all characters in the string.
ReplicateString(str, copies)	Returns multiple copies of a string.
Space(val)	Returns the specified number of spaces as a single string.
Join(list, delimiter)	Join an array of strings into one string and separate them with the specified delimiter.
Split(str, delimiter, count, compare)	Split a single string into an array of strings based upon the specified delimiter. The parameters count and compare are optional.
Picture(str, template)	Formats the characters in a string onto a template.

The Filter() function searches an array of strings for a matching sub-string. It returns an array of all the strings that have that sub-string in them. The first parameter is the string array and the second parameter is the sub-string to search for. Essentially, this function calls the InStr() function for every string in the array. If the InStr() doesn't return a zero, then the string is added to the result array.

The Filter() function has an optional include parameter that tells the function to return an array of strings that don't match the sub-string. Essentially, this would be the same as saying that it returns all strings where the InStr() function returns a zero. Pass the include parameter the value False to get an array of the strings that don't have the sub-string in them. If you don't pass a value for this parameter, then the default value of True is used. Listing 9-1 demonstrates using the Filter() function with different parameters.

Listing 9-1. Using the Filter() function

```
'Demonstrate the Filter() function
Dim StringArray() As String
Dim ResultArray() As String
StringArray = Array("abcd", "bcde", "cdef")
'This will return an array with two elements: "abcd", "bcde"
ResultArray = Filter(StringArray, "bc")
```

```
'This will return an array with one element: "cdef"
'This is because it is the only element that doesn't have the sub-string
ResultArray = Filter(StringArray, "bc", False)
```

The Replace() function searches for a sub-string within another string, and if it finds it then it will replace it.

The Replace() function has two optional parameters that are important: start and count. The count parameter lets you limit how many string replacements are done. If you pass a number for this parameter then the number of replacements done cannot exceed that value. If you don't pass a value for this parameter then all the sub-strings are replaced.

```
'Change the addresses so that they use abbreviations
Dim Streets As String
Streets = "123 Main Street, 456 Cherry Avenue, 999 Brook Street"
Streets = Replace(Streets, "Street", "St.")
Streets = Replace(Streets, "Avenue", "Ave.")
'Streets is now "123 Main St., 456 Cherry Ave., 999 Brook St."
Formula = Streets
```

The Split() and Join() functions work together nicely. The Split() function takes a string and splits it into a string array. This makes it is easy to work on the individual strings. After you get done making any necessary changes to the individual strings you can combine them back into one string using the Join() function. How convenient!

This example demonstrates combining the functionality of the Split() and Join() functions. A string with the names of customers is available. We want the string to only have names with a prefix of "Mr." This is done by splitting the names into an array of strings. Then the Filter() function is used to return an array with only the strings that match our criteria. This array is combined back into a comma-delimited string using the Join() function.

```
'Demonstrate the Split() and Join() functions
Dim Names As String
Dim NamesArray() as String
Names = "Mr. Jones, Sir Alfred, Ms. Bee, Mr. Smith"
NamesArray = Split(Names, ",")
'Get the names that only use Mr.
NamesArray = Filter(NamesArray,"Mr.")
'RJoin the array back into a comma-delimited string
Names = Join(NamesArray, ",")
'Names is now "Mr. Jones, Mr. Smith"
Formula = Names
```

The Picture() function maps a string onto a template. The first parameter is the source string and the second parameter is the template.

The template consists of a series of "x"s with other characters around it. Each character in the source string gets mapped onto each the "x"s in the template.

The source string can use any character and it will get mapped. If the source string has more characters than what can fit in the template, then all remaining characters are added to the end. If the template has any non-"x" characters, then they stay as they are.

```
'Demonstrate mapping a string with non-alphanumeric characters
Formula = Picture("ab&[{1234", "xxx..xx..x..")
'The result is "ab&..[{..1..234"
```

This example illustrates that all characters in the source string were mapped onto the "x"s. It also shows that since the source string has nine characters and the template has six "x"s, then the extra three characters are added to the end.

Converting Data Types

Basic syntax is a type safe language that requires all constants and variables in the same formula to be of the same data type. It also requires you to pass constants and variables as parameters using the exact data type that the formula expects. Even though the data types in Basic syntax are fairly simple, you still have to make sure that they are compatible. Fortunately, all the necessary type conversion formulas are available. Table 9-5 lists the conversion functions.

Table 9-5. Conversion Functions

Conversion Function	Description
CBool(number), CBool(currency)	Convert to Boolean.
CCur(number), CCur(string)	Convert to Currency.
CDbl(currency), CDbl(string), CDbl(boolean)	Convert to Number. Equivalent to ToNumber(). See the section "Formatting Values for Output".
CStr()	Convert to String. Equivalent to ToText().
CDate(string), CDate(year, month, day), CDate(DateTime)	Convert to Date.
CTime(string), CTime(hour, min, sec), CDate(DateTime)	Convert to Time.
CDateTime(string), CDateTime(date), CDateTime(date, time), CDateTime(year, month, day)	Convert to DateTime
CDateTime(year, month, day, hour, min, sec)	Convert to DateTime.
ToNumber(string), ToNumber(boolean)	Convert to a Number.

ToText()	Convert to String. Same as CStr().
IsDate(string), IsTIme(), IsDateTime()	Test a string for being a valid date/time.
IsNumber(string)	Test a string for being a valid number.
ToWords(number), ToWords(number, decimals)	Convert a number to its word equivalent.

Most of the above functions work the same as the similarly named .NET functions. The **CBool()** function takes a number or currency value and converts it to Boolean **True** or **False**. Any non-zero value is converted to **True** and zero is converted to **False**. When it is displayed on a report, it prints the words "True" or "False".

The **CCur()** function takes a number or string and converts it to the **Currency** data type. When converting a string, it can have formatting characters in it ("$", ",", etc.) and it will still be converted properly.

The **CDbl()** and **ToNumber()** functions are equivalent. Pass them a value and it gets converted to a number.

The **CDate()**, **CTime()** and **CDateTime()** are all similar. Pass all of them a string and it gets converted to the proper data type. The string parser for this function is very sophisticated. It will let you type in strings as diverse as "Jan 19, 1991", "5/26/1998" and "2002, Feb 04". You can also pass numbers as individual parameters for representing the different parts of a date and time. See Table 9-5 for the various parameter options.

When converting a string to a date or number, you run the risk of raising an error if the string isn't in the expected format. You can avoid this by testing the strings validity before converting it. The **IsDate()** and **IsNumber()** functions do this for you. They return **True** if the string can be properly converted. If not, they return **False**.

The **ToWords()** function takes a number and converts it to its equivalent in words. This is similar to writing an amount on a check and then spelling out the full amount in words. It will print the decimal portion as a being the "##/100". You can set the number of decimals it displays by passing a number to the second parameter, which is optional. Notice in the following example how the decimals are rounded up.

```
'Demonstrate the ToWords() formula
Formula = ToWords(123.45) 'Result is "one hundred twenty-three 45 / 100"
Formula = ToWords(123.45,1) 'Result is "one hundred twenty-three and 5 / 100
```

Formatting Values for Output

When formatting output to be displayed in a report, the output is usually a combination of string data variables. As the last section stated, Basic syntax is a type safe language. As a result, you can't concatenate strings with numbers or dates. To build an output string with a combination of data types, you have to convert everything to a string using the CStr() method. This method takes all data types and converts them to a string.

The CStr() function is usually passed the value to format as the first parameter and the formatting string as the second parameter. The formatting string is used as a template that describes how the value should look when it gets converted as a string. Table 9-6 shows the different formatting characters that can be used. Table 9-7 shows examples of how different values will look after being formatted.

Table 9-6. CStr() Formatting Characters

Format	Description
#	Use with formatting numbers. If the number isn't large enough, then spaces will be used instead. If the number is too large, then the integer part will still be fully displayed. Unused digits after the decimal are zero filled.
0	Use with formatting numbers. If the number isn't large enough, then it will be padded with zeros. If the number is too large, then the integer part will still be fully displayed. Unused digits after the decimal are zero filled.
,	Use with formatting numbers to designate the thousand separators.
.	Use with formatting numbers to designate the decimal separator.
d, M	Day and month as a number (without a leading zero).
dd, MM, yy	Day, month and year as a two digit number (with a leading zero when necessary).
ddd, MMM	Day and month as a three letter abbreviation.
dddd, MMMM, yyyy	Day, month and year fully spelled out.
h, m, s	Time portions as a number without a leading zero.
hh, mm, ss	Time portions as a two digit number (with a leading zero when necessary).
HH	Show hours using a 24 hour clock (military time).
T	Single character representation of AM/PM.
Tt	Two character representation of AM/PM.

Table 9-7. CStr() Example Output

#	CStr()	Output
1	CStr(1234, 2)	1,234.00
2	CStr(1234.567, 2)	1,234.57
3	CStr(1234.567, "#")	1234
4	CStr(1234.567, "0")	1234
5	CStr(1234, "0.##")	1234.00
6	CStr(1234, "0.00")	1234.00
7	CStr(1234.567, "#.##")	1234.57
8	CStr(1234.567, "0.00")	1234.57
9	CStr(1234.567, "#####")	1234
10	CStr(1234.567, "00000")	01234
11	CStr(1234.567, "#", 2)	1234
12	CStr(1234.567, "#.##", 2)	1234.57
13	CStr(1234.567, "#.###", 2)	1234.57
14	CStr(1234.567, "#.##", 2, ",")	1234.57
15	CStr(1234.567, "#.##", 2, ".", ",")	1234,57
16	CStr(1234.567, 2, ".", ",")	1.234,57
17	CStr(1234.567, "###,###.##")	1,234.57
17	CStr(#1/2/2003 04:05:06 am", "d/M/yy H/m/s t")	1/2/03 4: 5: 6 A
18	CStr(#1/2/2003 04:05:06 am", "dd/MM/yyyy HH/mm/ss tt")	01/02/2003 04:05:06 AM
19	CStr(#1/2/2003 04:05:06 am", "dd/MM/yyyy hh/mm/ss tt")	01/02/2003 04:05:06 AM
20	CStr(#3:20 PM#, "HH:mm")	15:20

Table 9-7 shows examples of many different CStr() function calls and the associated output. On the surface, this looks very straightforward and everything matches what was stated in Table 9-6. However, we know that in the world of software when you look below the surface things aren't always what they seem. You'll soon see that the simple CStr() function can get very complicated.[14]

---

[14] Who would have thought that a technical book would have foreshadowing in it?

Examples 1 and 2 are easy. The first parameter is the number to format and the second parameter is the number of decimals to display. If the number to format doesn't have any decimals, then they are zero filled. Notice that in these examples as well as all the others, the decimals are rounded up.

With one exception, examples 3 through 10 are easy as well. The exception is that unlike the first two examples, the second parameter is the format string. Using this format string lets you be very specific about how to format the number.

Stop for a moment and look at examples 1 and 5. Do you notice one thing different between them? The difference is that the output in example 5 doesn't have a thousands separator. In both example 1 and example 5, no thousands separator is specified, but example 1 has it by default. This isn't the case in when you use a format string. The documentation says that the format string needs to use an optional parameter to specify the thousands separator. But example 14 shows that Basic syntax has a bug that keeps this from working.[15]

Examples 5 and 6 show that if there aren't enough decimals then both the "#" and the "0" will zero fill their positions.

Examples 9 and 10 show that if there aren't enough digits to fill the whole number, then the "#" fills it with a space and the "0" fills it with a zero.

Examples 11 through 13 are where things really get interesting. These examples show that you can use the format string and also specify how many decimals to display. If you think about this for a minute, it may not make sense why you would do this. After all, if you were using a format string, you shouldn't have to specify the number of decimals because it is already part of the format string. The only time you will do this is when you pass the optional parameters that specify the thousands separator and decimal character. Then you are forced to list all optional parameters and this means also specifying the number of decimals.

When you do specify the number of decimals, you should specify the same number as what your format string allows. If you specify a number different than what is in this string, then it uses the lesser of the two. Example 11 shows that the format string doesn't allow any decimals and that is how it is displayed. Example 13 shows that the number of decimals is two, and the format string allows three decimals. Thus, two decimals are displayed.

Example 14 shows that you can have a third optional parameter that specifies the thousands separator. Unfortunately, the output shows you that it doesn't have any effect. Example 15 tries to illustrate how to show a number using the European format of using a period for the thousands separator and a comma

---

[15] The suspense keeps building...

for the decimal. The output shows that the comma is now the decimal, which is correct. But again, no thousands separator is shown.

Example 16 shows that if you don't use a format string then everything works out perfectly.

Does this mean that if you use the format string then you can't have a thousands separator? No. It just means you have to do it manually. Example 17 shows a working example where everything is typed in. The proper characters are entered exactly where they belong in the string. If you use this method, be sure that you specify enough characters for the largest number that could be displayed.

The good news is that these problems only happen when you are formatting numbers for international display. By default, Basic syntax uses the computers international settings to determine how to format the number and you don't have to specify the format string. If you must use a format string then you will have to do it all manually like example 17.

All these variations on how to use the format string and remember where the bugs are can be pretty confusing. Just remember that if your format string doesn't act the way you think it should, then come back to this section for a quick refresher.

Unfortunately, the preformatted date strings that are in .NET (e.g. LongDate, ShortDateTime, etc.) are not in Crystal Reports. You have to write the entire format string manually. Although this certainly isn't difficult, the .NET feature has me spoiled.

The dates that are illustrated in examples 18 and 19 are much easier to look at, but far from perfect. First of all, you need to be very careful about capitalization. The compiler is case sensitive when formatting date strings. When entering a format string, refer back to Table 9-6 so that you get it right.

Now let's look at a couple of problems with formatting dates. According to the documentation, using a single "h", "m" or "s" will not put leading zeros in front of the hour, minute or second. This is shown to be true in Example 17. However, you can also see that it does insert a leading space. Even though we specified that all the characters are to be adjacent, it inserts spaces anyway. This is not what we wanted and there is not an easy way to fix it. To get around this, you have to concatenate the values together using the Hour(), Minute() and Second() functions. Unfortunately, these functions return two decimal places so you have to work a little harder than expected. The solution is shown in Listing 9-2.

Listing 9-2. Displaying a time with no leading spaces

```
'Demonstrate displaying a time with no leading spaces
Dim Now As Time
Now = CTime("1:2:3 AM")
```

```
Formula = CStr(Hour(Now), 0) & ":" & CStr(Minute(Now), 0) & ":" & _
    CStr(Second(Now), "0") & " " & CStr(Now, "tt")
'Now is formatted as "1:5:4 AM"
```

Math Functions

Table 9-8. Math Functions

Function Name	Description
Abs(number)	Return the absolute value.
Fix(number, decimals)	Return a number with a specified number of significant digits.
Int(number), numerator \ denominator	Return the integer portion of a fractional number.
Pi	3.14...
Remainder(numerator, denominator),	Return the remainder of dividing the numerator by the denominator.
numerator Mod denominator	Return the remainder of dividing the numerator by the denominator.
Round(number, decimals)	Round up a number with a specified number of significant digits.
Sgn(number)	Return number's sign.
Sqr(number), Exp(number), Log(number)	The standard arithmetic functions.
Cos(number), Sin(number), Tan(number), Atn(number)	The standard scientific functions.

The math functions listed in Table 9-8 are similar to the corresponding functions in .NET. There are only a couple of interesting points to notice.

Working with whole numbers and decimals is done numerous ways. The Fix() and Round() functions take a fractional number and truncate it to a specified number of digits. The Round() function will round up to the nearest decimal. The number of decimals to display is optional and the default is zero. The Int() function is similar to the Round() function except that it only returns the whole number and will round down to the nearest whole number. Table 9-9 shows how the three functions will return a different number depending upon the decimal portion and whether the number is positive or negative.

Table 9-9. Examples of Truncating Decimals

Function	1.9	-1.9
Fix()	1	-1
Round()	2	-1
Int()	1	-2

If you want to get the whole number and you have the numerator and denominator available, you can use the \ operator to perform integer division. This does the division and only returns the integer portion of the result. The Mod operator and Remainder() function return the remainder after doing the division.

```
'Demonstrate the integer division and the Mod operator
Formula = 10 \ 3              'Returns 3
Formula = 10 mod 3           'Returns 1
Formula = Remainder(10, 3)    'Returns 1
```

Generating Random Numbers

Generating random numbers using the Rnd() function. When you use random numbers, you normally want to tell the computer to generate a new random number sequence based upon some internal method (usually using the system clock). This still applies with Basic syntax. The Rnd() function has an optional parameter that lets you tell the computer to generate a new random number sequence. With Basic syntax, you can pass your own random number seed value to generate the sequence. This is beneficial if you are writing a report that uses random numbers and want to test it using the same random number sequence each time. If you pass the Rnd() function a positive number, then it does just that. However, if you want your sequence to be different every time, and thus your report will have different numbers every time, pass the Rnd() function a negative number. This tells it to use the system clock to generate the random number sequence. This results in a pseudo-random sequence of numbers each time you call it. Once you have called Rnd() with a seed, call the Rnd() function without a seed to get the next random number in the sequence.

Date and Time Functions

Table 9-10. Date and Time Functions

Function Name	Description
CurrentDate, CurrentTime, CurrentDateTime	Returns the current date and/or time.
DateSerial(year, month, day), DateTime(hour, minute, second)	Returns a date or time.
DateAdd(interval, number, date)	Increases the date by a certain interval.
DateDiff(interval, startdate, enddate, firstdayofweek)	Finds the difference between two dates.
DatePart(interval, date, firstdayofweek, firstweekofyear)	Returns a number representing the current interval of a date.
MonthName(integer, abbreviate)	Returns the full month name. Return the 3-letter abbreviation if the second parameter is True.
Timer	The number of seconds that have elapsed since midnight.
WeekDay(date, firstdayofweek)	Returns a number representing the day of the week.
WeekdayName(weekday, abbreviate, firstdayofweek)	Returns the full month name. Return the 3-letter abbreviation if the second parameter is True.

Table 9-11. Interval Strings for DateAdd(), DateDiff() and DatePart()

String	Description
"yyyy"	Year
"q"	Quarter
"m"	Month (1 through 12)
"ww"	Week of the year (1 through 53)
"w"	Day of the week (1 through 7)
"y"	Day of year (1 through 366)
"d"	Day part of the date (1 through 31)
"h"	Hour
"n"	Minute
"s"	Second

The date and time functions that come with .NET pale in comparison to what you can do with Crystal Reports. Although many of the Basic syntax functions are similar to their .NET counterparts, they give you more functionality. You can also combine different functions together to create very powerful date calculations. There are a lot of new concepts to learn.

DateAdd( )

For adding and subtracting dates and times, the easiest function to use is the DateAdd() function. This is very similar to the functions AddDays(), AddMonths(), etc. found in the .NET DateTime class. Using the DateAdd() function requires passing a string representing the type of interval to modify, the number of units to add or subtract, and the date to modify. There are a number of different strings that designate the interval to modify. The interval strings are listed in Table 9-11. To subtract a date interval pass a negative number of units. The DateAdd() function returns a DateTime value and this may need to be converted to either a Date or a Time depending on how you intend to use the result.

Using one q interval unit is the same as using three m intervals. The benefit of using the q interval is that many financial reports are printed on a quarterly basis. After the user is prompted for how many quarters they wish to print, you can take their input and use it to calculate a final date. Although multiplying their input by 3 is fairly trivial, having a shortcut is nice and it helps makes your code self-documenting.

Rather than using the DateAdd() function to add and subtract days, it is just as acceptable to directly add a number to the Date variable. Since the date is stored as a number, adding another number to it will increase the date by that number of days. The following examples both produce the same result.

```
Formula = DateAdd("d", 10, #1/1/2002#)      'Returns 1/11/2002
Formula = #1/1/2002# + 10                    'Returns 1/11/2002
```

The benefit to using the DateAdd() function is that it takes into account how many days are in each month and it checks for valid dates. As an example, say that you want to find out the last day of the next month. To do this with the addition operator, you need to know how many days are in the next month so you will probably store that information in an array. You also need to track which years are leap years. Using the DateAdd() function is much easier because if you add one month to the current date, it will check that this returns a valid date. If there aren't enough days in the month then it will return the last valid day of the month. The same applies to using the quarter interval. The function adds three months to the current date and makes sure that this is a valid date. If not, it returns the last valid date of the quarter.

DateDiff( )

The DateDiff() function returns the difference between two dates or times. It can return the difference in different intervals. These intervals can be days, months, years or any of the intervals listed in Table 9-11.

Be careful when using the DateDiff() function for calculating an interval other than the number of days. When performing a difference calculation, it counts any interval less than a single unit as zero. For example, if want to find out how many months have elapsed between two dates, and the two dates are the first day of the month and the last day of the month, then the result is 0. This is because the interval is only a partial month and doesn't constitute a full month. The fact that the dates are 30 days apart is irrelevant. If you change this example so that rather than use the last day of the month, you use the first day of the next month, then the result is 1. Even though the two examples had final dates that only differed by one day, the result is different. This applies to all the intervals including dates and times.

There is an optional parameter that lets you specify the first day of the week. This is only used by the DateDiff() function when the interval is ww. This counts the number of times a particular day of the week appears within a date range. To pass this parameter to the function, prefix the day by cr For example, Friday is crFriday. The start date does not get counted when doing the calculation, but the end date does. Thus, if you pass the function a start date that falls on a Friday, and the parameter is crFriday, then the result will not include this date.

```
'Demonstrate counting the number of paydays
Dim StartDate as Date
Dim NumberOfFridays As Number
StartDate = DateSerial(Year(CurrentDate), 1,1)   'First day of year
```

```
NumberOfFridays = DateDiff("ww", #1/1/2002#, CurrentDate, crFriday)
'If the first date was a Friday, add it back
If WeekDay(StartDate) = 6 Then
    NumberOfFridays = NumberOfFridays + 1
End If
Formula = NumberOfFridays \ 2        'Paid on every other Friday
```

The DateDiff() function treats the w and ww intervals differently than the DateAdd() and DatePart() functions. In both the DateAdd() and DatePart() functions, the w interval represents a single weekday and the ww interval represents a seven day period. However, the DateDiff() function treats the w interval as the number of weeks between two dates and the ww interval counts the number of times a certain weekday appears. Thus, the ww interval counts the number of times a seven-day period occurs and the w interval counts the number of times a single day occurs. This is the exact opposite of how the other two functions treat these intervals.

DatePart( )

The DatePart() function returns a number representing the part of the date that you specify using the interval parameter. These intervals are listed in Table 9-11. Pass the interval as the first parameter and the date as the second parameter.

```
'Get the current quarter
Formula = DatePart("q", CurrentDate)  'Returns a number 1 – 4
```

Use interval "w" to display the weekday and it returns a number from 1 to 7. By default, Sunday is represented by a 1. The optional third parameter designates which day of the week is considered the first day of the week. If you passed this parameter crMonday, then Sunday is represented by a 7.

Use "ww" to display the week and it returns a number from 1 to 53. By default, the first week is the week that has January 1st in it. Use the optional fourth parameter to designate a different way of determining the first week of the year. There are two other methods to do this. The first method specifies that the first week is the one with at least four days in it. The second method specifies the first week as the first one to have seven full days in it. Table 9-12 lists the different constants that are used to specify the first week of the year parameter.

What happens if you specify the first week to be the first one with seven full days, and you pass it a date of 2/1/2002 that only has five days in the week? Does DatePart() return a 0? No, it returns 53 to let you know that the date falls before the first official week of the year.

Since the third and fourth parameters are both optional, if you want to specify the fourth parameter, then you are also required to specify the third parameter (the first day of the week). Although by default this is crSunday, you must still pass it to the function in order to be able to use the fourth parameter. In this circumstance the third parameter is ignored and the DatePart() function always assumes Sunday to be the first day of the week.

Table 9-12. First Week of the Year Constants

Constant	Description
crFirstJan1	The week that has January 1st.
crFirstFourDays	The first week that has at least four days in it.
crFirstFullWeek	The first week that has seven days in it.

MonthName( ), WeekDayName( ) and WeekDay( )

Just like the DatePart() function, these functions are given a date value and they return part of the date. The difference is that these functions are more specialized than the DatePart() function.

The MonthName() function is passed a number representing the month and it returns the name of the month fully spelled out. There is an optional second parameter that lets you specify whether it should be abbreviated to three letters. Pass True to the second parameter to get the abbreviated name. By default, this is False and it returns the full name.

The WeekDayName() function is passed a number representing the day of the week and it returns the name of the day fully spelled out. Just like MonthName(), you can pass True to the optional second parameter to get the 3 letter abbreviation.

The WeekDay() function is passed a date and it returns a number.

Both the WeekDayName() and WeekDay() functions use a number to represent the day of the week. By default, this number is a 1 for Sunday and a 7 for Saturday. As discussed for the DatePart() function, you can shift this number by specifying a different first day of the week. If you passed crMonday to the function, then Sunday is represented by a 7. You pass this as the third parameter for the WeekDayName() function and as the second parameter for the WeekDay() function.

```
'Demonstrate using the first day of the week parameter
Formula = WeekDayName(2, True, crMonday)    'Returns "Tue" for Tuesday
Formula = WeekDay(#1/6/2002#, crMonday)     'Returns 7 b/c it is a Sunday
```

DateSerial( ) and TimeSerial( )

The DateSerial() and TimeSerial() functions can be used to create a date or time by passing the parts of the value as separate parameters to the function. The DateSerial() parameters are the year, month and day. The DateTime() parameters are the hour, minute, and seconds.

In the simplest form, these functions create a date or time using three parameters. But these functions are also very powerful for adding and subtracting values to a Date and Time. They are different from the DateAdd() function in that they perform the calculations using a cumulative process. They start by calculating a partial date (or time) value and then build upon it and modify it each step of the way. It starts by calculating the year, then it calculates the month and finally the day. This is easiest to see by looking at a simple example first and then a more complex example. All of the examples use the following statements to declare and initialize the variable MyDate.

This code snippet shows the variable declaration that is used for the remaining examples.

```
'Declare the variable for use in the examples
Dim MyDate as Date
MyDate = CDate("2/4/2002")
```

This example gets the current year and month from the current date and passes them to the DateSerial() function. It passes the value 1 as the day parameter to force it to return the first day of the current month.

```
Formula = DateSerial(Year(MyDate), Month(MyDate), 1)    'Returns 2/1/2002
```

The next function calculates the last day of the prior month by using each parameter to create the next part of the date in sequence and then modifying the result according to the arithmetic.

```
Formula = DateSerial(Year(MyDate), Month(MyDate), 1 - 1)          'Returns 1/31/2002
```

How it calculates the result is best shown using the steps listed here.

1. Calculate the year. This returns a date with the year of 2002.

2. Calculate the month. This returns a date of 02/2002.

3. Calculate the day. The first part of the parameter is 1 and this returns a date of 02/01/2002.

4. The subtract operator tells it to subtract one day from the date as it has been calculated to this point. Thus, it subtracts one day from 02/01/2002 to give a date of 1/31/2002.

The next example is the most complex, but uses the same rules as the last example. It calculates the last day of the current month.

```
Formula = DateSerial(Year(MyDate), Month(MyDate) + 1, 1 - 1)        'Returns 2/28/2002
```

1. Calculate the year. This returns a date with the year of 2002.

2. Calculate the month. This returns a date of 02/2002

3. The addition operator tells it to add one month. This returns a date of 03/2002.

4. Calculate the day. The first part of the parameter is 1 and this returns a date of 03/01/2002.

5. The subtract operator tells it to subtract one day from the date as it has been calculated to this point. Thus, it subtracts one day from 03/01/2002 to give a date of 2/28/2002.

You can see from the three previous examples that using a cumulative approach to calculating the date is very powerful. It's almost like using a single function to write a simplified macro.

Timer

The Timer function returns the number of seconds that have elapsed since midnight. This can be used for doing performance evaluations. Unfortunately, it is only significant to the nearest second. So it is only useful for analyzing reports that have lengthy run times. The following code demonstrates timing how long it takes a report to run.

In the report Header put the following formula:

```
BeforeReadingRecords
Global StartTime as Number
StartTime = Timer
Formula = ""          'A necessary evil that won't effect the calculation
```

In the report Footer put the following formula:

```
WhilePrintingRecords
Global StartTime as Number
Formula = Timer – StartTime
'This returns the number of seconds it took to run the report
```

Other Functions

Although this chapter and the last two have listed many useful functions, Basic syntax still has many more to choose from. You've seen all the primary ones and I'm going to leave the remaining ones for you to explore on your own.

This page intentionally left blank

10
Charting Data

Visualizing data can have a tremendous impact compared to just printing raw numerical data. Adding a chart to a report makes it possible for readers to quickly grasp the important relationships between data. Many times reports are used with proposals to sell a reader on an idea or plan. Adding a colorful chart can sell your idea more effectively than a dry report filled with endless numbers. This chapter shows you what types of charts are available as well as how to modify their appearance so that they can make your report more appealing and quickly get your message across.

Choosing the Proper Chart

Charts are used to make it easy to compare sets of data. The visual aspect of a chart lets the reader immediately recognize things such as the differences in quantity, percentage of the whole or numerical trending. Depending upon the information you are trying to convey, certain chart styles are more effective at presenting this information than others. Table 10-1 lists different chart styles and what they are effective at presenting. This table gets you started in the right direction for choosing the proper chart.

Table 10-1. Effectiveness of different chart styles.

Chart Style	Effective at ...
Bar Chart	Comparing the differences between items and events.
	Comparing items and events against the same scale without relation to time.
	Showing relationships between sets of data using grouping.
	Note: The X-axis is generally non-numeric. When it is numeric, the interval isn't relevant.
Line Chart/Area Chart	Comparing continuous data over a period of time against a common scale.
	Tracking movement over time.
	Examining trends between two or more sets of data.
	Note: The X-axis represents a unit of time.
X-Y Scatter Chart	Charting a large quantity of values without relation to time.
	Finding groups of data where there is a large percentage of similar data points.
Bubble Chart	Similar to the X-Y chart, but with a third data point. The third data point determines the bubble's diameter. It is proportional to the value of this data point.
Pie/Doughnut Chart	Visualizing the percent of the whole.
	Examining relationships as part-to-whole.
	Note: There is only a single axis being represented. Thus, only one value is being charted.
Radar Chart	Comparing data sets in a star pattern. The importance/relationship of each data set is determined by having the target value start at either the center of the axis or the outside.
Stock Chart	Analyzing stock values. Shows the trading range for the day as well as first trade and last trade amounts.
3D Surface Chart	Showing trends with relationship to time.
	Note: It uses a three dimensional surface to makes it easy to analyze a large quantity of data.

To use Table 10-1, think about why you are using a chart to present your data, ask yourself what is the message you are trying to convey to the reader. Scan the list of reasons of why one chart is more effective than the other charts. Once you see a description that best matches your purpose, select that type of chart.

For example, assume that you have a report that prints the annual sales for each division in a corporation. The message you are conveying is which division had the largest sales volume as well as which division had the lowest sales. Three charts that are good at comparing different data sets is the bar chart, the line chart and the X-Y chart. The bar chart immediately looks good because it is effective at comparing differences between items. The line chart also compares data, but it does so over a period of time. This doesn't apply here because the data is within the same time period (i.e. the same year). So the line chart is not a good choice. The X-Y chart compares data, but it is done with respect to two data points. In other words, both the X and Y axis must represent numerical data. The sales report is charted with the sales volume and the division name. Since the division name isn't numerical data, it can't be used with the X-Y chart. The best choice for the division annual sales report is the bar chart.

Let's build on this example by saying that you are given a new requirement where the report has to be modified so that it is now a drill-down report. It currently shows the annual sales per division and it needs to be modified so that you can drill-down on a division and see its monthly sales. This helps the reader determine if the division had a particular month that was exceptionally better than the other months or if the division was consistently improving. The purpose of this chart is very similar to the first chart. You want to tell the reader how the total sales compare to each other. But this example has a slight variation: you are now charting for a single division and the individual months are being compared to each other. You are working with data that changes over a period of time and looking for the trend. The only reason we didn't use a line chart in the first example was because the data didn't relate to time. This example does relate to time and it is also looking at the sales trend. So the line chart is an excellent choice for presenting the monthly sales figures.

Adding a Chart

There are two ways to add a chart to a report: with the Report Expert and with the Add Chart Expert. If you are creating a report and you know in advance that it will use a chart, you can use the Report Expert to build the chart while performing the initial report design. If you decide to add a chart later in the report creation process, right-click on the report and select Insert | Chart. This brings up the Chart Expert. Both methods show the same dialog box (Figure 10-1) for creating a chart. The Report Expert displays it on the Chart tab.

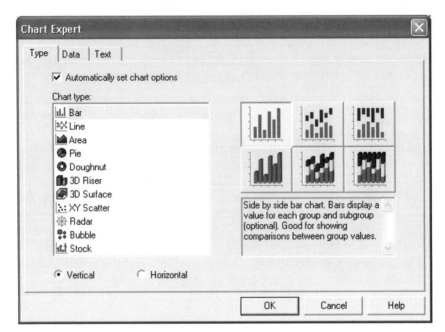

Figure 10-1. Chart Expert dialog box.

This dialog box has three tabs that are shown by default: Type, Data, and Text. There is also a checkbox on the Type tab titled Automatically Set Chart Options. It is checked by default. If you uncheck this option, then two additional tabs appear on the dialog box: Axes and Options.

Selecting a Chart with the Type Tab

Use the Type tab to select the type of chart to display. A sample of each chart is shown in Table 10-2. The Chart Expert shows many examples of each chart to the right of the list. As you click on each chart type in the list, the variations will change to reflect the available options. Charts that use an X-Y axis format have an option button that selects whether it is a vertical or horizontal chart. Vertical is chosen by default.

Table 10-2. Example chart types.

Chart Type	Sample	Chart Type	Sample
Bar Chart		Doughnut Chart	
Line Chart		3D Riser Chart	
Area Chart		3D Surface Chart	
Pie Chart		XY Scatter Chart	
Bubble Chart		Radar Chart	
Stock Chart			

Setting Data Points with the Data tab

The Data tab is the primary interface for configuring the chart and it is fairly complex. It sets the location of the chart, and the fields that determine the coordinates of each axis as well as map the data points. It also has three buttons for setting the properties of specialized charts.[16] The Advanced button shows the default layout and is available for every report. The Group button is enabled when your report has a grouping section and the Cross-Tab button is enabled when there is a cross-tab object on the report. The default layout, Advanced, is shown in Figure 10-2.

---

[16] There is actually a fourth button labeled OLAP. This isn't used with Visual Studio .NET and is always disabled.

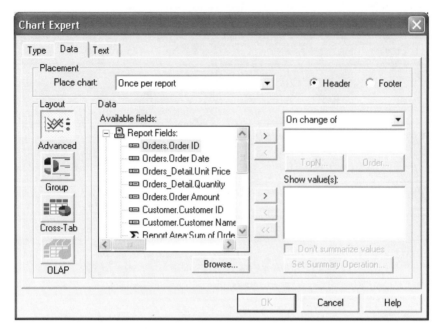

Figure 10-2. The Data tab with the Advanced button selected.

> ## Note
>
> The Advanced, Group and Cross-Tab buttons each create a different type of chart. Although they are all on the same Data tab and appear to work together, they are mutually exclusive. Only the last one selected will be used to create the chart. For example, say that you set some properties for the Advanced tab. You then decide that you would rather use a Group chart instead. So you click on the Group button and change the settings. When you run the report, the chart displayed on the report will be a group chart and reflect those settings. The settings you made with the Advanced button are ignored. In fact, when you close this dialog box and save your settings, only the settings for the current button are saved and any settings that were made with the other buttons are discarded.

The Placement frame controls which section the chart is placed in on the report. It is automatically placed there when you close the dialog box. The dropdown box sets whether the chart appears in the Report Header/Footer or whether it appears in the Group Header/Footer. When you click on it, it displays the options Once Per Report or For Each xxx. The Once Per Report option always puts the chart in the Report Header/Footer. There is one For Each xxx option listed for each group on your report. If there aren't any groups on your report then the only option listed will be Once Per Report. To the right of the dropdown are the options to select placement in either the Header or the Footer.

The Data frame lets you choose the fields to plot onto the chart. The Available Fields list shows all the fields that the chart can use. To the right of this list is an Evaluate option[17] and below that is the Show Value(s) list. Use the Available Fields list to select the fields to put in the two options on the right.

Setting the Evaluate Option

The Evaluate option determines when a new element is shown on the chart. On a standard vertical chart, this would be the elements listed on the X-axis. For example, this determines when a new bar is drawn on a bar chart. There are three options to choose from and they are listed in Table 10-3.

Table 10-3. The Evaluate options.

Evaluate Option	Description
On Change Of	A new element is created when the value of the field changes. The value plotted on the other axis is the sum of all fields that are in each group.
For Each Record	A new element is created for each detail record in the table. Check the number of detail records because too many records will over-crowd the chart.
For All Records	Shows a single element on the chart. The value plotted on the other axis is the grand total of each field selected in the Show Value(s) list.

The On Change Of option requires a little more explanation than the other two options, which are fairly straightforward. The On Change Of option is used in conjunction with one or more report fields. It creates chart-only groups and summarizes the values within the group. The groups in the chart have no effect on the rest of the report.

When selecting the On Change Of option, you add the field(s) to group onto the listbox below the option. The number of fields you add determines how many groups are in the report. If you only have one field, then each group name is listed as a single element on the chart. For example, Figure 10-3 shows

---

[17] The label "Evaluate" is assumed and isn't actually shown in the dialog box. It is the dropdown box at the top.

a chart with an Evaluate field of Customer Name and the Show Value field (discussed later) is Order Amount. This creates an element for each customer and it charts the total amount of all the orders in the report.

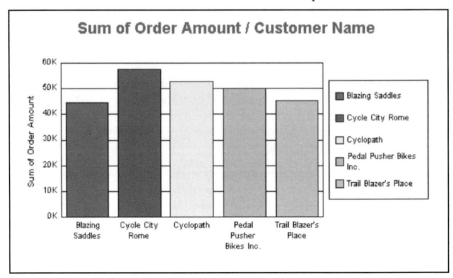

Figure 10-3. A chart with one field in the Evaluate list.

Having more than one field in the Evaluate list creates sets of data. Each set has the same number of elements in it and they are compared to each other as a group. The first element is the primary group and the second element is the sub-group. The primary group determines the sets that are charted. The sub-group charts each individual element within the primary group.

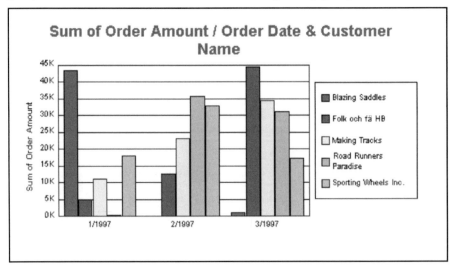

Figure 10-4. A chart with two fields in the Evaluate list.

The chart in Figure 10-4 also shows the total customer order amounts, but it does it per the month the order was placed. Putting two fields in the Evaluate list does this: The Order Date, by month, and the Customer Name. The Order Date is listed first so that the data sets are charted by month. The Customer Name is listed second so that it gets listed as a separate element on the chart.

For each field listed as an element, there are a few ways to customize it. Directly below the list are two buttons: TopN and Order. These are only enabled when you select one of the fields. These two buttons bring up the same dialog boxes that are used with formatting groups. The TopN button lets you filter the groups according to their overall ranking. The Order button lets you select whether the groups are sorted by Ascending, Descending, or Natural Order. You can also tell it to sort in a specified order. Please reference Chapter 4 if you need a refresher on how these dialog boxes work.

Setting the Show Value Fields

The Show Value list determines the fields that are plotted on the chart. On a standard vertical chart, this is where an element is plotted along the Y-axis. For example, this determines how high a bar is drawn on a bar chart. For each field listed, another element is drawn on the chart at each interval. If there is a line chart with three fields, then each field would have a separate line plotting its values.

The Show Value fields are charted using either their actual value or using a summary function. This is determined by what is selected for the Evaluate option. If this option is set to For Each Record, then each record gets charted according to its actual value. Thus, no summary calculation is performed. If the option selected is On Change Of or For All Records, then a summary calculation is performed to determine what value to plot. The On Change Of setting calculates a summary value each group. The For All Records setting plots a single summary value for the entire report. This has the effect of plotting one element for each field listed.

The default summary calculation is the Sum() function. If you had selected a text field for the Show Value field, then the summary function would be Count(). You can change this by selecting the field and clicking on the Set Summary Operation button. This brings up the standard Change Summary dialog box where you click on the dropdown box to select a different summary function.

Meeting the Minimum Field Requirements

The Evaluate setting and Show Value setting work together to determine the X, Y and Z axis on each chart. Due to the fact that each type of chart can be unique in how it uses the fields in these setting to create the chart, it is important to know many fields to put in each setting.

Charts have different requirements for the number of data values it needs to plot each point. For example, a line chart needs two values. The first value marks the time interval and the second value marks where on the chart the point will appear. A slightly more complicated chart, the X-Y Scatter chart, has different requirements. It needs a single value to set the intervals along the X-axis of the chart and it needs two values to mark where the point should appear on the chart. Table 10-4 shows the minimum number of fields required by each chart type.

Table 10-4. Required minimum number of fields for each type of chart.

Chart Type	# On Change Of	# Show Value
Bar/Line/Area	1	1
Pie/Doughnut	1	1
Pie/Doughnut multiple	1	Many
3D Riser	1	1
3D Surface	2	1
3D Surface	1	Many
XY Scatter	1	2
Bubble	1	3
Stock	1	2
Stock with open/close marks	1	4

The middle column, # of On Change Of fields, tells you how many fields are required when you have selected the On Change Of option in the drop-down box. This doesn't apply if you selected either For Each Record or For All Records. This is because these selections automatically set the interval along the X-axis and you aren't allowed to add new fields. However, if a chart type has a requirement of two fields, then you won't be able to use the For Each Record or For All Records options.

The last column, # of Show Value fields, tells you how many fields are required in the Show Values list. Each chart type requires at least one field and some charts allow you to add an unlimited number of fields. The only restriction is that it is limited to how many reasonably can fit on the chart.

Adding Group Charts

Below the Advanced button, on the Data tab of the Chart Expert, is the Group button. It is used to create a chart that shows each group and one of its summary fields. It can only appear within the Report Header/Footer. When you click on the button, the dialog interface changes to reflect options specific to grouping. This is shown in Figure 10-5.

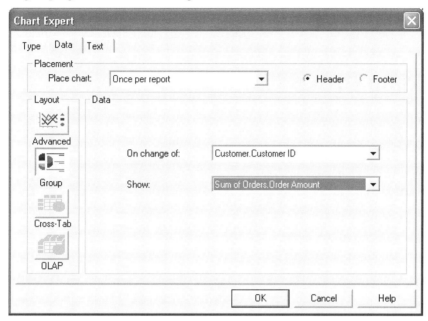

Figure 10-5. The grouping options of the Data tab.

The Group button presents a very simple interface when compared to the Advanced button. This is because the Group button is used for creating a simple chart. Whereas the Advanced button allows you a lot of variations on how many fields are charted on each axis, the Group button only lets you select a single group and a single summary field to chart.

There are two requirements for having the Group button enabled. The first requirement is that there is a group section. Of course, if your report doesn't have a group section then you certainly can't chart group values. The second requirement is that the group must use at least one summary field. This is because the group chart only plots summary fields. If you want to create a chart based on a group and your report doesn't meet these two requirements, then you can choose to place the chart within a Group Header/Footer and set the options using the Advanced button.

The top dropdown box lists the groups on your report. The groups that are listed here change depending upon where you place the chart. No matter how many groups are on your report, only two groups will be listed. These are the top two groups below the location that you are placing the chart. For example, if you place the chart in the Report Header/Footer section, then the first and second outer most groups are listed. However, if you place the chart in the first group's header/footer, then the next two groups directly below it will be listed in the dropdown box. If there is only one group below where the chart is located, then it will be the only one listed.

When you select the group, the lower dropdown box will show the summary fields for the group selected. From these summary fields, select which field to chart.

Adding Cross-Tab Charts

The Cross-Tab chart is similar to the Group chart because it takes one of the fields that the cross-tab object is grouped on and plots one of its summary fields. The related dialog box is shown in Figure 10-6.

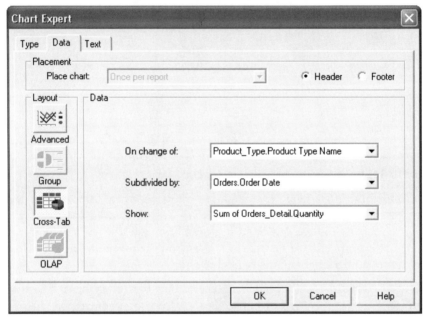

Figure 10-6. The cross-tab options of the Data tab.

The On Change Of dropdown box lists the two outer most group fields for the cross-tab object. If you have multiple fields listed for either the row or column setting, then the second and later fields are ignored and can't be used. The field selected in the dropdown box determines when a new element is drawn. Thus, the cross-tab chart can have either one element per row or per column.

The Show dropdown box, lets you select the summary field to plot. This serves the same purpose as the Show Value setting with the Advanced button. However, the Advanced setting lets you select multiple fields and the Cross-Tab settings only let you select one field.

The middle dropdown box, titled Subdivided By, lets you create a data set that is similar to having multiple fields in the Evaluate setting of the Advanced options.

Setting Captions with the Text tab

Use the Text tab to set the captions that appear on the chart as well as their fonts. This tab is shown in Figure 10-7. It is only visible when the Type tab option to automatically set chart options is unchecked.

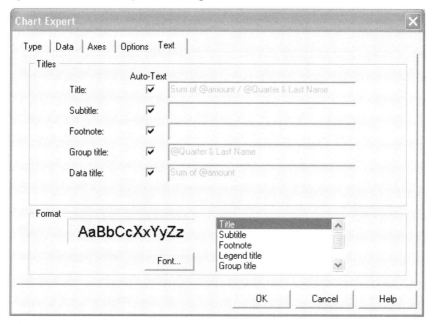

Figure 10-7. The Text tab of the Chart Expert.

The Text tab is very easy to understand and modify. It consists of two halves. The top half shows a checkbox for each title that appears on the chart. By default, each caption is set to Auto-Title. This means that the chart will set the caption when you print the report. It uses the chart's field names to determine what to print. For each caption, you can uncheck Auto-Title and enter your own caption. What you enter will override whatever the chart would have printed on its own. If you uncheck it, and leave the text blank then nothing is printed for that caption.

The lower half sets the font for each caption. To change the font, select the caption name from the list on the right and then click on the Font button. This brings up the standard Font dialog box and you can set the properties as you wish. When you click OK you are brought back to the Chart Expert and an example of how the new font settings look are shown above the Font button.

Using the Options Tab

The Options tab, shown in Figure 10-8, has a few miscellaneous options for customizing the layout of the chart. Like the Text tab, it is only visible when the Type tab option to automatically set chart options is unchecked.

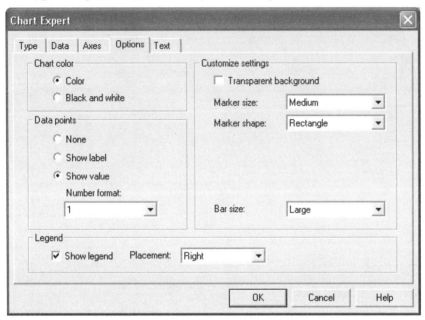

Figure 10-8. The Options tab of the Chart Expert.

There are four main areas on the Options tab. The Color Chart frame lets you set the chart to be in color or black and white. Black and white can be helpful when you are sending the report to the printer. The Data Points frame is used to toggle displaying the data point on or off. A data point is an identifier on a chart's element telling what the element represents. This can be its text value or its coordinate on the chart. Figure 10-9 shows a chart with the data points turned on.

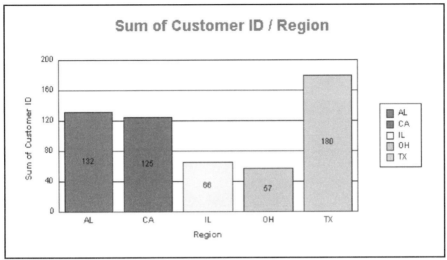

Figure 10-9. Displaying the data points on a chart.

The Customize Settings frame sets whether the chart background has a transparent background, how large the markers are and what shape the markers are. The Legend frame sets whether the legend is displayed, and where it is displayed. It can be displayed to the right or left of the chart or at the bottom.

Using the Format Menus

Once a chart is finished and the Chart Expert is closed, two new menu items become available. By right-clicking on the chart object in design mode, you are given two formatting specific menu options: Format and Format Chart. The Format menu gives you the standard formatting dialog box that you've already seen with the other report objects. It lets you select options such as suppressing the object and changing the border. These have already been discussed in detail in Chapter 4 and you can reference that chapter if you need more information.

The Format Chart menu item is specific to the chart object and it gives you four new menu items: Template, General, Titles and Grid. Each of these menu items opens a new dialog box with options that provide you with the ability to add a finer amount of customization to your chart. This menu is shown in Figure 10-10.

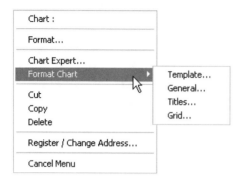

Figure 10-10. The Format Chart menu items.

You probably won't need to use these menu options with the majority of your reports. The formatting options provided by the Chart Expert will serve most of your needs on a daily basis. But there will be times when you want to take one of the options in the Chart Expert and fine tune it to a greater degree. That is when you will use these menu options.

A lot of the functionality in the Chart Expert is duplicated by these menu options. But in addition to that, they also give you many more selections to choose from. It's the multitude of selections that make these menu items powerful. Since you won't need to reference them very often and they are easy to understand, you are left to explore them in more detail on your own.

Creating Cross-Tab Reports

Cross-tab reports are a powerful way to create summaries of data in a spreadsheet style format. They generate summary data in a grid where the rows and columns represent groups of data. This provides the user with a report format that is easy to read and uses a small footprint.

Ask a programmer how he or she feels about cross-tab reports and you will probably get a variety of answers - both good and bad. I think that programmers can be put into three general categories about their experiences with cross-tab reports. Some programmers have tried using cross-tab reports and found them to be too confusing. They shrug them off as being unworthy of the effort to learn. Other programmers have successfully used cross-tab reports, but found a variety of problems in getting the data that they wanted. This group uses cross-tab reports only when absolutely necessary. And last, but not least, is the programmer who has successfully mastered the cross-tab report and found it to be a great way of producing reports that quickly summarize groups of data. They gladly use cross-tab reports whenever appropriate. The goal of this chapter is to take you from being a beginner in writing cross-tab reports to the level of an expert.

Understanding Cross-Tab Reports

Cross-tab reports are a way of reformatting a report that groups data into a grid format. This grid format is very similar to the way a spreadsheet represents data. It lets the user visually analyze the data in a way that makes it easy to compare values in one group against the values in another group. Let's look at the grouping report in Figure 11-1 and then we'll see it reformatted as a cross-tab report.

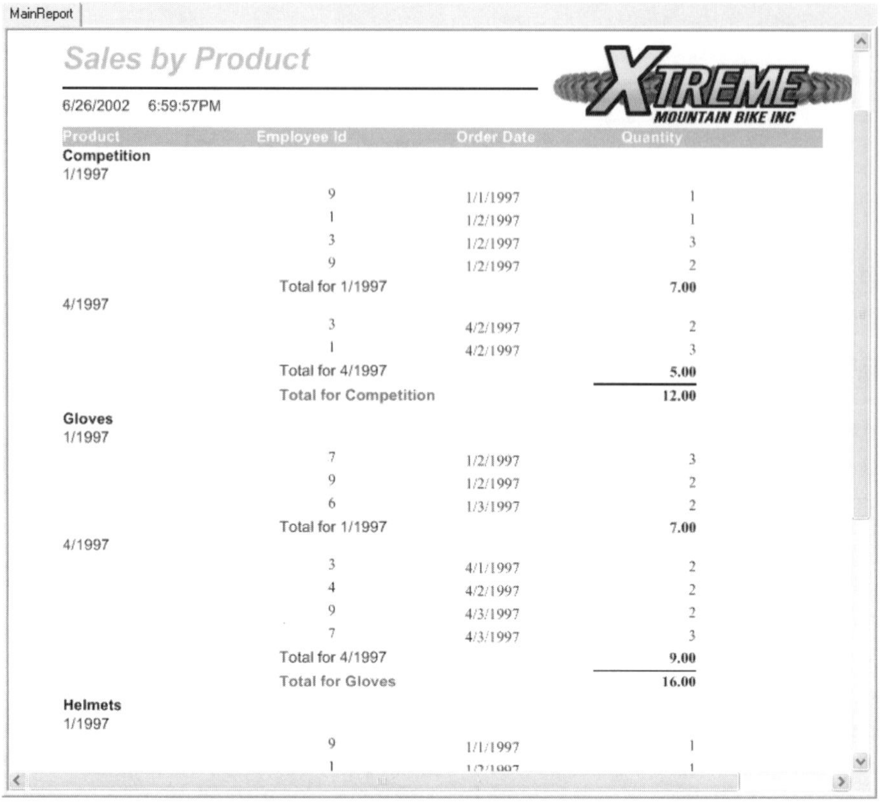
MainReport

Sales by Product

6/26/2002 6:59:57PM

Product	Employee Id	Order Date	Quantity
Competition			
1/1997			
	9	1/1/1997	1
	1	1/2/1997	1
	3	1/2/1997	3
	9	1/2/1997	2
	Total for 1/1997		7.00
4/1997			
	3	4/2/1997	2
	1	4/2/1997	3
	Total for 4/1997		5.00
	Total for Competition		12.00
Gloves			
1/1997			
	7	1/2/1997	3
	9	1/2/1997	2
	6	1/3/1997	2
	Total for 1/1997		7.00
4/1997			
	3	4/1/1997	2
	4	4/2/1997	2
	9	4/3/1997	2
	7	4/3/1997	3
	Total for 4/1997		9.00
	Total for Gloves		16.00
Helmets			
1/1997			
	9	1/1/1997	1
	1		1

Figure 11-1. Grouping by Product and Quarter.

This report has two grouping fields. The outermost group is by Product Type and the innermost group is the Order Date grouped quarterly. The group header for the Order Date is the first date in the period. The detail records show you the Employee ID, Order Date, and Quantity. There are two sub-totals of the quantity. The first occurs on the change of quarter and the next is on the change of product type.

This is a pretty standard grouping report and it shares a common problem with other grouping reports: the sub-total amounts are spread out across multiple pages. This makes it hard to compare numbers because they aren't consolidated into a single page.[18] A user reading this report will find that they are continuously flipping pages to see how the sales of one product compare to the sales of another product.

[18] Normally, the details for each group would span a page or more. To make the report small enough to fit onto a single page I had to filter the records down to just a few days in each month.

Re-writing this report as a cross-tab report eliminates this problem. Figure 11-2 shows the same report in cross-tab format.

Quarterly Sales by Product

6/26/2002   7:24:09PM

	1/1997	4/1997	Total
Competition	7.00	5.00	12.00
Gloves	7.00	9.00	16.00
Helmets	2.00	3.00	5.00
Locks	11.00	0.00	11.00
Mountain	5.00	2.00	7.00
Saddles	3.00	3.00	6.00
Total	35.00	22.00	57.00

Figure 11-2. Cross-tab report by Product and Quarter.

The cross-tab is much easier on the eyes. The outermost group field, Product Type, is represented on each row of the grid. The innermost group field, Order Date grouped by quarter, and makes each quarter a separate column. These columns span horizontally along the page. Although there are many detail records in the original report, these are ignored when generating the rows and columns. Only the values of the grouping fields are listed. The cross-tab report took two grouping fields and made them the X-axis and Y-axis of the grid.

The data inside the grid corresponds to the subtotals on the grouping report. The first row is for the Competition product type. It shows values of 5, 7 and a total of 12. When you look at the grouping report in Figure 11-1 you see that these match the subtotals for the Competition product type. Each row in the cross-tab report shows the same subtotals that are displayed in the grouping report for the product type groups. Thus, the cross-tab report took the sub-totals of a grouping report and formatted them as a grid. All the data is summarized into a very compact space and it doesn't span many pages like the grouping report would.

> **Note**
>
> It might help to think of a cross-tab report as taking a multi-group report and just copying the group footers into a grid.

The benefits of using a cross-tab report can be offset by the drawbacks. As powerful as the cross-tab report is for summarizing data, it has many limitations. These limitations are discussed throughout this chapter, but let's look at two obvious ones first.

The first limitation is that the original grouping report has a lot of data on it that isn't shown on the cross-tab. For example, the cross-tab report doesn't show the fields for Employee ID or the Shipping Date. In fact, it doesn't have any detail records shown. Although these fields are very important, the cross-tab report can't show individual detail records. This is because a cross-tab report can only show summary calculations.

The second limitation is that you can only print numbers in the summary fields. No text values are allowed. This is because each cell must calculate a summary function and summary functions can only return numbers. If you attempt to put a text field in the cell, then the report will default to printing a count of the text fields.

Given the benefits and drawbacks of cross-tab reports, you have to consider your alternatives before using the cross-tab report. The standard grouping report is great for showing as much information as necessary and having control over the format. But the data could span many pages and this makes it hard to do analysis with. The cross-tab report gives you the ability to quickly analyze summary data, but you have to give up looking at the detail records that make up the data.

Tip
If you have a report that needs to benefit from both types of reports, a solution is to combine the two reports. Create a grouping report that prints all the necessary detail information. Then add a cross-tab object to the report header. This lets a user see a summary of the critical information on the first page of the report and then dive into the details printed on the remaining pages.

Creating a Cross-Tab Object

The name "Cross-Tab Report" is a little misleading. It makes it sound like the whole report only shows the cross-tab grid and that no other data is printed. This isn't true. A cross-tab report refers to a report that has a cross-tab object in one of its sections. This object is similar to the other report objects on a report. It has properties that let you modify its fields and how it's formatted.

There are two ways to add a cross-tab object to your report. The first way is to add a new report to your application from the Project menu and choose the Cross-Tab Expert from the Crystal Report Gallery dialog box. This is shown in Figure 11-3.

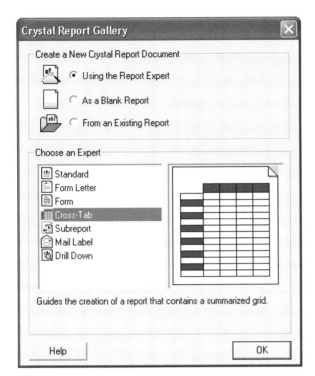

Figure 11-3. Choosing the Cross-Tab Expert from the Gallery.

You can also add a cross-tab object to an existing report by right-clicking on the report and selecting Insert | Cross-Tab. Both methods of adding a cross-tab object to your report gives you the dialog box shown in Figure 11-4.

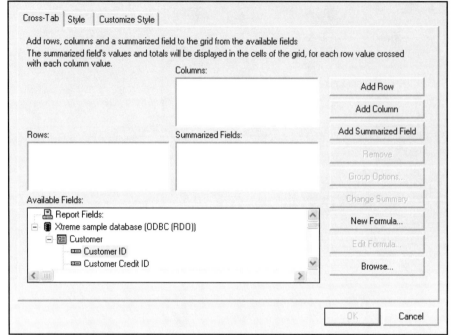

Figure 11-4. The Cross-Tab Expert dialog box.

There are three primary input areas on this dialog box: Rows, Columns, and Summarized Fields. Below these three sections is the list of available fields. Add fields from this list into the appropriate sections above it. Do this by either dragging and dropping the fields or by selecting a field and clicking one of the following Add buttons: Add Row, Add Column, or Add Summarized Field. If you want to see an example of the data that a field contains, click on the Browse button.

All three windows require you to add a minimum of one field to each before the cross-tab is functional. For example, you can't specify fields for the Rows and Summary Fields windows and not put a field in the Columns window. You can also add multiple fields to each window to make the cross-tab print additional data.

When you add a field to the Summarized Fields window, by default it assigns one of two different summary functions to the field. If the field is numeric, then the Sum() function is used. If the field is text, then the Count() function is used. You can change the default summary function after it has been added to the Summary Fields window by clicking on the Change Summary button.

When changing the summary function for a numeric field, all the summary functions in Crystal Reports are available. Summarizing on a text field is more restrictive. Remember that text fields aren't allowed to be printed in a cross-tab cell. Instead you have to choose from a list of text compatible summary functions. Not every function works with a text field. For example, it isn't possible to calculate the average value of a text field. However, you can determine the 5th largest item of all available items and print that. The text compatible functions that you can choose from are in Table 11-1.

Table 11-1. Summary functions available for text fields.

Function Name
Count()
DistinctCount()
Nth Largest()
Nth Smallest()
Nth Most Frequent()
Minimum()
Maximum()
Mode()

Summary functions are typically based on fields from a data source. But there are times when you need to summarize a custom formula field. You can select a formula that already exists or you can create a new formula from the Cross-tab Expert dialog box. When you click the New Formula button, it brings up the Formula Editor dialog box. This is the same dialog box discussed in Chapter 7. After you save and close this dialog box, that formula is added to the list of available fields at the bottom of the dialog box. You can then drag and drop the formula field into the Summary Fields window. Although this formula was created via the Cross-tab Expert, it will now be listed along with all the other formulas in your report. Thus, it can be placed on your report just like any other report object.

Caution

Crosstab summary functions can't perform many tasks that you take for granted with other types of reports. For example, it is a common error to attempt to devise formulas for a cross-tab report that calculates a value depending upon the value of another cell in the cross-tab or the sum of a group of cells in another row or column. You expect this to be possible because it is easy to do for a standard report. But a cross-tab report can't do this because it is built around the premise that each summary value is calculated independently of the other cells. Cross-tab summary fields are calculated during the report's first-pass and there is no mechanism to reference the value of any other field in the cross-tab. You can try to get creative and write a formula to emulate these tasks, but you will find that each formula relies upon having information about the other fields in the cross-tab. Thus, it won't succeed. The tasks that a cross-tab report can't perform are as follows: calculating second-pass formulas, calculating running sums, calculating percentages of the subtotal/grand total and sorting rows according to the row totals.

Once you are finished adding the fields, click the OK button. The cross-tab object is added to your report and you are put back at the report designer.

Adding additional summary fields to the cross-tab object results in the values being placed in the same cell. Each is stacked vertically on top of the other. The first field added is placed at the top.

Adding additional grouping fields for either the rows or columns creates a sub-group format. This is very similar to a standard report that uses multiple groups. The first field becomes the outermost group and the remaining fields are grouped based upon the subset of data. If you preview the report and find that the fields are not in the proper order, you can rearrange them by opening the Cross-tab Expert again and using the mouse to drag and drop the fields to the correct position in the list.

Figure 11-5 shows a cross-tab object in design mode that has two grouping fields in the row and two summary fields.

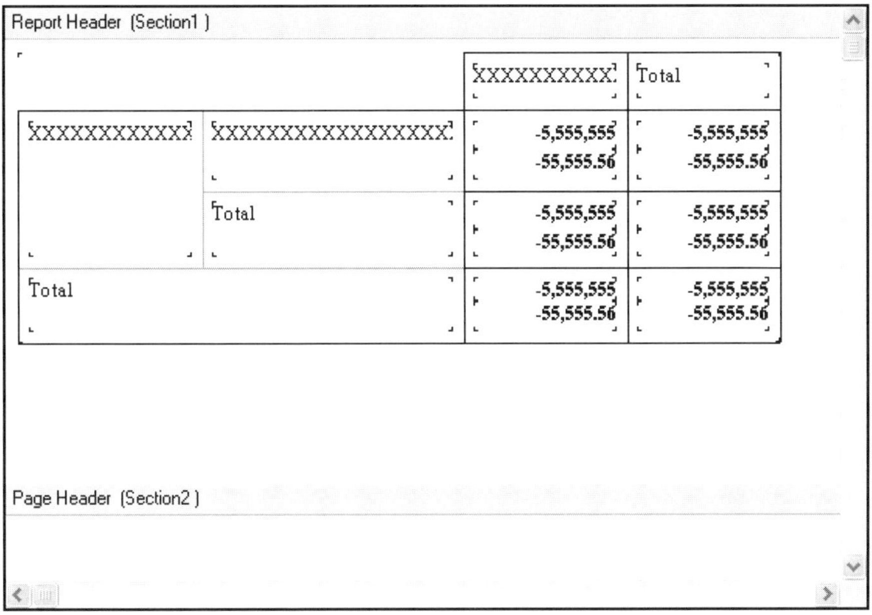

Figure 11-5. The cross-tab object using multiple fields.

The large, left-most block in the cross-tab object represents the outer-most group. The innermost group is represented by the two thinner blocks just to the right of it. Both groups have a subtotal field associated with them. This is similar to a standard multi-group report because when it prints there will be a group footer showing the subtotal for the group. The two summary fields are visually represented by the multiple fields filled with the number five. The top-most field is the first summary field that was added to the Summary Fields window. Running the report generates the output shown in Figure 11-6.

		2/21/1996	2/22/1996	2/24/1996	Total
Competition	Descent	1	1	0	2
		3.00	3.00	0.00	6.00
	Endorphin	0	1	0	1
		0.00	2.00	0.00	2.00
	Mozzie	3	1	1	5
		8.00	3.00	1.00	12.00
	Total	4	3	1	8
		11.00	8.00	1.00	20.00
Gloves	Active Outdoors Crochet Glove	0	1	0	1
		0.00	2.00	0.00	2.00
	Active Outdoors Lycra Glove	0	2	0	2
		0.00	2.00	0.00	2.00
	Total	0	3	0	3
		0.00	4.00	0.00	4.00
Helmets	Triumph Pro Helmet	0	1	0	1
		0.00	2.00	0.00	2.00
	Triumph Vertigo Helmet	0	3	0	3
		0.00	6.00	0.00	6.00
	Total	0	4	0	4
		0.00	8.00	0.00	8.00
Kids	Mini Nicros	0	0	1	1
		0.00	0.00	3.00	3.00
	Total	0	0	1	1
		0.00	0.00	3.00	3.00

Figure 11-6. The output of the cross-tab report using multiple fields.

There is no way to make a cross-tab object print the summary fields side by side. Each value is always stacked one on top of the other. You can get around this limitation by creating a duplicate cross-tab object, modifying its summary function, and then aligning it to be on top of the other cross-tab object. This gives the illusion of a single cross-tab object with multiple summary columns.

Follow these instructions to generate this type of output. Create a cross-tab object that is formatted exactly the way you want it. Make sure that the column widths are wide enough to support printing two fields side by side. Get this right the first time because if you later have to go back and reformat the cross-tab it will be much harder. Copy and paste the cross-tab object to the same section of the report. Modify the summary function to be the new calculation. Suppress all the fields except the summary fields and turn off all the grid lines. Left justify the summary field in one of the cross-tab objects and right justify the other summary field. This prevents the data from overlapping. Align the two cross-tab objects so that one is on top of the other. If all the steps were followed properly, you should not be able to tell that there are two objects on your report. You are now ready to print the report. A sample report is shown in Figure 11-7.

	2/21/1996		2/22/1996		2/24/1996		Total	
Competition	4	11.00	3	8.00	1	1.00	8	20.00
Gloves	0	0.00	3	4.00	0	0.00	3	4.00
Helmets	0	0.00	4	8.00	0	0.00	4	8.00
Kids	0	0.00	0	0.00	1	3.00	1	3.00
Locks	0	0.00	1	3.00	0	0.00	1	3.00
Mountain	1	1.00	4	8.00	1	2.00	6	11.00
Total	5	12.00	15	31.00	3	6.00	23	49.00

Figure 11-7. Output of printing summaries next to each other.

Placing the Cross-Tab Object

If you look back at the cross-tab report example from earlier in the chapter, you might realize that the cross-tab object as it appears in the report designer doesn't look like the cross-tab grid as it appears when printed on the report. This is because the report designer shows the cross-tab object as being a template for showing you what fields are used and how the cross-tab grid will be formatted. When the report is run the cross-tab object expands vertically and horizontally so that it can print as many columns and rows necessary to show each group. If you expect your report to have a lot of columns then make sure it is placed along the left side of the report to account for all the columns.

Tip

When you put a cross-tab object in a section, it will grow as large as necessary to print all the data. If you place other report objects below the cross-tab component, and in the same section, the cross-tab grid will probably overwrite them when it expands during the print process. Fix this by creating a second section in that area and place the lower data in the new section. This will let it appear just below the cross-tab grid without any overlapping.

The cross-tab object can only be placed in a certain sections: the Report Header/Footer and the Group Header/Footer. It can't be placed in the detail

---

section because it can't print detail records. It also can't be placed in the Page Header because it would be duplicated on each page without any of its data changing. This would create redundant information that wastes space.

Be careful about where you put the cross-tab object. Placing the cross-tab in the Report Header/Footer produces different results than putting it in the Group Header/Footer. It prints out whatever information is available to it. When placed in the Report Header, it has access to every record in your report. It summarizes all the data that is printed. When placed in the Group Header, it only has access to the data for that group. The cross-tab will be much smaller because it only prints a subset of all the report data.

Formatting the Cross-Tab Grid

As with every report object in Crystal Reports, the cross-tab object has many formatting options to make it look just the way you want. These changes can be categorized according to whether they affect the grid and its layout or whether they affect the individual fields within the grid.

Since the number of rows and columns of the cross-tab is dynamic, you can't control its final size on the report. But you can control the individual row and column widths. This has a direct effect on the total size of the cross-tab grid when it prints. When you select a field in the cross-tab object and resize it, the entire row and column changes to reflect this change. Changing the width changes the width of the entire column. Changing the height changes the height of the entire row. Thus, a change to one field affects all the fields that are in the same column and row.

Set the formatting properties by right-clicking on the cross-tab object and selecting Format. Be careful when doing this because if your cursor is positioned above one of the fields in the cross-tab, then you will get the format dialog boxes for that field. To set the formatting for the cross-tab object, position your cursor in the top left-hand corner of the object. This is where there are no other fields that could be selected by mistake.

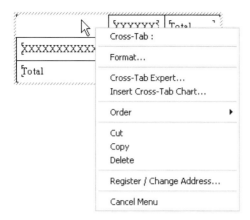

Figure 11-8. Selecting the Format menu item of the cross-tab object.

Both the grid and the fields within the grid can be formatted using the standard formatting properties. Some examples of these properties are suppressing the object, setting the font properties, changing the border, etc. Most of these properties have a formula button so that their value can be the result of a formula that you program.

There are two formatting related functions that can be used with cross-tab cells. As stated earlier, each cell has to display the output of the same formula. However, you can make each cell stand out by using the formulas with the formatting properties. Since each cell is identical, there are two formulas that let you identify what value is being displayed as well as identifying the current row and column values. The CurrentFieldValue() function returns the cell's current value. Use this to highlight values that fall within or outside of a certain range. The function GridRowColumnValue() returns the value of the row or column that the cell is in. Pass it the name of the group field, either the row's field name or the column's field name, and it returns the current value. For example, if the column groups by month of the year, then a cell in the third column will return the month name "March". If you want to refer to the row or column field as a different name, assign it an alias to make it easier to reference it. This is done via the style options in the Format Cross-Tab expert. That expert is shown next.

Formatting the Style Properties

The grid has some unique formatting properties that don't appear with other objects. These are called the Style properties. Right-click on the cross-tab object and select Cross-Tab Expert. The Cross-Tab tab is shown by default and this has already been discussed earlier. Click on the Style tab, the second tab, to choose from a list of more than a dozen predefined styles. As you click on each style, the right window shows a template of how your cross-tab object will be formatted.

Click on the Customize Style tab to make your own changes to the style. If you selected a predefined style in the previous tab, you will be prompted about whether you want to save that style. If you choose Yes, then the new style will be reflected on the Customize Style tab. If you choose No, then the Customize Style tab will reflect the formatting of the cross-tab object before you opened the Cross-Tab Expert.

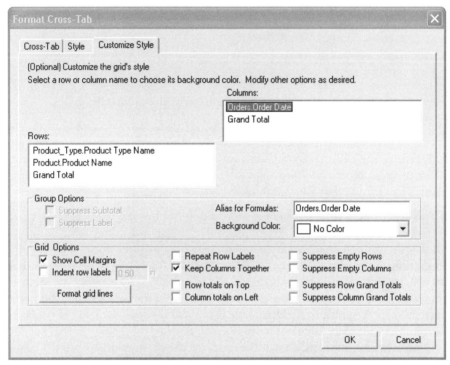

Figure 11-9. The CustomizeStyle tab of the Format Cross-Tab expert.

The Customize Style tab has numerous properties that you can use to format the cross-tab grid to look exactly like you want. There is a Rows window and a Columns window and within each window are the names of the grouping fields. Click on the field you want to format to change its properties. The properties and their descriptions are listed in the Group Options frame directly below those windows. Each of these properties only affects the group field that is currently selected. These style properties are listed in Table 11-2.

Table 11-2. Style formatting properties for cross-tab group options.

Style Property	Description
Suppress Subtotal	When you have multiple groups for a row or column, the cross-tab grid shows a subtotal for the top-most groups. This suppresses that subtotal from printing.
Suppress Label	This suppresses all data for that field from appearing in the cross-tab grid.
Alias for Formula	This changes the name that you use to reference the group in the conditional formatting formulas.
Background Color	Sets the background color for the cell.

At the bottom of the dialog box is a frame titled Grid Options. The properties listed in this frame apply to the entire cross-tab. These grid options are listed in Table 11-3.

Table 11-3. Grid options for the cross-tab object.

Grid Option	Description
Show Cell Margins	By default, each group field has a margin surrounding it. Turning this off makes the edge of the group field flush with the grid lines.
Indent Row Labels	The row labels can be indented so that they are offset from the Total row. This makes it easier to notice the Total row and it makes your report appear more professional. When this is checked, you can specify the indentation in inches.
Repeat Row Labels	When there are too many columns to fit on a single page, they will span across to the next page. Setting this option on causes the row values to be printed on the additional pages. This option is only available if you have the Keep Columns Together option enabled.
Keep Columns Together	Select this option (it is selected by default) to force columns that span multiple pages to stay intact. Unselecting this option could cause a column to be split in half.
Row/Column Totals on Top	Forces totals to be switched from their default position. Row totals will be at the top-most row and column totals will be left-most column.
Suppress Empty Rows/Columns	Don't print rows/columns with no data.
Suppress Row/Column Grand Totals	Don't print the grand-totals for rows and/or columns.

The Format Grid Lines button is used to set the line styles for the grid. Clicking on this button brings up the Format Grid Lines dialog box shown in Figure 11-10. For each grid line in the cross-tab object, you can set the color, style, and width properties. You can also suppress a line by unchecking both Draw options. If you don't want any grid lines to be shown then uncheck the Show Grid Lines option.

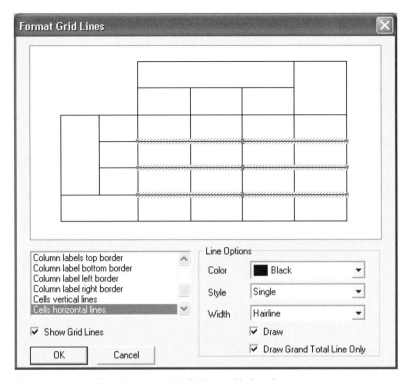

Figure 11-10. The Format Grid Lines dialog box.

Managing the Columns

One of the most interesting features of the cross-tab object is that it is dynamic. The number of columns changes according to the data being displayed. As an example, assume that you have a cross-tab report where the columns represent the historical sales figures per year. If a company has been in existence for five years, then there will be five columns printed. Once a new year starts, a new column is automatically added to the cross-tab. Columns are created on an as needed basis without requiring any additional work on your part.

Dynamic columns are a blessing and a curse. The fact that you can even have dynamic columns is great. Being able to have the number of columns grow and shrink according to the data in a table is very powerful. You can't do this with standard reports objects.[19] The drawback is that you can't control how many columns are created and you can't insert additional columns.

---

[19] Actually, you can create dynamic columns. But it requires writing some very advanced formulas and associating them to the columns. You also have to write formulas for the formatting properties of each column so that they are suppressed when necessary.

Having columns dynamically added to your report is a problem when you get more columns than you expected. For example, your company has twenty divisions world-wide and you formatted the cell's width so that there is just enough room on the page to represent each division. The report runs fine until six months later when your company acquires three new divisions. Now your columns run off the edge and onto a new page. The number of pages printed has just doubled and everyone is complaining to you about it. You have to watch out for this behavior and correct it, if necessary.

Tip

When a cross-tab object spans multiple pages, the only data printed on the "virtual" pages is what is generated by the cross-tab report. The other report objects on the report do not get printed. If there is a header value that should be printed above the cross-tab, it will not appear after the first page. You can simulate a report header by adding an additional column field to the cross-tab object that only prints the header text.

To simulate a cross-tab header, follow these instructions. Create a formula that generates the header text. Open the Format Cross-Tab Expert and add the formula as the first field in the Columns window. Go to the Customize Style tab and experiment with the grid settings to make the report look just the way you want. You will probably have to turn on Suppress Row Grand Totals and turn certain grid lines off. An example is shown in Figure 11-11.

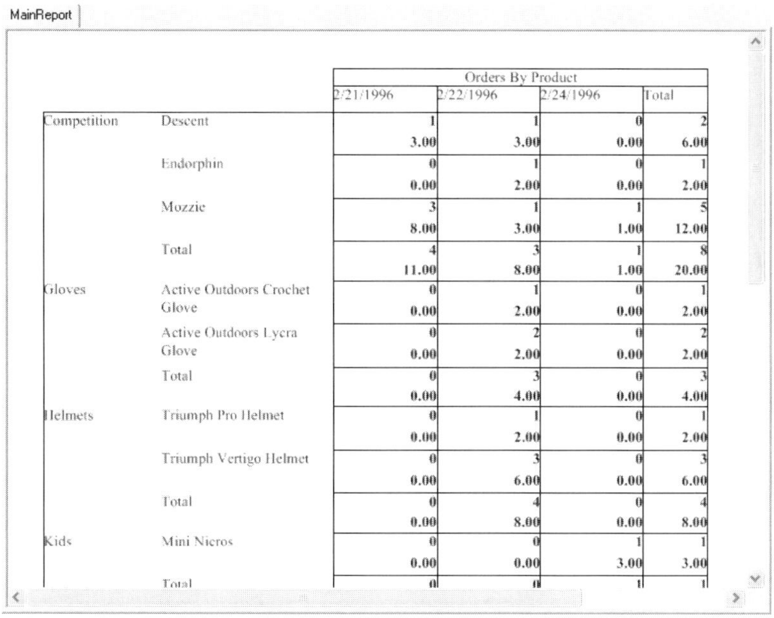

		Orders By Product			
		2/21/1996	2/22/1996	2/24/1996	Total
Competition	Descent	1	1	0	2
		3.00	3.00	0.00	6.00
	Endorphin	0	1	0	1
		0.00	2.00	0.00	2.00
	Mozzie	3	1	1	5
		8.00	3.00	1.00	12.00
	Total	4	3	1	8
		11.00	8.00	1.00	20.00
Gloves	Active Outdoors Crochet Glove	0	1	0	1
		0.00	2.00	0.00	2.00
	Active Outdoors Lycra Glove	0	2	0	2
		0.00	2.00	0.00	2.00
	Total	0	3	0	3
		0.00	4.00	0.00	4.00
Helmets	Triumph Pro Helmet	0	1	0	1
		0.00	2.00	0.00	2.00
	Triumph Vertigo Helmet	0	3	0	3
		0.00	6.00	0.00	6.00
	Total	0	4	0	4
		0.00	8.00	0.00	8.00
Kids	Mini Nicros	0	0	1	1
		0.00	0.00	3.00	3.00
	Total	0	0	1	1

Figure 11-11. Adding a heading to the cross-tab object.

Another problem with dynamic columns is that you can't insert additional columns in the grid. This is a common problem with reports that use the month of the year as the column. When the report is run as the end of the year there are twelve columns, and this is what you would expect. But when the report is run in February, only two columns are printed: January and February. Some people want their reports to show all twelve months even if they haven't occurred yet. Cross-tab reports won't do this. A similar problem is a report that uses the weeks of the year as the column heading. Assume a company is a production plant and they want to see the volume of units produced every week. Occasionally, the plant builds up too much inventory and is shut down for a week. The report should show a zero balance for the week that was shutdown. But since there wasn't any activity, no records exist for that week and a column won't be printed. The cross-tab report can't print a zero-filled column for that week because it doesn't have any data to even know that the week exists.

There really isn't an easy solution for this. The best advice is to write a SQL query that uses a creative Outer Join statement to generate zero value data for the missing records. Another option is to create a zero filled table with a record for each column. Use a SQL Union statement to join it with the live data. Each situation is unique and presents a new challenge.

This page intentionally left blank

12
Incorporating Subreports

Subreports are used to create multiple views of data on a single report. A limitation of the standard report is that only a single view of the data can be displayed. Rather than create one or more reports to present additional views of the data, subreports are used to present data that is independent of the main report or present multiple parent-child relationships.

From a functional and design standpoint, a subreport is virtually identical to a standard report. It has the same layout as a standard report and it uses the same report objects. The subreport differs from a standard report in that it is an object on a report. Thus, it is part of another report.

Adding subreports to a main report requires knowledge of three things: the options for linking subreports to the main report, how to add and edit a subreport object and whether it should be bound to the main report.

Linking Options

The most important aspect of subreports is the various options for linking them to the main report. Subreports are either linked or unlinked to the main report. A linked subreport relies upon the main report to tell it what to print. An unlinked subreport doesn't use any data from the main report to determine what to print.

If the subreport is linked to the main report, the subreport's data is dependent upon the data in the main report. For example, let's say that a subreport is linked to the main report via the Customer ID. The subreport's data will only display records related to the current Customer ID on the main report. When the Customer ID on the main report changes, so will the detail data that is displayed in the subreport. When the subreport is linked to the main report, the main report effectively acts as a filter for the subreport.

When the subreport is unlinked, it is independent from the main report. For example, assume that the main report is an employee sales report. It is grouped by sales person and it is broken apart to be distributed to each sales person. Within the group header is a chart showing the company's overall sales for the month. This chart will be added to the main report as an unlinked subreport. The chart prints the same data no matter which sales person is currently being printed.

For subreports that are linked to the main report, the main report needs a method of telling the subreport what data to print. One way of doing this is using a parameter field that is populated with information from the main report. Another way is to use shared variables. Shared variables are not normally used for filtering data, but they are used in formulas in the report. Table 12-1 is a summary of the different linking options between a main report and its subreports. A more thorough description of these options and related examples are listed after the table.

Table 12-1. Subreport linking options

Linking Option	Description
Linked with a data field	A field from the main report is passed to the subreport and this is used for filtering records. If the field is from a PC database (e.g. MS Access) then it must be indexed.
Linked with a formula field	A formula's value from the main report is passed to the subreport and this is used to filter records. Used to link to non-indexed fields in PC databases (e.g. MS Access, Excel).
Unlinked	The subreport is not connected to the main report. There is no data passed between the main report and the subreport. The subreport uses a data source that is independent of the parent report. This is used for combining unrelated reports into a single report.
Unlinked and using a formula field	A formula's value from the main report is passed to the subreport, but it doesn't effect record selection. It can be used for displaying non-critical data on the subreport.
Unlinked and using global variables	Multiple variables are used to pass data back and forth between the parent report and the subreport. This lets the parent report keep track of what the subreport is printing.

Linking with a Data Field

Linking subreports with a data field lets you filter the data in the subreport based upon the data that is in the main report. This is useful when you are printing data derived from tables that have a parent-child relationship.

First let's look at when a subreport isn't the best option. A simple report is useful when linking multiple tables together that have a one-to-one relationship or when two tables have a parent-child relationship. When tables have a one-to-one relationship, it is easy to match up the detail records and print them together. When two tables have a parent-child relationship, it is easy to group the records based on the parent data and print the associated child records within the detail section of each group.

Subreports become practical when there is a single parent table with more than one child table. If you tried to use a single report to print this data and you link the tables using the default inner join, then it is possible that not every record will print when there isn't a matching primary key in both child tables. If you use an outer join to link the tables, then you could get some records printed multiple times depending upon how many times the primary key appears in each child table.

Using a subreport with multiple child tables corrects these problems. Within the main report print the records from only one of the child tables in the detail table. For the other child tables, create a subreport for each one and use the main report's primary key to link them together. The subreports are placed in their own Details section so that their records are independent of the other sections and they print sequentially after the main report's detail records.

The drawback to linking with a data field is that if you are using a PC database (e.g. MS Access), then the fields must be indexed. You must create an index for each linking field before running the report.

An example of linking with a data field is shown in Figure 12-1. This report shows the sales detail for each customer. Below the detail records is a list of all the credits that has been issued to this customer. Since there are two listings of detail records, the second list must be printed as a subreport. In this example, the subreport is added to the main report's Group Footer section. It is linked via the Customer ID.

Customer Sales

ID	Customer Name	Order	Order Date	Ship Date	Amount
1	City Cyclists				
		1,143	06-Jan-1997	08-Jan-1997	$62.33
		1,246	30-Jan-1997	30-Jan-1997	$3,884.25
		1,296	16-Feb-1997	16-Feb-1997	$6,682.98
		1,387	01-Mar-1997	01-Mar-1997	$1,515.35
		1,717	14-Jun-1997	15-Jun-1997	$70.50
		1,763	24-Jun-1997	30-Jun-1997	$2,378.35
					$14,593.76

Credits Issued For City Cyclists	
Credit Authorization Number	Amount
CR1608	($1,792.91)
CR5241	($951.33)
CR6321	($1,484.68)
CR6592	($1,237.54)
CR6798	($727.56)

ID	Customer Name	Order	Order Date	Ship Date	Amount
2	Pathfinders				
		1,145	06-Jan-1997	17-Jan-1997	$27.00
		1,171	14-Jan-1997	14-Jan-1997	$479.85
		1,233	27-Jan-1997	29-Jan-1997	$139.48
		1,254	03-Feb-1997	04-Feb-1997	$2,497.05
		1,256	04-Feb-1997	04-Feb-1997	$70.50
		1,288	12-Feb-1997	12-Feb-1997	$8,819.55

Figure 12-1. Linked subreport in the Details section.

Linking with a Formula Field

Filtering records in a subreport is also done using a formula field. There are two benefits to using formula fields: they give you more flexibility because formulas can be customized to parse or join multiple data fields, and they can link non-indexed fields from PC databases.

Being able to parse or join multiple data fields and use the results to link to a subreport is very helpful. It is a common task to have to link tables from two different programs together and the data isn't compatible. This can happen when the programs were developed by different teams in the same company or when one company acquires another company and they have to consolidate their data. Formulas give you the flexibility to massage the data from one table into a format compatible with the data in another table. This can consist of converting the field to a different data type, concatenating multiple fields together or parsing a field to extract the extraneous characters.

Subreports aren't restricted to using indexed fields for linking tables. Linking with formulas lets you use any field in the table to link the two reports together.

Using Unlinked Subreports

An unlinked subreport is used when you want to combine two or more reports onto one report and these reports don't have any common data to create a relationship between them. The unlinked subreport is completely independent of the main report and the main report's data doesn't affect the subreport.

Figure 12-2 shows an example of an unlinked subreport. It is a customer sales report that shows the prior year sales amount for each customer.

Customer Sales Detail By Country

Summary of Sales by Country

Country	Sales
Australia	$40,446.64
Austria	$201,000.00
Bahamas	$14,463.35
Bangladesh	$4,683.50
Barbados	$4,443.80
Belgium	$200,000.00

	ID	Customer Name	Last Year's Sales
Australia	149	Tasmanian Devil Bikes	$1,739.85
	148	Koala Road Bikes	$6,744.80
	147	Peddles of Perth	$8,945.25
	146	Bruce's Bikes	$1,138.09
	145	Kangeroo Trikes	$9,594.70
	144	Canberra Bikes	$10,662.75
	143	Down Under Bikes	$1,621.20
			$40,446.64
Austria	66	Piccolo	$201,000.00
			$201,000.00
Bahamas	156	Beach Cycle and Sport	$14,463.35
			$14,463.35

Figure 12-2. Unlinked subreport being used in the report header.

The report is grouped by country and within each group it shows the customers from that country and what their sales were last year. At the top of the report it shows a summary of the prior year sales for each country. This lets you analyze how each country compares to the other before looking at detail records within each customer. Since there isn't a field that can be linked between the summary report and the customer detail report, these two reports are unlinked. This is implemented by adding the summary report as a subreport in the main report's header section.

Let's look at an example of an unlinked subreport that at first may appear to be a linked report. This example is a form letter that has a variable number of standard attachments printed at the end of it. This could be a legal document where each client needs to have signature pages attached to the end of it.

Within the Report Footer area, create multiple sections. Within each section add one subreport that represents a standard attachment. Set the conditional formatting to suppress the section if a field in the main report doesn't meet a certain value. In this case, the person receiving the form letter would have Boolean fields that are set to True for each attachment that should be included. If the proper field isn't True, then the section is suppressed and the attachment isn't printed. Although this may appear to be a linked subreport because data in the main report determines whether to print the subreport, it isn't. It is an unlinked subreport because there is no data that is being passed to the subreport. The Boolean field in the main report determines which sections get suppressed or printed. But this is all done at the main report level and not at the subreport level. The Boolean field never gets passed to the subreport and its value doesn't affect the content of what is printed.

Using Formula Fields without Linking

Formula fields can also be used by a subreport without linking them. This is used when you want to pass data to a subreport without filtering the data. For example, the main report can pass a string to the subreport so that the string gets printed in the subreport's header.

Passing Data Via Shared Variables

Shared variables let you share data between a main report and its subreports. This lets you perform calculations, track subtotals and create strings in one report and pass this data to the other report.

Adding a Subreport

A subreport is added to the main report in the same way that the other report objects are added: using the Insert menu item. Right-click on the main report and select Insert | Subreport. This gives you the outline of a subreport object attached to the mouse cursor and you move the cursor around to position it in the proper place on the report. Click the mouse to drop the subreport onto the report.

Subreports can only be one level deep. A subreport object can only be added to a main report and it can't be added to another subreport. If you right-click on a subreport and select Insert, the Subreport option will be disabled.

After placing the subreport object on the report, the Insert Subreport dialog box is opened. This dialog box, shown in Figure 12-3, gives you three ways of creating a subreport.

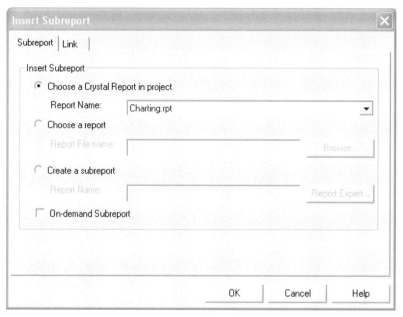

Figure 12-3. The Insert Subreport dialog box.

The first way is to select an existing report that is in the current project. Click on the dropdown box to see all the reports in your project. Select the one you want. The second way to create a subreport is to import one from outside the project file. The Browse button lets you find the report on your local computer or on the network. The third way is to create a report from scratch. When selecting this option you also have to click on the Create Report button to open the Report Expert dialog box. If you don't click this button then the OK button will stay disabled until you do so. The Report Expert button opens the Report Expert for a standard report. Once you are finished using it to build your report template, click Finish and you are brought back to the Insert Subreport dialog box. The OK button is now enabled, but don't click on it until you decide how to link the subreport to the main report.

When importing an existing report as a subreport, whether already in the project or external to the project, the subreport is a copy of the original report. When you make changes to the subreport, the original report is not modified. The subreport is saved within the same .rpt file as the main report.

After setting the report information on the main tab, go to the Links tab (shown in Figure 12-4) to set whether the report is linked or unlinked.

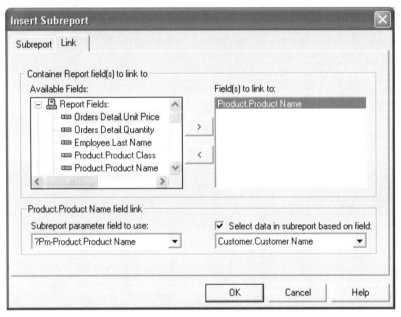

Figure 12-4. The Links tab of the Insert Subreport dialog box.

This dialog box is where you set the properties that determine how the subreport is linked to the main report. The Links tab has a list on the left side that shows the available report fields, formulas and data fields. The list on the right shows the fields from the main report that are selected to link to the subreport. At the bottom is a frame that shows the details of how the field(s) will be linked to the subreport. These linking options and how to set the properties for each are listed next.

Linked with a Data Field

Linking subreports with a data field lets you use a data field in the main report to filter the data in the subreport. The two fields must be of the same data type to link them together. If this is a PC database, then both fields must have an index already set up in the database.

To create a linked subreport, select the data field from the listbox on the left and add it to the listbox on the right. Once the data field is added, the linking frame at the bottom appears and shows you the parameter field name and the field in the subreport's data field to link to. The parameter name is automatically filled in for you. This parameter is used internally to pass the main report's field value to the subreport. Normally, when you have a parameter field on a report, the user is prompted to enter a value for the parameter before the report can be run. This is not the case with subreports. Subreports populate the parameter with the value of the field from the main report behind the scenes. You do not have to worry about this implementation.

The checkbox on the right tells the subreport that the main report's data field is being linked to a field in the subreport. This will be checked by default. Below the checkbox is a dropdown box listing the fields in the subreport. Select the one that is used to filter the data in the subreport. It must be of the same data type as the field from the main report.

Linked with a Formula Field

Linking a subreport with a formula lets you have more creativity for how it is linked to the main report. You can add a formula to the main report to convert the data type of a data field so that it is compatible with the field in the subreport. You can also have a formula field that is simply equal to the value of a data field in the main report. This gets around the restriction of having to use indexed fields for PC databases. Another reason for using formulas is to be able to either concatenate or parse fields so that their format matches the format of the field in the subreport.

To link with a formula field in the main report, make sure the formula field has already been created before adding the subreport object. If this has already been done, then the formula field will show up in the list of report fields. Select the formula field to link to and add it to the listbox on the right.

Once the formula field has been added, the frame at the bottom of the dialog box appears and it works the same as adding a data field: the parameter name is automatically filled in and the checkbox tells the subreport to link to the field that is listed in the dropdown box below it.

When you use the linking expert with either data fields or formulas, it defaults to filtering records that match the field you selected. But you aren't limited to filtering your report on exact matches to the field. You can change the filter so that it performs any type of filtering on the field (e.g. less than the field, greater than and equal to the field, etc.) When you are done using the linking expert on the main report, right-click on the subreport and select Report | Edit Selection Formula | Records. You can modify the formula to fit your needs

Unlinked Subreports

An unlinked subreport doesn't have a connection to the main report. It is totally independent. To create an unlinked subreport, do not set any properties on this dialog box. If you had already added fields to the listbox on the right, then remove them and this will remove any links between the main report and this subreport.

Unlinked with a Formula

Formulas are used with unlinked subreports so that information can be passed to the subreport without filtering any data. This is similar to the unlinked subreport because both subreports are independent of the main report. The benefit with using a formula is that although the subreport isn't linked, you can still pass information from the main report to the subreport. This information can be displayed on the report or used in the subreport's formulas.

To create an unlinked formula field, select the formula from the main report's list of available report fields. Once the formula has been selected, the frame at the bottom of the dialog box appears and the parameter name is already filled in. Since this is an unlinked report, uncheck the checkbox that is to the right of the parameter name. This causes the linking field dropdown box to become disabled and no linking field will be specified.

When the subreport runs, it can reference the parameter that is created by this dialog box to get the formula's value from the main report.

Unlinked with Shared Variables

Shared variables can be used to pass data between the main report and the subreport. The difference between using a parameter field and a shared variable is that shared variables can be used to pass data in both directions. When using parameter fields, data can only be passed from the main report to the subreport.

Since the subreport is not linked to the main report and no formulas are being passed to the subreport, then you shouldn't set any properties on this dialog box. The difference is that both reports have to have a formula that declares and uses the shared variable.

To illustrate how this works, let's modify the example report shown earlier that lists the customer sales and any credits issued to the customer. The report is also going to show the net amount of adding the total sales with the total credits issued. This revised report is shown in Figure 12-5.

Customer Sales

ID	Customer Name	Order	Order Date	Ship Date	Amount
1	City Cyclists				
		1,143	06-Jan-1997	08-Jan-1997	$62.33
		1,246	30-Jan-1997	30-Jan-1997	$3,884.25
		1,296	16-Feb-1997	16-Feb-1997	$6,682.98
		1,387	01-Mar-1997	01-Mar-1997	$1,515.35
		1,717	14-Jun-1997	15-Jun-1997	$70.50
		1,763	24-Jun-1997	30-Jun-1997	$2,378.35
					$14,593.76

Credit Authorization Number	Amount
CR1608	($1,792.91)
CR5241	($951.33)
CR6321	($1,484.68)
CR6592	($1,237.54)
CR6798	($727.56)
	($6,194.02)

Sub-Total of Net Orders For City Cyclists Is $8,399.74

ID	Customer Name	Order	Order Date	Ship Date	Amount
2	Pathfinders				
		1,145	06-Jan-1997	17-Jan-1997	$27.00
		1,171	14-Jan-1997	14-Jan-1997	$479.85
		1,233	27-Jan-1997	29-Jan-1997	$139.48
		1,254	03-Feb-1997	04-Feb-1997	$2,497.05
		1,256	04-Feb-1997	04-Feb-1997	$70.50
		1,288	12-Feb-1997	12-Feb-1997	$8,819.55
		1,399	02-Mar-1997	02-Mar-1997	$53.90

Figure 12-5. Calculate net sales amount using a subreport.

Since the sales amount is on the main report and the credits are listed on the subreport, it needs to use a shared variable so that the two reports can share their data. A formula is added to the subreport to calculate the total credit amount for the customer. The formula is placed in the report header of the subreport so that it gets calculated when the report is first run.

```
Shared TotalCredits as Currency
TotalCredits = Sum({Credits.Amount})
Formula = TotalCredits
```

The main report is modified so that it has a formula that declares the same shared variable and uses it in the calculation. If the main report didn't declare the variable as shared then it would always be zero. Notice in the formula that the TotalCredits variable is being added to the sum of the order amounts. It isn't being subtracted because it is already a negative number.

```
Shared TotalCredits as Currency
Formula = Sum({Orders.Order AMount}, {Customer.Customer ID}) + TotalCredits
```

A variation of using shared variables with subreports is to use a subreport to perform a particular calculation but not show the subreport on the report. The last example used a subreport to display and calculate the total credits given to a customer. However, you could have chosen to not show the details of the credits on the report and instead just use the total amount in the formula. If you try to do this by either hiding or suppressing the subreport or the section it is in, then the subreport won't calculate the shared variable. This is because the subreport has to be printed in order for the formulas on the subreport to be calculated. One alternative is to make the subreport object very small so that it isn't visible on the report. Depending upon how the subreport is designed, this may or may not print any extraneous graphics on the page. A better alternative is to modify the subreport object in your .NET application so that its height is set to 0 and the object isn't allowed to grow. The designer doesn't let you set the height to 0 but setting it via code gets around this limitation.

```
Dim rpt As CrystalDecisions.CrystalReports.Engine.ReportDocument
Dim rptObjects As CrystalDecisions.CrystalReports.Engine.ReportObjects
rpt = New SuppressSubreportDemo()
rptObjects = rpt.ReportDefinition.ReportObjects
rptObjects.Item("Subreport").ObjectFormat.EnableCanGrow = False
rptObjects.Item("Subreport").Height = 0
CrystalReportViewer1.ReportSource = rpt
```

Editing the Subreport

Once the subreport object has been added to the main report, you will probably need to edit it. Depending upon the types of changes you want to make to the subreport, there are different ways of editing it.

To edit the content of the subreport, from the main report either double-click on the subreport object or right-click on it and select Edit Subreport. This opens the subreport in the same design tab as the main report. The subreport is now treated the same as any other report. You can add new report objects, modify existing ones, or delete report objects.

When editing a subreport, the report designer changes so that it displays tabs at the bottom of the designer. Each tab lists the name of the main report and all open subreports. This lets you move back and forth between the main report and its subreports. This is shown in Figure 12-6.

Figure 12-6. The tabs that list the main report and open subreports.

If you have a main report that uses many subreports, you may find that you can't open them all and see their tabs listed at the bottom of the designer. As of now, Crystal Reports doesn't have a way to scroll to the other tabs. Thus, you will not be able to have all subreports open at one time. To make room for more tabs, go to a subreport that doesn't need to stay open and right-click on it to open the menu. Select Close Subreport. This closes the subreport and removes the associated tab from the designer. Now there is room for a new subreport to be opened.

You can also modify other aspects of the subreport. When viewing the main report in design mode, right-click on the subreport object and there are two menu options called Format and Change Subreport Links. The Format menu item opens the standard format dialog box where you set properties such as Suppress, Keep Object Together, etc. The formatting options on the Border, Subreport and Font tabs control how on-demand subreports are displayed on the main report. This is discussed in the next section. The Change Subreport Links menu item opens the Subreport Links dialog box. This lets you change the fields that are used to link the main report to the subreport.

One of the formatting oddities of subreports is there is no easy way to suppress a subreport with no data. Setting the formatting option Suppress Blank Section doesn't have any effect because the subreport is an object on the main report and the section isn't considered to be blank. Since subreports typically have column headings just like other reports, a subreport with no data will still print their column headings.

Getting around this problem requires making quite a few changes to trick the main report into not printing the subreport. The general idea is to make a copy of the subreport and put it in the next section on the main report. The first subreport has to set a shared Boolean variable that tells whether there are any records in the report. Then this subreport must be resized so that it doesn't take up any room on the main report. The next step is to use that shared variable on the main report so that the second subreport is conditionally suppressed when the variable is True.

To illustrate how to do this in your own reports, the customer sales report that has been used throughout this chapter is modified so that it won't show the subreport if there are no credits for a customer. As shown in Figure 12-7, customer Spokes 'N Wheels has no credits listed, but the subreport still shows the column headers.

Customer Sales

ID	Customer Name	Order	Order Date	Ship Date	Amount
	Sub-Total of Net Orders For Poser Cycles Is $8,955.01				
8	Spokes 'N Wheels Ltd.				
		1,224	23-Jan-1997	23-Jan-1997	$70.50
		1,472	31-Mar-1997	07-Apr-1997	$823.05
		1,504	08-Apr-1997	12-Apr-1997	$3,408.75
		1,517	11-Apr-1997	11-Apr-1997	$3,734.10
		1,739	19-Jun-1997	21-Jun-1997	$5,321.25
					$13,357.65
	Credit Authorization Number				Amount
	Sub-Total of Net Orders For Spokes 'N Wheels Ltd. Is $9,510.52				
9	Trail Blazer's Place				
		1,480	04-Apr-1997	07-Apr-1997	$14.73

Figure 12-7. An empty subreport still shows column headers.

The first step is to add a new section where the subreport is and insert a new copy of the subreport into this section. If the subreport was created from an existing report, then simply base the new subreport off the same report. If the subreport was created from scratch, then you have to run through the report expert again to recreate it.[20] This new subreport must have the same links to the main report as the original subreport.

When finished, the main report now has two sections with a subreport in each. The first section has the original subreport and the second section has the copy.[21] Figure 12-8 shows how the sample report looks. I put the copy of the subreport in Group Footer #1b (I used the template shortcut method) and Group Footer #1c has the original subreport.

---

[20] The copy of the subreport really only needs to have a single field in its Details section. To save yourself some time, you could use the report expert to just create a simple template of the subreport and only have one field listed in its detail section.

[21] If you took the shortcut mentioned in the last footnote and only made a template of the subreport, then you need to switch the sections that each subreport is in. Thus, the first section should have the template and the second section should have the original subreport.

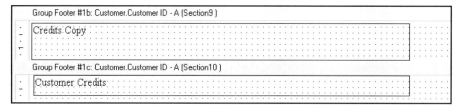

Figure 12-8. The subreports in the Group Footer sections.

The first subreport is responsible for determining if there are any records being printed and it sets a shared Boolean variable accordingly. You can test for the existence of any records by using either the IsNull() function or seeing if the Count() function returns 0. For this example, I used the IsNull() function and tested the Credit Authorization Number field.[22] This formula is placed in the Report Header section of the subreport.

```
Shared SuppressSub As Boolean
SuppressSub = IsNull({Credit.Credit Authorization Number})
Formula = SupressSub
```

The purpose of the first subreport is to determine whether there is any data that should be printed, but you don't want two copies of the same subreport to be shown to the user. So you have to hide the first subreport. As you learned earlier, if you hide or suppress a subreport, then its formulas won't be calculated. So you have to set the subreport object to have a height of 0 and set the section to Underlay Following Sections (so that the section doesn't take any space on the report). Setting the Underlay property is done via the format properties in the designer. To set the subreport height to 0, use the following code when opening the report in your .NET application.

```
Dim rpt As CrystalDecisions.CrystalReports.Engine.ReportDocument
Dim rptObjects As CrystalDecisions.CrystalReports.Engine.ReportObjects
rpt = New SuppressSubreportDemo()
rptObjects = rpt.ReportDefinition.ReportObjects
rptObjects.Item("SubreportCopy").ObjectFormat.EnableCanGrow = False
rptObjects.Item("SubreportCopy").Height = 0
CrystalReportViewer1.ReportSource = rpt
```

The subreport in the second section is the one that the user will see. It is modified so that it is only displayed if the first subreport determined that there are records to be printed. Use the shared Boolean variable in the conditional formatting formula of the Suppress (No Drill-Down) property for the section that has the subreport.

```
Shared SuppressSub As Boolean
```

---

[22] Since this function only tests one field on the subreport, the copy of the subreport really doesn't need any other fields in it. This is why the template shortcut method only has you add one field to the Details section.

Figure 12-9 shows the report after these changes have been made. You can see that the subreport is now suppressed for the customer Spokes 'N Wheels, and it is still visible for the next customer.

8	Spokes 'N Wheels Ltd.			
		1,224 23-Jan-1997	23-Jan-1997	$70.50
		1,472 31-Mar-1997	07-Apr-1997	$823.05
		1,504 08-Apr-1997	12-Apr-1997	$3,408.75
		1,517 11-Apr-1997	11-Apr-1997	$3,734.10
		1,739 19-Jun-1997	21-Jun-1997	$5,321.25
				$13,357.65

Sub-Total of Net Orders For Spokes 'N Wheels Ltd. Is $13,357.65

9	Trail Blazer's Place			
		1,480 04-Apr-1997	07-Apr-1997	$14.73
		1,513 11-Apr-1997	14-Apr-1997	$154.70
		1,515 11-Apr-1997	11-Apr-1997	$8,819.55
		1,645 23-May-1997	24-May-1997	$46.50
		1,768 24-Jun-1997	24-Jun-1997	$5,994.94
		1,767 24-Jun-1997	26-Jun-1997	$2,989.35
				$18,019.77

Credit Authorization Number	Amount
CR0194	($231.82)
CR1957	($572.67)
CR3276	($2,002.31)
CR6006	($1,119.82)
	($3,926.62)

Figure 12-9. The subreport is suppressed when there are no records.

Using On-Demand Subreports

By default, subreports are run at the same time as the main report. When you view or print the main report, the subreport information is printed as well. This may result in a performance decrease because the subreport could require just as much time, if not more, to process as the main report. If performance becomes a problem, declare the subreport so that it isn't bound to the main report. This is called an on-demand subreport.

An on-demand subreport doesn't print at the same time as the main report. Instead, a hyperlink that describes the subreport is shown where the subreport should appear.[23] When the user clicks on the hyperlink the subreport is processed and shown to the user. The on-demand subreport is shown on a separate tab in the viewer.

---

[23] A placeholder can be displayed instead of the hyperlink.

On-demand subreports are for reports viewed with the CrystalReportViewer control. If you send the report directly to the printer, only the placeholders are printed and not the subreport. This doesn't give the reader the detail information they are looking for.

To define a subreport as being an on-demand subreport, use the Subreport tab of the Insert Subreport dialog box. At the bottom of the dialog box is an On-Demand Subreport checkbox. It is unchecked by default. Click on it to make the subreport an on-demand subreport.

By default, an on-demand subreport is shown as a hyperlink on the main report. The text is the name of the subreport.

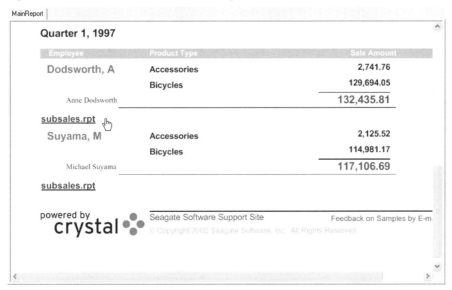

Figure 12-10. On-demand subreports shown as a hyperlink.

When you click on the hyperlink the subreport is processed and displayed on a new tab in the viewer. Each on-demand subreport is displayed on its own tab.

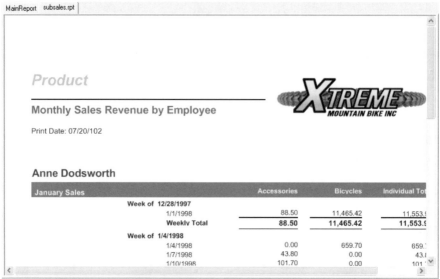

Figure 12-11. On-demand subreports shown on a separate tab.

If you feel that displaying a hyperlink isn't professional enough, you can display a customized placeholder instead. When you are in design mode, right-click on the subreport object and choose Format. Then go to the Subreport tab that is shown in Figure 12-12.

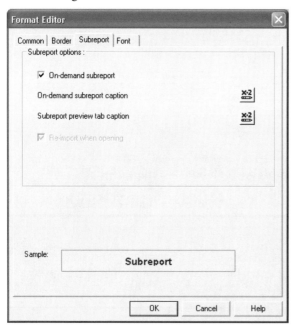

Figure 12-12. Formatting the subreport placeholder.

There is a formula button for modifying the caption that is displayed on the main report. You can enter a simple string in this formula or customize the string by concatenating data fields into it. The rest of the tabs on this dialog box can be used to format how the placeholder looks. For example, you can change the font, the background color and the border. Figure 12-13 shows the placeholder formatted with a border and a larger font size.

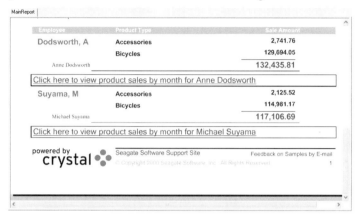

Figure 12-13. The subreport placeholder.

This page intentionally left blank

13
Data Connectivity

The backbone of every report is the data it prints. Large corporations merge data on servers into reports that consolidate and chart information from a dozen or more tables. Small businesses optimize their report distribution and expand their client base by providing their data in an XML format and letting companies from around the world generate reports on it. Home offices often do simple tasks such as tracking and printing monthly sales figures from an Access database or an Excel spreadsheet.

Crystal Reports is designed to work with many types of data. Reports can be generated regardless of where the data is stored; SQL Server, MS Access or even the Outlook email repository. Crystal Reports allows many ways to connect to databases; learning each method can be quite an undertaking. This chapter, along with Chapter 17, sorts out these options and presents them in an easy to read format. You can determine which method best meets your needs and how to quickly implement it.

All database connectivity is built around one of two models: the Pull Model and the Push Model. The Pull Model is the simplest to implement and is very easy to learn because it doesn't require writing any programming code. Reports designed to use the Pull Model make everything automatic. Crystal Reports does all the dirty work: creates the connection, reads the data, populates the report and then closes the connection. The Pull Model is covered in this chapter. The Push Model, which is covered in Chapter 17, is just the opposite. You write the code to do all the work in your program. You have to open the connection, get the data into memory, pass the data to the report, and close the connection.

So why would anyone ever want to use the Push Model? Who would want to when they know that the Pull Model Crystal will do everything for them? The answer is no different from any other choice your make when writing software. Tasks that require more effort allow more functionality. Since the Pull Model is very simple, it's less flexible than the code intensive Push Model.

This chapter focuses on connecting to databases using the Visual Studio IDE. The IDE makes it easy to connect to a data source and generate reports without having to write any programming code. Chapter 17 in Part II of this book shows the how to's of solving more complex reporting problems by writing programming codes that connects to data sources using the ReportDocument object.

Implementing the Pull Model

The Report Expert uses the simplest form of the Pull Model to create reports. Within the Report Expert is the Database Expert, where the data source(s) that the report connects to and the tables that have the data are defined. The Report Expert, generates a default report layout and builds, behind the scenes, all the data connections necessary. The only thing you have to do is call the proper method to either preview or print the report. All the examples in the book prior to this chapter used the Pull Model. This was done so that you could focus on report design and layout issues, unencumbered with worries about the intricacies of database. As you can see, implementing the examples didn't require any knowledge about data connectivity.

However, there are three aspects to the Pull Model you need knowledge of. They are: adding a data source, linking tables, and using multiple data sources.

Adding Data Sources

The Pull Model uses the Database Expert dialog box as the interface for selecting data sources for your report. It is a visual expert for opening data sources, finding tables within the data sources, and linking their related fields together. To get to it, run the Report Expert, or right-click on an existing report in design mode and select Database | Add/Change Database.

The Database Expert uses two tabs: the Data tab and the Links tab. The Data tab, shown in Figure 13-1, is the way to add data sources to the report. It shows two windows: Available Data Sources and Selected Data Sources.

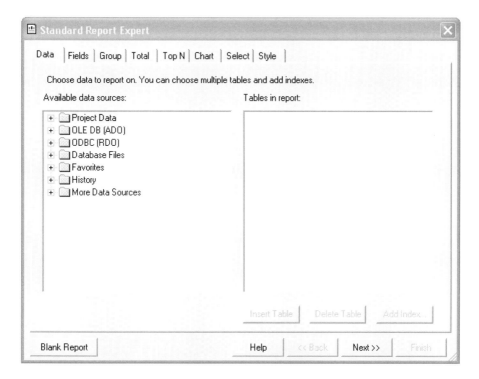

Figure 13-1. The Data Tab of the Database Expert.

The Available Data Sources window lists different categories of data sources. Table 14.1 lists these available data source categories.

Table 13-1. Available Data Sources

Data Source	Description
ADO.NET DataSets	Found within the Project Data category, these are the DataSet classes listed in the Visual Studio Project Explorer window. They give you the flexibility to tie your report to virtually any type of data.
Current Connections	Found within the Project Data category, select from any connections already established within the Server Explorer.
OLE DB (ADO)	Builds a connection string to access data sources using an OLE DB driver. It gives you a two screen wizard which asks you for the data source to connect to and any relevant information regarding its location and logon information.
ODBC (RDO)	Connect using an ODBC driver by selecting an existing System DSN[24].
Database Files	Select a PC database file using its file location.
Favorites	Choose from commonly used data sources you added to your Favorites list. Existing items can be added to the favorites list by right-clicking on them and selecting Add To Favorites. A Favorite can be renamed by clicking on it and pressing the F2 key.
History	Choose from data sources that have been used for other reports within the current project.
ADO.NET (XML)	Found within the More Data Sources category, it retrieves records by specifying an XML file path. You can also select an existing ADO.NET dataset.
Access/Excel (DAO)	Found within the More Data Sources category, it retrieves records using a DAO recordset that accesses a Microsoft Access database or Excel spreadsheet.
Field Definitions Only	Found within the More Data Sources category, it specifies a field definition file. Per the documentation, this is only for backwards compatibility and isn't used for new development.

To select the data source from the Database Expert dialog, click on the proper category node to expand it. This triggers a dialog box which asks for information about the data source. The dialog changes to match the needs of

---

[24] You should only use System DSN's. File DSN's and User DSN's are buggy.

each data source. This information can range from a simple file path to a database server name and the appropriate logon credentials. Upon entering the information, the dialog box closes and the data source name is shown in the Database Expert and listed under its category. Under the data source name is the list of available tables, views and stored procedures.[25] Click on the plus signs next to the individual items to expand the list.

Add the tables you need to your report by selecting them and clicking on the Add Table button. Double-clicking on the table will also add it to the list. When all have been added, go to the Links tab to establish the relationship between the tables.

Tip

There is one small quirk about the Available Data Sources window you should be aware of. It occurs when you click on the plus sign to expand a node and a data source dialog pops up. Once you close the dialog box there is no option to open the dialog box again. You have to click on the minus sign to close the node and then click on the plus sign to expand it again. This triggers the dialog box to open again. After adding a data source to that node, this isn't an issue because there will now be an item listed as the first item and clicking on it lets you add another data source.

Linking Tables

Whenever there are two or more tables, they need to be linked so that Crystal Reports knows how they are related. For example, a pet store that wants to print a list of its products by Animal ID needs to build a report using an animal table and a product table. To match the product to the appropriate type of animal, both tables will be linked by the Animal ID. It would be impossible to determine which products are associated with which animal without this link. The Links tab, shown in Figure 13-2, sets the linking fields.

---

[25] If you don't see everything listed in the Database Expert (particularly stored procedures), right-click the report and select Designer | Default Settings. Go to the Database tab and click on the items you want to see in Database Expert.

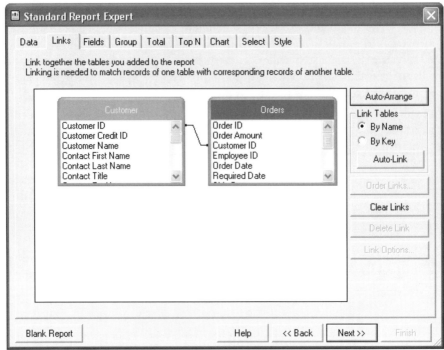

Figure 13-2. The Links tab.

When the Links tab is first displayed, it creates default links. This is the equivalent of Crystal's "best guess" for the relationships between the tables. In an effort to make it easier for you, Crystal Reports tries to figure out which fields in each table should be linked to each other. It does this based upon indexes and fields that have the same name and data type.

Tip

To get the most benefit out of the auto-arranged links, design your tables with field names that use a consistent naming convention and have well thought out indexes. This will result in a higher probability that Crystal Reports will create the appropriate default links.

The default links are not set in stone. You are free to delete or add more, according to your needs. To delete a link, simply click on it (to select it); then click on the button labeled Delete Link. You can also just press the Delete key after selecting it. To add a new link, drag and drop the field from one table onto the matching field in the other table.

There are a couple of buttons that are helpful for managing links. The Auto-Arrange button rearranges the tables into an easier-to-read layout, which is useful when handling a report with many tables. A multitude of tables makes difficult the visualization of their relationship with one another and the overall structure. The Auto-Link button rebuilds the links based on whether you want to link by field name or by index. This comes in handy for undoing any new links you added, should you want to start from scratch. The Clear Links button removes all the links between the tables. The Link Options button opens the Link Options dialog box, shown in Figure 14 -3.

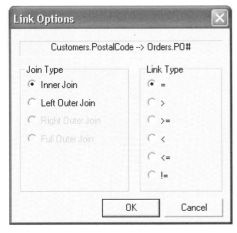

Figure 13-3. The Link Options dialog box.

The Link Options dialog box establishes the type of relationship between the two fields. It sets the type of join (Inner, Left Outer, Right Outer, or Full Outer) as well as how the fields are compared (equal to each other, less than, etc.). Table 13-2 shows a list of the different linking options and how they affect the resulting data.

Table 13-2. Join Options

Join Type	Resultset Description
Inner Join	Records from the left table are matched with records from the right table. Only records with an exact match are included.
Left Outer Join	All records from the left table are included. Field values are included if there is a matching record in the right table . NULL values are stored in the corresponding fields if there is no matching record in the right table..
Right Outer Join	All records from the right table are included. Field values are included if there is a matching record in the left table. NULL values are stored in the corresponding fields if there is no matching record in the left table.
Full Outer Join	Every record from both tables is included. When records from both tables match, the fields in the new recordset are filled in as normal. The other fields are set to NULL if there is no matching record for one of the tables.

The Order Links button sets the order in which the links between the tables are created. This is used only when there is more than one link shown. The tables will be linked automatically, in the order that they are shown in the dialog box. The default linking order processes the links on the left before the links on the right. Changing the default linking order is useful when there is a hierarchy of tables joined together and the order to which they are joined is important. This can happen when you are using a link to return a subset of records from two tables, and these records must therefore be linked to another table. Changing the order of the links changes the resulting data.

Using Multiple Data Sources

Complex reports often require printing data of different origins. This can happen when you have tables in a SQL Server database and they need to be linked to tables in an Oracle database. There can also be SQL Server databases on different servers on the network. Although Crystal Reports is capable of printing such reports, it doesn't always run flawlessly. Using multiple data sources has the potential for a variety of problems. There is no easy fix.

Crystal Reports, by design, takes the data connectivity information that is saved with a report and generates SQL statements with it. The statements are then delivered to the database server. Although every major database vendor claims to be compliant with the SQL standard, they each have their own subtle differences that can cause them to reject the SQL language of another database.

But Crystal Reports doesn't have the capability to, within a single report, generate SQL that is compatible with multiple variations of the SQL specification. It will inevitably create non-compatible SQL for one of the databases. You will have a compatibility issue.

That is not all. Different database servers manage their standard data types differently, chiefly in the way they store them internally. The way one database represents an Integer can be totally different from another database. When Crystal Reports tries to link these two fields together, it won't be able to because they look like different data types.

While it is true that Crystal Reports is designed to work with the majority of database servers, it doesn't imply that the database servers themselves will work with one another. Since every database tries to be better than the next database, companies are more concerned about performance than compatibility. There are limitations with reports using different databases.

Fortunately, there are some general rules you can follow to reduce the headaches caused by these problems. You should be able to generate the reports you need if you follow the following rules (with a little trial and error).

When linking tables together, only use fields that are of the String data type. String is the most consistent data type among different database servers and has the least likelihood of causing problems. This is no guarantee against all problems, however. For example, a string can be represented by variable and fixed length data type and this can create incompatibilities.

Rather than try to link tables from different data sources together, use subreports to print the same data. The benefit of using subreports is that they are treated individually. When Crystal Reports generates the SQL statements for the sub-report, it does so independently of the main report. Also, it has only to worry about working with a single database driver. This independence eliminates a lot of potential problems. Using subreports also allows for more flexible linking options between a main report and subreport. You aren't limited to linking with strings and you can also use formulas to perform data type conversions when necessary.

There are reports where using a subreport isn't an option. For example, if all the detail fields need to be printed side by side, you can't use subreports because the fields will have to be printed underneath the others. In this circumstance, find out if your database lets you create links to outside databases. Putting the links within the database server itself puts the responsibility of managing this data within the server. Crystal Reports benefits because now it only has to use one database driver to retrieve the data. You also get better performance because the database server maintains the additional connection and links.

Secured Databases

Most databases have security implemented in them. They require valid user credentials before accessing the data. This means that you have to pass a User ID and Password to the database prior to printing the report. Crystal Reports handles security differently, depending upon how the report is bound and the database used.

In most circumstances, a Windows application displays a login dialog box prompting the user to enter their user credentials. After entering the credentials, the user can login. However, this isn't always the case. If you are using an MS Access database with a database password or if you are printing from an Excel spreadsheet using OLE DB, the login dialog box isn't compatible. If you are writing an ASP.NET application, it doesn't have the capability to prompt the user for their credentials. In both of these examples the user won't be able to print the report. Rectifying this problem requires passing the user credentials during runtime. See Chapter 17 for a thorough discussion of connecting to every type of data source during runtime.

Caution

When using integrated security with ASP.NET applications, the SQL Server database should be on the same server as the web server. There are known issues when IIS tries to connect to SQL Server and then Crystal Reports tries to connect again. It can't perform a "double-hop" and the connection fails. See Microsoft Knowledge Base article 176377 for more information.

Connecting with Stored Procedures

As mentioned earlier in the chapter, stored procedures can be used as a data source just like a table. Crystal Reports can open a stored procedure, retrieve the data and print it. The one thing that can make a stored procedure unique is if it has input parameters.

For a stored procedure to execute, it must have a value for every input parameter. Crystal Reports automatically creates report parameters when it sees that the stored procedure has one or more input parameters. There is one report parameter for every stored procedure parameter and they will have identical names and data types. When the report runs, the user is prompted to enter a value for each parameter. Internally, Crystal Reports passes these report parameters to the stored procedure.

The following code is a sample stored procedure from the Northwind database.

```
CREATE PROCEDURE CustOrderHist
@CustomerID nchar(5)
AS
SELECT ProductName, Total=SUM(Quantity)
FROM Products P, [Order Details] OD, Orders O, Customers C
WHERE C.CustomerID = @CustomerID
AND C.CustomerID = O.CustomerID
```

In this stored procedure, there is one input parameter called @CustomerId that is a 5 character string. When this report is selected as the data source for a report, Crystal Reports automatically creates a parameter called @CustomerID as a String data type. The report prompts the user to enter a Customer ID when it is run. The report passes this value to the stored procedure; the stored procedure only returns records with a matching ID.

Note

If you want your application to directly pass the parameters to the stored procedure, you have to set the parameter objects during runtime. The user won't be prompted with the parameter dialog boxes and the report will run seamlessly. See Chapter 17 for the steps to set report parameter values during runtime.

If you are using two stored procedures and linking them together, make sure that the parameters have different names. When Crystal Reports creates parameters for each stored procedure, it doesn't have the capability to create a new alias for the parameter names. Consequently, it will only create one report parameter with that name and it won't know which stored procedure to assign the parameter to. Make sure that parameters use unique names.

Working with SQL Statements

Reports connect to databases, which in turn, return a set of records. The portion of the report's design that works with data is translated into a SQL statement that is syntactically valid for each specific data source.

Crystal Reports gives you many ways to customize the SQL statement that is passed to the database. This can be done while designing a report as well as during runtime. A few reasons for customizing the SQL is to create more sophisticated SQL queries, increase the database's performance, or to perform runtime customization according to a user's input.

Crystal Reports breaks a SQL statement into three distinct parts: table selection, filtering records, and sorting/grouping. Each of these parts is identified by a SQL keyword. The SELECT keyword specifies the tables and fields to use. The WHERE keyword specifies which records should be included and which should be filtered out. The SORT BY and GROUP ON keywords specify how to perform the sorting and grouping of the records. The following sections explain these three parts of the SQL statement and show the options for customizing them.

Selecting Tables and Fields

The Database Expert dialog box makes the selection of tables and fields a piece of cake. You get to select the tables to use, how the tables are linked, and the fields to print by nothing more than a mere point and click action. As to the final SQL statement that your report passes to the data source, this is the SELECT part of the SQL statement.

There are times when doing simple joins between tables isn't sufficient for your reporting needs. For example, Crystal Reports doesn't support the UNION statement for doing a non-linked merge of two tables. In these circumstances, you can specify your own SQL statement rather than use the one that Crystal creates.

Note

The SELECT portion of the SQL statement can only be customized while the report is being designed. There is no functionality in Crystal Reports to modify the SELECT statement during runtime.

When creating custom SQL statements for a report, it's critical that you are well versed in the proper syntax for the database you are using. Although most databases state that they are ANSI SQL-92 compliant, there are minor differences between each implementation as well as enhancements to the standards. You should, if you aren't familiar with these differences, familiarize yourself with the SQL language reference guide that came with the database.

A good way to learn how SQL works is to look at the SQL statements that Crystal creates for your reports. Right-click on the report in design mode and select Database | Show SQL Query. This opens the dialog box (Figure 13-8) that shows the SELECT portion of the SQL statement that is passed to the database.

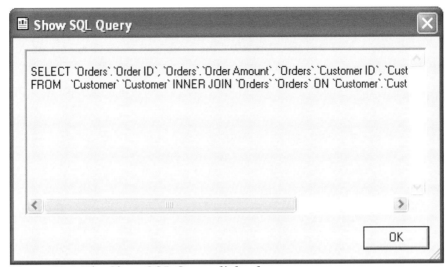

Figure 13-4. The Show SQL Query dialog box.

This dialog box displays the SELECT portion of the SQL statement, but it doesn't let you change it (it is read only). Writing a custom SQL statement for your report requires creating a new data source based on a Command object rather than modifying an existing connection.

Enter a custom SQL statement by opening the Database Expert and selecting the OLE DB (ADO) category and creating a new connection to the server. If the connection you want already exists, you can use it. Once the connection is created, double-click on the Add Command option to open the Add Command To Report dialog box. Enter a SQL statement and click OK.

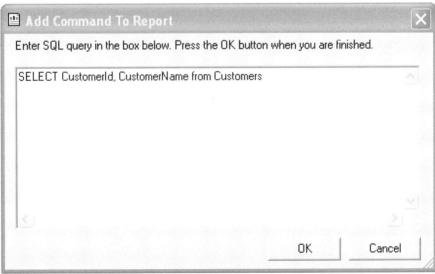

Figure 13-5. The Add Command To Report dialog box.

The new command is listed under the connection node, and the available fields are listed under the command node. At this point the command is treated as a standard data source and you can select the fields you want to appear on the report.

Filtering Records

When printing records from one or more tables, you probably don't need to print every single record. It is common to print only a subset of the original records. For example, rather than print every customer in the database, the report prints customers that have been added within the past thirty days. SQL statements use the WHERE statement to filter out records that aren't relevant to your query.

Crystal Reports uses selection formulas for data filtering. Selection formulas can be created at two dialog boxes designed for just such a purpose: the Select Expert and the Record Selection Formula Editor. As explained before, the Select Expert sets the fields and criteria used in the selection formula. It automatically builds the selection formula in Crystal Syntax. This makes it easy for you to quickly create filters without having to know the programming syntax.

When a report is run, all the records that are returned from the database are processed by the report engine and tested against the selection formula. Records meeting the conditions in the selection formula are printed on the report. This method of processing records is reliable, but slow.

It is slow because the way the selection formulas are processed makes for three bottlenecks. Firstly, the server passes all the records to the client computer. The speed at which these records are transferred is constrained by the physical limitations of the network design as well as the traffic already on the network. Secondly, the report engine has to process all the records through the selection formula. Depending on the complexity of the formula and the number of records being processed, this can be a very time intensive process. Lastly, the passing of all these records across the network can hinder the performance of other applications on the network. As the report designer, your goal is to design a report that is displayed as efficiently as possible. These three bottlenecks can be major stumbling blocks to that reality.

The solution is to transfer the workload from the client machine to the server. This is called "pushing down data" to the server. Pushing down data derives a big improvement in performance by having the server perform the filtering. Database servers are designed to provide the optimum performance when processing massive quantities of data. It can filter out records that don't meet a certain criteria in a fraction of the time that the report engine would take. Pushing down data has the secondary benefit of passing less data along the network back to the client. The report gets the data quicker and there is less traffic on the network that would affect other users.

Pushing down data to the server requires the server to take the record selection formula you created and test each record against it. The formula you created is saved internally using Crystal syntax. Since databases only understand SQL and not Crystal syntax, the Crystal formula gets converted to SQL. Crystal Reports tries to do this conversion with every selection formula because pushing down data gives the best performance.

Converting a formula involves the creation of the equivalent of a WHERE clause in SQL. The WHERE statement gets appended to the SELECT statement, which Crystal Reports always passes to the database server. Any one familiar with SQL would know that not only is it totally different from Crystal syntax, it also has a lot less functionality than Crystal syntax. The upshot: these differences can create problems when the formula is being converted to SQL. In fact, since Crystal Reports has a function library that is much more robust than the SQL language, it is very possible that the selection formula can't be converted into a valid WHERE clause.

When a formula can't be converted to a valid WHERE clause, it won't be included in the SQL string passed to the database server. Only the SELECT portion of the SQL statement is sent. This results in the database server passing all the records from the SELECT statement back to the client computer. The report has to manually process all the records with the selection formula to find those that ought to be printed. The result is a much slower performance than what would have been, had all the filtering been done on the server.

Now that you know that not every selection formula can be converted to SQL, let's look at how to make this happen as frequently as possible.

Before any formula can be converted to SQL, the report needs the feature to be turned on. The option "Use Indexes or Server for Speed" must be enabled for the report to push data down to the server. This option tells the report to use indexes when selecting records from a database and it tells it to use the server to improve performance whenever possible. You can set this option to be turned on by default for all reports or for just the current report. To make it the default setting, right-click on a report and select Designer | Default Settings. Go to the database tab and look at whether it is checked or unchecked. If it is unchecked, click on it to select it. It will now be selected for every report. If you want to set it for just the current report, right-click on a report and select Report | Report Options. The checkbox is listed near the bottom.

PC databases (e.g. MS Access) have an additional restriction for pushing down data. The fields in the record selection formula must be indexed.

After enabling this option for the report, you want to create a selection formula that would deliver the best performance for your report. The optimum selection formula is one that can be converted to SQL completely. However, you may not have a choice in whether you can write a formula that can be converted to SQL or not. As mentioned earlier, Crystal syntax has a lot more functionality than SQL. Since the purpose of a formula is to carry out the requirements of the report's design, you don't have a lot of choice about what will be in the formula. You have to write it so that it performs the required functionality. Converting the selection formula to SQL is a great benefit, but it is secondary to generating the necessary data.

One way to ensure the selection formula gets converted into SQL is to write it using SQL Expressions. An SQL Expression is a formula that is built using only valid SQL functions. Since it only has valid SQL functions, Crystal Reports will always be able to convert it to a valid WHERE clause. SQL Expressions are explained in greater detail in a later section.

A general rule of thumb to follow is that if you use the Select Expert, it usually results in a valid WHERE clause that will be sent to the database server. This is because the Select Expert doesn't do anything complex. It uses basic comparison operators that can be easily converted into SQL. A good rule to follow when using the Select Expert is to only specify database fields in the criteria. Since formulas generally use functions that can't get translated into SQL, including them in the selection could result in it not being converted. Restricting the selection formula to only database fields ensures its convertibility.

When a formula uses multiple conditions, they can be joined with either the AND operator or the OR operator. Each affects performance differently. To understand how this works, you have to understand how each operator is used.

When two or more conditions are combined using the AND operator, Crystal looks at each condition independently. If a condition can be converted to SQL, it is appended to the WHERE clause and passed down to the server. Any conditions that can't be converted are left for the report engine to process. Crystal will pass as many conditions down to the server as it can and leave the rest for the client. The result is improved performance because, even though the client has to process some of the records, there will be fewer to process. Many records have already been filtered out by the server.

The OR operator works differently from the AND operator. When using the OR operator, Crystal Reports looks at all the conditions as a whole. Like the AND operator, it tries to convert each condition into SQL. But this time, if it finds that any of the conditions can't be converted, none of them will be converted. For example, assume a record selection formula has three conditions and they are joined using the OR operator. If the first two conditions can be converted to SQL, but the last one can't, then none of them will be passed down to the server. The entire record selection formula will be processed by the client.

The reason for this is that when using the OR operator, all records are tested for each of the stated conditions. Only passing some of the conditions doesn't reduce the number or records that need to be passed to the client. For example, assume that there are two conditions and one of the two conditions was passed to the server. After the server processes the SELECT statement, it is left with 100 records. Even if the server performs the first test and 70 records fail, there is still a chance that these 70 records will pass the second test. However, the second test is on the client, which means the 70 records have to get passed to the client for testing. In effect, the server ends up passing all the records to the client. Using the OR operator didn't speed up the processing at all.

If you are using a PC database, then those rules don't apply. Using a PC database means you can't use the OR operator at all. Whether the individual conditions can be converted to SQL or not won't have any effect.

> **Tip**
>
> If you want to find out whether a selection formula was converted into SQL, right-click on the report and select Database | Show SQL Query. If you see that the query includes the WHERE clause, then it was successfully converted. If the WHERE clause isn't included, then one of the formulas or functions couldn't get converted.

Record Grouping and Sorting

When Crystal Reports generates a report that uses fields for grouping and sorting, it has to collect all the data within the client's computer and process each record. It takes a lot of resources to organize and sort each record as well as perform any necessary summary calculations. This section elaborates on the how-tos of enabling reports to optimize grouping and sorting, the restrictions of doing so, and how to customize the grouping formula during runtime.

Optimizing and modifying a report's grouping and sorting is very similar to working with the record selection formulas. You want to push down data to the server for processing. You learned in the last section, that for Crystal Reports to push data down to the server, you have to turn the feature on. The same goes for grouping records. Enable the option called "Perform Grouping on Server". This makes the server do as much of the grouping, summarizing and subtotaling as possible.

> **Note**
>
> You can't select the option to perform grouping on the server unless the option to use the server for performance is also turned on. If it isn't selected, the grouping option is disabled.

To turn it on by default, right-click on a report and select Designer | Default Settings. Go to the database tab and click on the "Perform Grouping on Server" option if it isn't already checked. If you want to set the options for just the current report, right-click on a report and select Report | Report Options. Both options are listed near the bottom of the dialog box. There is also a short-cut just for the grouping option. Right-click on the report and select Database | Perform Grouping On Server. This toggles the grouping option on or off. A check is shown next to the menu option so you can see its current value.

Restrictions on Grouping and Sorting

Having the server perform the grouping has certain restrictions associated with it. These restrictions are as follows:

- The goal of performing grouping and sorting on the server is to reduce the number of records passed back to the client and consequently reduce the amount of processing the client has to do. To make this possible, the report is restricted to printing only the group fields and summary fields. The Details section must be hidden and there can't be any detail fields in any of the header or footer sections.

- The report derives all its data from a single data source or stored procedure. You can't have two different data sources linked together.

- Grouping can't be performed on a formula, and formulas can't be used in summary fields. If either one of these is true, then all records will be passed back to the client for processing. This probably comes as a surprise since some formulas can be used in a record selection formula and can be passed to the server for processing. It is not the case with grouping.

- Sorting can't be done using specified order. It is impossible for Crystal Reports to convert the logic required to perform specified order sorting into valid SQL statements. This is always done on the client's machine.

- Running total fields must be based on summary fields. If a running total is based on a detail field, all the detail fields will be passed to the client to perform the calculation.

- The report cannot use summaries based on Average or Distinct Count.

- The fields that are being grouped must either be the actual database fields or SQL Expressions. SQL Expressions can always be sent to the server because they are built using valid SQL functions. This is discussed in the next section.

Using SQL Expressions

SQL Expressions are report formulas that only use SQL compatible functions. As mentioned in the last section, many formulas written with Crystal syntax don't have a SQL compliant equivalent. Thus, the report engine has to take the data returned from the server and process it on the client's computer. SQL Expressions alleviate this problem because they are passed directly to the server for processing. The data returned to the client computer has already been processed. SQL Expressions can be used as formulas that are used directly on the report output, or they can be included as part of the formulas.

Writing reports requires achieving a balance of functionality and performance. Many reports need to use custom formulas and functions to produce the proper output. But this can result in slower performance because it requires the report engine to do more work on the client computer. Thus, you would want to, whenever possible, push as much work as possible onto the database server. The drawback to using SQL Expressions is that they aren't as robust as formulas written with Crystal syntax or Basic syntax. Crystal Reports has an extensive library of functions that isn't matched in other programs. The functions found in the SQL language pale in comparison to Crystal Reports. Many formulas can't be rewritten using a SQL Expression.

When deciding when to use SQL Expressions instead of the standard formulas, you have to decide which gives you the best cost-benefit ratio. There are three places where formulas are used: as part of the report output, in the record selection formula, and as a sorting/grouping field. You should focus your attention on using SQL Expressions in formulas that are used for either record selection or sorting/grouping. Formulas that are used as part of the report output don't have a major effect on report performance because the report engine can quickly calculate these as it processes each record. The additional overhead incurred isn't significant. SQL Expressions should definitely be used to replace formulas that are used for record selection or sorting/grouping. Both of these tasks are very resource intensive and can affect the number of records that are passed from the server back to the client. The database server is optimized to perform record selection and sorting/grouping on a large number of records very quickly. Replacing these formulas with SQL Expressions can result in noticeable improvements in report performance.

To create a SQL Expression, look in the Field Explorer window for the SQL Expressions category.[26] Right-click on the SQL Expressions category and select New. A SQL Expression Name dialog box opens where you enter a name for the expression. Once you click the OK button the SQL Expression Editor window opens. You can see that the SQL Expression Editor looks almost identical to the Formula Editor.

Figure 13-6. The SQL Expression Editor dialog box.

The process of creating a SQL Expression is the same as creating other formulas. You select the functions to use and apply them to the listed database fields. The important difference between regular formulas and SQL Expressions is that SQL Expressions have a more limited functionality. The only fields that you can use in a SQL Expression are database fields. You can't use other formulas, parameters or special fields. The available functions are also limited to SQL specific functions.

---

[26] If you don't see SQL Expressions, then you are either using a PC Database or another non-compatible database. In general, you have to be using SQL Server or an ODBC database to create a SQL Expression.

The list of available functions is specific to the database server you are connected to. If you create a SQL Expression and later change database servers, the expression may not be valid if the new database doesn't support one of the functions used.

After adding a SQL Expression to the report, the SELECT statement passed to the database server is modified to include the SQL Expression. It becomes an additional field that is requested from the server. If you also include the SQL Expression in a record selection formula, or sorting/grouping formula, then this is also added to the query. Figure 13-7 shows how the formula is used as part of the SELECT portion of the query as well as the WHERE clause.

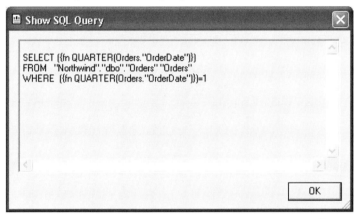

Figure 13-7. The SQL Query using a SQL Expression.[27]

Changing the Data Source

Many reports are very simple and all the tables come from the same data source. The tables that are used when you designed the report are the same tables that will be used when the application is put into production. But this isn't always the case. It is common for the requirements to change and for a report to use a data source different from what it was designed with. Or, you may have a development server that is used for designing the application and a production server that is used when the application is finished.

---

[27] Due to the fact that the Show SQL Query dialog box doesn't scroll its text, for the purpose of this illustration all the other fields in the report were removed before doing this screenshot. Otherwise the SQL Expression wouldn't be visible.

Crystal Reports has a number of features that make it easier to change the location of the tables. It lets you set the location of a data source, change the name that a table is referenced by, and verify whether a database is valid.

Set Location Dialog Box

The Set Location dialog box, shown in Figure 13-8, is used to change the data source of an existing table. You might need to do this when the reporting requirements change, or when you find that, after having used one data source for coding and testing, you have to change to the production data source before releasing the program.

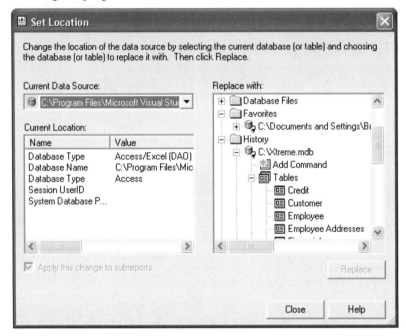

Figure 13-8. The Set Location dialog box.

The Set Location dialog box lets you replace an existing data source with a new data source. You can switch the database server so that all the tables from one server are switched to a different server. You can also change the data source for just one table and it won't affect the other tables in that report. This includes changing the database server for that table or switching out the table for a totally different table.

Open the Set Location dialog box by right-clicking on the report and selecting Database | Set Location. It has a combobox on the left hand side labeled "Current Data Source". This lists the current connections and any tables that are being used with that connection. The window on the right is labeled

"Replace With". It lists the same data sources that are displayed in the Database Expert dialog box.

To replace the entire data source for all the tables, select that database server from the Current Data Source window on the left.

To replace a single table, drill down to select that table from the combo box. The window below the combo box is refreshed to display the information about the table.

The Replace With window on the right is where you select the data source that will replace what was selected in the combo box. Scroll through this window to find the new data source. If the Current Data Source combobox lists a database server, choose a database server within the Replace With window. If the Current Data Source is a table, you have to have a table selected within the Replace With window.

Caution

When you open the Set Location dialog box and click on one of the database servers, a list of all the available tables in the database is created. If at a later point you go into the database server to make changes to the tables (e.g. adding or deleting tables), the Set Location dialog box won't recognize those changes. It will still show the original list of tables. The Set Location dialog box only queries the database server the first time it is opened. To force the table names to be refreshed you have to close and reopen Visual Studio.

When both the current data source and the new data source are selected, click the Replace button. The existing data source gets replaced with the new data source. The information on the left is updated to reflect the properties of the new data source.

If you find that the Replace button isn't enabled, you haven't selected data sources that are compatible with each other. For example, if you have a table selected in the combo box, then you have to have a table selected in the Replace With window. If the combo box has a data source selected, then the Replace With window can't have a table selected.

Verifying Changes to the Data Source

If you make changes to a table and its fields using the management console of the database, this will impact the reports that use that table. Modifying a field's data type can affect how the report formats the data. Changing a field's name causes the report to lose its reference to the field.

Crystal Reports has a Verify Database function that checks whether the fields in a report match the fields in the current data source. This should be done whenever you suspect that the tables have been modified. Access this function by right-clicking on your report and selecting Database | Verify Database. It will display a confirmation box if the database is up to date. If Crystal Reports determines that the fields in your report do not match, it lets you re-map them to their equivalent fields in the new table structure.

Re-mapping Fields

When replacing one table with another table, it is possible that one or more of the fields on the report won't have exact matches in the new table. If the fields in a table are renamed or deleted, this can affect the existing fields on your report. When this happens, Crystal Reports gives you the option to remap the existing fields to the new fields in the database.

After using the Set Location dialog box or when using the Verify Database function, Crystal Reports checks if any changes have been made to the table. If it detects that a change has occurred that effects fields being used on the report, it opens the Map Fields dialog box shown in Figure 13-9. It shows the fields that don't have a matching field in the current table. It also shows you the new fields in the data source so that you can match the old fields to the new fields. Crystal replaces them accordingly.

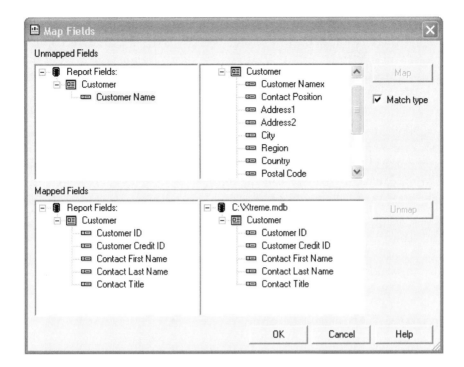

Figure 13-9. The Map Fields dialog box.

This dialog box is only displayed when necessary. If changes are made to fields that have not been added to the report yet, then it isn't necessary to re-map these fields. Fields that only have their data types changed are not mapped either, but you should check their output when the report runs to make sure they are formatted properly.

The Map Fields dialog box is divided into two halves. The top half shows the unmapped fields. The left-most window shows the fields that are in the report but don't have a matching field in its assigned table. The right-most window shows all the fields from the currently selected tables. Select one of the unmapped fields in the left window and then select one of the available fields in the right window. Click on the Map button to replace the old field with the new field. You might notice that not all the fields are listed in the right-most window. This is because the checkbox to the right, labeled "Match type" is checked by default. This requires you to only match fields that have the same data type. It won't list the fields that don't have the same data type. If you uncheck this checkbox then all fields are displayed and you can replace a field with a field of a different data type. If you do this, you should go back to the report and make sure that the formatting and spacing of the new field are appropriate. The formatting of the old field may not have carried over properly.

If there are fields that are currently mapped, but you still want to replace them, use the window in the lower half of the dialog box. In the left-most window click on the field to replace and then click the Unmap button. This moves the field to the Unmapped window in the top half and you can now follow the previous steps to re-map it with a new field.

After you accept the mapping changes, the report is automatically updated so that all report fields and formulas have the old field name replaced with the new field name. This saves you the trouble of going back through a report and modifying all formulas that referenced that field. This is the same effect as using a program like MS Word and using the Search and Replace function.

Setting a Table's Alias

When fields are added to a report, they are referenced by a combination of their table name and their field name. During the course of designing a report and making updates to it, the fields can have the table renamed or the table can be replaced with a different table. If you created formulas based upon a field in a table that has changed, then these formulas could potentially become invalid. In this situation, you would expect to have to go back through the formulas and update the table names for each field. Fortunately, Crystal Reports has thought of a way around this problem.

In the prior discussion about re-mapping old field names to new field names, you learned that Crystal Reports automatically performs a search-and-replace to change the old field names with new field names. It handles changes to the name of a table differently. The report still uses the old table name in the formulas. But now these table names reference the new table name behind the scenes. On the surface, it appears that the table still references the old table because its name hasn't changed. This new table name is called an alias.

An alias is a name that is assigned to a database table that isn't the actual name of the table. If you replace a table with a new table, Crystal Reports refers to the new table using the same name as the original table. You can think of an alias as a variable that points to a table. You can change which table the variable points to, but the name of the variable never changes.

Every table in a report is referred to by an alias. When a table is first added to a report, an alias is created and its name matches the name of the table. Since they are the same, you don't even realize that an alias is being used. When you use the Set Location dialog box to change a data source's table to a new table, the alias name stays the same, but the table it refers to is now different.

As an example, consider a report that prints fields from a table called CustomerData. The table is later modified so that the name is now called Customer. You use the Set Location dialog box to change the CustomerData table to the Customer table. When you close the dialog box you will see that the formulas still reference the table using CustomerData name. You might incorrectly think that the table name wasn't changed. But it was.

You can also use aliases to make it easier to design a report. For example, if you are using a table name that is extremely long, you can use an alias that is a shorter name. If you have a table name that uses a cryptic naming schema, you can use the alias to give the table a more useful name. For example, rather than referring to a table as "AR970EOY" you could refer to it as "Accts Receivable Year End". Everywhere in your report where this table is referenced, you will see the alias name that you assigned it rather than the actual name of the table used in the database.

The interesting thing about having an alias in a formula is that unlike re-mapping fields, aliases don't change anything on the surface. Since formulas reference the name of the alias and this name never changes, then you don't have to worry about updating the formulas.

Tip

If you are going to rename a table's alias to make it easier to work with, make sure you do so before creating any formulas with that table. When you change a table's alias, the formulas are not updated. Your formulas will quit working until you modify them to use the new alias name.

Another reason to use an alias is when want to use a table for a self-join SQL statement. You need to rename the alias of one of the tables before linking them together. The alias that the table is named doesn't have any effect on the table's actual name in the database. When you give a table an alias, Crystal Reports modifies the **SELECT** statement so that it uses the new alias name.

To manually change the alias of a table, right-click on the report and select Database | Set Alias. This opens the Database Expert dialog box with the current connections shown in the right-most window. Click on the table that you want to assign an alias to and press the F2 key. This puts the name in edit mode and you can change it.

If you are using multiple data sources, it's possible that you will add two tables with the same name to your report. Crystal Reports forces you to give one of the tables an alias so that there isn't a naming conflict. Before it lets you add the table, it prompts you with the Database Warning dialog box in Figure 13-10. It tells you that there is already a table with that same alias and asks if you really want to add it to your current connections. If you click Yes, then it prompts you to enter a new alias name. The table gets added to your current connections using the new alias name.

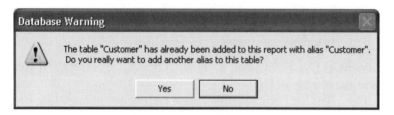

Figure 13-10. The Database Warning dialog box.

Tip

It isn't obvious when a table is using an alias that is different than the actual table name. If you are given a report that you didn't design, a table that uses an alias can make it difficult to determine what the actual table is. To find out which tables have aliases and what table is used, open the Set Location dialog box. The drop down box lists the table aliases that are associated with each data source. When you click on the table name, the detail section below the drop-down box changes to show you the details about the alias. The actual table name is shown in this information. The following figure shows that the alias CustomerData references the Customer table.

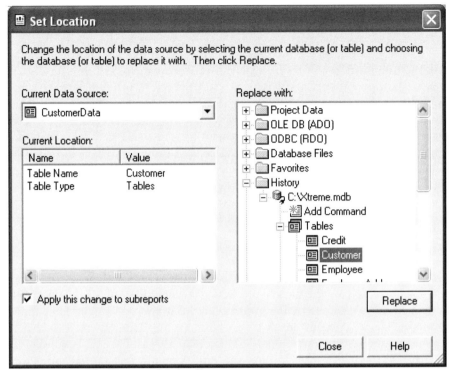

Figure 13-11. Finding a table's alias.

Printing with MS Excel Files

One of the data sources that you can print from is a MS Excel file. Crystal makes it simple to print using the worksheets within a spreadsheet file. It references each worksheet as if it were a table within the data source. However, there are a few quirks that you have to work around to make it function properly.

The most obvious way of printing from an Excel file is to use the Database Expert and go to the category called More Data Sources. Within this category you find an option for connecting to MS Excel via DAO (data access objects). Select this option and then find the Excel file you want to print from. It will list each worksheet that has data on it. Add the worksheets to print from into the Selected Tables window. Once the worksheets have been selected, proceed to design the report as normal.

At this point, if you run your program and try to print the report, a Database Login dialog box appears. It is asking you to enter the user credentials for the Excel spreadsheet. Of course, there are no user credentials to enter so you just click on Finish. This causes a Logon Failed dialog box to appear and it won't let you print the report. The problem is that as of the time this book was printed, Crystal Reports can't print from an Excel file via OLE DB. Of course, this will be corrected in a future service pack.

Crystal Reports can only print Excel files via a DSN that was created using the ODBC Administrator.[28] Unfortunately, if you create the report using a DSN as your data source then Crystal Reports can't query the file to determine what spreadsheets are available. This means that there won't be a list of tables that can be moved to the Selected Tables window within the Database Expert. You have to manually enter a SQL statement that extracts the data from the spreadsheet. While this is certainly possible, it isn't pleasant. For example, the following listing shows the SQL statement to select two columns from Sheet1 and one column from Sheet2. It joins the two sheets via the ISBN column.

```
SELECT `Sheet1_`.`Title`, `Sheet1_`.`Publisher`, `Sheet2_`.`ISBN`
  FROM  `Sheet1$` `Sheet1_` INNER JOIN `Sheet2$` `Sheet2_`
  ON `Sheet1_`.`ISBN`=`Sheet2_`.`ISBN`
  ORDER BY `Sheet1_`.`Publisher`
```

In summary, each option has pros and cons. Adding an Excel file to the report via DAO gives you the benefit of letting Crystal Reports create the SQL statement to pull data from the spreadsheet and it also queries the spreadsheet to determine what fields are available for printing. The drawback is that it crashes when running the report. The other alternative is to connect via ODBC. The benefit is that this lets you print a report, but the tradeoff is that you have to do all the work of creating the SQL statement and debugging it.

The optimum solution is to use a combination of the two methods. The workaround involves the following steps.

Connect to the Excel file using DAO. In the Database Expert, choose the More Data Sources category and then select the Excel option. Use the Browse button to find the file on the hard drive. Behind the scenes, Crystal Reports builds a valid SQL statement to select data from the spreadsheet.

Design the report as you normally would with the DAO connection. All the fields will be listed in the report's Field Explorer window and you can drag and drop them onto the report as you would any other data source.

Once you are finished designing the report and you want to run it, you have to swap out the DAO connection for the ODBC connection. This gets around the problem of not being able to run the report using DAO. If you haven't created the System DSN via the ODBC Administrator, then do so now. When the DSN has been created, right click on the report and select Database | Set Location. Within this dialog box, choose the System DSN you created as the new connection and click on Replace to swap it with the OLE DB connection.

---

[28] The ODBC is accessed via the Control Panel option found by clicking the Start button on the Windows taskbar.

Now you can run the report without being asked to enter logon credentials for the spreadsheet. Of course, once a service pack is released to fix the problem with DAO then this work-around won't be necessary.

Chapter 13

PART II
Programming Reports

Advanced report designers aren't satisfied with using the built-in functions to customize reports. They want to integrate their .NET applications with Crystal Reports during runtime. Part II shows you how to seamlessly integrate your reports into .NET with runtime customization of report objects and modifying parameters. Dynamic data connections let you connect to virtually any data source. For the most advanced reporting functionality, develop Report Web Services or upgrade to the stand-alone version of Crystal Reports and use .NET to program the RDC and the RAS. Part II shows you how to take your reporting skills to the expert level.

This page intentionally left blank

14

Learning the Report Object Models

Part I of this book taught the details of designing reports by laying out the report objects in the different report sections and connecting to data sources. When the report was finished, its design and layout stayed the same every time it was run. The data that it prints will change, but the report format is locked. With Crystal Reports .NET, reports have the flexibility to be dynamic. .NET programmers have full access to the properties of a report and the underlying report objects. These properties can be read and many of them can be written. You get the power to create a reporting solution that takes user input and customizes each report prior to printing it. This can range from changing the formatting of report objects, modifying the grouping and sorting, and changing the data source. The more you learn about runtime customization, the more you will find out what you can do. This chapter serves as the foundation for building your knowledge throughout the rest of the book.

The reason that you have so much power to modify reports is because .NET treats every report as an object-oriented class. The entire object model is exposed to your .NET program. Whether you program with VB.NET or C# isn't important. The object model can be accessed by any of the .NET languages.

There are three ways to use the Crystal Reports object model. The first is to use the ReportDocument class to reference virtually every class and property of the report. The second way is to use the methods and properties of the CrystalReportViewer control. When compared to the ReportDocument class, the viewer only has a small subset of properties and methods. The viewer lets you modify the properties that effect logging in to a data source, setting report parameters, and deciding which report to preview. The last way to work with the object model is to subscribe to the events that are triggered while the report is previewed and printed. These events are useful for knowing what part of the report is being looked at and what the user is doing. This chapter goes into detail on all three ways of working with the report classes.

If you have experience with Crystal Reports 8.5 Developer Edition, then you are probably familiar with modifying reports during runtime. One of the key features of the Developer Edition was that the Visual Studio 6.0 developer had a greater amount of control over the report during runtime. In fact, a developer could write an entire report from scratch during runtime! The report classes that come with .NET are not this sophisticated. While you do have a lot of flexibility with modifying an existing report, you are limited to using the existing report objects. You can't create new report objects nor can you change the fields that the current objects link to. If you want to create reports and add new report objects, you have to purchase a separate developer's license. However, this license is extremely expensive and is only practical for companies with a large budget.

Basic Customization

No matter what type of runtime customization you want to perform, there are three basic steps that you need to know. Customizing reports always starts with the same premise: declare and instantiate a ReportDocument object, modify its properties, and print or preview it.

Chapter 3 gave a thorough explanation of the different ways to integrate reports into an application (Strongly-Type versus Untyped). If you need a refresher, refer to the sections on binding reports for a discussion of the pros and cons of the different methods of binding reports.

Note

The code that implements runtime customization is the same for both WinForms development and ASP.NET applications. The ReportDocument class is used with both types of applications. ASP.NET will only be mentioned when special circumstances necessitate it.

Step 1: Declare and instantiate the ReportDocument object variable.

An object variable can either instatiate the report class directly (Strongly-Typed reports) or it can instantiate the ReportDocument class and then load the report into memory (Untyped reports). Since runtime customization requires the use of Strongly-Typed reports, the examples in this chapter will use this binding method.

Note

In the examples throughout this chapter and the rest of the book, the report class being referenced is called CrystalReport1. This is the default report name that is given by the report wizard. When you implement the sample code in your applications, replace the name CrystalReport1 with the class name of the report you want to print. All the code samples are generic and will work with every report.

```
'Declare and instantiate an object variable of the report class
Dim MyReport As New CrystalReport1
```

Step 2: Modify the properties of the report object.

After instantiating the report variable, all the properties and methods of the ReportDocument object are available to you. Set the properties that need to be modified. The different properties of the report object are explained throughout all the chapters in Part II of this book.

In this example, the record selection formula is changed. The report variable MyReport (from Step 1) is used to get a reference to the DataDefinition object and change its RecordSelectionFormula property.

```
MyReport.DataDefinition.RecordSelectionFormula = "{Orders.Order Date}>#01/01/2004#"
```

The above line of code is very simplistic for purposes of illustrating how to change a property of the ReportDocument class. Real applications aren't so simple and you can save yourself effort by using the same code in different projects. A lot of times you will find yourself taking a specific piece of code and rewriting it so that it can be generic enough to be used by multiple applications or put into a reporting library. In many of the examples in this book, I do this by writing a method that gets passed the report object and any necessary parameters. The method modifies the properties of the report object that was passed to it and exits. In these examples, the method's code will be shown but not the code that calls it. I won't repeat the code that declares and initializes the report variable and previews it. It is assumed that you know that these methods should be called after the report object is declared and initialized, but before previewing the report. If you need a refresher, you can refer back to this chapter.

Step 3: Print or preview the report.

To preview the report, pass the report variable to the viewer control. To print the report, call the PrintToPrinter() method of the report variable. To be consistent, my examples always preview the report. Thus, the sample code will assign the report variable to the viewer control.

```
CrystalReportViewer1.ReportSource = MyReport
```

Those three steps are always used for performing runtime customization. The next question you might be asking yourself is where to put the code. You can put this code anywhere in the form. If you want to load the form immediately and customize the report, put it in the Load() event. There are times that you are going to call this code after the user has entered various data that specifies how the report should be customized. If that's the case, put the code in response to the click event of an OK button that confirms they are finished inputting data. The following code sample shows you a complete code listing and it demonstrates where to put the code for calling a generic method to modify report properties.

Listing 14-1. A template for modifying reports.

```
Private Sub Form1_Load(ByVal sender As System.Object, _
    ByVal e As System.EventArgs) Handles MyBase.Load
    Dim MyReport As New CrystalReport1
    'Call all report modification code here.
    'As mentioned in Step 2 above, this can be a method that is passed the report variable.
    'For illustration purposes, I'm calling a generic method that changes
    'the report title. The code for ModifyTitle() isn't shown here.
    ModifyTitle(MyReport, "Runtime Demo")
    CrystalReportViewer1.ReportSource = MyReport
End Sub
```

If you are writing an ASP.NET application, this code can be put in the Page_Load() event. See Chapter 3 for more information about writing ASP.NET applications.

Note
All report customization must be done prior to previewing or printing the report. No changes are allowed once the report is generated. For example, you can't use .NET to change the way a field is formatted depending upon the current group value. Making dynamic report changes while the report is running requires writing formulas and using conditional formatting (discussed in Chapters 7, 8, and 9).

ASP.NET Template

Printing reports within an ASP.NET application requires a slightly different template than the Windows template shown in Listing 14-1. Reports shown on an ASP.NET page are unique in that each time the user moves to a new report page, the web page gets reloaded. If a report is resource intensive, then this can slow performance or tie up resources. For example, a report that connects to SQL Server will open a new connection each time the page is loaded. Fixing this problem requires saving the report to the Session collection and using the IsPostBack function.[29] When doing ASP.NET development, use the template in Listing 14-2 for optimizing reports.

Listing 14-2. Template for ASP.NET pages.

```
Private Sub Page_Load(ByVal sender As System.Object, ByVal e As System.EventArgs) Handles
MyBase.Load
    Dim MyReport As CrystalDecisions.CrystalReports.Engine.ReportDocument
```

---

[29] The Session object was typically avoided when doing ASP development. However, with ASP.NET, Microsoft has rewritten the Session object so that its memory problems have largely been done away with.

```
If Not IsPostBack Then
    MyReport = New CrystalReport1
    'Call all report modification code here.
    'For illustration purposes, I'm calling a generic method that changes
    'the report title. The code for ModifyTitle() isn't shown here.
    ModifyTitle(MyReport, "Runtime Demo")
    Session("MyReport") = MyReport
Else
    'Get the report object from the Session collection
    MyReport = CType(Session("MyReport"), CrystalDecisions.CrystalReports.Engine.ReportDocument)
End If
CrystalReportViewer1.ReportSource = MyReport
End Sub
```

Caution

The template modifies the report's properties after the ReportDocument is loaded into memory. If you later call the viewer's Refresh() method, the viewer loads the report back into memory again and loses all changes you made to the report. You will have to set the properties again.

If a report connects to an MS Access database, you might notice that the record lock file (.MDL) isn't released when the page unloads. If the report connects to SQL Server, then it leaves the connection open. This is because the connection is closed when the report is disposed of during .NET's garbage collection process. To dispose of an object when the page unloads, you have to force garbage collection during the Unload() event. Listing 14-3 shows how this is done.

Listing 14-3. Forcing garbage collection in an ASP.NET page.

```
Private Sub Page_Unload(ByVal sender As Object, ByVal e As System.EventArgs) Handles MyBase.Unload
    MyReport.Close()
    MyReport.Dispose()
    GC.Collect()
End Sub
```

There are a couple points of interest here. The first assumes that the MyReport object variable has been declared at the class level. The template shown in Listing 14-2 declares the MyReport object variable at the procedure level. This declaration will have to be moved to the class level. The second point is that if you are connecting to SQL Server and using VB.NET, this code doesn't work. Disposing the report object closes the connection to the database and you have to login again (thus defeating the purpose of Listing 14-2). You have to clean up resources on another web page. If you are using the C# listings shown at the end of this chapter, this code will work for SQL Server.

The ReportDocument Object

The ReportDocument class is the base class for all reports. Its properties give an application the ability to thoroughly examine all the report objects. Many of these properties, but not all of them, have write capabilities so that you can modify their values.

Each report is a class that inherits from the ReportDocument class. Figure 14-1 shows the Object Browser window with the class for a blank report, CrystalReport1. You can see that ReportClass is the base class for the report. This class is derived from the ReportDocument class. The members listed to the right of the figure belong to the ReportDocument class.

Figure 14-1. Object Browser view of the ReportDocument class.

The ReportDocument class has seven other classes that it references. Figure 14-2 shows the ReportDocument object model. The class thoroughly exposes all the objects of a report. Since the coverage is so broad and hits many topics covered in this book, the relevant classes are covered in different chapters. This chapter gives you an overview of all the classes and goes into detail on the two generic classes SummaryInfo class and ReportOptions class.

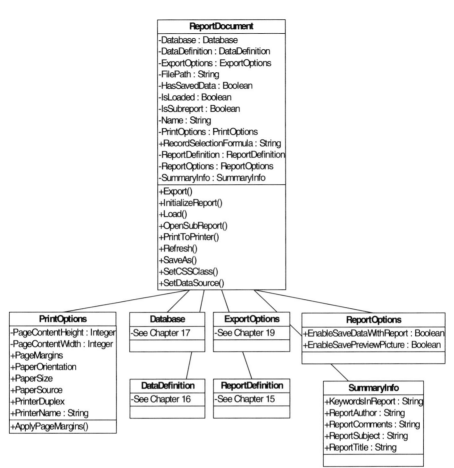

ReportDocument

-Database : Database
-DataDefinition : DataDefinition
-ExportOptions : ExportOptions
-FilePath : String
-HasSavedData : Boolean
-IsLoaded : Boolean
-IsSubreport : Boolean
-Name : String
-PrintOptions : PrintOptions
+RecordSelectionFormula : String
-ReportDefinition : ReportDefinition
-ReportOptions : ReportOptions
-SummaryInfo : SummaryInfo

+Export()
+InitializeReport()
+Load()
+OpenSubReport()
+PrintToPrinter()
+Refresh()
+SaveAs()
+SetCSSClass()
+SetDataSource()

PrintOptions

-PageContentHeight : Integer
-PageContentWidth : Integer
+PageMargins
+PaperOrientation
+PaperSize
+PaperSource
+PrinterDuplex
+PrinterName : String
+ApplyPageMargins()

Database

-See Chapter 17

ExportOptions

-See Chapter 19

ReportOptions

+EnableSaveDataWithReport : Boolean
+EnableSavePreviewPicture : Boolean

DataDefinition

-See Chapter 16

ReportDefinition

-See Chapter 15

SummaryInfo

+KeywordsInReport : String
+ReportAuthor : String
+ReportComments : String
+ReportSubject : String
+ReportTitle : String

Figure 14-2. The ReportDocument object model.

Every report in Visual Studio is saved as a class. Since it is a class, you have to declare an object variable and instantiate it. There are two ways to create this object variable. You can declare and instantiate it yourself, or you can add a ReportDocument component to your form. Both of these methods were discussed in Chapter 3. Either method gives you access to the properties of the object variable to manage the different collections.

Retrieving Summary Information

Every report has a variety of summary information saved with it. This information is set by the report designer and it usually consists of things such as the report author, the report title and report comments. This information is set during design mode by right-clicking on the report and selecting Report | Summary Info. The class that maintains this summary information is the SummaryInfo class. Although you can override the property values, more than likely, you will only want to read from these values. This information was set by the report designer and won't need to change during runtime. There are only a half dozen properties that this class exposes (see Table 14-1).

Table 14-1. Properties of the SummaryInfo class.

Property	Description
KeywordsInReport	The keywords in the report.
ReportAuthor	The author of the report.
ReportComments	Comments about the report.
ReportSubject	The subject of the report.
ReportTitle	The title of the report.

The following example displays a message box showing the author of a report. You can see that accessing these properties is very simple. CrystalReport1 is the class for a generic report. Replace it with the class name of your own report.

```
Dim MyReport As New CrystalReport1
MessageBox.Show(MyReport.SummaryInfo.ReportAuthor)
```

Setting the Report Options

The ReportOptions class only has a few properties that can be set. They are listed in Table 14-2. This information is set during design mode by right-clicking on the report and selecting Designer | Default Settings and selecting the Reporting tab. These properties were discussed in Chapter 2.

Table 14-2. Properties of the ReportOptions class.

Property	Description
EnableSaveDataWithReport	Saves the latest data with the report. Allows report to be opened without a live data connection.
EnableSavePreviewPicture	Saves a thumbnail picture of the report.
EnableSaveSummariesWithReport	Saves data summaries with the report.

The following example sets the EnableSaveDataWithReport property to True.

```
Dim MyReport As New CrystalReport1
MyReport.ReportOptions.EnableSaveDataWithReport = True
```

Connecting to the Data Sources

The Database class is used for examining the tables used in a report and their relationships with each other. It's also used for setting the login information before opening the report. This class is described in Chapter 17.

Modifying the Printing Options

The PrintOptions class stores the options for how a report is sent to the printer. This can consist of the destination printer, the paper orientation or the page margins. This is normally set during design mode. While the majority of an application's reports will use the same settings, you can override the default settings for specific reports. Table 14-3 lists the properties.

Table 14-3. PrintOptions properties.

Property	Description
PageMargins	Gets the page margins.
ApplyPageMargins()	Sets new page margins.
PaperOrientation	Switch between Landscape and Portrait.
PaperSize	Set the paper size using pre-defined size constants.
PaperSource	Set the tray that the paper is printed from.
PrinterName	Change the printer by passing a string that exactly matches the printer name listed in the Printers Control Panel.

Each of these properties is easy to modify. In same cases you will have to use a predefined constant to set the property (e.g. PaperOrientation and PaperSize).

Caution

Changing the printer name can cause the report output to be scrambled. Each printer uses a unique printer language for producing output. If the new printer doesn't use the same printer language as the default printer that the report was designed to use, then the report will not print correctly. For example, if a report was designed for use with an HP printer, then it is okay to switch between similar models of an HP printer. But printing this report to Acrobat PDFWriter will result in an unreadable PDF file.

Listing 14-4. Change a report's printer settings.

```
Dim MyReport As New CrystalReport1
MyReport.PrintOptions.PaperOrientation = CrystalDecisions.[Shared].PaperOrientation.Landscape
MyReport.PrintOptions.PrinterName = "HP LaserJet510"
MyReport.PrintToPrinter(1, False, 0, 0)
```

Exporting Reports

If your application only sends reports to the printer, it is lacking the functionality to make your data accessible to a variety of applications. Crystal Reports lets you export a report in many different formats so that different applications can read the data. For example, you can export report data to an Excel spreadsheet so that an end user can perform a statistical analysis on the data. The ExportOptions class has the properties that specify the exporting options. This is discussed in Chapter 19.

Referencing and Formatting the Report Objects

The ReportDefinition class is responsible for maintaining the collections of the basic report objects. These objects consist of the Areas collection, Sections collection and the ReportObjects class. Each Section class contains the report objects that are within that section. You can modify the formatting properties of any of these objects. This is discussed in Chapter 15.

Changing Report Objects

Every report can have many types of fields that are used to generate the report, but don't have to appear directly on the report. Some examples are grouping fields, parameter fields, and formula fields. Even though these fields may not be shown directly on the report, they are updateable during runtime and can be used to change the report's appearance. For example, you can change the grouping field so that the report sorts and summarizes in a new way. The DataDefinition class manages the collections that control these aspects of the report. These collections are discussed in the appropriate chapters throughout the book.

CrystalReportViewer Object Model

Previewing reports is done with the CrystalReportViewer control. The viewer can be used as an alternative to the ReportDocument class for modifying reports during runtime. It is a lightweight control and only exposes a few properties. You can use it when you only need want to perform basic tasks.

The viewer exposes three properties for modifying a report. The RecordSelection property filters the report data. The ParameterFieldInfo property is the ParameterFields collection (discussed in Chapter 16). The LogOnInfo property (discussed in Chapter 17) is a collection of TableLogOnInfo objects for setting the user credentials for each table. These collections are already found in the ReportDocument class, but they are provided in this class in case you don't need to work directly with the ReportDocument class.

CrystalReportViewer
+DisplayBackgroundEdge : boolean
+DisplayGroupTree : boolean
+DisplayToolbar : boolean
+EnableDrillDown : boolean
-LogOnInfo : TableLogonInfos
-ParameterFieldInfo : ParameterFields
+ReportSource
+RightToLeft
+SelectionFormula : String
+ShowCloseButton : boolean
+ShowExportButton : boolean
+ShowGotoPageButton : boolean
+ShowGroupTreeButton : boolean
+ShowPrintButton : boolean
+ShowRefreshButton : Border
+ShowTextSearchButton : boolean
+ShowZoomButton : boolean
-ViewCount : Integer
+CloseViews()
+DrillDownOnGroup()
+ExportReport()
+GetCurrentPageNumber()
+PrintReport()
+RefreshReport()
+SearchForText()
+ShowFirstPage()
+ShowGroupTree()
+ShowLastPage()
+ShowNthPage()
+ShowPreviousPage()
+Zoom()

Figure 14-3. The CrystalReportViewer object model.

Tip

I prefer making all runtime modifications using only the ReportDocument object and not the CrysalReportViewer control. It is by far the most robust of the two objects. By learning the ReportDocument properties and methods, you don't have to learn the viewer class. The only time you can't perform modifications with the ReportDocument object is when you are writing Report Web Services. This requires using the viewer object to make runtime modifications.

Responding to Events

Report classes are built with events that let you respond to the actions that the user is doing as they preview a report. Your application can subscribe to these events and be alerted when they occur. The events that can be subscribed to are primarily associated with the actions that a user takes while previewing a report. Since a user can only preview a report using the CrystalReportViewer, the events are written for this class. The ReportDocument class only has the InitReport() event that can be subscribed to. Table 14-4 lists the reporting related events.

> **Note**
>
> The CrystalReportViewer also has the standard events associated with all controls (e.g. Click, GotFocus, etc.) However, these are not unique to Crystal Reports, so if you need more information about them, please consult MSDN.

Table 14-4. The primary events for reports.

Event	Description
InitReport()	Fired after a report has been successfully loaded. This is the only event available for the ReportDocument class. This is not available for the CrystalReportViewer class.
Drill()	Fired when the user drills down on a field.
DrillDownSubReport()	Fired when the user drills down on a subreport.
HandleException()	Fired when an exception occurs.
Navigate()	Fired when a user moves to another page on the report.
ReportRefresh()	Fired when the user refreshes the report data.
Search()	Fired when the user enters a search string.
ViewZoom()	Fired when the user changes the zoom percentage.

The Drill() event is fired whenever a user clicks on a field to drill down on it. It passes an object of type DrillEventArgs. This object can be examined to find the group level the user is currently looking at as well as the new group level being moved to. Table 14-5 lists the properties of the DrillEventArgs event type.

Table 14-5. Properties of the DrillEventArgs event type.

Property	Description
CurrentGroupLevel	Returns an integer representing the current group level.
CurrentGroupName	Returns a string representing the name of the current group level.
NewGroupLevel	Returns an integer representing the new group level.
NewGroupName	Returns a string representing the group level name.

The DrillDownSubReport() event is similar to the Drill() event and it is fired when the user drills down on a subreport. Although the functionality is similar, this event passes an object of the DrillDownSubreportEventArgs type. It gives you information such as the subreport name and the page number. Table 14-6 lists the properties of this event type.

Table 14-6. Properties of the DrillDownSubreportEventArgs event type.

Property	Description
CurrentSubreportName	The name of the current subreport.
CurrentSubreportPageNumber	The page number that the subreport is on.
CurrentSubreportPosition	Returns a Point object that tells the position of the subreport on the viewer.
Handled	Set to true if you do not want the subreport to be drilled down to.
NewSubreportName	The name of the new subreport.
NewSubreportPageNumber	Sets the page number to drill down into.
NewSubreportPosition	Returns a Point object that tells the position of the new subreport on the viewer.

The HandleException() event is used for capturing exceptions and handling them. This is discussed in detail in the section Handling Exceptions.

The Navigate() event is fired when the user moves to another page in the report. This can be done by paging forward through the report or jumping to the beginning or end of the report. Table 14-7 lists the properties for the NavigateEventArgs event type.

Table 14-7. Properties of the NavigateEventArgs event type.

Property	Description
CurrentPageNumber	The page number that the report is on.
Handled	Set to True if you do not want to move to the new page.
NewPageNumber	The page number that the user is moving to.

The ReportRefresh() event is fired when the user refreshes the report data. The only property for this event is the Handled property. It is the same as the other events.

The Search() event is fired when the user searches for text within the report. Table 14-8 lists the properties for this event type.

Table 14-8. Properties of the SearchEventArgs event type.

Property	Description
Direction	Gets or sets the direction to be backward or forward. Use a variable of the SearchDirection type.
Handled	Set to True if you do not want to search for the text.
PageNumberToBeginSearch	Gets or sets the page number to start searching.
TextToSearch	Gets or sets the string to search for.

The ViewZoom() event is fired when the user changes the zoom level of the preview image. This event lets you find out the current zoom level and what the new zoom level will be. Table 14-9 lists the properties for this event type.

Table 14-9. Properties of the ZoomEventArgs event type.

Property	Description
CurrentZoomFactor	Gets the current zoom factor.
Handled	Set to true if you do not want to change the zoom factor.
NewZoomFactor	Gets the new zoom factor.

Handling Exceptions

Crystal Reports gives you the ability to handle any errors that might occur while printing and previewing. The benefit to handling the error yourself is that you can customize the error handling process. For example, you could write the error to a log file or you can gracefully exit the process without throwing an error message at the user.

The CrystalReportViewer class has a HandleException() event that you can subscribe to. It is fired whenever an error occurs. This event has properties to tell you the exception class that was raised and lets you specify a new text message for the error. Table 14-10 lists the properties for the ExceptionEventArgs() type.

Table 14-10. Properties of the ExceptionEventArgs event type.

Property	Description
Exception	The class of exception that was raised.
Handled	Set to True if you do not want to the error triggered.
UserData	Overrides the error message.

Unfortunately, the HandleException() event is not available if you are using the ReportDocument class. If you are printing a report directly with the ReportDocument class, there is no error-related event that you subscribe to. You have to use the standard Try-Catch error handling statements that you use for the rest of your application.

```
Try
    Dim myReport As New CrystalReport1()
    myReport.PrintToPrinter(1, False, 0, 0)
Catch
    ... do error handling here
End Try
```

C# Code Listings

The C# code listings are equivalent to the VB.NET code listings.

Listing 14-1. A template for modifying reports.

```
private void Form1_Load(object sender, System.EventArgs e)
{
    CrystalReport1 MyReport = new CrystalReport1();
    //Call all report modification code here.
    //For illustration purposes, I'm calling a generice method that changes the report title.
    //The code for ModifyTitle() isn't shown here.
    ModifyTitle(MyReport, "Runtime Demo");
    crystalReportViewer1.ReportSource = MyReport;
}
```

Listing 14-2. Template for ASP.NET pages.

```
private void Page_Load(object sender, System.EventArgs e)
{
    CrystalDecisions.CrystalReports.Engine.ReportDocument MyReport;
    if (!IsPostBack) {
        MyReport = new CrystalReport1();
        //Call all report modification code here.
        //For illustration purposes, I'm calling a generice method that changes the report title.
        //The code for ModifyTitle() isn't shown here.
        ModifyTitle(MyReport, "Runtime Demo");
        Session["MyReport"] = MyReport;
    } else {
        MyReport = (CrystalDecisions.CrystalReports.Engine.ReportDocument)Session["MyReport"];
    }
    CrystalReportViewer1.ReportSource = MyReport;
}
```

Listing 14-3. Forcing garbage collection in an ASP.NET page.

```
private void WebForm1_Init(object sender, System.EventArgs e)
{
    if (MyReport!=null) {
        MyReport.Close();
        MyReport.Dispose();
        GC.Collect();
    }
}
```

Listing 14-4. Change a report's printer settings.

```
CrystalReport1 MyReport = new CrystalReport1();
MyReport.PrintOptions.PaperOrientation = CrystalDecisions.Shared.PaperOrientation.Landscape;
MyReport.PrintOptions.PrinterName = "HP LasterJet510";
MyReport.PrintToPrinter(1, false, 0, 0);
```

Runtime Customization

This chapter builds on the basic report customization shown in Chapter 14. It focuses on working with the DataDefinition and ReportDefinition classes. The DataDefinition class controls Record selection, Grouping and Sorting, and Parameters/Formulas.[30] The ReportDefinition class handles the functionality for report sections, grouping/sorting and running totals. With respect to the number of objects contained within it, an object variable of the ReportDefinition type is the largest report object by far. It manages the collection objects for all the areas, sections, and report objects within a report.

If you learn best by seeing sample code, this chapter is for you!

Modifying the Record Selection

There are two types of record selection formulas. The first type selects records based upon data that is available during the first-pass stage. This consists of raw data and fields/formulas that don't use summary information. The second type of formula is a group selection formula that is based on second-pass data (e.g. summary fields and subtotals). Selecting records during the first-pass is done with the RecordsSelectionFormula property. Figure 15-1 shows the properties that modify the record selection formulas.

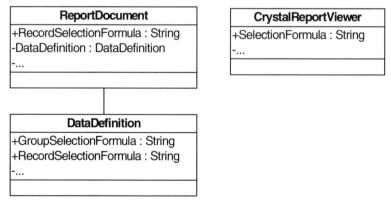

Figure 15-1. Properties used in selecting records.

---

[30] Parameters are discussed in Chapter 16.

The record selection formula is modified in two places: the ReportDocument class and the DataDefinition class. The properties are identical and you can use either class. Setting the group selection is done with the GroupSelectionFormula and it is only found in the DataDefinition class.

Modifying the record selection formulas is one of the easiest runtime changes to make to a report. The selection formula is a string and all you have to do is assign a new string to it. The formula syntax must be Crystal syntax. Basic syntax isn't allowed for selection formulas. The following code listings set the formulas to filter on records that are within a certain date range. The listings demonstrate making the change with the DataDefinition class as well as the CrystalReportViewer class.

Listing 15-1. Changing the selection formula via the ReportDocument.

```
Dim myReport As New CrystalReport1()
MyReport.DataDefinition.RecordSelectionFormula = _
"{Orders.Order Date} in Date (1996, 02, 19) to Date (1996, 03, 28)"
CrystalReportViewer1.ReportSource = myReport
```

Listing 15-2. Changing the selection formula with the viewer control.

```
Dim myReport As New CrystalReport1()
CrystalReportViewer1.ReportSource = myReport
CrystalReportViewer1.SelectionFormula = _
"{Orders.Order Date} in Date (1996, 02, 19) to Date (1996, 03, 28)"
```

Mapping the ReportDefinition Classes

The ReportDefinition class manages everything printed on a report. It has collection classes for storing each area, section, and object shown on the report. You can map out every detail about your report. Leaning how to map these collections teaches you how they are organized. This is necessary for learning how to modify the individual report objects.

Figure 15-2 shows the object model for the ReportDefinition classes. It uses three collections for managing the objects: Areas, Sections and ReportObjects. You can see that the class tree is only a couple levels deep and that each collection is similar to the others. This makes them easy to understand.

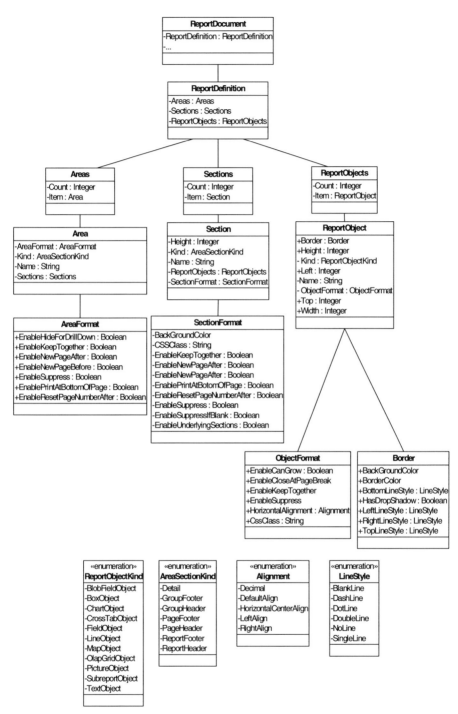

Figure 15-2. The ReportDefinition object model.

The Areas collection stores the Area object. This Area object has a property that lets you access its formatting properties. The Sections collection class stores the Section object. The ReportObjects collection manages the ReportObject object. It is the final object in the object model and it only has formatting properties.

Each of the collections can be referenced directly or through its parent collection. For example you can go directly to each report object via the ReportObjects collection. You can also reference each report object via the section it is in. Each Section object has a ReportObjects collection that references just the report objects that are within that section.

Mapping out the report objects consists of looping through each collection and printing out the properties of each object. To be concise, this code only prints a few properties for each object. If you want to modify the code to print more properties, you can look at the object model to see the names of the additional properties and add them.

The sample program is a Windows program that uses a listbox, lstMapping, for the output. Each property is printed as a string in the listbox. Indentation is used to offset the object from its properties so that it is easier to read. Notice that all the parameters and variables are declared using the full namespace. You can see that this is quite lengthy and that the code could be shortened considerably by using the VB.NET Imports (or C# using) statement at the beginning of the program. However, in this book I always use the full namespace for learning purposes. The program also uses a generic Output() procedure for printing this information. This makes it easy for you to modify the program so that it can fit your needs. You could modify the code to save it an XML file or print to a console window.

Listing 15-3. Mapping the ReportDefinition object model.

```
Private Sub Form1_Load(ByVal sender As System.Object, _
    ByVal e As System.EventArgs) Handles MyBase.Load
    Dim MyReport As CrystalDecisions.CrystalReports.Engine.ReportDocument
    MyReport = New CrystalReport1()
    MapAreas(MyReport.ReportDefinition.Areas, 0)
End Sub
Sub MapAreas(ByVal Areas As _
    CrystalDecisions.CrystalReports.Engine.Areas, ByVal Indent As Integer)
    Dim Area As CrystalDecisions.CrystalReports.Engine.Area
    For Each Area In Areas
        MapArea(Area, Indent)
    Next
End Sub
Sub MapSections(ByVal Sections As _
    CrystalDecisions.CrystalReports.Engine.Sections, ByVal Indent As Integer)
    Dim Section As CrystalDecisions.CrystalReports.Engine.Section
    For Each Section In Sections
        MapSection(Section, Indent)
```

```
      Next
  End Sub
  Sub MapReportObjects(ByVal ReportObjects As _
      CrystalDecisions.CrystalReports.Engine.ReportObjects, _
      ByVal Indent As Integer)
      Dim ReportObject As CrystalDecisions.CrystalReports.Engine.ReportObject
      For Each ReportObject In ReportObjects
          MapReportObject(ReportObject, Indent + 2)
      Next
  End Sub
  Sub MapArea(ByVal Area As CrystalDecisions.CrystalReports.Engine.Area, _
      ByVal Indent As Integer)
      Dim Section As CrystalDecisions.CrystalReports.Engine.Section
      'Print the Area properties
      Output("Area: " & Area.Name, Indent)
      Output("Kind: " & Area.Kind.ToString, Indent + 2)
      Output("Suppress: " & Area.AreaFormat.EnableSuppress.ToString, Indent + 2)
      Output("Keep Together: " & Area.AreaFormat.EnableKeepTogether.ToString, _
          Indent + 2)
      For Each Section In Area.Sections
          MapSection(Section, Indent + 2)
      Next
  End Sub
  Sub MapSection(ByVal Section As _
      CrystalDecisions.CrystalReports.Engine.Section, ByVal Indent As Integer)
      Dim ReportObject As CrystalDecisions.CrystalReports.Engine.ReportObject
      'Print the Section properties
      Output("Section: " & Section.Name, Indent)
      Output("Suppress: " & _
      Section.SectionFormat.EnableSuppress.ToString, Indent + 2)
      Output("Keep Together: " & _
      Section.SectionFormat.EnableKeepTogether.ToString, Indent + 2)
      For Each ReportObject In Section.ReportObjects
          MapReportObject(ReportObject, Indent + 2)
      Next
  End Sub
  Sub MapReportObject(ByVal ReportObject As _
      CrystalDecisions.CrystalReports.Engine.ReportObject, _
      ByVal Indent As Integer)
      'Explicitly cast the ReportObject as its native data type
      Select Case ReportObject.Kind
          Case CrystalDecisions.[Shared].ReportObjectKind.TextObject
              MapTextObject(CType(ReportObject, _
              CrystalDecisions.CrystalReports.Engine.TextObject), Indent)
          Case CrystalDecisions.[Shared].ReportObjectKind.FieldObject
              MapFieldObject(CType(ReportObject, _
              CrystalDecisions.CrystalReports.Engine.FieldObject), Indent)
      End Select
  End Sub
```

```
Sub MapTextObject(ByVal TextObject As _
   CrystalDecisions.CrystalReports.Engine.TextObject, _
   ByVal Indent As Integer)
   Output("Name: " & TextObject.Name, Indent)
   Output("Kind: " & TextObject.Kind.ToString(), Indent + 2)
   Output("Text: " & TextObject.Text, Indent + 2)
End Sub
   Sub MapFieldObject(ByVal FieldObject As _
   CrystalDecisions.CrystalReports.Engine.FieldObject, _
   ByVal Indent As Integer)
   Output("Name: " & FieldObject.Name, Indent)
   Output("Kind: " & FieldObject.Kind.ToString(), Indent + 2)
   Output("DataSource.Name: " & FieldObject.DataSource.Name, Indent + 2)
   Output("DataSource.Formula: " & FieldObject.DataSource.FormulaName, _
   Indent + 2)
End Sub
Sub Output(ByVal Line As String, ByVal Indent As Integer)
   lstMapping.Items.Add(New String(" "c, Indent) & Line)
End Sub
```

Most of this code is pretty simple. It consists of procedures that use For Each
loops to traverse a collection. While traversing the collection, the object's
properties are printed and if there is a sub-collection then that is traversed as
well.

There are some interesting aspects of the code that need to be explored. Notice
that there are three main mapping procedures: MapAreas, MapSections, and
MapReportObjects. These directly correspond to the three distinct collections of
the ReportDefinition class. The top-most collection is the Areas collection. This
collection can be used to reference the Sections collection, which is used to
reference the ReportObjects collection. But when you look at the object model
previously shown in Figure 15-2, these collections each have their own
property in the ReportDefinition class. Thus, you can also go directly to the
Sections or ReportObjects collections.

This example uses the form's Load() event to call the MapAreas() procedure so
that you can see how the entire object hierarchy is mapped out. But you can
isolate the individual collections by replacing the MapAreas() call with a call to
either MapSections() or MapReportObjects().

The MapReportObject() procedure (near the end of the listing) also deserves
mentioning. The ReportObject class isn't used to represent any actual objects on
your report. Instead, it is the base class for those objects. You have to explicitly
cast the object as the proper data type before working with it. The actual report
objects are shown in Figure 15-3. They are all very similar to each other, and
some properties are even repeated. But each one has at least a few properties
that make it unique from the other classes.

FieldObject
+Border
+Color
-DataSource : FieldDefinition
-FieldFormat
+Font
+Height : Integer
-Kind : ReportObjectKind
+Left : Integer
-Name : String
+ObjectFormat : ObjectFormat
+Top : Integer
+Width : Integer
+ApplyFont()

FieldDefinition
-FormulaName : String
-Kind : FieldKind
-Name : String
-ValueType : FieldValueType

BlobFieldObject
+Border
-DataSource : FieldDefinition
+Height : Integer
-Kind : ReportObjectKind
+Left : Integer
-Name : String
+ObjectFormat : ObjectFormat
+Top : Integer
+Width : Integer

TextObject
+Border
+Color
- Font
+Height : Integer
- Kind : ReportObjectKind
+Left : Integer
-Name : String
+ObjectFormat : ObjectFormat
+Top : Integer
+Width : Integer
+Text : String
+ApplyFont()

SubreportObject
+Border
+EnableOnDemand : Boolean
+Height : Integer
-Kind : ReportObjectKind
+Left : Integer
-Name : String
+ObjectFormat : ObjectFormat
+Top : Integer
+Width : Integer
+OpenSubreport()

LineObject
+Border
+EnableExtendToBottomOfSection : Boolean
+EndSectionName : String
+Height : Integer
-Kind : ReportObjectKind
+Left : Integer
+LineColor
+LineStyle : LineStyle
+LineThickness : Integer
-Name : String
+ObjectFormat : ObjectFormat
+Top : Integer
+Width : Integer

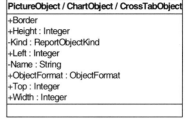

PictureObject / ChartObject / CrossTabObject
+Border
+Height : Integer
-Kind : ReportObjectKind
+Left : Integer
-Name : String
+ObjectFormat : ObjectFormat
+Top : Integer
+Width : Integer

BoxObject
+Border
+EnableExtendToBottomOfSection : Boolean
+EndSectionName : String
+FillColor
+Height : Integer
-Kind : ReportObjectKind
+Left : Integer
+LineColor
+LineStyle : LineStyle
+LineThickness : Integer
-Name : String
+ObjectFormat : ObjectFormat
+Top : Integer
+Width : Integer

Figure 15-3. The report classes that inherit from the ReportObject class.

When mapping out the report objects, there is no immediate way to know what type of object is being referenced. Fortunately, the ReportObject class has a property that identifies this. The Kind property tells you what type of object it is. The MapReporObject() procedure uses a Select Case statement to determine what type of report object it is and then calls the proper mapping procedure. When it calls the mapping procedure, the report object variable is cast as the proper class within the parameter list. This listing only shows the code for mapping the TextObject and the FieldObject, but it is simple to add the other objects if you wish.

Let's run this program on a sample report. I made a few changes to the label report from Chapter 6. The names of the sections were changed so that they are descriptive. By default, when you create a report the section names are given generic names such as Section1, Section2, etc. Since the Crystal Reports designer prints a section description next to the section name, this normally isn't a problem. But the mapping example prints out raw text and doesn't have the designer available, so the names were changed to make it easier to read the output. The changes to the section names are shown in Figure 15-4. The area names can't be changed, so they will always use the generic naming convention.

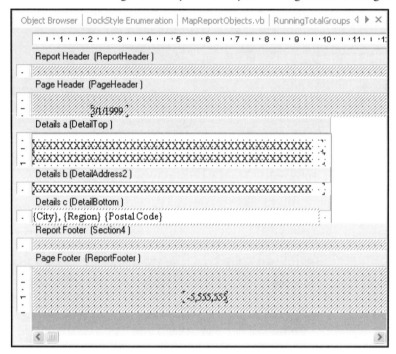

Figure 15-4. The report designer for the labels report.

This example is fairly simple so that most of the important output can be shown here. Most of the sections simply show a text box that represents a field of the customer's address. The different headers and footers are suppressed so that only the Detail sections are shown. There are three Detail sections and they are all part of the same area. Thus, the output should show a single Area object with three detail sections listed.

The section DetailBottom is a text field that is composed of three fields and a comma to separate the City from the Region[31]. When you look at this field in the example's output, it only shows a comma. Thus, the actual composition of

---

[31] Normally, this is shown in the designer as "XXXXX". But for the illustration I double-clicked on it so that it would be placed in edit mode. This lets you see how the field is composed.

the field is stored in an internal format that you can't access. This is shown near
the bottom of the output.

```
Area: Area1
  Kind: ReportHeader
  Suppress: False
  Keep Together: False
  Section: ReportHeader
    Suppress: True
    Keep Together: True
Area: Area2
  Kind: PageHeader
  Suppress: False
  Keep Together: True
  Section: PageHeader
    Suppress: True
    Keep Together: True
    Name: Field5
      Kind: FieldObject
      DataSource.Name: PrintDate
      DataSource.Formula: PrintDate
Area: Area3
  Kind: Detail
  Suppress: False
  Keep Together: False
  Section: DetailTop
    Suppress: False
    Keep Together: True
    Name: Field9
      Kind: FieldObject
      DataSource.Name: Name
      DataSource.Formula: {@Name}
    Name: Field10
      Kind: FieldObject
      DataSource.Name: Address1
      DataSource.Formula: {Employee_Addresses.Address
  Section: DetailAddress2
    Suppress: False
    Keep Together: True
    Name: Field11
      Kind: FieldObject
      DataSource.Name: Address2
      DataSource.Formula: {Employee_Addresses.Address
  Section: DetailBottom
    Suppress: False
    Keep Together: True
    Name: Text1
      Kind: TextObject
      Text: ,
Area: Area4
  Kind: ReportFooter
```

Figure 15-5. Mapping the objects of the the label report.

Programming ReportDefinition Objects

The ReportDefinition classes are used for modifying all the report objects. With
every object, you can modify the formatting properties to change its
appearance. Some of the objects such as the TextObject and FieldObject, can
have their content modified. This isn't the case for every report object. This

section shows you how to get a reference to the report object and how to modify its properties.

Before learning the details of the ReportDefinition object, you need to understand the limitations. First of all, the object model is designed so that you can modify the objects, but not add new ones. In other words, none of the collections have an Add() method. For example, if your report has two text objects, you are free to change what they display, but you can't add any additional text objects.

Secondly, not all properties can be modified. Flip back at Figures 15-2 and 15-3. The properties with a + next to them are read-write. The properties with a - are read-only. As you can see, most properties are read-only. Although you can't modify everything, many important properties can be changed.

Referencing the Report Objects

To modify any of the objects, declare an object variable of the proper data type and have it reference the report object. Referencing the report object is done by passing the object name to the Item property of the collection and assigning this to the object variable. Of course, use the appropriate collection to get a reference to the object you want. Don't try to reference a Section object with the Areas() collection.

Listing 15-4. Get a reference to the ReportFooter section.

```
Dim myReport As New CrystalReport1()
Dim mySection As CrystalDecisions.CrystalReports.Engine.Section
mySection = myReport.ReportDefinition.Sections.Item("ReportFooter")
```

Report object variables can be declared as either the ReportObject base class or the classes for the specific object (e.g. TextObject, BoxObject, etc.) The benefit to using the object's specific class is that you have access to its unique properties. The ReportObject class has generic properties that apply to all the report objects, but not to the specific ones.

Listing 15-5. Get a reference to the report object State using the ReportObject data type.

```
Dim myReport As New CrystalReport1()
Dim myObject As CrystalDecisions.CrystalReports.Engine.ReportObject
myObject = myReport.ReportDefinition.ReportObjects.Item("State")
```

Listing 15-6. Get a reference to the State object using the object's specific data type.

```
Dim MyReport As New CrystalReport1()
Dim MyField As CrystalDecisions.CrystalReports.Engine.FieldObject
MyField = CType(MyReport.ReportDefinition.ReportObjects.Item("State"), _
CrystalDecisions.CrystalReports.Engine.FieldObject)
```

Referencing a section can be a little tricky because you might use the wrong name for it. When you look at the report in design mode, a section appears to have two names. The first name is a description of the section (e.g. Page Header, Details, etc.) but this isn't the name that it's referenced by. It's simply a description so that you know what the purpose of the section is. Right after the description is the name enclosed in parentheses: Page Header (Section2). In this example, Section2 is the name that you should use when referencing the section from the Sections collection. You will also see the section name listed in the properties window under the Name property.

Modifying the Report Object Properties

The Area class and Section class have similar properties to each other. You can enable or disable formatting properties such as suppressing the object, keeping the object on the same page, and printing it at the bottom of the page. The difference between the two is that every section has to be within an area. Any formatting done to the area will affect all the sections within the area. But formatting done to a section will not affect the area it is in. Nor will other sections in the area be affected.

The ReportObject class is the base class for the objects that are used in a report. It has some of the basic formatting options that are common to all objects. For example, there are properties in the class for changing the objects positioning on the report. You can modify the Top and Left properties as well as the Left and Width properties. You can also modify the object's border using the Border property and its various Enable related options (Suppress, KeepTogether, etc.) using the ObjectFormat property.

To modify the properties that are unique to an individual report object, the object variable must be declared as the proper data type. For example, declaring an object variable of the type LineObject lets you modify the LineThickness property. Assign the report object to the variable by explicitly casting it as the proper data type. The next few examples demonstrate modifying different objects on a report.

Listing 15-7. Modify properties of the ReportFooter section.

```
Dim myReport As New CrystalReport1()
Dim mySection As CrystalDecisions.CrystalReports.Engine.Section
mySection = myReport.ReportDefinition.Sections.Item("ReportFooter")
mySection.SectionFormat.EnableKeepTogether = True
```

```
mySection.SectionFormat.EnableSuppress = False
CrystalReportViewer1.ReportSource = MyReport
```

Listing 15-8. Modify the border of the report object State using the ReportObject data type.

```
Dim myReport As New CrystalReport1()
Dim myObject As CrystalDecisions.CrystalReports.Engine.ReportObject
myObject = myReport.ReportDefinition.ReportObjects.Item("State")
myObject.Border.TopLineStyle = CrystalDecisions.[Shared].LineStyle.SingleLine
myObject.Border.BottomLineStyle = CrystalDecisions.[Shared].LineStyle.DoubleLine
CrystalReportViewer1.ReportSource = MyReport
```

Listing 15-9. Modify the line properties of the object Line using the object's specific data type.

```
Dim myReport As New CrystalReport1()
Dim myLine As CrystalDecisions.CrystalReports.Engine.LineObject
myLine = CType(myReport.ReportDefinition.ReportObjects.Item("Line1"), _
CrystalDecisions.CrystalReports.Engine.LineObject)
myLine.LineStyle = CrystalDecisions.[Shared].LineStyle.DashLine
CrystalReportViewer1.ReportSource = MyReport
```

The TextObject lets you modify the content that an object displays on the report. It has a Text property that sets what is displayed. Simply assign a string to it to change its contents.

Listing 15-10. Modify the Text property of a TextObject located in ReportHeader.

```
Dim myReport As New CrystalReport1()
Dim myText As CrystalDecisions.CrystalReports.Engine.TextObject
myText = CType(myReport.ReportDefinition.ReportObjects.Item("HeaderText"), _
CrystalDecisions.CrystalReports.Engine.TextObject)
myText.Text = "New Report Header"
CrystalReportViewer1.ReportSource = MyReport
```

The FieldObject object is used to print fields from a data source. You can't modify it. The DataSource property is a FieldDefinition class and this is where the content is stored. Unfortunately, it is a read-only property and you aren't allowed to modify it. This applies to database fields, running totals, summary fields, etc. The only way to modify these fields is to base them off of a formula and modify that formula during runtime. This is discussed in Chapter 16.

Grouping and Sorting Data

The Crystal Reports object model lets you examine how a report is sorted, grouped and what type of data is summarized. You can change many of these properties prior to running the report.

Since the sorting and grouping features of a report are so closely related, it makes sense that their classes are also closely related. Within these classes there is overlap because grouping is an advanced form of sorting. Grouping has more features and within each group you have to sort the records that it prints. The respective classes for sorting and grouping are shown in Figure 15-6.

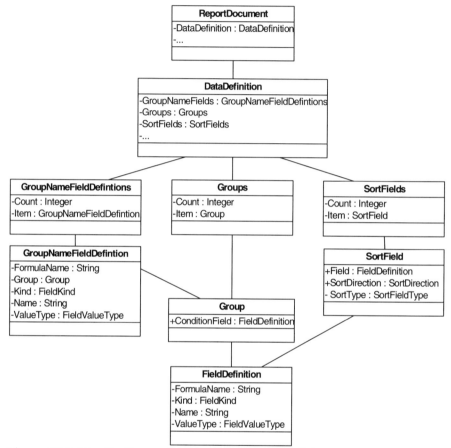

Figure 15-6. The Sorting and Grouping object model.

Many of the classes have properties that are enumeration constants. These are documented in Figure 15-7.

«enumeration» FieldKind	«enumeration» FieldValueType	«enumeration» SortFieldType	«enumeration» SortDirection
-DatabaseField	-BitmapField	-GroupSortField	-AscendingOrder
-FormulaField	-BlobField	-RecordSortField	-BottomNOrder
-GroupFieldName	-BooleanField		-DescendingOrder
-ParameterField	-ChartField		-TopNOrder
-RunningTotalField	-CurrencyField		
-SpecialVarField	-DataField		
-SQLExpressionField	-DateTimeField		
-SummaryField	-IconField		
	-Int32Field		
	-NumberField		
	-OleField		
	-StringField		
	-TimeField		

Figure 15-7. Sorting and Grouping enumeration constants.

Sorting and grouping are both based on one thing: a field. The field determines what the sort order is and how the records are grouped. Whether this field is a report field, database field or a formula field isn't important. But without a field you can't have sorting or grouping. Thus, the field classes are shared throughout the class diagram and you need to understand how they are organized before you can work with sorting and grouping.

The ReportDocument.DataDefinition class has the collections that manage the sorting and grouping fields. Groups are managed with the Groups collection and the GroupNameFieldDefinitions collection. The primary means of working with these collections is by using a For Each loop.

The sort fields are referenced using the SortFields collection. The SortFields collection is a property of the DataDefinition object. Navigate through this collection using a For Each loop.

The SortFields collection stores SortField objects. The SortField object has properties that determine the sort field, sort direction, and whether it represents a simple record sort or a group. The SortField class is defined in the namespace CrystalDecisions.CrystalReports.Engine.

An interesting aspect about the SortFields collection is that it assigns a SortField object for each group in the report. This is because group fields have to be sorted prior to determining what order the groups are printed in.

The grouping fields are referenced using two collections: Groups and GroupNameFieldDefinitions. These collections are a property of the DataDefinition object. Navigate through these collections using a For Each loop.

Both group collections have properties for storing the object's name, the formula, the data type and whether it is a report field, formula field, etc. Since both collections give you the same information, the one you decide to use is more of a personal preference than a hard and fast rule. Each collection has its own pros and cons.

The GroupNameFieldDefinitions collection gives you more direct access to the group properties (e.g. the name, field kind, etc.). However, this collection has a lot of redundancy in it because it also has a reference to the Group object. Within the Group object is the ConditionField object and this object gives you the same information already in the GroupFieldNameDefinition object.

The Groups collection is pretty simple because it only references the Group object. Each Group object has all the information that you need and there is no redundancy. Another benefit is that the FieldDefinition class is the same class used to map the report fields and formula fields. This lets you quickly change the fields that a group is based on. You can also do this with the GroupNameFieldDefinitions collection, but not as direct.

To keep things simple, I will only use the Groups collection to work with the group objects. If you prefer to use the GroupNameFieldDefinitions collection, it is easy to modify the sample code.

Mapping the Grouping and Sorting Objects

To learn how to use the different sorting and grouping classes, let's start with some generic procedures that traverse the collections in a report and print out the various properties. The code isn't very complicated because it primarily consists of For Each loops to traverse the collection objects and print out the properties of each object. The important part is to look at which collections manage which objects and see how the object variables are declared.

Listing 15-11. Mapping the sorting and grouping objects.[32]

```
Private Sub Form1_Load(ByVal sender As System.Object, _
    ByVal e As System.EventArgs) Handles MyBase.Load
    Dim MyReport As New CrystalReport1()
    MapSortFields(myReport.DataDefinition.SortFields, 0)
    Output("-----", 0)
    MapGroups(MyReport.DataDefinition.Groups, 0)
End Sub
Sub MapSortFields(ByVal SortFields As _
    CrystalDecisions.CrystalReports.Engine.SortFields, _
    ByVal Indent As Integer)
    Dim SortField As CrystalDecisions.CrystalReports.Engine.SortField
    Output("Total SortFields: " & SortFields.Count, Indent)
    For Each SortField In SortFields
        MapSortField(SortField, Indent)
```

---

[32] The sample code only prints out a few of the properties for each object. This example is not meant to be comprehensive.

```
        Next
    End Sub
    Sub MapSortField(ByVal SortField As _
        CrystalDecisions.CrystalReports.Engine.SortField, _
        ByVal Indent As Integer)
        MapFieldDefinition(SortField.Field, Indent)
        Output("Direction:" & SortField.SortDirection.ToString, Indent + 2)
        Output("Type:      " & SortField.SortType.ToString(), Indent + 2)
    End Sub
    Sub MapGroups(ByVal Groups As _
        CrystalDecisions.CrystalReports.Engine.Groups, ByVal Indent As Integer)
        Dim Group As CrystalDecisions.CrystalReports.Engine.Group
        Output("Total Groups: " & Groups.Count, Indent)
        For Each Group In Groups
            MapGroup(Group, Indent)
        Next
    End Sub
    Sub MapGroup(ByVal Group As CrystalDecisions.CrystalReports.Engine.Group, _
        ByVal Indent As Integer)
        MapFieldDefinition(Group.ConditionField, Indent)
    End Sub
    Sub MapFieldDefinition(ByVal FieldDefintion As CrystalDecisions. _
        CrystalReports.Engine.FieldDefinition, ByVal Indent As Integer)
        Output("Field Name: " & FieldDefintion.Name, Indent)
        Output("Formula:" & FieldDefintion.FormulaName, Indent + 2)
        Output("Kind:      " & FieldDefintion.Kind.ToString(), Indent + 2)
        Output("Value Type: " & FieldDefintion.ValueType.ToString(), Indent + 2)
    End Sub
    Sub Output(ByVal Line As String, ByVal Indent As Integer)
        lstMapping.Items.Add(New String(" "c, Indent) & Line)
    End Sub
```

Mapping the properties of the sort objects is done by instantiating the report object and passing the DataDefinition.SortFields collection to the MapSortFields() procedure. This procedure prints the number of sort fields in the collection and then traverses the collection. It calls MapSortFields() which then calls MapSortField() for each object in the SortFields collection. The MapSortField() procedure calls the MapFieldDefinition() procedure to print out the details of the field object. Then it prints the sort direction and whether this is a group sort or a record sort.

Mapping the properties of the group classes is done by instantiating the report object and passing the DataDefinition.Groups collection to the MapGroups() procedure. This procedure prints the number of groups in the report and then traverses the collection. The MapGroups() procedure then calls the MapGroup() procedure for each group object. The Group object has one property, ConditionField, which is of type FieldDefinition. So the MapGroup() procedure only calls the MapFieldDefinition() procedure to print out the properties of the field.

To see the output created by this program, I created a simple report.[33] The report is a sales report that prints the order detail from the Extreme.mdb database. It prints all the orders for each month. The group field is the Order Date and it groups the date by month. The most recent month is printed first, so a descending sort order is used. Within each group, the details of the order for each product are shown. These records are sorted by order date. Thus, the order date is being used in two different ways. The groups are sorted by month in a descending fashion and the detail records are sorted by the individual order date in an ascending order. Figure 15-8 shows the report designer and Figure 15-9 shows the report preview.

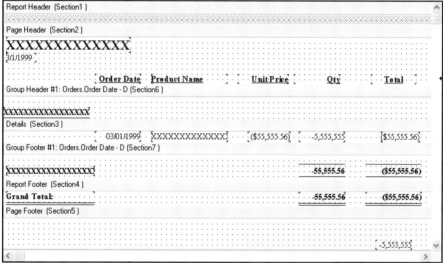

Figure 15-8. The Sales Report in the report designer.

---

[33] I'm not going into the details of how to create the sample report. The important part is to understand the general structure of the report so that the program's output makes sense.

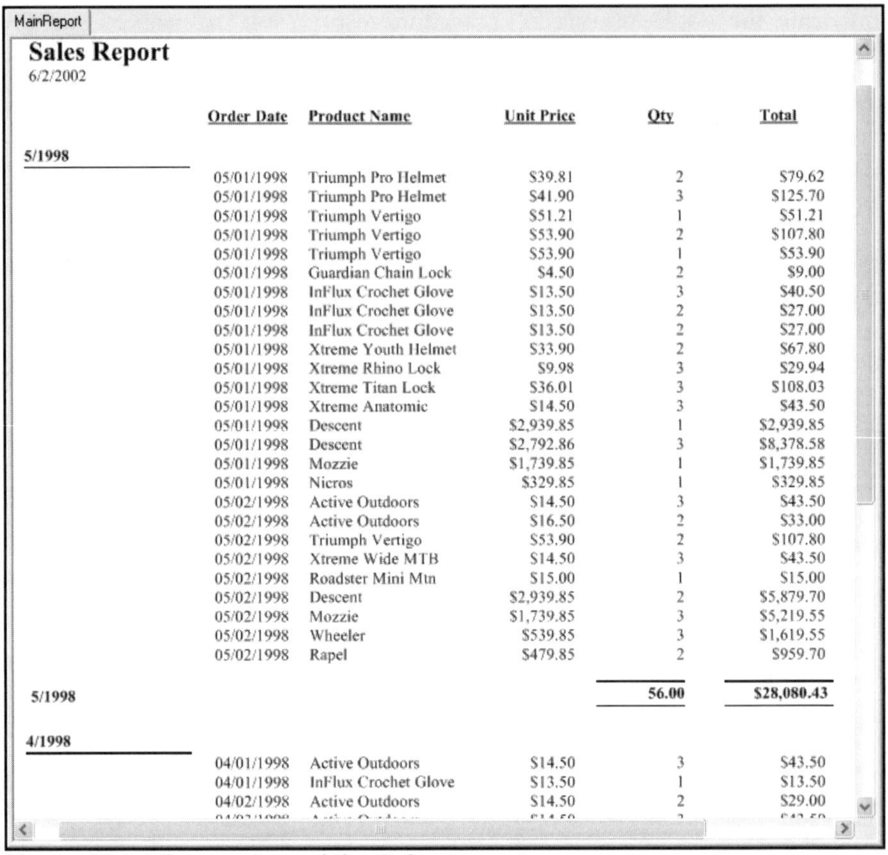

MainReport

Sales Report

6/2/2002

	Order Date	Product Name	Unit Price	Qty	Total
5/1998					
	05/01/1998	Triumph Pro Helmet	$39.81	2	$79.62
	05/01/1998	Triumph Pro Helmet	$41.90	3	$125.70
	05/01/1998	Triumph Vertigo	$51.21	1	$51.21
	05/01/1998	Triumph Vertigo	$53.90	2	$107.80
	05/01/1998	Triumph Vertigo	$53.90	1	$53.90
	05/01/1998	Guardian Chain Lock	$4.50	2	$9.00
	05/01/1998	InFlux Crochet Glove	$13.50	3	$40.50
	05/01/1998	InFlux Crochet Glove	$13.50	2	$27.00
	05/01/1998	InFlux Crochet Glove	$13.50	2	$27.00
	05/01/1998	Xtreme Youth Helmet	$33.90	2	$67.80
	05/01/1998	Xtreme Rhino Lock	$9.98	3	$29.94
	05/01/1998	Xtreme Titan Lock	$36.01	3	$108.03
	05/01/1998	Xtreme Anatomic	$14.50	3	$43.50
	05/01/1998	Descent	$2,939.85	1	$2,939.85
	05/01/1998	Descent	$2,792.86	3	$8,378.58
	05/01/1998	Mozzie	$1,739.85	1	$1,739.85
	05/01/1998	Nicros	$329.85	1	$329.85
	05/02/1998	Active Outdoors	$14.50	3	$43.50
	05/02/1998	Active Outdoors	$16.50	2	$33.00
	05/02/1998	Triumph Vertigo	$53.90	2	$107.80
	05/02/1998	Xtreme Wide MTB	$14.50	3	$43.50
	05/02/1998	Roadster Mini Mtn	$15.00	1	$15.00
	05/02/1998	Descent	$2,939.85	2	$5,879.70
	05/02/1998	Mozzie	$1,739.85	3	$5,219.55
	05/02/1998	Wheeler	$539.85	3	$1,619.55
	05/02/1998	Rapel	$479.85	2	$959.70
5/1998				56.00	$28,080.43
4/1998					
	04/01/1998	Active Outdoors	$14.50	3	$43.50
	04/01/1998	InFlux Crochet Glove	$13.50	1	$13.50
	04/02/1998	Active Outdoors	$14.50	2	$29.00

Figure 15-9. The preview of the Sales Report.

The sample application is run using this report and the output is shown in Figure 15-10. You can see that the SortFields collection has two items in it: the group field and the sort field. The last property listed for each field tells whether it belongs to a group or is an individual sort record. After listing the sort objects, the program lists the group objects. In this example, the report only has one group. You can see that there isn't as much information for the group field. Although it tells you about the field that is being grouped, it doesn't tell you what direction the sort is. You can only find this out by browsing the SortFields collection.

```
Total SortFields: 2
Field Name: Order Date
  Formula:     {Orders.Order Date}
  Kind:        DatabaseField
  Value Type:  DateTimeField
  Direction:   DescendingOrder
  Type:        GroupSortField
Field Name: Order Date
  Formula:     {Orders.Order Date}
  Kind:        DatabaseField
  Value Type:  DateTimeField
  Direction:   AscendingOrder
  Type:        RecordSortField
-----
Total Groups: 1
Field Name: Order Date
  Formula:     {Orders.Order Date}
  Kind:        DatabaseField
  Value Type:  DateTimeField
```

Figure 15-10. The output of the mapping application.

Programming the Grouping and Sorting Objects

The sorting and grouping objects in a report can be modified during runtime. You can use a form to have the user enter criteria to modify the default properties of a report and your program can change the report to meet these criteria. Modifying the objects during runtime is very powerful, but it requires you to understand what the limitations are.

Just like you learned at the beginning of the chapter, you can't add new report objects to the report. Secondly, only certain properties can be modified. The properties with a + can be modified and the ones with a – are read-only.

The SortField class controls how the fields are sorted. You can modify the SortDirection property to set whether it is ascending or descending. Listing 15-12 shows how to modify the SortDirection property.

Although the Groups collection appears to give you complete access to the group objects, it is missing the sort direction. You can't use the Groups collection exclusively and find out the whether the group is being sorted ascending or descending. You have to use the SortFields collection to modify a group's sort order.

Listing 15-12. Changing the sort direction of a field

```
Private Sub btnModifySorting_Click(ByVal sender As System.Object, _
    ByVal e As System.EventArgs) Handles btnModifySorting.Click
    Dim myReport As New CrystalReport1()
    Dim crSortFields As CrystalDecisions.CrystalReports.Engine.SortFields
    Dim crSortField As CrystalDecisions.CrystalReports.Engine.SortField
    'Modify the sort order of the OrderDate field to be Descending
    'Access the fields by traversing the sort fields collection
```

```
    crSortFields = myReport.DataDefinition.SortFields
    For Each crSortField In crSortFields
        If crSortField.Field.Name = "Order Date" Then
            'There are two differnt sorts with this field name.
            'Make sure its a record sort
            If crSortField.SortType = _
                CrystalDecisions.[Shared].SortFieldType.RecordSortField Then
                crSortField.SortDirection = _
                CrystalDecisions.[Shared].SortDirection.DescendingOrder
            End If
        End If
    Next
    CrystalReportViewer1.ReportSource = myReport
End Sub
```

This example uses a form with a button on it which changes the sorting order of the report used in the last example. When the user clicks on the button, it loads the report into the object variable myReport. The SortFields collection is traversed looking for the SortField with a name property of "Order Date". In this example report, there are two fields with this name. This is because the group section is based upon the order date's month, and within the group the individual records are sorted by the day of the order date.

Once it matches the name of the field, it has to check if this is the field for the group section or the individual record. When it is certain that it has the object for the individual record, it changes the sort order to descending. Once this is finished, the report object is assigned to the viewer. If you wanted to modify the sort order for the group section, you would do it here, but instead you would check if the field is of type GroupSortField. The report output is shown in Figure 15-11.

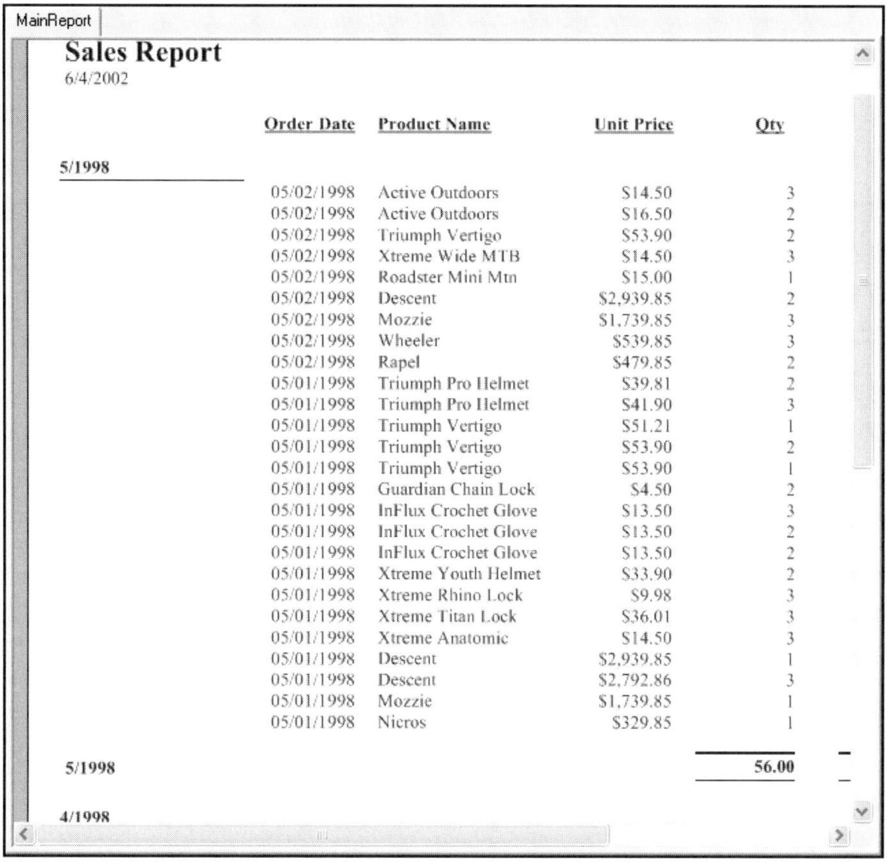

MainReport

Sales Report

6/4/2002

	Order Date	Product Name	Unit Price	Qty
5/1998				
	05/02/1998	Active Outdoors	$14.50	3
	05/02/1998	Active Outdoors	$16.50	2
	05/02/1998	Triumph Vertigo	$53.90	2
	05/02/1998	Xtreme Wide MTB	$14.50	3
	05/02/1998	Roadster Mini Mtn	$15.00	1
	05/02/1998	Descent	$2,939.85	2
	05/02/1998	Mozzie	$1,739.85	3
	05/02/1998	Wheeler	$539.85	3
	05/02/1998	Rapel	$479.85	2
	05/01/1998	Triumph Pro Helmet	$39.81	2
	05/01/1998	Triumph Pro Helmet	$41.90	3
	05/01/1998	Triumph Vertigo	$51.21	1
	05/01/1998	Triumph Vertigo	$53.90	2
	05/01/1998	Triumph Vertigo	$53.90	1
	05/01/1998	Guardian Chain Lock	$4.50	2
	05/01/1998	InFlux Crochet Glove	$13.50	3
	05/01/1998	InFlux Crochet Glove	$13.50	2
	05/01/1998	InFlux Crochet Glove	$13.50	2
	05/01/1998	Xtreme Youth Helmet	$33.90	2
	05/01/1998	Xtreme Rhino Lock	$9.98	3
	05/01/1998	Xtreme Titan Lock	$36.01	3
	05/01/1998	Xtreme Anatomic	$14.50	3
	05/01/1998	Descent	$2,939.85	1
	05/01/1998	Descent	$2,792.86	3
	05/01/1998	Mozzie	$1,739.85	1
	05/01/1998	Nicros	$329.85	1
5/1998				56.00
4/1998				

Figure 15-11. Report output after modifying the sort order.

Both the SortField class and Group class have a property that lets you modify the field they are based on. It is called Field in the Sort class and called ConditionField in the Group class. Both are of the type FieldDefinition. To modify this property, you have to set it to a reference of an existing field object. Thus, the field must already exist somewhere on the report. This field could be a field from one of the report tables or a formula field. Listing 15-13 demonstrates how to change the field by modifying the group object. This code works the same way for modifying a sort field.

Listing 15-13. Modifying a group's field

```
Private Sub btnModifyGrouping_Click(ByVal sender As System.Object, _
    ByVal e As System.EventArgs) Handles btnModifyGrouping.Click
    Dim myReport As New CrystalReport1()
    Dim crGroups As CrystalDecisions.CrystalReports.Engine.Groups
    Dim crGroup As CrystalDecisions.CrystalReports.Engine.Group
    Dim crField As CrystalDecisions.CrystalReports.Engine.DatabaseFieldDefinition
    'Modify the group to use CustomerName rather than OrderDate
    'Get the field to base the group on
```

```
crField = myReport.Database.Tables("Customer").Fields("Customer Name")
'Access the group by traversing the groups collection
crGroups = myReport.DataDefinition.Groups
For Each crGroup In crGroups
  If crGroup.ConditionField.Name = "Order Date" Then
     crGroup.ConditionField = crField
  End If
Next
CrystalReportViewer1.ReportSource = myReport
End Sub
```

This example uses another button on the same form as the last example and it also modifies the original report example. It changes the group from being based on Order Date to using the Customer Name field.

It first uses the Tables collection to get a reference to the Customer Name field from the Customers table.[34] It loops through the Groups collection to find the correct Group object. The field is changed by setting the ConditionField to the field object variable. Once this is finished, the report object is assigned to the viewer and the viewer is refreshed. The output is shown in Figure 15-12.

---

[34] See Chapter 17 for a discussion of tables.

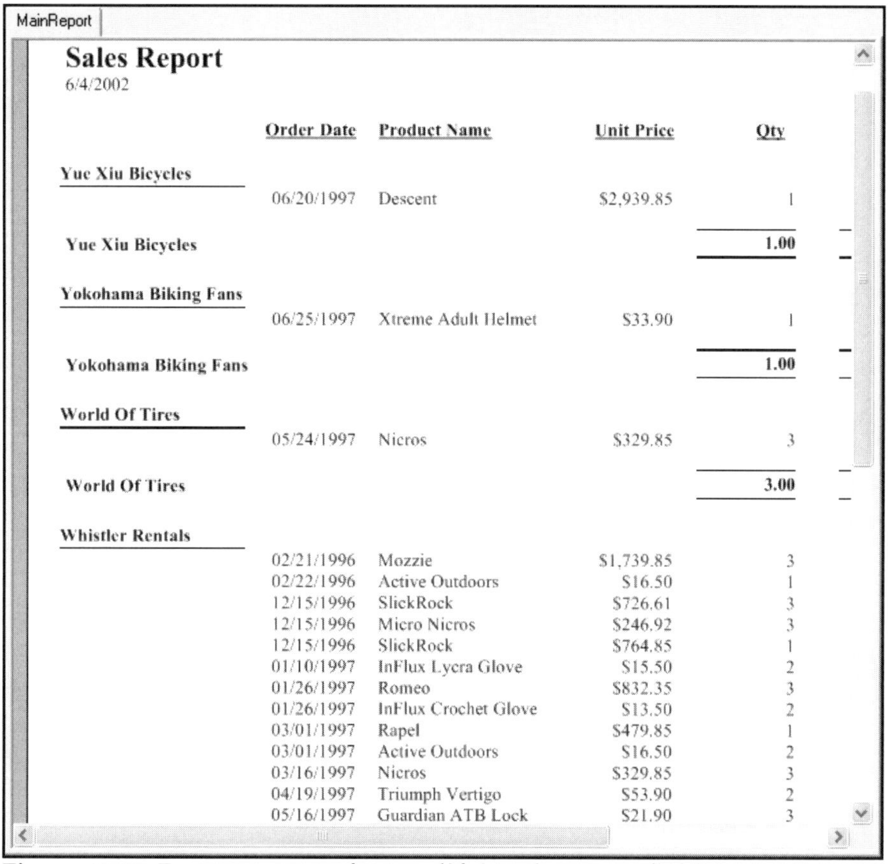

Sales Report

6/4/2002

	Order Date	Product Name	Unit Price	Qty
Yue Xiu Bicycles				
	06/20/1997	Descent	$2,939.85	1
Yue Xiu Bicycles				**1.00**
Yokohama Biking Fans				
	06/25/1997	Xtreme Adult Helmet	$33.90	1
Yokohama Biking Fans				**1.00**
World Of Tires				
	05/24/1997	Nicros	$329.85	3
World Of Tires				**3.00**
Whistler Rentals				
	02/21/1996	Mozzie	$1,739.85	3
	02/22/1996	Active Outdoors	$16.50	1
	12/15/1996	SlickRock	$726.61	3
	12/15/1996	Micro Nicros	$246.92	3
	12/15/1996	SlickRock	$764.85	1
	01/10/1997	InFlux Lycra Glove	$15.50	2
	01/26/1997	Romeo	$832.35	3
	01/26/1997	InFlux Crochet Glove	$13.50	2
	03/01/1997	Rapel	$479.85	1
	03/01/1997	Active Outdoors	$16.50	2
	03/16/1997	Nicros	$329.85	3
	04/19/1997	Triumph Vertigo	$53.90	2
	05/16/1997	Guardian ATB Lock	$21.90	3

Figure 15-12. Report output after modifying the group field.

Understanding the Summary Field Classes

The summary field classes are referenced with the SummaryField property of the DataDefinition class.

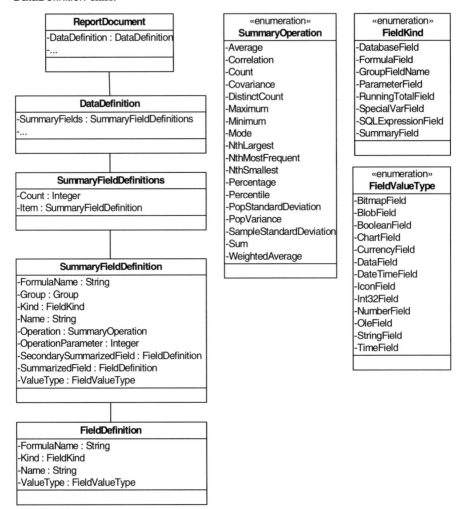

Figure 15-13. The Summary Field classes.

The SummaryField property is a collection of SummaryFieldDefinition objects. Each object contains all the information about each summary field: the field, the summary operation, etc. Unfortunately, it is missing one key piece of data: the section it is located in. There are no properties to tell you if it is a subtotal or a grand total. This is an important piece of information that you need to know about a field. To see how much information is provided to you, look at Figure 15-14. It is the output of the Mapping application for the SummaryField collection. You can see that there is no way to determine which fields are subtotals and which ones are grand totals.

```
Total SummaryFieldDefinitions: 4
Field Name: {Orders_Detail.Quantity}
  Formula:     {Orders_Detail.Quantity}
  Kind:        DatabaseField
  Value Type:  Int32sField
  Operation:   Sum
  Parameter:   0
  Value Type:  NumberField
Field Name: {@ItemTotalPrice}
  Formula:     {@ItemTotalPrice}
  Kind:        FormulaField
  Value Type:  CurrencyField
  Operation:   Sum
  Parameter:   0
  Value Type:  CurrencyField
Field Name: {Orders_Detail.Quantity}
  Formula:     {Orders_Detail.Quantity}
  Kind:        DatabaseField
  Value Type:  Int32sField
  Operation:   Sum
  Parameter:   0
  Value Type:  NumberField
Field Name: {@ItemTotalPrice}
  Formula:     {@ItemTotalPrice}
  Kind:        FormulaField
  Value Type:  CurrencyField
  Operation:   Sum
  Parameter:   0
  Value Type:  CurrencyField
```

Figure 15-14. The summary fields mapping output.

While accessing all the summary fields from the DataDefinition class is possible, you aren't given enough information to make it practical. It is better to reference these fields from within the sections that they are located in.

Modifying Subreports

Modifying the properties of a subreport is the same as modifying the properties of any report. Throughout this book there is code for modifying report objects such as the fields, groups and formatting, and there is code for setting login information. Every line of the code samples can be used on a subreport without making any changes. This is because subreports are also derived from the ReportDocument class just like the main report is.

The only difference with modifying subreports is how you get a reference to them. When you add a subreport to the main report, it is derived from the class SubReportObject. But the SubreportObject class doesn't let you modify the report objects. Instead, you have to instantiate the subreport as a new

ReportDocument object variable. Use this object variable to modify the all properties and objects of the subreport.

There are two ways of getting a reference to subreport objects. The first way is to call the ReportDocument.OpenSubreport() method and pass it the subreport name. The second way is looping through the ReportObjects collection of the main report and finding each subreport. Referencing the subreport by name is much easier because you only have to call a single method. But that doesn't mean that looping through the ReportObjects collection is frivolous. There is a reason for using both methods.

Use the OpenSubreport() method when you want to modify the properties of only one of the subreports. For example, you could have a subreport with salary information and it gets suppressed if the user doesn't have permission to view it.

Looping through the ReportObjects collection is used when you want to apply the same modification to all the subreports. As each subreport is found, call a method which performs an operation on it and then returns back to look for more subreports. An example of this is setting the login credential for every subreport.

Let's look at a couple of examples to see how it all works. The first example opens a subreport using the subreport's name.

Listing 15-14. Open a subreport using the subreport name.

```
Dim MyReport As New CrystalReport1
Dim MySubReport As CrystalDecisions.CrystalReports.Engine.ReportDocument
Dim MyReportObject As CrystalDecisions.CrystalReports.Engine.ReportObject
Dim MyTextObject As CrystalDecisions.CrystalReports.Engine.TextObject
MySubReport = MyReport.OpenSubreport("Sales Subreport")
MyReportObject = MySubReport.ReportDefinition.ReportObjects.Item("Text3")
MyTextObject = CType(MyReportObject, CrystalDecisions.CrystalReports.Engine.TextObject)
MyTextObject.ObjectFormat.EnableSuppress = True
CrystalReportViewer1.ReportSource = MyReport
```

After declaring the necessary variables, the first line of code calls the OpenSubreport() method of the report. This method takes the name of the subreport and instantiates a new ReportDocument object for the subreport. Notice that the variable MySubReport is declared as a ReportDocument class. In this example I used "Sales Subreport", but you should replace this with the name of your subreport.

At this point, the variable MySubReport is just like any ReportDocument object variable that is used throughout this book. Modify its properties as you normally would. For example purposes, I get a reference to the Text3 object and suppress it. The last step is assigning the main report object variable to the viewer so that the user can preview it.

As you can see, using the OpenSubreport() method is very simple. But there is one part that could cause you some confusion: figuring out the report name. The subreport has multiple names depending upon what part of the report designer you are looking at. The most obvious way of getting the report name is to look at the report object on the designer.

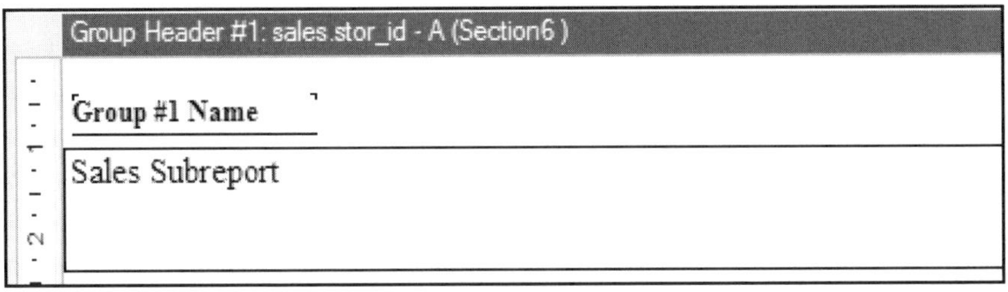

Figure 15-15. The subreport object in the designer.

In Figure 15-15 the subreport's name is Sales Subreport. Luckily, if you get the name in this way, then you are correct. The tricky part is if you look in the Properties Window. The name is listed here as Subreportx (e.g. Subreport1). This is not the name that should be passed to the OpenSubreport() method. To make things even more unusual, try double-clicking on the subreport to open it in the designer. Then look at the Properties Window under the Report property. The Report property for the subreport lists the main report's name, not its own name.

The second way of referencing a subreport is to loop through the ReportObjects collection and find each subreport. The next example uses this technique to clear the record selection formula of all subreports.

Listing 15-15. Find subreports using the ReportObjects collection.

```
Dim MySubReport As CrystalDecisions.CrystalReports.Engine.ReportDocument
Dim MySubReportObject As CrystalDecisions.CrystalReports.Engine.SubreportObject
Dim MyReportObject As CrystalDecisions.CrystalReports.Engine.ReportObject
Dim MyReport As New CrystalReport1
For Each MyReportObject In MyReport.ReportDefinition.ReportObjects
    If MyReportObject.Kind = CrystalDecisions.[Shared].ReportObjectKind.SubreportObject Then
        MySubReportObject = CType(MyReportObject, CrystalDecisions.CrystalReports.Engine.SubreportObject)
        MySubReport = MyReport.OpenSubreport(MySubReportObject.SubreportName)
        MySubReport.RecordSelectionFormula = ""
    End If
Next
CrystalReportViewer1.ReportSource = MyReport
```

Listing 15-15 gets a reference to each report object in the ReportObjects collection. It tests the Kind property to see if the object is a subreport. If it is, assigns the report object to a variable by explicitly casting it as the SubreportObject class. You need to cast it as the SubreportObject class because this class has a property called SubreportName. Pass the SubreportName property to the main report's OpenSubreport() method. The object variably MySubReport is a ReportDocument object that holds the subreport. Just like the last listing, you can now modify the properties of the subreports using the properties and methods of the ReportDocument class. This example clears the record selection formula so that none of the subreports use any filtering. Once all the report objects have been examined and all the subreports have been modified, assign the main report object variable to the ReportSource property of the viewer so that the report can be previewed.

C# Code Listings

The C# code listings are equivalent to the VB.NET code listings.

Listing 15-1. Changing the selection formula with the ReportDocument object.

```
CrystalReport1 MyReport = new CrystalReport1();
MyReport.DataDefinition.RecordSelectionFormula =
"{Orders.Order Date} in Date (1996, 02, 19) to Date (1996, 03, 28)";
crystalReportViewer1.ReportSource = MyReport;
```

Listing 15-2. Changing the selection formula with the viewer control.

```
CrystalReport1 MyReport = new CrystalReport1();
crystalReportViewer1.ReportSource = MyReport;
crystalReportViewer1.SelectionFormula =
"{Orders.Order Date} in Date (1996, 02, 19) to Date (1996, 02, 20)
```

Listing 15-3. Mapping the ReportDefinition object model.

```
private void Form1_Load(object sender, System.EventArgs e)
{
    CrystalReport1 MyReport = new CrystalReport1();
    MapAreas(MyReport.ReportDefinition.Areas, 0);
}
public void MapAreas(CrystalDecisions.CrystalReports.Engine.Areas Areas, int Indent)
{
    foreach(CrystalDecisions.CrystalReports.Engine.Area Area in Areas)
    {
        MapArea(Area, Indent);
    }
}
public void MapSections(CrystalDecisions.CrystalReports.Engine.Sections Sections, int Indent)
{
    foreach(CrystalDecisions.CrystalReports.Engine.Section Section in Sections)
    {
        MapSection(Section, Indent);
    }
}
public void MapReportObjects(CrystalDecisions.CrystalReports.Engine.ReportObjects ReportObjects, int Indent)
{
    foreach(CrystalDecisions.CrystalReports.Engine.ReportObject ReportObject in ReportObjects)
    {
        MapReportObject(ReportObject, Indent + 2);
    }
}
public void MapArea(CrystalDecisions.CrystalReports.Engine.Area Area, int Indent)
{
    Output("Area: " + Area.Name, Indent);
```

```csharp
        Output("Kind: " + Area.Kind.ToString(), Indent+2);
        Output("Suppress: " + Area.AreaFormat.EnableSuppress.ToString(), Indent + 2);
        Output("Keep Together: " + Area.AreaFormat.EnableKeepTogether.ToString(), Indent + 2);
        foreach(CrystalDecisions.CrystalReports.Engine.Section Section in Area.Sections)
        {
            MapSection(Section, Indent + 2);
        }
    }
    public void MapSection(CrystalDecisions.CrystalReports.Engine.Section Section, int Indent)
    {
        //Print the Section properties
        Output("Section: " + Section.Name, Indent);
        Output("Suppress: " + Section.SectionFormat.EnableSuppress.ToString(), Indent);
        Output("Keep Together: " + Section.SectionFormat.EnableKeepTogether.ToString(), Indent);
        foreach(CrystalDecisions.CrystalReports.Engine.ReportObject ReportObject in Section.ReportObjects)
        {
            MapReportObject(ReportObject, Indent + 2);
        }
    }
    public void MapReportObject(CrystalDecisions.CrystalReports.Engine.ReportObject ReportObject, int Indent)
    {
        switch(ReportObject.Kind)
        {
            case CrystalDecisions.Shared.ReportObjectKind.TextObject:
            {
                MapTextObject(((CrystalDecisions.CrystalReports.Engine.TextObject)ReportObject), Indent);
                break;
            }
            case CrystalDecisions.Shared.ReportObjectKind.FieldObject:
            {
                MapFieldObject(((CrystalDecisions.CrystalReports.Engine.FieldObject)ReportObject), Indent);
                break;
            }
        }
    }
    public void MapTextObject(CrystalDecisions.CrystalReports.Engine.TextObject TextObject, int Indent)
    {
        Output("Name: " + TextObject.Name, Indent);
        Output("Kind: " + TextObject.Kind.ToString(), Indent + 2);
        Output("Text: " + TextObject.Text, Indent + 2);
    }
    public void MapFieldObject(CrystalDecisions.CrystalReports.Engine.FieldObject FieldObject, int Indent)
    {
        Output("Name: " + FieldObject.Name, Indent);
        Output("Kind: " + FieldObject.Kind.ToString(), Indent + 2);
        Output("DataSource.Name: " + FieldObject.DataSource.Name, Indent + 2);
        Output("DataSource.Formula: " + FieldObject.DataSource.FormulaName, Indent + 2);
    }
    public void Output(string Line, int Indent)
```

```
{
    lstMapping.Items.Add(new string(' ',Indent) + Line);
}
```

Listing 15-4. Get a reference to the ReportFooter section.

```
CrystalReport1 MyReport = new CrystalReport1();
CrystalDecisions.CrystalReports.Engine.Section MySection;
MySection = MyReport.ReportDefinition.Sections["ReportFooter"];
```

Listing 15-5. Get a reference to the report object State using the ReportObject data type.

```
CrystalReport1 MyReport = new CrystalReport1();
CrystalDecisions.CrystalReports.Engine.ReportObject MyObject;
MyObject = MyReport.ReportDefinition.ReportObjects["State"];
```

Listing 15-6. Get a reference to the State object using the object's specific data type.

```
CrystalReport1 MyReport = new CrystalReport1();
CrystalDecisions.CrystalReports.Engine.FieldObject MyField;
MyField = (CrystalDecisions.CrystalReports.Engine.FieldObject)
    MyReport.ReportDefinition.ReportObjects["State"];
```

Listing 15-7. Modify properties of the ReportFooter section.

```
CrystalReport1 MyReport = new CrystalReport1();
CrystalDecisions.CrystalReports.Engine.Section MySection;
MySection = MyReport.ReportDefinition.Sections["ReportFooter"];
MySection.SectionFormat.EnableKeepTogether = true;
MySection.SectionFormat.EnableSuppress = false;
```

Listing 15-8. Modify the border of the report object State using the ReportObject data type.

```
CrystalReport1 MyReport = new CrystalReport1();
CrystalDecisions.CrystalReports.Engine.ReportObject MyObject;
MyObject = MyReport.ReportDefinition.ReportObjects["State"];
MyObject.Border.TopLineStyle = CrystalDecisions.Shared.LineStyle.SingleLine;
MyObject.Border.BottomLineStyle = CrystalDecisions.Shared.LineStyle.DoubleLine;
crystalReportViewer1.ReportSource = MyReport;
```

Listing 15-9. Modify the line properties of the object Line using the object's specific data type.

```
CrystalReport1 MyReport = new CrystalReport1();
CrystalDecisions.CrystalReports.Engine.LineObject MyLine;
MyLine = (CrystalDecisions.CrystalReports.Engine.LineObject)
MyReport.ReportDefinition.ReportObjects["Line1"];
MyLine.LineStyle = CrystalDecisions.Shared.LineStyle.DashLine;
crystalReportViewer1.ReportSource = MyReport;
```

Listing 15-10. Modify the Text property of a TextObject located in ReportHeader.

```
CrystalReport1 MyReport = new CrystalReport1();
CrystalDecisions.CrystalReports.Engine.TextObject MyText;
MyText = (CrystalDecisions.CrystalReports.Engine.TextObject)
MyReport.ReportDefinition.ReportObjects["HeaderText"];
MyText.Text = "New Report Header";
crystalReportViewer1.ReportSource = MyReport;
```

Listing 15-11. Mapping the sorting and grouping objects.

```
private void Form1_Load(object sender, System.EventArgs e)
{
    CrystalReport1 MyReport = new CrystalReport1();
    MapSortFields(MyReport.DataDefinition.SortFields, 0);
    Output("---",0);
    MapGroups(MyReport.DataDefinition.Groups, 0);
}
public void MapSortFields(CrystalDecisions.CrystalReports.Engine.SortFields SortFields, int Indent)
{
    Output("Total SortFields: " + SortFields.Count, Indent);
    foreach(CrystalDecisions.CrystalReports.Engine.SortField SortField in SortFields)
    {
        MapSortField(SortField, Indent);
    }
}
public void MapSortField(CrystalDecisions.CrystalReports.Engine.SortField SortField, int Indent)
{
    MapFieldDefinition(SortField.Field, Indent);
    Output("Direction: " + SortField.SortDirection.ToString(), Indent + 2);
    Output("Type: " + SortField.SortType.ToString(), Indent + 2);
}
public void MapGroups(CrystalDecisions.CrystalReports.Engine.Groups Groups, int Indent)
{
    Output("Total Groups: " + Groups.Count, Indent);
    foreach(CrystalDecisions.CrystalReports.Engine.Group Group in Groups)
    {
        MapGroup(Group, Indent + 2);
    }
}
public void MapGroup(CrystalDecisions.CrystalReports.Engine.Group Group, int Indent)
{
    MapFieldDefinition(Group.ConditionField, Indent);
}
public void MapFieldDefinition(CrystalDecisions.CrystalReports.Engine.FieldDefinition FieldDefinition,
int Indent)
{
    Output("Field Name: " + FieldDefinition.Name, Indent);
    Output("Formula: " + FieldDefinition.FormulaName, Indent + 2);
    Output("Kind: " + FieldDefinition.Kind.ToString(), Indent + 2);
    Output("Value Type: " + FieldDefinition.ValueType.ToString(), Indent + 2);
}
```

```csharp
public void Output(string Line, int Indent)
{
    lstMapping.Items.Add(new string(' ',Indent) + Line);
}
```

Listing 15-12. Changing the sort direction of a field

```csharp
private void btnModifySorting_Click(object sender, System.EventArgs e)
{
    CrystalReport1 MyReport = new CrystalReport1();
    //Modify the order of the OrderDate field to Descending
    //Reference the fields by traversing the sort fields collection
    foreach(CrystalDecisions.CrystalReports.Engine.SortField MySortField in
        MyReport.DataDefinition.SortFields)
    {
        if (MySortField.Field.Name == "Last Name")
        {
            //There are two different sort objects with this name
            //Make sure its a record sort.
            if (MySortField.SortType ==
            CrystalDecisions.Shared.SortFieldType.RecordSortField)
            {
                MySortField.SortDirection =
                CrystalDecisions.Shared.SortDirection.DescendingOrder;
            }
        }
        crystalReportViewer1.ReportSource = MyReport;
    }
}
```

Listing 15-13. Modifying a group's field

```csharp
private void btnModifyGrouping_Click(object sender, System.EventArgs e)
{
    CrystalReport1 MyReport = new CrystalReport1();
    CrystalDecisions.CrystalReports.Engine.DatabaseFieldDefinition MyField;
    //Modify the group to use CustomerName rather than Orderdate
    //Get the field to base the group on
    MyField = MyReport.Database.Tables["Employee"].Fields["First Name"];
    //Reference the group by traversing the Groups collection
    foreach(CrystalDecisions.CrystalReports.Engine.Group MyGroup in MyReport.DataDefinition.Groups)
    {
        if (MyGroup.ConditionField.Name == "Last Name")
        {
            MyGroup.ConditionField = MyField;
        }
    }
    crystalReportViewer1.ReportSource = MyReport;
}
```

Listing 15-14. Open a subreport using the subreport name.

```
CrystalReport1 MyReport = new CrystalReport1();
CrystalDecisions.CrystalReports.Engine.ReportDocument MySubReport;
CrystalDecisions.CrystalReports.Engine.ReportObject MyReportObject;
CrystalDecisions.CrystalReports.Engine.TextObject MyText;
MySubReport = MyReport.OpenSubreport("Sales Subreport");
MyText = (CrystalDecisions.CrystalReports.Engine.TextObject)
    MyReport.ReportDefinition.ReportObjects["Text3"];
MyText.ObjectFormat.EnableSuppress = true;
crystalReportViewer1.ReportSource = MyReport;
```

Listing 15-15. Find subreports using the ReportObjects collection.

```
CrystalReport1 MyReport = new CrystalReport1();
CrystalDecisions.CrystalReports.Engine.SubreportObject MySubreportObject;
CrystalDecisions.CrystalReports.Engine.ReportDocument MySubreport;
foreach(CrystalDecisions.CrystalReports.Engine.ReportObject MyReportObject in
MyReport.ReportDefinition.ReportObjects)
{
    if (MyReportObject.Kind == CrystalDecisions.Shared.ReportObjectKind.SubreportObject){
        MySubreportObject = (CrystalDecisions.CrystalReports.Engine.SubreportObject)MyReportObject;
        MySubreport = MySubreportObject.OpenSubreport(MySubreportObject.SubreportName);
        MySubreport.RecordSelectionFormula = "";
    }
}
crystalReportViewer1.ReportSource = MyReport;
```

Modifying Parameters and Formulas

Using parameters is a critical part of report writing. They are the only way for a user to send input to a report prior to it printing. For each parameter, the user is prompted with a separate dialog box to enter either discrete values or a range of values.

The problem with parameters is that the user interface for prompting the user to enter a value isn't very exciting. There is a separate dialog box for each parameter and it is generic and bland. There is no way to customize them to make them fit in with the look and feel of your application. Fortunately, Crystal Reports .NET lets you override a parameter's default behavior. When opening a report with parameters, you can use a form in your project that prompts the user for all the relevant data and pass this directly to the report. This gives the user a clean interface for entering the data. You also get the benefit of validating the user input prior to printing the report. This reduces the chances of an error occurring when running reports.

Replacing Parameters with Formulas

Before getting into a discussion of how to modify parameters, you first need to know that parameters are very complicated to work with. Changing them involves a lot of steps and it is easy to make a mistake. You also have to make sure you have the parameter name and data type exact. If anything goes wrong, your code won't work and the user is still prompted with the dialog box to enter the parameter value. There is a simple solution to all of this: Don't use parameters. If you think that was a typographical error, then let me repeat it. Don't use parameters.

Since parameters are the only way to let a user input data directly into a report, most people assume that they are very important. And they are important for non-programmers. But with .NET's ability to directly modify report objects prior to printing a report, parameters have lost their significance. With a little thought, you can eliminate most parameters from your reports.

Let's look at a couple of examples. Suppose you have a parameter that prompts the user for a special comment that should appear at the bottom of the report. Rather than making this a parameter field, use a Text object instead and programmatically modify the text via the ReportDocument object. As another example, take a parameter that is used to let a user choose whether a sort will be ascending or descending. Instead of using a parameter, programmatically get a reference to the sort object and modify the sort direction.

The majority of parameters in a report represent a discrete value. Some examples of discrete values are a date, a dollar amount, or an ID of a product or company. These parameters are easily replaced with formulas. A formula doesn't have to be a complex algorithm of functions or programming code. It can be a simple number, date or string. Wherever you need to use a discrete parameter value, use a formula instead.

Modifying formulas is simple. It only takes one line of code. Here is an example of modifying the formula CustomerId to be the value 999.

```
MyReport.DataDefinition.FormulaFields("CustomerId").Text = "999"
```

The FormulaFields collection stores each formula in the report. Formulas are referenced by passing the formula name as the indexer to the FormulaFields collection. The above sample code passes the string "CustomerId" to the FormulaFields collection and modifies the Text property of the formula.

"The remaining text does not appear to be part of the formula"

When there are problems with modifying a formula during runtime, you get this error. Unfortunately, the error doesn't give you any indication of what is wrong. The easiest way to debug formulas is to use the report designer. It gives you the exact error message and is much easier to figure out. Go into design mode for the report and copy the problem text into a dummy formula. It checks the formula's syntax and gives you a better error message. If it says that there are no syntax errors with the formula, then the error is most likely because you are using Basic syntax. Changing formulas during runtime requires using Crystal syntax. The runtime engine only has access to the Crystal syntax compiler and it can't interpret Basic syntax. You can only use Basic syntax when you are in design mode of a report. Even if a formula was originally written using Basic syntax, overriding a formula during runtime require using Crystal syntax.

There is one flaw in my theory of not using parameters: formulas can't be modified using the viewer control. Formulas can only be modified using the DataDefinition class found within the ReportDocument object. The DataDefinition class doesn't exist in either the WinForms viewer control or the ASP.NET viewer control. The viewer control can only modify parameters. You are only required to use the viewer control when modifying Report Web Services. Due to the limitations that using the viewer control puts on you, it is preferable to make runtime customization changes using the ReportDocument class.

Understanding the Parameter Classes

The parameter object model is designed to give you complete control over almost every property of the parameter. The majority of the class properties have write access. This lets you modify parameters during runtime so that you can set the current value and the user isn't prompted to enter it via the parameter dialog boxes. If you still want the user to use the parameter dialog boxes, you can modify the default values so that you have control over what values they choose from.

The object model uses three different collections to manage parameters. These collections are listed in Table 16-1. The ParameterFieldDefinitions collection manages the parameters in the ReportDocument class. The ParameterFields collection manages the parameters in the CrystalReportViewer class. A parameter can store one value or multiple values. Since a parameter can store multiple values, a collection is used to save this data. This collection is called the ParameterValues collection. It is shared between both ParameterFieldDefinitions and ParameterFields for storing CurrentValues and DefaultValues collections (both are a ParameterValues collection).

Table 16-1. The three types of parameter collections.

Collection	Purpose
ParameterFieldDefintions	Manages the parameters in the ReportDocument class. It is fully populated with all the parameters. Found in the CrystalDecisions.CrystalReports. Engine namespace.
ParameterFields	Manages parameters in the CrystalReportViewer class. It is empty by default. Found in the CrystalDecisions.Shared namespace.
ParameterValues	Manages the values stored within each parameter object. The ParameterFieldDefinitions collection and the ParameterFields collection both use this class. Found in the CrystalDecisions.Shared namespace.

It's important to know which namespace the collections are in. When writing an application, you will refer to these namespaces to access the collections. As an alternative, you can always use the Imports statement (using in C#) so that you don't have to write out the full namespace name. The code samples in this chapter declare the full namespace so that you can learn them.

The naming convention for the parameter classes gives them the potential to be confusing to learn. The class DataDefinition uses the classes ParameterFieldDefinitions and ParameterFieldDefinition. The CrystalReportViewer class has similar class names: ParameterFields and ParameterField. The names are almost the same except that the DataDefinition classes have the word 'Definition' appended to them. This helps make it clear which class each is associated with. However, the property name in the DataDefinition class for the ParameterFieldDefinitions collection is called ParameterFields. This is the same name as the collection class in the viewer classes. Having a property that has the same name as a non-compatible class can be very confusing. If you aren't careful, you might see the ParameterFields property in the DataDefinition class and accidentally look at the object model for the ParameterFields class in the CrystalReportViewer class instead.[35]

The parameter classes are designed with two approaches in mind. The first approach is that you are using the CrystalReportViewer control to preview the report. The second approach is modifying parameters with the ReportDocument object. Both approaches can be used to modify the current value or the default values. But they do so in different ways.

The object model in Figure 16-1 shows two columns of classes. The left column has the classes related to the ReportDocument object. The right column has the classes for the CrystalReportViewer class. At the bottom of the diagram are the classes that store the actual parameter values. These classes are shared by both columns.

---

[35] When I first stared working with parameters, I didn't notice that the names were identical, but the classes were different. This caused me many headaches until I realized what the problem was.

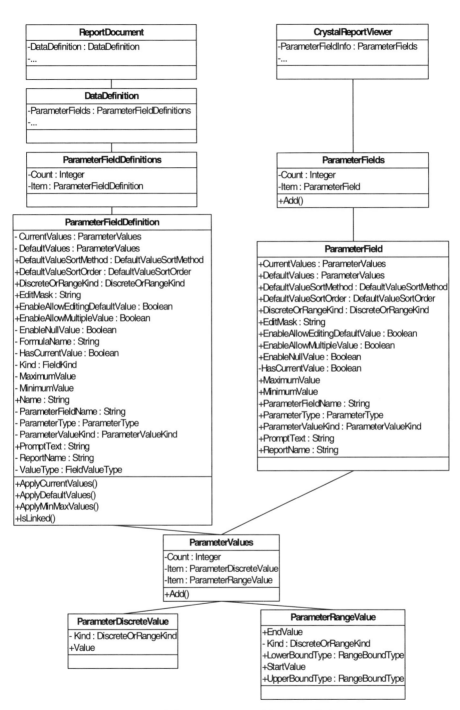

Figure 16-1. The classes of the Parameter object model.

When looking at the individual classes of both columns in more detail, you see that there are a lot of similarities between them. Let's start at the top and work our way down. The top most classes are the ReportDocument class and CrystalReportViewer class. Below the ReportDocument class is the DataDefinition class. Below each class is a collection class that stores the parameters. Under the collection class is the actual parameter field class. The two parameter field classes, ParameterFieldDefinition and ParameterField, have all the properties that you set when using the Create New Parameter dialog box in design mode (e.g. prompt text, min and max values, sort order, etc.). You can see that they have many properties in common.

The parameter field classes use a collection class to store the current values and the default values. The ParameterValues collection holds ParameterValue objects. Since the current value and default value of a parameter can store either a single discrete value or a range of values, there are two classes that are used to represent this. The ParameterDiscreteValue class only holds a single value. The ParameterRangeValue class stores a range value (it has an upper and lower range).

All of the parameter classes have a variety of properties that are enumeration data types. These enumerations are used to store a pre-determined set of values that the property can have. Since there are so many of the enumeration types, they are listed separately from the main parameter object model. See Figure 16-2 for each enumeration used. Since these represent the options that you can set for a parameter, they have already been discussed earlier in Chapter 5.

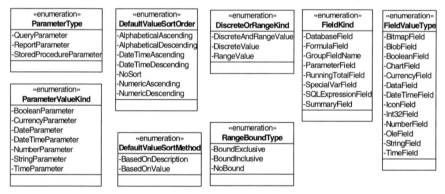

Figure 16-2. The enumeration constants of the Parameter object model.

Mapping the Parameter Classes

To get an overall understanding of how the parameter classes are organized, mapping out the parameters is a good way to start. This section shows you the code to print out all the report parameters and their properties.

The code to print out the parameters is very simple. The classes are composed of two collections. There is a collection for storing the parameter fields, and there is a collection for storing the values that each parameter has. The main logic consists of For Each loops to process each element in the collection.

The ReportDocument class is the only class that is mapped in this chapter because it is the most frequently used class for modifying reports. Mapping out the CrystalReportViewer class would prove to be mostly redundant.

Parameters in the ReportDocument class are managed with two collection classes. The ParameterFieldDefinitions collection stores all the parameters as ParameterFieldDefinition objects. The ParameterValues collection manages the value objects within each parameter of type ParameterValue. Listing 16-1 shows the code for mapping out the parameters.

Listing 16-1. Mapping the parameters in the ReportDocument class.

```
Dim MyReport As New CrystalReport1()
MapParameterFieldDefinitions(MyReport.DataDefinition.ParameterFields, 0)
...
Sub MapParameterFieldDefinitions(ByVal ParameterFieldDefintions As _
    CrystalDecisions.CrystalReports.Engine.ParameterFieldDefinitions, _
    ByVal Indent As Integer)
    Dim ParameterFieldDefinition As _
        CrystalDecisions.CrystalReports.Engine.ParameterFieldDefinition
    For Each ParameterFieldDefinition In ParameterFieldDefintions
        MapParameterFieldDefinition(ParameterFieldDefinition, Indent)
    Next
End Sub
Sub MapParameterFieldDefinition(ByVal ParameterFieldDefinition As _
    CrystalDecisions.CrystalReports.Engine.ParameterFieldDefinition, _
    ByVal Indent As Integer)
    Output("Name: " & ParameterFieldDefinition.ParameterFieldName, Indent)
    Output("PromptText: " & ParameterFieldDefinition.PromptText, Indent + 2)
    Output("ValueType: " & _
        ParameterFieldDefinition.ParameterValueKind.ToString(), Indent + 2)
    Output("Kind : " & _
        ParameterFieldDefinition.DiscreteOrRangeKind.ToString(), Indent + 2)
    If ParameterFieldDefinition.CurrentValues.Count > 0 Then
        Output("Current Values", Indent + 2)
        MapParameterValues(ParameterFieldDefinition.CurrentValues, Indent + 4)
    End If
    If ParameterFieldDefinition.DefaultValues.Count > 0 Then
        Output("Default Values", Indent + 2)
        MapParameterValues(ParameterFieldDefinition.DefaultValues, Indent + 4)
    End If
End Sub
Sub MapParameterValues(ByVal ParameterValues As _
    CrystalDecisions.Shared.ParameterValues, ByVal Indent As Integer)
    Dim ParameterValue As Object
```

```
For Each ParameterValue In ParameterValues
    If TypeOf ParameterValue Is _
        CrystalDecisions.Shared.ParameterRangeValue Then
        MapParameterRangeValue(CType(ParameterValue, _
            CrystalDecisions.Shared.ParameterRangeValue), Indent)
    Else
        MapParameterDiscreteValue(CType(ParameterValue, _
            CrystalDecisions.Shared.ParameterDiscreteValue), Indent)
    End If
    Next
End Sub
Sub MapParameterDiscreteValue(ByVal ParameterValue As _
    CrystalDecisions.Shared.ParameterDiscreteValue, ByVal Indent As Integer)
    Output("Value : " & ParameterValue.Value.ToString(), Indent)
End Sub
Sub MapParameterRangeValue(ByVal ParameterValue As _
    CrystalDecisions.Shared.ParameterRangeValue, ByVal Indent As Integer)
    Output("Value : " & ParameterValue.StartValue.ToString() & _
    " to " & ParameterValue.EndValue.ToString(), Indent)
End Sub
```

The first procedure, MapParameterFieldDefinitions(), loops through every parameter object in the ParameterFieldDefinitions collection and calls MapParameterFieldDefinition(). This procedure prints out a few properties (you can add more if you wish) and then calls MapParateterValues() for both the CurrentValues and DefaultValues collections. Each of these collections are of the data type ParameterValues.

The MapParameterValues() procedure loops through every parameter value. Notice that the variable it uses for the loop is of type Object. As you will see in the section on programming the classes, parameter values are added using either the ParameterDiscreteValue class or the ParameterRangeValue class. However, at this point we don't know which class was used. So we declare a generic Object variable and then use the TypeOf keyword to see which interface it supports. This lets us call the proper procedure to map it out.

To see the output, I ran this code against a report that has two parameters. The first parameter is a string that can accept a single value and has no default values. The second parameter is a date range that has multiple default values. Notice that even though the date range has multiple default values, they are all discrete. The output is shown in Figure 16-3.

```
Name: Location
  PromptText: Corporate location
  ValueType: StringParameter
  Kind : DiscreteValue
Name: DateRange
  PromptText: Historical archive date
  ValueType: DateParameter
  Kind : RangeValue
  Default Values
    Value : 1/19/1991 12:00:00 AM
    Value : 5/26/1998 12:00:00 AM
    Value : 2/4/2002 12:00:00 AM
```

Figure 16-3. The output from mapping the parameters.

Programming the Parameter Classes

Before you can use the parameter classes to pass values to the parameter objects, you need to understand how values are classified. When a report with parameters loads, the user is shown a dialog box to enter values for each parameter. The dialog box frequently shows a pre-populated list of values to choose from. The values in the list are called Default Values. When the user enters a value for a parameter, it could be a single value or possibly multiple values. The value that the user enters is called the Current Value.

A .NET program can modify either the default values or the current values. To design your application so that the user enters all the values on a .NET form and doesn't get the parameter dialog box, set the current values with your application. On the other hand, you might let the user get prompted with the parameter dialog box but you want to set the default values listed. For example, you can simulate a data-bound listbox by setting the default value list to show data in a table. This is done by overriding the default values that were assigned to the parameter when the report was designed.

Note

When setting parameter values, either set the current value or the default values, but not both. Setting the current value and setting the default values are mutually exclusive operations. If you set a parameter's current value, then the user never sees the dialog box and the default values are ignored. When you want the user to enter a parameter, set the default values but not the current values. Since there is no current value, the user will be prompted to enter it.

Considering that the parameter field classes of the ReportDocument class and the CrystalReportViewer class look so similar, you might assume that once you learn how to program with one class, you automatically know how to program with the other class. Unfortunately, this is not the case. Although there are many similarities, the differences are significant enough that you have to be very careful to make sure you understand the nuances between them. Paying close attention to the code examples in this section will save you headaches.

Tip
From a conceptual standpoint, the parameter objects in the ReportDocument class and the CrystalReportViewer class are the same. Both of them can modify the current values and default values of a parameter. This leads to the question of which one should you use in your application. This is determined by the other functionality your application implements. If your application only needs to modify the parameters, then you can use the CrystalReportViewer class to make these changes. However, if you are making other changes that can only be implemented with the ReportDocument class (e.g. changing formulas or the formatting of report objects) then you have to use the ReportDocument class. The logic is that if you are already working with the ReportDocument classes, then you should continue using these classes to modify the parameters as well. Crystal Decisions officially states that you cannot make report modifications with both classes simultaneously. You have to use one or the other.

Programming with the ReportDocument Class

The ReportDocument class manages every report object in the report. It has a collection class that is fully populated with every report parameter. Each parameter object can be assigned a value prior to printing the report.

To set a parameter's value, first get a reference to parameter field object. In the ReportDocument class, a parameter field is represented with the ReportFieldDefinition class. Once you have a reference to it, you can modify any of its properties.

The ReportFieldDefinition class has two properties that you are most concerned with: the CurrentValues and DefaultValues collections. Both of these collection objects are of the ParameterValues class. If you recall from Chapter 5, a parameter can have a single value or it can have multiple values. Since it can have more than one value then a collection is needed to store the values. The ParameterValues collection class is where these values are stored.

A parameter is either a discrete value or a range value and each is represented by a different class. The ParameterDiscreteValue class is for discrete values. The ParameterRangeValue class is for range values.

The ParameterDiscreteValue class only has one property to set: Value. This is the parameter's value. It is of type Object so that you can assign any data type to it as long as it is compatible with the data type that the parameter uses.

The ParameterRangeValue class has four values to set: StartValue, EndValue, LowerBoundType and UpperBoundType. The two value parameters are used to define the lower and upper bounds of the range. The two bound-type parameters are used to set whether the endpoint is inclusive or exclusive. If it is inclusive, then the value is included as part of the range. If it is exclusive, then the endpoint is not included as a part of the range. For example, let's say the range is 0 to 10 and the LowerBoundType is BoundExclusive and the UpperBoundType is BoundInclusive. This range would include all numbers from 1 to 10. If the bound-type is NoBound, then there will be no bounds for that parameter and you do not need to enter a value for it.[36]

After populating the ParameterValues collection with one or more values, you have to assign it to either the CurrentValues property or the DefaultValues property. Do this by calling the ApplyCurrentValues() method or the ApplyDefaultValues() method. Pass each method the ParameterValues collection object.

Programming parameters with the ReportDocument class consists of 8 steps:

1. Get a reference to the parameter field object that you want to modify. Use caution when declaring the variables because you have to declare an object of the ParameterFieldDefinition class, but get a reference to it using the ParameterFields property.
2. Instantiate a ParameterValues collection object.
3. Instantiate a parameter value object. This will either be of the ParameterDiscreteValue class or the ParameterRangeValue class.
4. Set the properties of the new parameter value object.
5. Add the parameter value object to the ParameterValues collection using the Add() method.
6. Repeat steps 3-5 for each parameter value object.
7. Assign the ParameterValues collection to the appropriate parameter field property using either the ApplyCurrentValues() method or the ApplyDefaultValues() method.

---

[36] See Chapter 5 for a discussion of bound-types.

8. Set the ReportSource property of the CrystalReportViewer
   object so that the report gets displayed.

Listing 16-2 illustrates these steps. It creates two parameters that are discrete values and assigns them to the DefaultValues collection. Since we want the user to be prompted with the new default values, then there is no need to modify the CurrentValues property. The inline comments explain the steps that are taking place.

Listing 16-2. Use the report document to modify a discrete parameter.

```
'Use the ReportDocument object to create two default parameters
Dim MyReport As New CrystalReport1()
Dim ParameterFieldDefinition As _
    CrystalDecisions.CrystalReports.Engine.ParameterFieldDefinition
Dim ParameterValues As CrystalDecisions.Shared.ParameterValues
Dim ParameterDiscreteValue As _
    CrystalDecisions.Shared.ParameterDiscreteValue
'Step 1:Get a reference to the parameter field to modify
ParameterFieldDefinition = _
    MyReport.DataDefinition.ParameterFields.Item("Location")
'Step 2: Instantiate a ParameterValues collection object.
ParameterValues = New CrystalDecisions.Shared.ParameterValues()
'Step 3: Instatiate a ParameterValue object.
'This example uses a discrete value
ParameterDiscreteValue = _
    New CrystalDecisions.Shared.ParameterDiscreteValue()
'Step 4: Assign a value to the object
ParameterDiscreteValue.Value = "Louisville, KY"
'Step 5: Add it to the ParameterValues collection using the Add() method
ParameterValues.Add(ParameterDiscreteValue)
'Step 6: Repeat steps 3-5 for additional parameters
ParameterDiscreteValue = _
    New CrystalDecisions.Shared.ParameterDiscreteValue()
ParameterDiscreteValue.Value = "San Diego, CA"
ParameterValues.Add(ParameterDiscreteValue)
'Step 7: Assign the ParameterValues collection to the parameter field.
'Do this with either the CurrentValues or DefaultValues collection
ParameterFieldDefinition.ApplyDefaultValues(ParameterValues)
'Step 8: Print or Preview the report
CrystalReportViewer1.ReportSource = MyReport
```

Programming the CrystalReportViewer Control

Programming with the viewer has some similarities to programming with the report document, but there are differences. From a high level, the viewer is similar to the report object because you have to get a reference to the parameter object and assign a value to its CurrentValues collection.[37] From an implementation standpoint, the viewer is different because it uses different parameter classes. You'll find it easier to program parameters using the viewer control than using the report document.

The viewer uses the ParameterFields collection to manage the properties of each parameter in a report. The ParameterFields collection manages the ParameterField object. It is easier to work with the ParameterField object (compared to the ParameterFieldDefinition object of the report document) because the ParameterField object lets you reference the CurrentValues collection directly. This makes more sense conceptually and it saves you some coding.

The viewer also requires you to assign the report object to the ReportSource property first. The viewer examines the report object and builds a list of parameters in the report. It has to build this list before you can reference the individual parameter objects. The last step is to assign a value to the parameter object's CurrentValues collection.

Programming with the CrystalReportViewer consists of 8 steps:

1. Declare and instantiate a ReportDocument object variable.
2. Assign the ReportDocument object to the ReportSource property of the viewer control.
3. Get a reference to the viewer's ParameterFields collection.
4. Get a reference to the ParameterField object you are modifying.
5. Instantiate a parameter value object. This will either be of the ParameterDiscreteValue class or the ParameterRangeValue class.
6. Set the properties of the new parameter value object.
7. Use the Add() method to add the parameter value object to the CurrentValues collection.
8. Repeat steps 4-6 for each parameter value object.

Caution

In Step 4 (getting a reference to the ParameterField object), the parameter name is case sensitive. Passing a string to the ParameterFields() indexer that doesn't match the parameter name results in the error System.ArgumentOutOfRange being raised. Note that this rule only applies when using the viewer object. The ParameterFieldDefinitions collection of the ReportDocument class is not case sensitive.

---

[37] If you recall, the viewer control doesn't use the DefaultValues collection because it can't prompt the user to enter a value.

Listing 16-3 illustrates these steps. It creates a parameter that is a range value and assigns it to the CurrentValues collection. The in-line comments explain the steps that are taking place.

Listing 16-3. Use the viewer to modify a range parameter.

```
Dim ParameterFields As CrystalDecisions.Shared.ParameterFields
Dim ParameterField As CrystalDecisions.Shared.ParameterField
Dim ParameterRangeValue As CrystalDecisions.Shared.ParameterRangeValue
'Step 1: Assign the report object to the viewer
Dim MyReport As New CrystalReport1
CrystalReportViewer1.ReportSource = MyReport
'Step 2: Reference the ParameterFields collection
ParameterFields = CrystalReportViewer1.ParameterFieldInfo
'Step 3: Reference the ParameterField object
ParameterField = ParameterFields("DateRange")
'Step 4: Create a ParameterValue object.
'This example uses a RangeValue object
ParameterRangeValue = New CrystalDecisions.Shared.ParameterRangeValue
'Step 5: Assign a value to the object
ParameterRangeValue.StartValue = "1/4/1997"
ParameterRangeValue.EndValue = "2/2/1997"
'Step 6: Add the ParameterValue object to either the
'CurrentValues or DefaultValues collection
ParameterField.CurrentValues.Add(ParameterRangeValue)
```

Caution

If you are programming the viewer control with C#, there is a serious bug you need to be aware of. The ParameterField object model doesn't expose all the properties and methods that it is supposed to. Many of the properties are hidden and won't appear when using Intellisense. To fix this you have to declare parameter field variables using the IParameterField interface. If you look at the classes with the Object Browser you'll see that the ParameterField class implements the IParameterField interface but it doesn't expose all its properties. Compare the properties of the ParameterField class listed in the Object Browser to the properties listed in the help file. You'll see that they look like totally different classes. Fortunately, the work-around only requires a minor change to the code, but it's very important nonetheless. See C# Listing 16-3.

Remember that this bug only happens for C# and only when using the viewer control. VB.NET has access to all the documented properties.

Modifying Subreport Parameters

Modifying the parameters of a subreport is the same as modifying any report object within a subreport. The code from Chapter 15 that references and instantiates subreport objects works with parameters as well.

Using the code in Chapter 15 as a basis to modify subreport parameters works great. But it can only be used with the ReportDocument object. If you recall from the discussion about modifying the viewer object, it limits what you can do. You can't reference the more sophisticated ReportDocument object with the viewer control. So how are you supposed to modify the parameters of a subreport if the viewer doesn't give you access to the ReportDocument object?

The ParameterFields collection of the viewer object has an overloaded indexer. In addition to passing it the parameter name, you can also pass the name of a subreport. Passing the subreport name gives you access to all the parameters on a subreport. If you pass an empty string as the subreport name, the main report's parameters are referenced.

As an example, Step 3 from Listing 16-3 has been modified to demonstrate getting a parameter from a subreport. The rest of the code in Listing 16-3 works as is and modifies the subreport parameter as expected.

```
'Step 3: Reference the ParameterField object
ParameterField = ParameterFields("ParameterName", "SubReportName")
```

Even though you really only need to use this trick when modifying parameters with the viewer control, you can also do it with the ParameterFieldDefinition collection of the ReportDocument object. This is a nice shortcut compared to looping through all the report objects in the main report looking for the subreport object.

Simplifying Parameters

If you found that programming parameters was difficult to understand, you are not alone. There are a lot of steps to learn and it doesn't help that the ReportDocument object is programmed differently than the viewer control. To try and simplify this, I wrote some generic methods that can be added to your reporting library and be used by many projects. These methods modify discrete and range parameters for both the ReportDocument object and the viewer control. If you want the fastest way to modify parameters with no bugs, just copy this code into your own project and see how much easier it is to start using parameters.

All the methods are written so that you can pass a subreport name as the last parameter. To reference parameters on the main report, pass the empty string as the subreport name. Remember that ParameterFields collection is case sensitive for parameter names. This applies to the subreport names as well.

Note
This code is just a variation on what you've already seen. To understand how it works, see the previous sections in this chapter. This code only works for the CurrentValues collection. As a .NET developer it is unlikely you will do much programming with the DefaultValues collection. If you want to use this code for updating the DefaultValues collection, it is easy enough to modify it on your own.[38]

Listing 16-4 and 16-5 modify parameters using the report object. They modify discrete values and range values. Pass each method the report object, the parameter field's name and any information necessary to fill the parameter's value. Notice that in Listing 16-5 the method definition for updating a range parameter is quite large. This is because a range parameter has many properties that need to be set.

Listing 16-4. Modify a discrete parameter using the report object.

```
Public Sub SetParameterDiscreteWithReport(ByVal MyReport As
CrystalDecisions.CrystalReports.Engine.ReportDocument, ByVal ParameterName As String, ByVal Value As
Object, ByVal SubreportName as String)
    Dim MyParameterFieldDefinition As _
        CrystalDecisions.CrystalReports.Engine.ParameterFieldDefinition
    Dim MyParameterValues As CrystalDecisions.Shared.ParameterValues
    Dim MyParameterDiscreteValue As _
        CrystalDecisions.Shared.ParameterDiscreteValue
    MyParameterFieldDefinition = _
        MyReport.DataDefinition.ParameterFields.Item(ParameterName, SubreportName)
    MyParameterValues = New CrystalDecisions.Shared.ParameterValues
    MyParameterDiscreteValue = _
        New CrystalDecisions.Shared.ParameterDiscreteValue
    MyParameterDiscreteValue.Value = Value
    MyParameterValues.Add(MyParameterDiscreteValue)
    MyParameterFieldDefinition.ApplyCurrentValues(MyParameterValues)
End Sub
```

---

[38] Don't you hate how some books tell you about a really interesting problem and then say, "I leave it as an exercise for the reader to write the code." Arghh! In my case, I'm not trying to avoid work. It's unlikely that you will need this code for default values.

Listing 16-5. Modify a range parameter using the report object.

```
Public Shared Sub SetParameterRangeWithReport(ByVal MyReport As
CrystalDecisions.CrystalReports.Engine.ReportDocument, ByVal ParameterName As String, ByVal StartValue
As Object, ByVal EndValue As Object, ByVal LowerBoundType As CrystalDecisions.Shared.RangeBoundType,
ByVal UpperBoundType As CrystalDecisions.Shared.RangeBoundType, ByVal SubreportName as String)
    Dim MyParameterFieldDefinition As _
        CrystalDecisions.CrystalReports.Engine.ParameterFieldDefinition
    Dim MyParameterValues As CrystalDecisions.Shared.ParameterValues
    Dim MyParameterRangeValue As _
        CrystalDecisions.Shared.ParameterRangeValue
    MyParameterFieldDefinition = _
        MyReport.DataDefinition.ParameterFields.Item(ParameterName, SubreportName)
    MyParameterValues = New CrystalDecisions.Shared.ParameterValues
    MyParameterRangeValue = _
        New CrystalDecisions.Shared.ParameterRangeValue
    MyParameterRangeValue.StartValue = StartValue
    MyParameterRangeValue.EndValue = EndValue
    MyParameterRangeValue.LowerBoundType = LowerBoundType
    MyParameterRangeValue.UpperBoundType = UpperBoundType
    MyParameterValues.Add(MyParameterRangeValue)
    MyParameterFieldDefinition.ApplyCurrentValues(MyParameterValues)
End Sub
```

Listing 16-6 and 16-7 modify parameters using the viewer control. Pass it the viewer control, the parameter name, and any information necessary to fill the parameter's value. Before calling this method, you have to instantiate the report object and assign it to the viewer's ReportSource property.

Listing 16-6. Modify a discrete parameter using the viewer control.

```
Public Sub SetParameterDiscreteWithViewer(ByVal CrystalReportViewer1 As
CrystalDecisions.Windows.Forms.CrystalReportViewer, ByVal ParameterName As String, ByVal
ParameterValue As Object, ByVal SubreportName as String)
    Dim MyParameterFields As CrystalDecisions.Shared.ParameterFields
    Dim MyParameterField As CrystalDecisions.Shared.ParameterField
    Dim MyParameterDiscreteValue As CrystalDecisions.Shared.ParameterDiscreteValue
    MyParameterFields = CrystalReportViewer1.ParameterFieldInfo
    MyParameterField = MyParameterFields(ParameterName, SubreportName)
    MyParameterDiscreteValue = New CrystalDecisions.Shared.ParameterDiscreteValue
    MyParameterDiscreteValue.Value = ParameterValue
    MyParameterField.CurrentValues.Add(MyParameterDiscreteValue)
    CrystalReportViewer1.ParameterFieldInfo = MyParameterFields
End Sub
```

Listing 16-7. Modify a range parameter using the viewer control.

```
Public Sub SetParameterRangeWithViewer(ByVal CrystalReportViewer1 As
CrystalDecisions.Windows.Forms.CrystalReportViewer, ByVal ParameterName As String, ByVal StartValue As
Object, ByVal EndValue As Object, ByVal LowerBoundType As CrystalDecisions.Shared.RangeBoundType,
ByVal UpperBoundType As CrystalDecisions.Shared.RangeBoundType, ByVal SubreportName as String)
    Dim MyParameterFields As CrystalDecisions.Shared.ParameterFields
    Dim MyParameterField As CrystalDecisions.Shared.ParameterField
    Dim MyParameterRangeValue As CrystalDecisions.Shared.ParameterRangeValue
    MyParameterFields = CrystalReportViewer1.ParameterFieldInfo
    MyParameterField = MyParameterFields(ParameterName, SubreportName)
    MyParameterRangeValue = New CrystalDecisions.Shared.ParameterRangeValue
    MyParameterRangeValue.StartValue = StartValue
    MyParameterRangeValue.EndValue = EndValue
    MyParameterRangeValue.LowerBoundType = LowerBoundType
    MyParameterRangeValue.UpperBoundType = UpperBoundType
    MyParameterField.CurrentValues.Add(MyParameterRangeValue)
End Sub
```

Listing 16-8 and 16-9 show how to use the above methods in an application. To keep the examples simple, they pass the empty string as the subreport name. If a report has subreports with parameters, you should pass the subreport name instead. Notice that these example uses date parameters. I did this because many people have trouble working with dates and this shows how easy it is to do.

Listing 16-8 demonstrates using the report object to update parameters. It instantiates a new report object and sets the values for a discrete and range parameter.

Listing 16-8. Modify parameters using the report object.

```
Dim MyReport As New CrystalReport1
SetParameterDiscreteWithReport(MyReport, "CustomerId", "DotNetTech", "")
SetParameterRangeWithReport(MyReport, "DateRange", #2/1/1997#, #2/15/1997#, _
CrystalDecisions.[Shared].RangeBoundType.BoundInclusive, _
CrystalDecisions.[Shared].RangeBoundType.BoundExclusive, "")
CrystalReportViewer1.ReportSource = MyReport
```

Listing 16-9 demonstrates using the viewer to update parameters. It instantiates a new report object and assigns it to the viewer. Then it calls the methods to update the parameters.

Listing 16-9 Modify parameters using the viewer control.

```
Dim MyReport As New CrystalReport1
CrystalReportViewer1.ReportSource = MyReport
SetParameterDiscreteWithViewer(CrystalReportViewer1, "MyBirthday", #5/23/1968#, "")
SetParameterRangeWithViewer(CrystalReportViewer1, "DateRange", #2/1/1997#, _
#2/15/1997#, CrystalDecisions.[Shared].RangeBoundType.BoundInclusive, _
CrystalDecisions.[Shared].RangeBoundType.BoundExclusive, "")
```

C# Code Listings

The C# code listings are equivalent to the VB.NET code listings.

Listing 16-1. Mapping the parameters in the ReportDocument class.

```
CrystalReport1 MyReport = new CrystalReport1();
MapParameterFieldDefinitions(MyReport.DataDefinition.ParameterFields, 0);
...
public void MapParameterFieldDefinitions(
    CrystalDecisions.CrystalReports.Engine.ParameterFieldDefinitions
    ParameterFieldDefinitions, int Indent)
{
    foreach(CrystalDecisions.CrystalReports.Engine.ParameterFieldDefinition
    ParameterFieldDefinition in ParameterFieldDefinitions)
    {
        MapParameterFieldDefinition(ParameterFieldDefinition, Indent);
    }
}
public void MapParameterFieldDefinition(
    CrystalDecisions.CrystalReports.Engine.ParameterFieldDefinition
    ParameterFieldDefinition, int Indent)
{
    Output("Name: " + ParameterFieldDefinition.ParameterFieldName, Indent);
    Output("PromptText: " + ParameterFieldDefinition.PromptText, Indent + 2);
    Output("ValueType: " +
    ParameterFieldDefinition.ParameterValueKind.ToString(), Indent + 2);
    Output("Kind: " +
    ParameterFieldDefinition.DiscreteOrRangeKind.ToString(), Indent + 2);
    if (ParameterFieldDefinition.CurrentValues.Count>0)
    {
        Output("Current Values: ", Indent + 2);
        MapParameterValues(ParameterFieldDefinition.CurrentValues, Indent + 4);
    }
    if (ParameterFieldDefinition.DefaultValues.Count>0)
    {
        Output("Default Values", Indent + 2);
        MapParameterValues(ParameterFieldDefinition.DefaultValues, Indent + 4);
    }
}
public void MapParameterValues(CrystalDecisions.Shared.ParameterValues ParameterValues, int Indent)
{
    foreach(CrystalDecisions.Shared.ParameterValue ParameterValue in
    ParameterValues)
    {
        if (ParameterValue is CrystalDecisions.Shared.ParameterRangeValue)
        {
            MapParameterRangeValue((CrystalDecisions.Shared.ParameterRangeValue)
            ParameterValue, Indent);
```

```
    }
    else
    {
      MapParameterDiscreteValue(
      (CrystalDecisions.Shared.ParameterDiscreteValue)ParameterValue,
      Indent);
    }
  }
}
public void MapParameterDiscreteValue(
CrystalDecisions.Shared.ParameterDiscreteValue ParameterValue, int Indent)
{
    Output("Value: " + ParameterValue.Value.ToString(), Indent);
}
public void MapParameterRangeValue(
CrystalDecisions.Shared.ParameterRangeValue ParameterValue, int Indent)
{
    Output("Value: " + ParameterValue.StartValue.ToString() + " to " + ParameterValue.EndValue.ToString(),
Indent);
}
```

Listing 16-2. Use the report document to modify a discrete parameter.

```
CrystalDecisions.Shared.ParameterDiscreteValue ParameterDiscreteValue;
CrystalDecisions.Shared.ParameterValues ParameterValues;
//Use the ReportDocument object to create two default parameters
CrystalReport1 MyReport = new CrystalReport1();
CrystalDecisions.CrystalReports.Engine.ParameterFieldDefinition ParameterFieldDefinition;
//Step 1: Get a reference to the property field to modify
ParameterFieldDefinition = MyReport.DataDefinition.ParameterFields["Location"];
//Step 2: Instantiate a ParameterValues collection object
ParameterValues = new CrystalDecisions.Shared.ParameterValues();
//Step 3: Instantiate a ParameterValue object
//This example uses a discrete value
ParameterDiscreteValue = new CrystalDecisions.Shared.ParameterDiscreteValue();
//Step 4: Assign a value to the object
ParameterDiscreteValue.Value = "Louisville, KY";
//Step 5: Add it to the ParameterValues collection using the Add() method
ParameterValues.Add(ParameterDiscreteValue);
//Step 6: Repeat steps 3-5 for additional parameters
ParameterDiscreteValue = new CrystalDecisions.Shared.ParameterDiscreteValue();
ParameterDiscreteValue.Value = "San Diego, CA";
ParameterValues.Add(ParameterDiscreteValue);
//Step 7: Assign the ParameterValues collection to the parameter field
//Do this for either the CurrentValues or DefaultValues collection
ParameterFieldDefinition.ApplyDefaultValues(ParameterValues);
//Step 8: Print or Preview the report
crystalReportViewer1.ReportSource = MyReport;
```

Listing 16-3. Use the viewer to modify a range parameter.

```
CrystalDecisions.Shared.ParameterFields ParameterFields;
CrystalDecisions.Shared.IParameterField ParameterField;
CrystalDecisions.Shared.ParameterRangeValue ParameterRangeValue;
//Step 1: Assign the report object to the viewer
CrystalReport1 MyReport = new CrystalReport1();
crystalReportViewer1.ReportSource = MyReport;
//Step 2: Reference the ParameterFields collection
ParameterFields = crystalReportViewer1.ParameterFieldInfo;
//Step 3: Reference the ParameterField
ParameterField = ParameterFields["DateRange"];
//Step 4: Create a ParameterValue object
//This example uses a range value object.
//You could also use a discrete value object.
ParameterRangeValue = new CrystalDecisions.Shared.ParameterRangeValue();
//Step 5: Assign a value to the object
ParameterRangeValue.StartValue = "1/4/1997";
ParameterRangeValue.EndValue = "1/20/1997";
//Step 6: Add the ParameterValue object to either the
//CurrentValues or DefaultValues collection
ParameterField.CurrentValues.Add(ParameterRangeValue);
```

Listing 16-4. Modify a discrete parameter using the report object.

```
public void SetParameterDiscreteWithReport(
CrystalDecisions.CrystalReports.Engine.ReportDocument MyReport,
string ParameterName, object ParameterValue, string SubreportName)
{
    CrystalDecisions.CrystalReports.Engine.ParameterFieldDefinition
    ParameterFieldDefinition;
    CrystalDecisions.Shared.ParameterDiscreteValue ParameterDiscreteValue;
    CrystalDecisions.Shared.ParameterValues ParameterValues;
    ParameterFieldDefinition =
    MyReport.DataDefinition.ParameterFields[ParameterName, SubreportName];
    ParameterValues = new CrystalDecisions.Shared.ParameterValues();
    ParameterDiscreteValue =
    new CrystalDecisions.Shared.ParameterDiscreteValue();
    ParameterDiscreteValue.Value = ParameterValue;
    ParameterValues.Add(ParameterDiscreteValue);
    ParameterFieldDefinition.ApplyCurrentValues(ParameterValues);
}
```

Listing 16-5. Modify a range parameter using the report object.

```
public void SetParameterRangeWithReport(
CrystalDecisions.CrystalReports.Engine.ReportDocument MyReport,
string ParameterName, object StartValue, object EndValue, CrystalDecisions.Shared.RangeBoundType
LowerBoundType, CrystalDecisions.Shared.RangeBoundType UpperBoundType, string SubreportName)
{
    CrystalDecisions.CrystalReports.Engine.ParameterFieldDefinition
    ParameterFieldDefinition;
    CrystalDecisions.Shared.ParameterRangeValue ParameterRangeValue;
```

```
CrystalDecisions.Shared.ParameterValues ParameterValues;
ParameterFieldDefinition = MyReport.DataDefinition.ParameterFields
[ParameterName, SubreportName];
ParameterValues = new CrystalDecisions.Shared.ParameterValues();
ParameterRangeValue = new CrystalDecisions.Shared.ParameterRangeValue();
ParameterRangeValue.StartValue = StartValue;
ParameterRangeValue.EndValue = EndValue;
ParameterRangeValue.LowerBoundType = LowerBoundType;
ParameterRangeValue.UpperBoundType = UpperBoundType;
ParameterValues.Add(ParameterRangeValue);
ParameterFieldDefinition.ApplyCurrentValues(ParameterValues);
}
```

Listing 16-6. Modify a discrete parameter using the viewer control.

```
public void SetParameterDiscreteWithViewer(
CrystalDecisions.Windows.Forms.CrystalReportViewer crystalReportViewer1,
string ParameterName, object ParameterValue, string SubreportName)
{
    CrystalDecisions.Shared.IParameterField ParameterField;
    CrystalDecisions.Shared.ParameterDiscreteValue ParameterDiscreteValue;
    ParameterField = crystalReportViewer1.ParameterFieldInfo[ParameterName,
    SubreportName];
    ParameterDiscreteValue =
    New CrystalDecisions.Shared.ParameterDiscreteValue();
    ParameterDiscreteValue.Value = ParameterValue;
    ParameterField.CurrentValues.Add(ParameterDiscreteValue);
}
```

Listing 16-7. Modify a range parameter using the viewer control.

```
public void SetParameterRangeWithViewer(
CrystalDecisions.Windows.Forms.CrystalReportViewer crystalReportViewer1,
string ParameterName, object StartValue, object EndValue, CrystalDecisions.Shared.RangeBoundType
LowerBoundType, CrystalDecisions.Shared.RangeBoundType UpperBoundType, string SubreportName)
{
    CrystalDecisions.Shared.IParameterField ParameterField;
    CrystalDecisions.Shared.ParameterRangeValue ParameterRangeValue;
    ParameterField = crystalReportViewer1.ParameterFieldInfo
    [ParameterName, SubreportName];
    ParameterRangeValue = new CrystalDecisions.Shared.ParameterRangeValue();
    ParameterRangeValue.StartValue = StartValue;
    ParameterRangeValue.EndValue = EndValue;
    ParameterRangeValue.LowerBoundType = LowerBoundType;
    ParameterRangeValue.UpperBoundType = UpperBoundType;
    ParameterField.CurrentValues.Add(ParameterRangeValue);
}
```

Listing 16-8. Modify parameters using the report object.

```
CrystalReport1 MyReport = new CrystalReport1();
SetParameterDiscreteWithReport(MyReport, "MyBirthday", new DateTime(1968,5,23), "");
```

```
SetParameterRangeWithReport(MyReport, "DateRange",new DateTime(1997,2,1), new DateTime(1997,3,1),
CrystalDecisions.Shared.RangeBoundType.BoundInclusive,
CrystalDecisions.Shared.RangeBoundType.BoundExclusive, "");
crystalReportViewer1.ReportSource = MyReport;
```

Listing 16-9 Modify parameters using the viewer control.

```
CrystalReport1 MyReport = new CrystalReport1();
crystalReportViewer1.ReportSource = MyReport;
SetParameterDiscreteWithViewer(crystalReportViewer1, "CustomerId",
"DotNet Tech", "");
SetParameterRangeWithViewer(crystalReportViewer1, "DateRange",
new DateTime(1997, 1, 1),new DateTime(1997, 2, 1),
CrystalDecisions.Shared.RangeBoundType.BoundInclusive,
CrystalDecisions.Shared.RangeBoundType.BoundExclusive, "");
```

This page intentionally left blank

Dynamic Data Sources

Connecting to databases during runtime gives a reporting solution great flexibility for using a single report to print with different data sources and dynamic queries. Reports can dynamically print data from different servers, different types of databases, and customized queries.

To be honest, this chapter has a lot of meat on its bones. There are many variations for performing data connectivity and it can be overwhelming at first. It's best to read this chapter in its entirety to get a good understanding of how everything works. Then decide the best option for implementing your report. Scan through the chapter and look for the code examples labeled for your chosen interface method. Each piece of the code is complete and the sample report it runs against is deliberately kept simple. Most of the code can be used with any report without modifications.

Chapter 13 showed how to connect to data sources using the Visual Studio IDE. This consisted of using the different wizards to select the data source, specify the fields to print, and work with SQL statements. This chapter focuses on changing the data source of an existing report during runtime. Using the Crystal Reports object during runtime gives you more power than working solely with the Visual Studio IDE.

Implementing the Push Model

Reports can either use the Pull Model or the Push Model for retrieving data. The Pull Model links to a data source and retrieves the data automatically. This was discussed in Chapter 13. The Push Model is based upon generating reports from a manually populated dataset. It requires you to create the dataset object, populate it with the appropriate data, and pass it to the report object for printing. You have complete control over how it works and can optimize the data connections. Since a dataset is designed to link to many types of data sources and you code the connection string, the Push Model gives you the flexibility to link to almost any type of data source as well as create custom datasets that link to proprietary data sources. This isn't always possible with the Pull Model.

Using the Push Model results in the worst performance possible. Datasets are new to Crystal Reports and consequently they have terrible performance. The report has to process the data manually on the client. The performance might change in a future release, but for now Crystal Reports has been optimized to use the Pull Model with ODBC and OLE DB connections. The Push Model should only be used when the standard methods of connecting to data sources don't work.

In certain circumstances, datasets can improve the scalability of ASP.NET applications. Datasets can be saved to the ASP.NET cache and used by multiple reports. For queries that either require a lot of processing by the server or return a large resultset, this results in a considerable improvement in performance. The first report runs as expected, but all reports after that benefit by having the dataset already populated and available in the web server's memory. Use the Cache.Insert() method to save the DataSet object and use the Cache.Item() method to retrieve it.

The Push Model is more complicated than the Pull Model, and as a result there are more steps to learn. These steps are implemented in two stages. The first stage is creating the report for use with the Push Model. This consists of creating a dataset and specifying it as the report's data source. Then design the report using the fields from this dataset. The second stage is writing the code to populate the dataset and pass it to the report. There are a total of four steps, which are listed and explained in detail next.

Stage	Steps
Report Creation	1. Define the dataset schema file.
	2. Build the report using the dataset schema file as the data source.
Running the Report	3. Populate the dataset.
	4. Bind the dataset to the report.

Define the Dataset Schema File

When designing a report using the Report Expert you assign it an existing data source and it uses this information to determine which fields are available. When you are using the Push Model you don't have this luxury. Instead, you have to create a dataset schema file that defines the fields and assign it to the report. The report examines the dataset schema to get a field list.

A dataset schema is a fully compliant XML file that defines the properties of the data source. It has a file extension of '.xsd'. Listing 17-1 shows an excerpt of the XML code that is in the dataset file.

Listing 17-1. The XML schema from a dataset file.

```
<xs:element name="Customers">
    <xs:complexType>
        <xs:sequence>
            <xs:element name="CustomerID" type="xs:string" />
            <xs:element name="CompanyName" type="xs:string" />
            <xs:element name="ContactName" type="xs:string" minOccurs="0" />
        </xs:sequence>
    </xs:complexType>
</xs:element>
```

A dataset schema file can be created in two different ways. The first method uses the Visual Studio IDE and the second way uses the ADO.NET methods to create it. The method you use depends upon your preferences.

Using the IDE to Create a Dataset File

The Visual Studio IDE makes it easy to create a dataset file. Right-click on the menu Project | Add New Item. The Add New Item dialog box lists Dataset File as an option. Click on this option, give it an appropriate file name and click OK. The dataset file is created and added as an item in the Solution Explorer window. As you can see in Figure 17-1, the dataset is represented in the IDE as an empty screen.

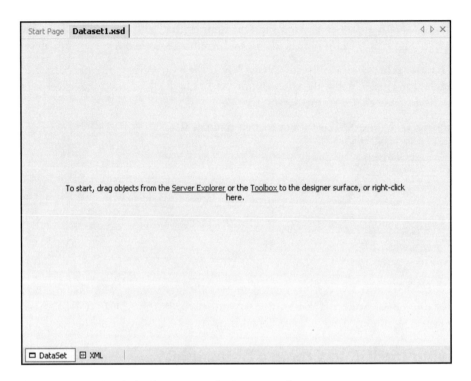

To start, drag objects from the <u>Server Explorer</u> or the <u>Toolbox</u> to the designer surface, or right-click here.

□ DataSet │ ⊞ XML

Figure 17-1. The default Dataset designer surface.

At this point, the IDE is ready to build a new dataset file from scratch. Open the Server Explorer and drill down to the appropriate data source to find the table(s) you need. Drag one or more tables from the Server Explorer window onto the dataset surface. Behind the scenes the IDE generates the appropriate code to represent the table(s) with XML. To see what the XML source looks like without opening the file, right-click anywhere on the designer and select the option View XML Source.

Tip
The dataset has a dropdown box for the data type. You can click on this dropdown box to change the data type for the field. If you have a table that is similar to the dataset you want to create, but not exact, add it to dataset and make any changes to it. This is easier than creating the tables in the dataset from scratch.

Once finished adding the appropriate tables to the dataset your screen will look similar to the one in Figure 17-2.

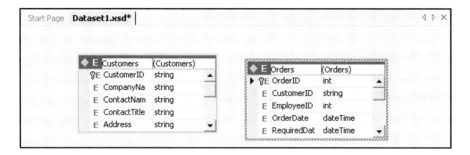

Figure 17-2. The Dataset designer surface with two tables.

Clicking on the Save button in the toolbar causes the IDE to save the XML source to the dataset file. The file is ready to be linked to the report.

> **Caution**
>
> It is easy to forget to save the schema file before linking it to the report. But if you don't save the file, the Report Expert won't know what the fields are. It will show an empty table with no fields listed. There must be a physical .xsd file prior to running the Report Expert.

Creating a DataSet Manually with the IDE

The last method of building a dataset assumed that you have a table that can be dragged and dropped onto the designer. There are times you want to build without an existing data source. This could be a report based on user input or internal calculations. No worries, you can still use the IDE to create a dataset manually.

Just like before, add a DataSet object to your project. Right-click on the menu item Project | Add New Item. The Add New Item dialog box lists Dataset File as an option. Select this option, give it an appropriate filename and click OK.

The designer shows a blank screen. Right-click anywhere on the designer and select Add | New Element. In the first column of the first row type in the table name and press the Tab key twice. In Figure 17-3 I named the table ManualTable.

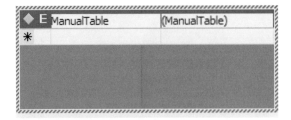

Figure 17-3. A new DataSet table.

Each field in a table is defined as an XML Element with a field name and data type. On the second row click on the first column and a dropdown list appears. Select the Element item.

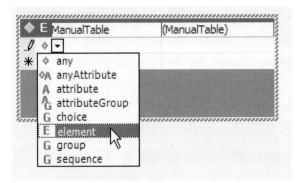

Next enter a field name and a data type. In this example I created a field EmployeeId of type int and EmployeeName of type string.

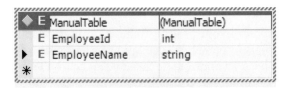

The dataset is complete. After saving the file it can be referenced by a report.

Note
If you make changes to the dataset schema after creating the report, the report will not recognize these changes. It keeps the schema in its cache and doesn't refresh. The only way to force it to renew the cache is to completely close the Visual Studio IDE, re-open the project, right-click on the report and select Database	Verify Database.

Creating a Dataset File with ADO.NET Methods

The last way to create a dataset file is to use the methods of the ADO.NET classes. The ADO.NET namespace is designed to make working with XML files almost effortless. It converts XML schema to and from the internal representation. Use the WriteXMLSchema() method to save the schema to a file. Simply pass it the filename to save it to.

First create a dataset object that links to the data you want to report on. Since the dataset object can be used to connect to a wide variety of data sources, this gives you great flexibility for what your report prints. Once the dataset is created, call the WriteXMLSchema() method and pass it the filename. This saves the XML schema to the file to be used by your report.

The code in listing 17-2 gives you a simple example of how to implement this. It takes a filename and a DataSet object and creates an XML schema file. Make sure that the DataSet object has been populated elsewhere in your application before calling this procedure. Also make sure that the filename has a .ds extension.

Listing 17-2. Creating an XML schema file from a dataset object.

```
'Write a populated dataset object to an XML schema file
'The XmlFileName should have a ".ds" file extension
Public Sub CreateXmlFile(ByVal XmlFileName As String, ByVal XmlDataset As DataSet)
    XmlDataset.WriteXmlSchema(XmlFileName)
End Sub
```

The code in this listing is very generic and can be used anywhere in your application. It is meant to be executed once prior to creating the report. It doesn't have to be part of your final application and you can comment it out.

Build the Report Using the Dataset File

For a report to use the Push Model, it has to be designed using a dataset as the data source. The previous section showed three different ways to create the dataset schema file. The way that you created the dataset determines how it links to the report.

If you used the IDE to create a dataset, open the Database Expert[39], and expand the category ADO.NET Datasets. This lists all the datasets in the project. Expand the dataset you created to see the list of tables within it. Add the appropriate tables to the Selected Tables window on the right. Go to the Links tab to establish relationships between the tables.

---

[39] As mentioned earlier, the Database Expert can be reached by either using the Report Expert or by right-clicking on a report and selecting Database | Add Database.

If you created a dataset file manually, open the Database Expert and click on the category called "More Data Sources". Under it you will see "ADO.NET (XML)". Click on this and the dialog box in Figure 17-4 will open.

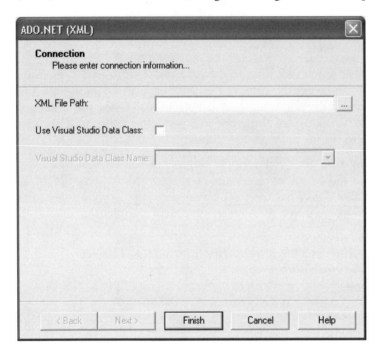

Figure 17-4. The ADO.NET (XML) dialog box.

This dialog box lets you browse the dataset files on your computer. It also has the option of letting you select a dataset that was created using the IDE. This is the same as the category "ADO.NET Datasets" which was discussed previously. These options are mutually exclusive and you can only use one of them. Choosing to enter the path of a dataset file lets you use the dataset file you just created or you can use a dataset file that already exists. This lets you re-use a dataset file that has been created for other projects or by other teams. If you want to use a dataset object that is part of your project, then select the checkbox "Use Visual Studio Data Class" and select the class name from the dropdown list.

After linking the report to a dataset, design the report as normal. When finished with the report layout, go to the next steps to populate the dataset.

Note

Once the report is bound to a dataset file, the file is no longer used by the report. The schema information is saved within the report file. You can delete the dataset file after binding it and it will have no effect.

Populate the DataSet Object

At this point in the process, you've created the proper dataset files and designed the report to use the datasets. If you run the report, nothing is printed. This is because the datasets don't have any data in them. You have to manually populate the datasets prior to opening the report.

Populating the dataset objects is coded differently for each type of data source you are connecting to. It is not within the scope of this book to discuss the best way to connect to a data source.

The code in this section shows the basic ways of populating a dataset for various data sources. Each procedure is called FillDataset() and takes an empty Dataset object. It populates it with the appropriate data. This procedure is called by the code in the next section "Bind the Dataset".

The purpose of each of these procedures is to give you a quick way to copy and paste this code into your own application and quickly be productive. This should give you a good starting point and serve as a quick reference without having to look up the code in other books.

Caution

Within these examples, notice that the Fill() method of the DataAdapter object is always passed the table name. This is the name the report associates with each table. If you give a table an alias (discussed Chapter 13), then the Fill() method must be passed the original table name. You can't pass the alias name to the Fill() method. Also note that per the documentation, the table name is case sensitive.

MS Access

Connecting to an MS Access database requires using the OLEDB provider in the .NET Framework. The critical parts of the code are specifying the connection string and the SQL statement. The SQL statement can be any valid SQL statement that MS Access accepts. The connection string uses the standard tags, but notice that the password tag is more complex than you might expect and you also have to specify where the system database (System.MDW) is located. If the Access database hasn't been secured, then leave the ID, password, and system database tags out of the connection string.

Listing 17-3. Populating a dataset with a MS Access table.

```
Private Sub FillDataset(ByVal myDataset As DataSet)
    Dim myConnectionString As String
    Dim myDataAdapter As OleDbDataAdapter
    Dim SQL As String = "SELECT * FROM Customer"
    Dim myDataSet As DataSet = New DataSet()
    myConnectionString = "Provider=Microsoft.Jet.OLEDB.4.0; " & _
        "Data Source=C:\Xtreme.mdb;User ID=Admin;" & _
        "Jet OLEDB:Database Password=pw;Jet OLEDB:System database=" & _
        "C:\Program Files\Office2000\Office\system.mdw"
    MyDataAdapter = New OleDbDataAdapter(SQL, MyConnectionString)
    myDataAdapter.Fill(myDataSet, "Customer")
End Sub
```

You can use MS Access to help you build SQL statements. Use the visual query designer to build and test a query. This is a simple matter of adding the tables to the designer and linking the fields together. When finished, click on the View button in the top left hand corner and select the SQL option. This shows you the corresponding SQL statement to generate the query. Copy and paste this to your application. If you are familiar enough with SQL that you don't need to use the visual query designer, you can still use Access to test the code you wrote. Open a new query and don't add any tables to it. Click on the view button in the top left hand corner and select the SQL option. Copy the SQL statement from your program into the Access query window. Click on the view window again to see the query results. It will immediately tell you if there is a syntax error. If there is no syntax error, you can look at the results of the query to see if it generated the expected results.

SQL Server

Connect to SQL Server using the SqlClient provider in the .NET Framework. Notice that the SQL statement in Listing 17-4 joins the Customers table and the Orders table by the CustomerId. This is much faster than creating two dataset objects and having the report join them on the client machine.

Listing 17-4. Populating a dataset with a SQL Server table.

```
Private Sub FillDataset(ByVal myDataSet As DataSet)
    Dim myConnectionString As String
    Dim myDataAdapter As SqlClient.SqlDataAdapter
    Dim SQL As String
    SQL = "SELECT Customers.*, Orders.* " & _
        "FROM Customers INNER JOIN Orders " & _
        "ON Customers.CustomerId = Orders.CustomerId"
    myConnectionString = "Data Source=(local);UID=sa;pwd=pw;Database=Northwind"
    myDataAdapter = New SqlClient.SqlDataAdapter(mySQL, myConnectionString)
    myDataAdapter.Fill(myDataSet, "Customers")
End Sub
```

XML file

Printing from an XML file is very easy. The DataSet object has a ReadXML() method that loads XML data into the dataset object. In this example, the ReadXML() method is passed a fully qualified filename.

Listing 17-5. Populating a dataset with an XML file.

```
Private Sub FillDataset(ByVal myDataSet As DataSet, ByVal myFileName As String)
   myDataSet.ReadXML(myFileName)
End Sub
```

Manually Populated

Crystal Reports doesn't have to print from an existing data source. It's easy to report on data that is dynamically created as your application runs. There are a couple different ways where this can be useful. The first is reports based upon user input. For example, an application can have a user enter the details of a bank loan and it prints the amortization schedule. Since the input is dynamic, there is no database to print from. You have to calculate the amortization formulas that generate the data while the application is running and send it to the report for printing.

Another example is to manipulate data before it prints. Although Crystal Reports has a multitude of options for writing formulas and creatively using subreports, there are times when this doesn't meet your needs. For example, a mailing label report could need to print each label a certain number of times. The number of times to print each one is stored in the database. It isn't possible to use formulas or subreports to change the number of times a record is printed on a report. To create this report, you would first create a new dataset. Then loop through the records in the original dataset while copying each record into the new dataset as many times as necessary. The report now prints each label multiple times because there are multiple records for each one.

The DataSet class has methods to create a new dataset object within memory and populate it manually. Pass this manual dataset to Crystal Reports for printing. Listing 17-6 shows a simple example of how this is done. It creates a simple array with a customer's ID and their last name. Then it builds a new DataTable object with two fields in it and adds it to the dataset. The last step is to copy the array into the dataset. Now it's ready for printing!

Listing 17-6. Manually populating a dataset.

```
Private Sub FillDataset(ByVal myDataSet As DataSet)
   Dim Customers(,) As String = {{"123", "Jones"}, {"456", "Smith"}}
   ' Create a new DataTable.
   Dim myDataTable As DataTable = New DataTable("Customers")
   Dim myDataColumn As DataColumn
   Dim myDataRow As DataRow
```

```
' Create first column
myDataColumn = New DataColumn()
myDataColumn.DataType = System.Type.GetType("System.String")
myDataColumn.ColumnName = "CustomerID"
myDataTable.Columns.Add(myDataColumn)
' Create second column
myDataColumn = New DataColumn()
myDataColumn.DataType = System.Type.GetType("System.String")
myDataColumn.ColumnName = "LastName"
myDataTable.Columns.Add(myDataColumn)
myDataSet.Tables.Add(myDataTable)
'Copy the array into the datatable
Dim ixCustomers As Integer
For ixCustomers = 0 To 1
   myDataRow = myDataTable.NewRow()
   myDataRow("CustomerID") = Customers(ixCustomers, 0)
   myDataRow("LastName") = Customers(ixCustomers, 1)
   myDataTable.Rows.Add(myDataRow)
Next
End Sub
```

DataGrid Control

Similar to printing a manually populated dataset is printing the contents of a DataGrid control. You can have a datagrid on a form and give the user the option to send the datagrid contents to a report. The user modifies the datagrid and sends its values to a report without having to save it first.

Fortunately, this is very easy because the datagrid is designed to work with datasets. The datagrid has a DataSource property that can be explicitly cast as a DataSet object. In Listing 17-7, the MyDataSet parameter is set to the DataSource property.

Listing 17-7. Getting the DataSet object from a DataGrid control.

```
Private Sub FillDataset(ByVal MyDataSet As DataSet)
   MyDataSet = CType(DataGrid1.DataSource, DataSet)
End Sub
```

DataView Object

The DataView object is useful for taking an existing Dataset object and filtering or sorting its records. You have three options for doing this. The first is to create a new dataset and populate it with the filtered/sorted data. This isn't a very good idea because the server has to process the request a second time and send the results back to the client. This unnecessarily ties up resources on the server as well as the network. Another option is to change the properties of the report object so that it uses a record selection formula or adds sort fields. The third way is to create a DataView object that is based off the original dataset. This optimizes performance by keeping the server from having to do any additional work as well as saving the network from the additional throughput. Another benefit is that the ADO.NET classes are optimized for doing this type of processing. So you will reap better performance by using a DataView object rather than asking the report to process the same data.

Caution

As of when this book was published, there is a bug with Crystal Reports that doesn't let it print from a DataView object. My technical contact has logged this issue and it will be corrected in a future service pack. This code will be functional once the proper service pack is released.

Listing 17-8. Printing from a DataView object.

```
Private Sub PrintDataView(myDataSet As DataSet)
    Dim myDataView as DataView
    Dim myReport As New CrystalReport1()
    myDataView = New  DataView(myDataSet.Tables("TableName"), _
        "CompanyName > 'B'", "", DataViewRowState.CurrentRows)
    myReport.SetDataSource(myDataView)
    CrystalReportViewer1.ReportSource = myReport
End Sub
```

The code in Listing 17-8 deviates from the other examples shown so far. All the examples so far are passed a null DataSet object and they populate it so it can be used by the calling method. Since the DataView object needs an existing DataSet object to work, this method is passed a DataSet object that is already populated. You can only create a DataView object after creating a DataSet object elsewhere in your program.

This method creates a DataView object to create a subset of the records, and binds the DataView object to the report using the SetDataSource() method (explained in the next section). Then it prints the report.

In the spirit of never letting a bug defeat me, I wrote a short procedure to convert the DataView object into a new DataTable object. It creates a new DataTable based on the columns in the DataView and then copies the DataView rows into the DataTable. Pass it a DataView object and it returns the corresponding DataTable object. Since this code isn't specific to Crystal Reports, I'm not going to go into the details of how it works. Just copy and paste the code into your project if you need to use it.

Listing 17-9. Convert the DataView object into a DataTable

```
'Take a dataview and return a table with the same data
'This is necessary b/c reports can't print views
```

```
Private Shared Function ConvertViewToTable(ByVal dv As DataView) As DataTable
    Dim Col, Row As Integer
    Dim NewRow() As Object
    Dim NewTable As New DataTable(dv.Table.TableName)
    'Copy the column objects into the table
    For Col = 0 To dv.Table.Columns.Count - 1
        NewTable.Columns.Add(dv.Table.Columns.Item(Col).ColumnName,
        dv.Table.Columns.Item(Col).DataType)
    Next Col
    'Create each row and copy the column data into a new row object
    For Row = 0 To dv.Count - 1
        ReDim NewRow(dv.Table.Columns.Count - 1)
        For Col = 0 To dv.Table.Columns.Count - 1
            NewRow(Col) = dv.Item(Row).Item(Col)
        Next Col
        NewTable.Rows.Add(NewRow)
    Next Row
    Return NewTable
End Function
```

As far as performance is concerned, you need to test you own data and compare this to modifying the sorting and filtering with the report object.

Arrays and Collections

A lot of people ask if they can print a report using an array or collection as a data source. Unfortunately, this is not possible. The best option is to copy the array to a dataset and build the report using this dataset.

Bind the Dataset to the report

The last step in using the Push Model is writing the code to link the fully populated dataset to the report. The ReportDocument class has a SetDataSource() method that takes a populated DataSet object and uses it as the data source for the report. After calling this method the report is bound to the dataset and is able to print the records.

Listing 17-10. Linking the dataset file to the report and previewing it.

```
Dim myReport as New CrystalReport1
Dim myDataSet As New DataSet()
'Use the appropriate FillDataSet() method from the previous section
FillDataSet(myDataSet)
'Uncomment the following line if you need to create a new dataset file
'CreateXmlFile("C:\FileName.ds", myDataSet)
myReport.SetDataSource(myDataSet)
CrystalReportViewer1.ReportSource = myReport
```

The code first creates an instance of the report and assigns it to the myReport object variable. Then it creates a new DataSet object and passes it to the FillDataSet() method. This method is from the code listings in the prior section. Use the one that matches your data source and modify it for any special needs you have. There is also a call to the procedure WriteXmlFile() and it is commented out. As mentioned earlier, before you build a report you need to have a dataset file that the report can reference. It is commented out so that you can run it again if you need to rebuild the dataset file.

The SetDataSource() method is passed the populated dataset. This binds the data to the report.

> **Tip**
>
> It is common to bind the report to the dataset and get the error "Logon Failed". This occurs when the table name wasn't specified when the dataset was populated with the data table. It can also occur when the table name doesn't match what the report is expecting. Examine the dataset object in debug mode and see what those table names are.

The Database Class

The ReportDocument class, shown in Figure 17-5, manages the connections to your report's data sources. It gives you runtime access to the methods and properties to dynamically manipulate and optimize the connections.

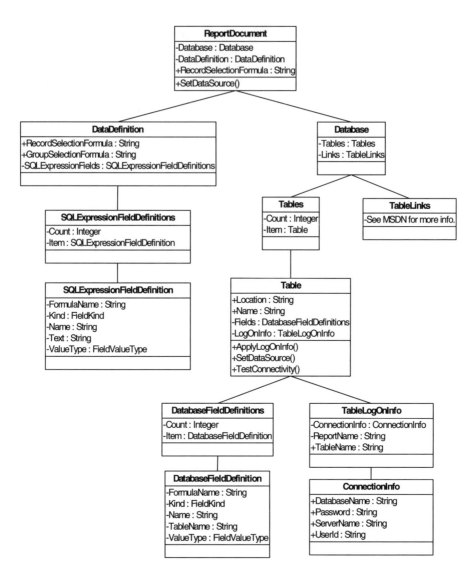

Figure 17-5. The Database class diagram.

This diagram shows the ReportDocument class and the two properties that work with data sources. The first is the Database property. It is a collection of tables and table links. Each table has properties that set the relevant information for connecting to the table as well as the fields in each table. This is the class that this chapter focuses on. The second property of the ReportDocument class is the DataDefinition class. It has the SQL expression field.

The following sections discuss the different topics for working with and manipulating a report's data sources. Each topic makes use of different properties and methods of the ReportDocument classes.

Logging on to Secure Data Sources

Using secure data sources with your report can be an initial source of confusion. There are a lot of types of data sources and just as many ways to connect to them. This is a lot of information to comprehend.

Crystal Reports is designed so that the user ID you entered at design time is saved with the report file, but not the password. This is done so that the security of your database isn't compromised. If you are printing from a non-secure data source, then the report prints fine. If the data source is secure, then you are prompted with a dialog box to enter the login credentials. You can prevent the dialog box from appearing by setting the user credentials during runtime. This lets you manage security in a way that conforms to your corporation's policies.

Note

This section only applies to reports that use the Pull Model. The Pull Model saves connection information with the report and you have to modify the connection properties to set the user credentials. This doesn't apply if you are using the Push Model because you had to connect to the data source manually. The report doesn't save any of the connection information and consequently there is nothing for you to change.

Logging on to a secure data source uses two classes: Table and ConnectionInfo. The Table class is the primary class. The report object stores each table that it uses within a Tables collection. Loop through the Tables collection to reference each Table object. The Name property identifies which database table it is. If you want to apply different login credentials for each table, then examine the Name property to identify each table.

Within the Table object is the LogOnInfo object. This is only used to get a reference to the ConnectionInfo object. The ConnectionInfo object has the properties UserId and Password. The UserId property is already set to the user ID that you entered during design mode. If this is what you want, then you do not have to change it. However, you probably want to reassign it with the current user's credentials. The Password property is always empty. You have to assign it with the current user's password.

When the UserId and Password properties are set, call the ApplyLogOnInfo() method of the Table object. After this is done for each table, the report is ready to print. Crystal Reports attempts to log on to the data source when it prints. If the information is valid, then the user is logged in and the report prints. If the information isn't valid, then a login dialog box is displayed so that new user information can be entered.

> **Tip**
>
> If you want to find out if the user credentials are valid before opening the report, call the TestConnectivity() method of the Table object. It returns True if there was a successful login.

Setting the logon properties is done differently depending upon whether you are doing so with the ReportDocument object or if you are using the viewer control. Although both use the same objects and properties, the way you get to this information is different. This is explained in detail in the next two sections.

Logging On with the ReportDocument

The ReportDocument object has a Tables collection that stores each table in a report. The program loops through each table in this collection and sets the logon properties for it. Listing 17-11 shows how to loop through each data source and set these properties. It sets different login credentials based upon the table.

Listing 17-11. Logging in to multiple tables.

```
Private Sub LoginToTables(ByVal UserId As String, ByVal Password As String)
    Dim myReport As New CrystalReport1()
    Dim myTable As CrystalDecisions.CrystalReports.Engine.Table
    Dim myLogonInfo As CrystalDecisions.Shared.TableLogOnInfo
    'Changing the logon info
    For Each myTable In myReport.Database.Tables
        myLogonInfo = myTable.LogOnInfo
        If myTable.Name = " CorpStandards" Then
            With myLogonInfo.ConnectionInfo
                .UserID = G_UserId
                .Password = G_Password
            End With
        Else
            With myLogonInfo.ConnectionInfo
                .UserID = UserId
                .Password = Password
            End With
        End If
        myTable.ApplyLogOnInfo(myLogonInfo)
```

```
'Test if the user credentials are valid
If Not myTable.TestConnectivity() Then
    MessageBox.Show("Invalid user credentials for table: " & myTable.Name)
End If
Next myTable
CrystalReportViewer1.ReportSource = myReport
End Sub
```

This example illustrates how each table is treated separately. It uses a table called CorpStandards that has public access for everyone in the company. It uses a global user account to login to it. All other tables have specific security and use the current user's login information. This is managed elsewhere in the program and is passed to this procedure via its parameter list.

The code loops through each table in the ReportDocument.Database. Tables collection and gets a reference to the TableLogOnInfo object. If the table name is "CorpStandards" it applies the generic login information. For all other tables it uses the login parameters passed to the procedure. After setting the properties, it calls the ApplyLogOnInfo() method of the Table class. This updates the table with the new login properties. The TestConnectivity() method is used to determine whether the user credentials are valid or not. If they aren't, then a message box is displayed that tells which table failed. The report viewer is assigned the report document and this forces the report to open the database connections using the user credentials and display the report.

Logging on with the Viewer Control

Setting the login credentials using the viewer control uses the same objects as the ReportDocument objects. It does so in a slightly different manner because the viewer control doesn't have any knowledge of the tables in a report. You can't loop through the Tables collection because the viewer doesn't have access to it. You have to create the collection yourself and set the properties of each table.

The TableLogOnInfos collection is the viewer's collection object. It is initially empty and it needs to have a separate Table object for each table in the report. Create a new Table object for each table and set the UserId and Password properties of the ConnectionInfo object. Call the Add() method to add the table to the TableLogOnInfos collection.

Listing 17-12. Setting the Logon credentials with the viewer control.

```
Public Sub PrintPreview(ByVal UserId As String, ByVal Password As String)
    Dim myReport As New CrystalReport1()
    Dim myLogonInfo As CrystalDecisions.Shared.TableLogOnInfo
    CrystalReportViewer1.LogOnInfo = _
        New CrystalDecisions.Shared.TableLogOnInfos()
    'Create the Customer table and set its properties
```

```
myLogonInfo = New CrystalDecisions.Shared.TableLogOnInfo()
myLogonInfo.TableName = "Customers"
With myLogonInfo.ConnectionInfo
  .UserID = UserId
  .Password = Password
End With
CrystalReportViewer1.LogOnInfo.Add(myLogonInfo)
'Create the Orders table and set its properties
myLogonInfo = New CrystalDecisions.Shared.TableLogOnInfo()
myLogonInfo.TableName = "Orders"
With myLogonInfo.ConnectionInfo
  .UserID = UserId
  .Password = Password
End With
CrystalReportViewer1.LogOnInfo.Add(myLogonInfo)
'Show the report
CrystalReportViewer1.ReportSource = myReport
End Sub
```

The first step is to create a new instance of the TableLogOnInfos() object and assign it to the viewer. This is the collection that stores the table information for the report. The code then creates the Customer table by creating a new instance of a TableLogOnInfo() object and assigning its properties. The three important properties are TableName, UserID, and Password. As mentioned earlier in the chapter, the TableName property is case sensitive and must match the table name in the report exactly. After the properties are set, this object gets added to the TableLogOnInfos collection by calling the Add() method. This is repeated for the Orders table. After all the tables have been added, the report object is assigned to the viewer and the report is displayed.

Caution

The choice of names for the viewer properties can be confusing if you aren't careful. The name of the collection class is called TableLogOnInfos(). Notice that it has an "s" at the end of it. It stores a collection of TableLogOnInfo() objects. Notice that this object name is singular. Now for the confusing part: the viewer's property name that represents the TableLogOnInfos() collection is called LogOnInfo. Notice that this name doesn't have the "s" at the end. Thus, the viewer's collection property doesn't have the same name as the collection class. Rather it has a similar name as the objects it manages. Be careful or else you might think that the collection is the object it stores.

Parameters and Stored Procedures

A common hurdle that developers have is figuring out how to print reports connected to stored procedures using parameters. But it really isn't hard once you understand how it works. Reports that use stored procedures as their data source are no different than reports that use any other data source. When you open the report, it automatically calls the stored procedure, retrieves the data, and populates the report with this data. The difference between using a stored procedure and using a table is that stored procedures accept parameters as input.

When a report is designed with a stored procedure, Crystal Reports examines the stored procedure to see if it uses parameters. If so, the designer automatically creates a report parameter for each parameter in the stored procedure. There is a one-to-one mapping of report parameters to stored procedure parameters. When the report runs, the report engine takes the value of each of these parameters and automatically passes them to the stored procedure.

As you saw in Chapter 16, the user is always prompted to enter the parameters before the report can execute. Of course, you probably don't want to prompt the user for this information because your application has already done so via the user interface. To prevent this from happening, manually populate the parameter(s) via code with the information the user has already provided. After the parameters are filled, the report connects to the database, passes the parameters to the stored procedure and previews the report.

Listing 17-13 is the complete code for using the viewer control to connect to a stored procedure that uses a parameter.

Listing 17-13. Connecting to a stored procedure using parameters.

```
Private Sub SpWithViewer(ByVal UserId As String, ByVal Password As String, _
    ByVal SpParameter As String)
    'Logon to the server
    Dim crReport As New CrystalReport1()
    Dim crLogonInfo As New CrystalDecisions.Shared.TableLogOnInfo()
    CrystalReportViewer1.LogOnInfo = _
        New CrystalDecisions.Shared.TableLogOnInfos()
    crLogonInfo.TableName = "spCustomers;1"
    With crLogonInfo.ConnectionInfo
        .UserID = UserId
        .Password = Password
    End With
    CrystalReportViewer1.LogOnInfo.Add(crLogonInfo)
    'Create the parameter
    Dim ParameterFields As CrystalDecisions.Shared.ParameterFields
```

```
Dim ParameterField As CrystalDecisions.Shared.ParameterField
Dim spValue As CrystalDecisions.Shared.ParameterDiscreteValue
ParameterFields = New CrystalDecisions.Shared.ParameterFields()
ParameterField = New CrystalDecisions.Shared.ParameterField()
ParameterField.ParameterFieldName = "@CustPattern"
spValue = New CrystalDecisions.Shared.ParameterDiscreteValue()
spValue.Value = SpParameter
ParameterField.CurrentValues.Add(spValue)
ParameterFields.Add(ParameterField)
CrystalReportViewer1.ParameterFieldInfo = ParameterFields
'Show the report
CrystalReportViewer1.ReportSource = crReport
End Sub
```

This code is a compilation of code you've already seen. The first half logs onto
the data source with the appropriate server name, database name, and login
credentials. Notice that the TableName property is the name of the stored
procedure with ;1 shown at the end of it. Crystal Reports always puts ;1 at the
end of the procedure name and if you forget to include it then it won't work.
The second half of the code creates a new parameter field, adds it to the
parameter field collection and assigns this collection to the report viewer. If you
want to pass parameters using the ReportDocument object instead, then replace
the parameter code with the code from Listing 16-1.

Tip

If you want to pass a NULL value to a stored procedure
parameter, set the parameter's Value property to Nothing in
VB.Net and null in C#.

Set NoCount On

Although this chapter assumes you are already familiar with stored procedures,
there is one statement that doesn't get much attention. I think it is very
important to be aware of it.

SET NOCOUNT ON

The Set NoCount On statement prevents extraneous messages from being output
by SQL Server. By default, Sql Server outputs status messages while it executes
a stored procedure. These often state how many records were affected by the
last statement. Unfortunately, these status messages confuse Crystal Reports
and it thinks that they are part of the recordset. This obviously isn't the case
and the report won't generate any output.

If you are working with simple stored procedures, then the majority of them
consist of a SELECT statement followed by a list of tables, fields and a join
method. Crystal Reports handles this type of stored procedure fine. Once you

start getting into writing more complex stored procedures you will find that you often need to execute multiple SQL statements within one stored procedure. This happens when you are using temporary tables or updating data prior to executing the final SELECT statement.

```
'SET NOCOUNT ON
INSERT INTO AuditLog ...
SELECT * FROM tblSales WHERE ...
```

In the above code, the SET NOCOUNT ON statement is commented out. Running this code will generate two output messages for each statement. They will be in the format of xx records affected. This message is passed prior to the records being returned from the stored procedure. This conflicts with what the report is expecting. Thus, it doesn't use the data from the SELECT statement as the recordset. By removing the comment from the first line, you tell the database server not to report how many records are affected. This eliminates Crystal Reports from incorrectly using these messages as part of the database. Ideally, this statement would be the first statement in every stored procedure.

Programmatically Changing the Data Source

Some programs require changing the data source of a table while the application is running. Although this isn't common, it does happen. An example is an application that wants to use the same report for multiple data sources. For example, a sales application could offer the user two reports: a sales report that shows current year data and a sales report that shows historical data. By changing the data source during run-time, you can design a single report that handles both options.

Note

You can only change the data source when using the Pull Method. The Pull Method stores the data source information you set at design time and this is what is used by default. The nature of the Push Method is that no data source information is saved with the report. It only knows the XML schema for a table. Thus, you always have to manually set the data source information every time you run the report.

The two classes that were used earlier in the chapter to modify logon information are the same classes used to change a table's data source: Table and ConnectionInfo. But this time, rather than modify the UserId and Password properties, modify the ServerName and DatabaseName properties.

The ServerName and DatabaseName properties represent different values depending upon which data source you are connecting to. Table 17-3 shows what belongs in each property.

Table 17-3. The properties for each type of data source.

Data Source	ServerName	DatabaseName
MS Access	The fully qualified file path	Leave it blank
SQL Server[40]	The server name	The database name
ODBC Driver	The DSN name	Leave it blank

Note

The data source isn't designed to have its connection type changed. For example, if the report is connected to SQL Server with an ODBC connection, then you can't modify the connection during runtime to use OLE DB or any other type of connection. This would require the report engine to change the DLL it uses to process the data source. This is set when the application is compiled and can't be changed.

The data source can only be changed using the ReportDocument object. You can't use the viewer control to modify the data source during runtime.

Using the ReportDocument Object

Listing 17-14 shows how to change the data source of a table as well as set the user credentials. This is very similar to Listing 17-10 which only demonstrated how to set the logon credentials. In that listing, different logon credentials were applied depending upon the table name. In this listing, all tables are treated the same and they are all set to the same data source.

Listing 17-14. Changing the location of a data source.

```
Private Sub LogonToTables(ByVal UserId As String, ByVal Password As String, _
    Optional ByVal ServerName As String = "", Optional ByVal DatabaseName _
    As String = "")
    Dim MyReport as New CrystalReport1()
    Dim MyTable As CrystalDecisions.CrystalReports.Engine.Table
    Dim MyConnectionInfo As New CrystalDecisions.Shared.ConnectionInfo
    Dim MyLogonInfo As New CrystalDecisions.Shared.TableLogOnInfo
```

---

[40] Changing the server name also requires setting the Location property. Otherwise the changes will be discarded.

```
If ServerName <> "" Then
    MyConnectionInfo.ServerName = ServerName
    MyConnectionInfo.DatabaseName = DatabaseName
End If
MyConnectionInfo.UserID = UserId
MyConnectionInfo.Password = Password
For Each MyTable In MyReport.Database.Tables
    MyLogonInfo = myTable.LogOnInfo
    MyLogonInfo.ConnectionInfo = MyConnectionInfo
    MyTable.ApplyLogOnInfo(MyLogonInfo)
    'Note: The next line is only necessary for SQL Server
    If ServerName <> "" Then
        MyTable.Location = MyTable.Location.Substring(MyTable.Location.LastIndexOf(".") + 1)
    End If
Next
CrystalReportViewer1.ReportSource = MyReport
End Sub
```

Since the code is very similar to the code in Listing 17-11, only a few differences need to be mentioned. The parameters being passed to the procedure are a user ID, password, server name and database name. Both the server name and database name are optional. If they are passed a value, then the report is assigned the new data source. If nothing is passed, then those properties aren't modified and the report uses the default server and database that was assigned during design time.

Just as before, the code loops through each table in the report and sets its properties. In addition to setting the UserId and Password properties of the ConnectionInfo object, it also sets the ServerName and DatabaseName properties (assuming that they were passed as parameters). Lastly, it calls the ApplyLogOnInfo() method to save the property values.

A very important piece of code is the assignment of the myTable.Location property near the end of the listing. A requirement for changing the data source of a SQL Server table is that you must also change the Location property of the Table object. The Location property is a string value that has the name of the server as part of the string. It lists the database name, the table owner and the table name. For example, it looks similar to the following:

```
pubs.dbo.Customers
```

If you leave the Location property alone and don't overwrite it, then the report's server and database name won't change. Instead, you have to reset it to just the table name. By removing the database name from the string, the report has to look at the new properties you just set to get this information. This results in the server and database changing.

The easiest change to make would be to overwrite the Location property with a string constant. For example, the following line of code would overwrite it with the Customers table.

```
myTable.Location = "Customers"
```

This works fine if the report only uses one table. But when you have multiple tables, you have to get more creative because you can't assign the same table name to every table object. Rather than use a string constant, the code parses out the table name from the Location property and reassigns it to itself. This has the effect of resetting the value, but dropping the database name and table owner from the string.

```
myTable.Location = myTable.Location.Substring(myTable.Location.LastIndexOf(".") + 1)
```

Setting each Table to a Different Data Source

If you are changing all tables to the same server and database, then the code in Listing 17-11 works fine. But if the individual tables are being changed to different servers or databases, then the report might not work properly. The way a report is designed determines whether the individual tables can use different data sources or whether they have to all use the same server and database. You need to make sure that your report is set up to handle this situation.

> **Note**
>
> If your report always uses the same server and database, then this section won't apply.

First, lets look at an example of when a sales report with two tables needs to use different locations. The report uses two tables: Customers and Orders. The Customers table has its individual records updated regularly, but its size only grows a small amount each year. Thus, it requires no special attention. The Orders table is fairly large and every year its size gets significantly larger. To keep the Orders table optimized, all prior year data is archived on a server on the network that is separate from the current year data. You want your report to have the ability to either print from the current Orders table or pull the data from the archived Orders table. This isn't necessary for the Customers table because it is relatively small and is only on one server.

To implement this, the application presents the user with a selection form that lets the user choose whether they want to print current data or historical data. When the user clicks the OK button, the application looks at which option the user selected and changes the server name and database name to either the current database or the archived database.

The problem with assigning tables to different locations is that your report has only allocated enough memory for one server name and database name property for all the tables. Even though your code appears to be modifying different ConnectionInfo objects for each table, behind the scenes they are all referencing the same object. In other words, if you have two tables in your report, changes made to the second table will override the changes made in the first table.[41] When you design a report and Crystal Reports sees that the tables have the same data source, it internally creates a single ConnectionInfo object that is shared among all tables.

To fix this, the report has to be designed so that it is forced to allocate separate ConnectionInfo objects for each table. Do this by using the Set Location dialog box to set each table to use a different data source. Since the report is set to use two different data sources at design time, each table is allocated the required memory to track its own server and database properties. Now you can modify each table independently of the other during runtime and they will work as expected.

Let's look at how this is implemented with the sales report example. The default behavior of the report is to print a sales report for current data. In this case, it will link the Customers and Orders table from the Northwind database on the local server. In Figure 17-6, The Set Location dialog box is shown and you can see that the Customers and Orders table are both coming from the local server and the Northwind database.

---

[41] This only applies to the ServerName and DatabaseName properties. The UserId and Password properties don't have this problem.

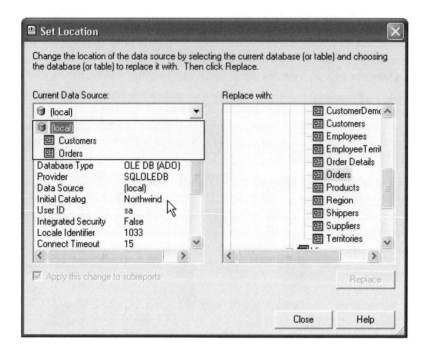

Figure 17-6. Both tables use the same data source.

After testing the report you determine that everything works as expected. The next step is to write the code so that the user can run the same report but have the option to print historical data. For this example, we will say that the historical data is in the pubs database and still on the local server. The way the report is currently designed, if you write code to change the data source for the Orders table to the pubs database, then the Customers table will also change to the pubs table. To fix this problem, you have to re-map the tables so that the Orders table already points to the pubs database.

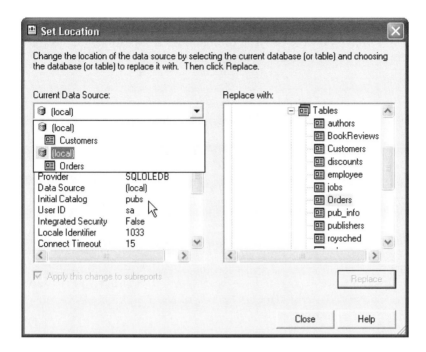

Figure 17-7. The two tables use different data sources.

In Figure 17-7, you have the same Customers and Orders tables as before, but now they are from different data sources. Both of the tables are still on the local server, but the Orders table is from the pubs database and the Customers table is still from the Northwind database. Now that both tables reference a different ConnectionInfo object, the code that changes the data source for the Orders table won't overwrite the Customers table data source. Each table is independent of the other.

Unfortunately, the drawback is that this change makes the report's default behavior print the historical data. Luckily, this is an easy fix. Put a condition in your code that sets the DatabaseName property depending upon the user's choice.

Working with Subreports

When you open a report and set its data connectivity properties, you have to do the same with any subreports that are used. Subreports have the same data connectivity issues that standard reports have. You have to do things such as log on to one or more data sources and change the record selection formula. Fortunately, the subreport object is based on the same class as the main report (the ReportDocument class). Modifying the properties of a subreport uses the same code that was written for the main report. The only difference being that you have to first drill down to the subreport object and create a reference to an instance of it. Drilling down to find the subreport object was shown in Chapter 15.

> **Note**
>
> If the subreport uses the same database as the main report, you can skip setting the subreport's logon properties. By logging on to the main report you are automatically logged on to the subreport. If the subreport uses a different database than the main report, you have to set the logon properties for both reports.

If a subreport uses the Push Model, you have to pass a populated dataset to the subreport. This is easily accomplished with the SetDataSource() method. Pass this method the dataset object. The following code demonstrates setting the data source for the main report and two subreports. Please note that I don't show the code to populate the datasets here. Call the appropriate FillDataSet() methods for your data sources.

Listing 17-15. Set subreport credentials

```
Dim MyReport As New CrystalReport1
Dim ds0, ds1, ds2 As DataSet
FillDataSet(ds0)
FillDataSet(ds1)
FillDataSet(ds2)
MyReport.SetDataSource(ds0)
MyReport.OpenSubreport("subreport1").SetDataSource(ds1)
MyReport.OpenSubreport("subreport2").SetDataSource(ds2)
CrystalReportViewer1.ReportSource = MyReport
```

Printing Dynamic Images

I've received many email requests from people wanting to know how to print dynamic images on a report. If you've used previous versions of Crystal Reports with VB6, you know that there is a method that lets you load a new image onto the report for every record printed. Many people want that functionality back. Others want to have a field that serves as a link to an image. Rather than printing the link, they want the report to print the image that the link points to. Unfortunately, neither of these options is possible with .NET.[42] There are only two ways to print dynamic images on a report. The first way is to store the

---

[42] If you have CR9, you can dynamically load images during runtime like you did with VB6. See Chapter 20 for more information.

---

image in a blob field in SQL Server or MS Access. Add this field to the report just like any other field and it is printed on the report.

If the images aren't stored in the database table, then they have to be located on the local computer or network drive. To print these files you have to create a DataTable in memory and load these images into each row of the DataTable.

I'm going to show you an example of how to implement the second option where the images are loaded into a datatable. But this example requires that you modify it for your particular circumstance. It's not possible to illustrate all the ways you could add dynamic images to a report. More than likely you will have the file path stored in one of the fields in a table. I'm going to assume that is the case in this example and if you get your field names from somewhere else (e.g. hard-coded in the project, by reading the file list from the current directory, etc.) then you can modify the example for your needs.

The overall process works as follows:

Load the existing dataset into memory. This is probably done by calling one of the FillDataSet() methods shown earlier.

Add a new column to the DataTable with a data type of Byte(). This column is where the image is stored.

Save this new table structure as an XML file using the DataSet.WriteXmlSchema() method (only do this the first time).

Create a new report using the schema file. Place all fields (including the image field) on the report.

When the application runs, read each record in the table and get the file path of the image. Use the file path to load the image into memory and save it to the new column of the row.

After looping through each row assign the DataTable's DataSet to the ReportSource property of the report.

Preview or print the report.

Wow! That's a lot of steps. I'm going to show you the final code that makes all this work and try to explain it as concisely and clearly as possible.[43]

First of all, let's create a new DataSet and load a DataTable. I'm going to make this simple by creating a new DataTable manually and populate it with a couple records. In your application, replace this code with a call to FillDataSet().

Listing 17-16. Printing dynamic images with a DataSet object.

```
Dim MyDataSet As New DataSet
```

---

[43] In VB6 this was so simple! Oh well, I guess this is what we call progress…

```
Dim MyDataTable As DataTable
Dim MyDataRow As DataRow
Dim MyDataColumn As DataColumn
MyDataTable = New DataTable("ImageTable")
' Create first column
MyDataColumn = New DataColumn("PicNumber", GetType(System.Int32))
MyDataTable.Columns.Add(MyDataColumn)
'Field that points to the image file
MyDataColumn = New DataColumn("ImagePath", GetType(System.String))
MyDataTable.Columns.Add(MyDataColumn)
'Populate the table with dummy data
'Make sure your C Drive has two files called Image1.jpg and Image2.jpg
MyDataRow = MyDataTable.NewRow()
MyDataRow("PicNumber") = 1
MyDataRow("ImagePath") = "C:\Image1.jpg"
MyDataTable.Rows.Add(MyDataRow)
MyDataRow = MyDataTable.NewRow()
MyDataRow("PicNumber") = 2
MyDataRow("ImagePath") = "C:\Image2.jpg"
MyDataTable.Rows.Add(MyDataRow)
MyDataSet.Tables.Add(MyDataTable)
'Add the image column to the table - See Listing 17-17.
AddImageColumn(MyDataTable)
'Only do this when you first design the report
MyDataSet.WriteXmlSchema("ImageTable.xsd")
'Open the report and preview it
Dim MyReport as New CrystalReport1
MyReport.SetDataSource(MyDataSet)
CrystalReportViewer1.ReportSource = MyReport
```

This code creates a DataTable with two columns: PicNumber and ImagePath. The ImagePath column points to the location of the image. I put two images on the root directory of the C drive.

The next step adds a column to the table to hold the image. The following code is in a generic method so you can easily drop it into your own project with no modifications.

Listing 17-17. Create a table column for the image.

```
Public Shared Sub AddImageColumn(ByVal MyDataTable As DataTable, ByVal FieldName As String)
    'Create the column to hold the binary image
    Dim MyDataColumn As DataColumn = New DataColumn(FieldName, GetType(System.Byte()))
    MyDataTable.Columns.Add(MyDataColumn)
End Sub
```

This procedure takes a DataTable object and the name of the column that holds the binary image. It creates a new column of type Byte().

After adding the new column, write the XML schema file and build the report using this schema file. Don't forget to comment out this line after you create the schema file!

> **Note**
>
> Even though the new column is of type Byte(), when this is saved to an XML schema file the column data type is automatically changed to base64Binary. If you are creating the DataSet manually with the IDE you have to specify the data type to be base64Binary.

Once the report is designed, open the DataTable again and load in the images.

Listing 17-18. Process each row in the table.

```
Public Shared Sub LoadAllImages(ByVal MyDataTable As DataTable, ByVal FilePathField As String, ByVal
ImageField As String)
    'Loop through all the rows and load the images
    For Each MyDataRow As DataRow In MyDataTable.Rows
        LoadImage(MyDataRow, ImageField, MyDataRow.Item(FilePathField))
    Next
End Sub
```

The LoadAllImages() procedure loops through each row in the DataTable and calls the LoadImage() procedure to load a single image. Pass the LoadAllImages() procedure the DataTable object, the name of the column that has the image location, and the name of the column that will hold the binary image.

Listing 17-19. Load a single image into a DataRow.

```
Public Shared Sub LoadImage(ByVal MyDataRow As System.data.DataRow, ByVal FilePath As String, ByVal
ImageField As String)
    Dim fs As New System.IO.FileStream(FilePath, IO.FileMode.Open, System.IO.FileAccess.Read)
    Dim Image(fs.Length) As Byte
    fs.Read(Image, 0, fs.Length)
    fs.Close()
    MyDataRow.Item(ImageField) = Image
End Sub
```

The LoadImage() procedure creates a new FileStream object and loads the image into a Byte array. Then it saves this Byte array to the DataRow in the column.

Once all the rows have been updated with their appropriate image, pass the DataSet to the report and preview or print it.

C# Code Listings

The C# code listings are equivalent to the VB.NET code listings.

Listing 17-2. Creating an XML schema file from a dataset object.

```
//Write a populated dataset object to an XML schema file
//The XmlFileName should have ".ds" file extension
public void CreateXMLFile(string XmlFileName, DataSet XmlDataSet)
{
    XmlDataSet.WriteXmlSchema(XmlFileName);
}
```

Listing 17-3. Populating a dataset with a MS Access table.

```
public void FillDataSet(ref DataSet MyDataSet)
{
    OleDbDataAdapter MyDataAdapter;
    string MyConnectionString;
    string SQL = "SELECT * FROM Customer";
    MyDataSet = new DataSet();
    MyConnectionString = "Provider=Microsoft.Jet.OLEDB.4.0;" +
    "Data Source=C\\Xtreme.mdb;User Id=Admin;" +
    "Jet OLEDB:Database Password=;Jet OLEDB:System database=" +
    "C:\\ProgramFiles\\Office2000\\Office\\System.mdw";
    MyDataAdapter = new OleDbDataAdapter(SQL, MyConnectionString);
    MyDataAdapter.Fill(MyDataSet, "Customer");
}
```

Listing 17-4. Populating a dataset with a SQL Server table.

```
public void FillDataSet(ref DataSet MyDataSet)
{
    string MyConnectionString;
    System.Data.SqlClient.SqlDataAdapter MyDataAdapter;
    MyDataSet = new DataSet();
    string MySql = "SELECT Customers.*, Orders.* " +
        "FROM Customers INNER Join Orders " +
        "ON Customers.CustomerId = Orders.CustomerId";
    MyConnectionString = "Data Source=(local);UID=sa;pwd=pw;Database=Northwind";
    MyDataAdapter = new SqlDataAdapter(MySql, MyConnectionString);
    MyDataAdapter.Fill(MyDataSet, "Customers");
}
```

Listing 17-5. Populating a dataset with an XML file.

```
public void FillDataset(DataSet MyDataSet, string XmlFileName)
{
    MyDataSet.ReadXml(XmlFileName);
}
```

Listing 17-6. Manually populating a dataset.

```
public void FillDataSet17_6(ref DataSet MyDataSet)
{
    MyDataSet = new DataSet();
    string[,] Customers = new string[,]{{"123","Jones"},{"456","Smith"}};
    //Create a new Data Table
    DataTable MyDataTable = new DataTable("TableName");
    DataColumn MyDataColumn;
    DataRow MyDataRow;
    //Create first column
    MyDataColumn = new DataColumn();
    MyDataColumn.DataType = System.Type.GetType("System.String");
    MyDataColumn.ColumnName = "CustomerId";
    MyDataTable.Columns.Add(MyDataColumn);
    //Create the second column
    MyDataColumn = new DataColumn();
    MyDataColumn.DataType = System.Type.GetType("System.String");
    MyDataColumn.ColumnName = "LastName";
    MyDataTable.Columns.Add(MyDataColumn);
    MyDataSet.Tables.Add(MyDataTable);
    //Copy the array into the datatable
    int ixCustomers;
    for (ixCustomers=0; ixCustomers<=1; ixCustomers++)
    {
        MyDataRow = MyDataTable.NewRow();
        MyDataRow["CustomerId"] = Customers[ixCustomers, 0];
        MyDataRow["LastName"] = Customers[ixCustomers, 1];
        MyDataTable.Rows.Add(MyDataRow);
    }
}
```

Listing 17-7. Getting the dataset object from a datagrid control.

```
public void FillDataset(DataSet MyDataSet)
{
    MyDataSet = (DataSet)DataGrid1.DataSource;
}
```

Listing 17-8. Printing from a DataView object.

```
public void PrintDataView(DataSet MyDataSet)
{
    DataView MyDataView;
    CrystalReport1 MyReport = new CrystalReport1();
    MyDataView = new DataView(MyDataSet.Tables["TableName"],
        "CompanyName > 'b'","", DataViewRowState.CurrentRows);
    MyReport.SetDataSource(MyDataView);
    crystalReportViewer1.ReportSource = MyReport;
}
```

Listing 17-9. Convert the DataView object into a DataTable

```
public DataTable ConvertViewToTable(DataView MyDataView)
{
    int Col, Row;
    Object[] NewRow;
    DataTable NewTable = new DataTable(MyDataView.Table.TableName);
    //Copy the column objects into the table
    for (Col=0; Col<MyDataView.Table.Columns.Count; Col++)
    {
        NewTable.Columns.Add(
            MyDataView.Table.Columns[Col].ColumnName,
            MyDataView.Table.Columns[Col].DataType);
    }
    //Create each new row and copy the column data into
    //a new row object
    for (Row=0; Row < MyDataView.Count; Row++)
    {
        NewRow = new Object[MyDataView.Table.Columns.Count];
        for (Col=0; Col < MyDataView.Table.Columns.Count; Col++)
        {
            NewRow[Col] = MyDataView[Row][Col];
        }
        NewTable.Rows.Add(NewRow);
    }
    return NewTable;
}
```

Listing 17-10. Linking the dataset file to the report and previewing it.

```
private void mnuCh17_10_Click(object sender, System.EventArgs e)
{
    CrystalReport1 MyReport = new CrystalReport1();
    DataSet MyDataSet = null;
    //Use the appropriate FillDataSet() method
    //from the previous sections
    FillDataSet(ref MyDataSet);
    //Uncomment the following line if you need to create
    //a new dataset file
    //CreateXMLFile("C:\\FileName.ds", MyDataSet);
    MyReport.SetDataSource(MyDataSet);
    crystalReportViewer1.ReportSource = MyReport;
}
```

Listing 17-11. Logging in to multiple tables.

```
public void LoginToTables(string UserId, string Password)
{
    CrystalReport1 MyReport = new CrystalReport1();
    CrystalDecisions.Shared.TableLogOnInfo MyLogonInfo;
```

```
//Change the logon info
foreach (CrystalDecisions.CrystalReports.Engine.Table MyTable in MyReport.Database.Tables)
{
    MyLogonInfo = MyTable.LogOnInfo;
    if (MyTable.Name == "CorpStandards")
    {
        MyLogonInfo.ConnectionInfo.UserID = G_UserId;
        MyLogonInfo.ConnectionInfo.Password = G_Password;
    }
    else
    {
        MyLogonInfo.ConnectionInfo.UserID = UserId;
        MyLogonInfo.ConnectionInfo.Password = Password;
    }
    MyTable.ApplyLogOnInfo(MyLogonInfo);
    //Test the user credentials
    if (!MyTable.TestConnectivity())
    {
        MessageBox.Show("Invalid user credentials for table: " + MyTable.Name);
    }
}
crystalReportViewer1.ReportSource = MyReport;
}
```

Listing 17-12. Setting the Logon credentials with the viewer control.

```
public void PrintPreview(string UserId, string Password)
{
    CrystalReport1 MyReport = new CrystalReport1();
    CrystalDecisions.Shared.TableLogOnInfo MyLogonInfo;
    crystalReportViewer1.LogOnInfo = new CrystalDecisions.Shared.TableLogOnInfos();
    //Create the Customer table and set its properties
    MyLogonInfo = new CrystalDecisions.Shared.TableLogOnInfo();
    MyLogonInfo.TableName = "Customer";
    MyLogonInfo.ConnectionInfo.UserID = UserId;
    MyLogonInfo.ConnectionInfo.Password = Password;
    crystalReportViewer1.LogOnInfo.Add(MyLogonInfo);
    //Create the Orders table and set its properties
    MyLogonInfo = new CrystalDecisions.Shared.TableLogOnInfo();
    MyLogonInfo.TableName = "Orders";
    MyLogonInfo.ConnectionInfo.UserID = UserId;
    MyLogonInfo.ConnectionInfo.Password = Password;
    crystalReportViewer1.LogOnInfo.Add(MyLogonInfo);
    //Show the report
    crystalReportViewer1.ReportSource = MyReport;
}
```

Listing 17-13. Connecting to a stored procedure using parameters.

```
public void SpWithViewer(string UserId, string Password, string spParameter)
```

```
{
    //Login to the server
    CrystalReport1 MyReport = new CrystalReport1();
    crystalReportViewer1.ReportSource = MyReport;
    CrystalDecisions.Shared.TableLogOnInfo MyLogonInfo;
    crystalReportViewer1.LogOnInfo = new CrystalDecisions.Shared.TableLogOnInfos();
    //Create the Customer table and set its properties
    MyLogonInfo = new CrystalDecisions.Shared.TableLogOnInfo();
    MyLogonInfo.TableName = "spCustomers;1";
    MyLogonInfo.ConnectionInfo.UserID = UserId;
    MyLogonInfo.ConnectionInfo.Password = Password;
    crystalReportViewer1.LogOnInfo.Add(MyLogonInfo);
    //Create the parameter
    CrystalDecisions.Shared.ParameterFields ParameterFields;
    CrystalDecisions.Shared.IParameterField ParameterField;
    CrystalDecisions.Shared.ParameterDiscreteValue spValue;
    ParameterFields = crystalReportViewer1.ParameterFieldInfo;
    ParameterField = ParameterFields["@CustPattern "];
    spValue = new CrystalDecisions.Shared.ParameterDiscreteValue();
    spValue.Value = spParameter;
    ParameterField.CurrentValues.Add(spValue);
    crystalReportViewer1.ReportSource = MyReport;
}
```

Listing 17-14. Changing the location of a data source.

```
public void LoginToTables(string UserId, string Password, string ServerName, string DatabaseName)
{
    CrystalReport1 MyReport = new CrystalReport1();
    CrystalDecisions.Shared.TableLogOnInfo MyLogonInfo;
    CrystalDecisions.Shared.ConnectionInfo MyConnectionInfo = new
CrystalDecisions.Shared.ConnectionInfo();
    if (ServerName != "")
    {
        MyConnectionInfo.ServerName = ServerName;
        MyConnectionInfo.DatabaseName = DatabaseName;
    }
    MyConnectionInfo.UserID = UserId;
    MyConnectionInfo.Password = Password;
    foreach (CrystalDecisions.CrystalReports.Engine.Table MyTable in MyReport.Database.Tables)
    {
        MyLogonInfo = MyTable.LogOnInfo;
        MyLogonInfo.ConnectionInfo = MyConnectionInfo;
        MyTable.ApplyLogOnInfo(MyLogonInfo);
        //Note: The next line is only necessary for SQL Server
        if (ServerName != "")
        {
            MyTable.Location = MyTable.Location.Substring(MyTable.Location.LastIndexOf(".")+1);
        }
```

```
  }
  crystalReportViewer1.ReportSource = MyReport;
}
```

Listing 17-15. Set subreport credentials

```
CrystalReport1 MyReport = new CrystalReport1();
DataSet ds0=null, ds1=null, ds2=null;
FillDataSet(ds0);
FillDataSet(ds1);
FillDataSet(ds2);
MyReport.SetDataSource(ds0);
MyReport.OpenSubreport("subreport1").SetDataSource(ds1);
MyReport.OpenSubreport("subreport2").SetDataSource(ds2);
crystalReportViewer1.ReportSource = MyReport;
```

Listing 17-16. Printing dynamic images with a DataSet object.

```
DataSet MyDataSet = new DataSet();
DataTable MyDataTable;
DataRow MyDataRow;
DataColumn MyDataColumn;
MyDataTable = new DataTable("ImageTable");
//Create the first column
MyDataColumn = new DataColumn("PicNumber", Type.GetType("System.Int32"));
MyDataTable.Columns.Add(MyDataColumn);
//Field that points to the image file
MyDataColumn = new DataColumn("ImagePath",Type.GetType("System.String"));
MyDataTable.Columns.Add(MyDataColumn);
//Populate the tabel with dummy data
//Make sure your C Drive has two files called Image1.jpg and Image2.jpg
MyDataRow = MyDataTable.NewRow();
MyDataRow["PicNumber"] = 1;
MyDataRow["ImagePath"] = "C:\\Image1.jpg";
MyDataTable.Rows.Add(MyDataRow);
MyDataRow = MyDataTable.NewRow();
MyDataRow["PicNumber"] = 2;
MyDataRow["ImagePath"] = "C:\\Image2.jpg";
MyDataTable.Rows.Add(MyDataRow);
MyDataSet.Tables.Add(MyDataTable);
//Add the image column to the table
AddImageColumn(MyDataTable, "Image");
//Only do this when you first design the report
MyDataSet.WriteXmlSchema(@"c:\ImageTable.xsd");
//Load the images into the datatable
LoadAllImages(MyDataTable,"ImagePath", "Image");
//Open the report and preview it
CrystalReport1 MyReport = new CrystalReport1();
MyReport.SetDataSource(MyDataSet);
crystalReportViewer1.ReportSource = MyReport;
```

Listing 17-17. Create a table column for the image.

```
public void AddImageColumn(DataTable MyDataTable, string FieldName)
{
    //Create the column to hold the binary image
    DataColumn MyDataColumn = new DataColumn(FieldName, Type.GetType("System.Byte[]"));
    MyDataTable.Columns.Add(MyDataColumn);
}
```

Listing 17-18. Process each row in the table.

```
public void LoadAllImages(DataTable MyDataTable, string FilePathField, string ImageField)
{
    //Loop through the rows and load the images
    foreach(DataRow MyDataRow in MyDataTable.Rows)
    {
        LoadImage(MyDataRow, ImageField, MyDataRow[FilePathField].ToString());
    }
}
```

Listing 17-19. Load a single image into a DataRow.

```
public void LoadImage(DataRow MyDataRow, string ImageField, string FilePath)
{
    System.IO.FileStream fs = new System.IO.FileStream(FilePath, System.IO.FileMode.Open,
    System.IO.FileAccess.Read);
    Byte[] Image = new Byte[fs.Length];
    fs.Read(Image, 0, (int)fs.Length);
    fs.Close();
    MyDataRow[ImageField] = Image;
}
```

18
Report Web Services

Creating reports as Report Web Services (RWS) enables you to deliver reports using SOAP via an HTTP protocol. There are no issues with worrying about the report being blocked by security or network constraints.

There are two parts to viewing reports as a web service. The first part is to build the web service application and publish the report. The second is creating an application that consumes the report. Fortunately, Visual Studio .NET makes creating and consuming web services almost trivial.

First create a new Web Services project using the Visual Studio IDE.

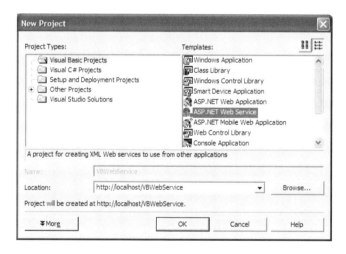

Figure 18-1. Create new web services project

When the project opens, add a new report to it. Use the Report Wizard to build the report from scratch or add an existing report.

In my example, I selected the EmployeeList report I built in an earlier chapter. Right click on the project name in the Solution Explorer window and select Add | Add Existing Item. After the dialog box opens browse to where your report is located and select it.

To publish the report as a web service, right-click on it in the Solution Explorer window and select Publish as Web Service.

Figure 18-2. Publish the report as a web service.

This adds a new web service class to your project. It is automatically named the same as the report name with "service" appended to it. The file extension is .asmx.

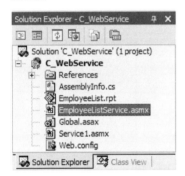

Figure 18-3. The new report web service class.

That's all there is to it! Test the report web service by right-clicking on it in the Solution Explorer and selecting Set As Start Page. Then run the application. A web browser will open up with the following page displayed.

Caution
Reports that are published as a web service cannot have a comment on the first line of the record selection formula. The first line should be a standard formula.

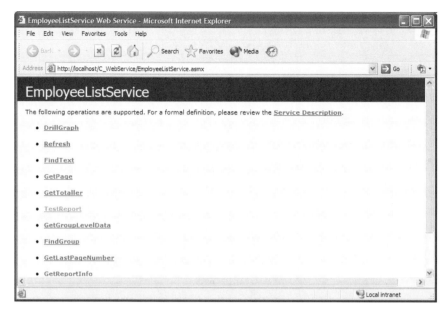

Figure 18-4. Testing the Report Web Service with a browser.

The browser shows you all the operations that the report supports. You can click on each one and find see a sample SOAP request and response. Look in the address bar for the full URL of the report web service. This is the URL that is assigned to the viewer control of the application that consumes this service.

The second part is creating an application to consume the web service. To create an application that consumes the web service, open a new instance of the Visual Studio IDE and create a new Windows application (or an ASP.NET application).

Right-click on the project and select Add Web Reference. You are prompted to enter the location of where to look for the web service.

Start Browsing for Web Services

Use this page as a starting point to find Web services. You can click the links below, or type a known URL into the address bar.

Browse to:

- Web services on the local machine

- Browse UDDI Servers on the local network
  Query your local network for UDDI servers.

- UDDI Directory
  Query the UDDI business registry to find companies and production Web services.

- Test Microsoft UDDI Directory
  Locate test Web services to use during development.

Figure 18-4. Browse the existing web services.

Click on the option "Web Services on the local machine".

This shows you a list of the available web services that have been installed on your computer. Select the web service that you just created.

Click the Add Reference button to close the dialog box and create the web reference in your project.

Add a CrystalReportViewer control to your form and bind it to the web service. The following code performs the binding.

Listing 18-1. Consuming a project's web service

```
Private Sub Form1_Load(ByVal sender As
    CrystalReportViewer1.ReportSource = New localhost.EmployeeListService
End Sub
```

This code creates a new instance of the EmployeeListService class and passes it to the ReportSource property of the viewer. Of course, you will want to replace the EmployeeListService name with the name of the report class being used in your application.

Run the application and the viewer will display the report.

You can bind to a report web service using only the URL. This lets you consume any report web service without having to add it to your project.

Listing 18-2. Preview a report using the web service's URL.

```
Private Sub Form1_Load(ByVal sender As System.Object, ByVal e As System.EventArgs) Handles _
    MyBase.Load
    CrystalReportViewer1.ReportSource = "http://localhost/VBWebService/EmployeeListService.asmx"
End Sub
```

Notice that when setting the ReportSource property with a URL, the viewer doesn't need to have any special properties set. In other words, a viewer can display any web service report as long as it's passed the URL. This lets you create an application that is a generic report viewer and display a number of reports. You could have one web service which returns a list of all the reports on the server and an application which retrieves this list and previews whichever one the user chooses.

Web services can only be consumed by the viewer control. Passing the web service URL to a ReportDocument results in an error. The only time you really need to use a ReportDocument object is when you want to print the report without previewing it first. To get around this problem, load the report into the viewer, call the PrintReport() method and then assign the ReportSource property to Nothing.

Listing 18-3. Print a web service report without previewing it.

```
Private Sub Form1_Load(ByVal sender As System.Object, ByVal e As System.EventArgs) _
Handles MyBase.Load

    CrystalReportViewer1.ReportSource =
    "http://localhost/VBWebService/EmployeeListService.asmx"
    CrystalReportViewer1.PrintReport()
    CrystalReportViewer1.ReportSource = Nothing
End Sub
```

Making Client Side Runtime Modifications

Report web services can have a minor number of modifications made to them during runtime. As you learned in Chapter 14, the most flexible way to make runtime report modifications is by using the ReportDocument class. It is far more robust than the viewer control which only has a few properties. Unfortunately, a web service report is generated on the server and consequently this is where the ReportDocument object is instantiated. The client is restricted to using the viewer control and doesn't have any access to the ReportDocument object.

Only being able to use the viewer control is disappointing. It can only do three things: set the record selection formula, set parameters, and set user credentials for logging into the data source.[44] It can't get direct access to all the report objects and their properties.

All the code samples that use the viewer to make runtime modifications will work unchanged for report web services. Here is a quick example just to illustrate it. Listing 18-4 demonstrates adding a discrete parameter. It uses the EmployeeList web service created earlier.

---

[44] Each of these was discussed in a prior chapter along with complete source code.

Listing 18-4. Setting the parameter of a report web service.

```
Private Sub Form1_Load(ByVal sender As System.Object, _
ByVal e As System.EventArgs) Handles MyBase.Load
    CrystalReportViewer1.ReportSource = _
    "http://localhost/VBWebService/EmployeeListService.asmx"
    Dim ParameterField As CrystalDecisions.Shared.ParameterField
    Dim DiscreteValue As New CrystalDecisions.Shared.ParameterDiscreteValue
    ParameterField = CrystalReportViewer1.ParameterFieldInfo ("LastName")
    DiscreteValue.Value = "B*"
    ParameterField.CurrentValues.Add(DiscreteValue)
End Sub
```

The first step is to assign the web service to the viewer. Then it gets a reference to the report parameter LastName and gives it a filter string. When the application runs it displays the report using the LastName parameter as a filter. This example could have just as easily logged into a database or set the record selection formula.

Making Server Side Report Modifications

The last section showed how the client is limited to using the viewer control for making runtime modifications. This doesn't give you many options for making runtime modifications. But that doesn't mean that it is impossible to make changes using the ReportDocument class. You just have to do it on the server within the web service application.

Making changes on the server side is very powerful because you get full access to the ReportDocument class. You can make changes to the report objects so that the report is completely dynamic. And you don't have to learn any new coding practices because you can use same code shown throughout this book. The only difference is how you reference the ReportDocument object. That is the tricky part!

Before showing you how to make server side modifications, you need to understand that there is one major problem with this approach. The server can't communicate with the client because the client can't pass information to the report web service. If this were a typical application, the user would enter information on a form and this information is used to modify the ReportDocument object prior to printing the report. But you can't do this with report web services. If you try to pass information on the query string then the web service returns an error. You also can't use cookies because these are strictly client based. You are restricted to making changes to the ReportDocument object that aren't user specific.

The one trick around this is to use multiple web services that open the same report. Each web service can perform a different modification to the report object prior to previewing it. For example you could have one web service show the default report and another web service modify the default grouping of a report. This lets one report be used by different web services and the end user thinks that they are looking at different reports. As another example, you could also have different web services specific to individual clients. Each client gets the same report, but you can charge them an additional fee if they want it customized to match their corporate image.

Modifying the ReportDocument object is done within the CreateReport() method of the web service. The CreateReport() method declares and instantiates the report object.

The CreateReport() method is within the web service's underlying .asmx.vb file (.asmx.cs for C# programs). By default the .asmx.vb file is hidden from the IDE. To see this file, click on the menu option Project | Show All Files. Go to the Solution Explorer window and find the web service file (it has the .asmx extension). Click on the + sign to the left of it. This lists the underlying .asmx.vb file for the web service. Right-click on this .asmx.vb file and select View Code. Scroll through the code till you find the method CreateReport(). It's probably near the end.

Here is the CreateReport() method code for the EmployeeList web service report that was created earlier in this chapter.

```
Protected Overridable Function CreateReport() As ReportDocument _
    Implements ICachedReport.CreateReport
    Dim report As EmployeeList = New EmployeeList
    AddHandler report.InitReport, New EventHandler( _
    AddressOf Me.webService.OnInitReport)
    Return report
End Function
```

The important part of this code is that it declares and instantiates a report object variable of the EmployeeList class. Then it returns this report object to the calling method. All you have to do is put your changes after the report variable is instantiated. Any of the code in this book can be put here and it will work without changes.

Being able to modify the ReportDocument on the server is crucial if you have a report based on a DataSet. If you recall from Chapter 17, datasets have to be manually populated by the application and assigned to the report using the SetDataSource() method of the ReportDocument object. You also know from the previous section that the viewer class can only set login credentials for a report. It can't set the data source property. If a report uses a dataset and you make it into a web service, the viewer is going to give you an error. To make it work you have to set the report's data source within the CreateReport() method of the web service. Listing 18-5 shows how this is done.

Listing 18-5. Assign a DataSet object to the report's data source

```
Protected Overridable Function CreateReport() As ReportDocument _
    Implements ICachedReport.CreateReport
    Dim report As EmployeeList = New EmployeeList
    AddHandler report.InitReport, New EventHandler(AddressOf
    Me.webService.OnInitReport)
    'Put all your report modification code here
    Dim MyDataSet as New DataSet
    'Call one of the sample methods from Chapter 17 for populating
    'the DataSet object
    FillDataSet(MyDataSet)
    Report.SetDataSource(MyDataSet)
    Return report
End Function
```

At this point in the book, this code shouldn't need much explanation. After declaring the report variable, the MyDataSet variable is declared and instantiated. The method FillDataSet() is called to populate the MyDataSet variable. This method can be any of the sample methods from Chapter 17 that populate a DataSet object. After MyDataSet has data, it is assigned to the report using the SetDataSource() method. A viewer control can now call this web service and display the report without getting an error.

C# Code Listings

The C# code listings are equivalent to the VB.NET code listings.

Listing 18-1. Consuming a project's web service

```
private void Form1_Load(object sender, System.EventArgs e)
{
    crystalReportViewer1.ReportSource = new localhost.EmployeeListService();
}
```

Listing 18-2. Preview a report using the web service URL.

```
private void Form1_Load(object sender, System.EventArgs e)
{
    crystalReportViewer1.ReportSource =
    "http://localhost/VBWebService/EmployeeListService.asmx";
}
```

Listing 18-3. Print a web service report without previewing it.

```
private void Form1_Load(object sender, System.EventArgs e)
{
    crystalReportViewer1.ReportSource =
    "http://localhost/VBWebService/EmployeeListService.asmx";
    crystalReportViewer1.PrintReport();
    crystalReportViewer1.ReportSource = null;
}
```

Listing 18-4. Setting the parameter of a report web service.

```
private void Form1_Load(object sender, System.EventArgs e)
{
    CrystalDecisions.Shared.IParameterField ParameterField;
    CrystalDecisions.Shared.ParameterDiscreteValue DiscreteValue =
    new CrystalDecisions.Shared.ParameterDiscreteValue();
    crystalReportViewer1.ReportSource =
        "http://localhost/C_WebService/EmployeeListService.asmx";
    ParameterField = crystalReportViewer1.ParameterFieldInfo["LastName"];
    DiscreteValue.Value = "B*";
    ParameterField.CurrentValues.Add(DiscreteValue);
}
```

Listing 18-5. Assign a DataSet object to the report's data source

```
public virtual ReportDocument CreateReport()
{
    EmployeeList   report = new EmployeeList();
    //Put all your report modification code here
    DataSet MyDataSet = new DataSet();
    //Call one of the sample methods from Chapter 17 for populating
    //the DataSet object
```

```
    FillDataSet(MyDataSet);
    report.SetDataSource(MyDataSet);
    report.InitReport += new EventHandler( this.webService.OnInitReport );
    return ( report );
}
```

Exporting and Deploying Reports

Crystal Reports gives you two ways of delivering reports. The first way is exporting them to different formats. This is similar to a web service in that a report can be viewed on many platforms with different applications. But this time the reports are delivered as a physical entity. This can be a file, an email attachment, an Exchange folder or a binary stream. The second way of delivering reports is by deploying them with your application. This involves modifying the setup files so that the reports and related libraries are included on the destination computer. This chapter covers both exporting and deploying reports.

Exporting Reports

Printing and previewing reports is a great way of presenting data to users. But there is one big problem: the user has to have a copy of your application to do it. If you want to show someone what a report looks like, you can't email them your application or ask everyone to sit at your computer. That is where exporting comes in. You can export reports in a variety of formats that are displayed by common applications that most people already have (Adobe Acrobat, Excel, HTML, etc.). This lets people see and understand your data without having a copy of the application on their computer. For example, the PDF format is the most common way of presenting data via the web. In fact, it has become the defacto standard and most users already have the Adobe Acrobat viewer installed on their computer. If you want to deliver reports that let users work with the data so that it is dynamic, you can export them to an Excel spreadsheet and give your users the ability to perform more advanced data analysis.

In one respect, exporting a report could seem like a frivolous task. Consider that a report is just output data that you had to assimilate with your code. Rather than generate a report, you could skip that step entirely and use a SQL query to export the raw data into another table or as XML. However, using Crystal Reports gives you many advantages. The most obvious advantage is that it has the export functionality built-in and this saves you time programming. A less obvious benefit is that it gives you the ability to quickly customize how the data is presented. Use the powerful report engine to perform the sorting and grouping and other functionality without having to worry about the implementation details. Without a doubt, being able to export report data to different formats is a very powerful feature.

Crystal Reports gives you many different formats for exporting your reports. The following formats can be exported to: MS Excel, HTML 3.2/4.0, PDF, RichText, MS Word, Microsoft Mail (MAPI), and Exchange Folder.

There are two ways to export a report. The first is using the built-in export capabilities of the Windows Report Viewer. The second is to write the code to export the report. Although this is more work, you'll see in a later section that it gives you more control over how the exported report is formatted.

Note
The Web Viewer control doesn't have an export button. Crystal Reports is installed on the server and the browser is a client tool. If the server tried to export the report then it would be saved on the server and not on the client's computer. If you want to export reports using the browser, you have to do it on the server and stream the results to the client computer. This is discussed at the end of this chapter.

Exporting with the Viewer

The easiest way to export a report is to have the users do it themselves by using the Windows Report Viewer. The viewer has a built-in export button that lets the user export the current report to the file format of their choice.

Figure 19-1. The Export button on the Windows Report Viewer toolbar.

When the user clicks on the export button, the Export Report dialog box appears. The user selects the file format and enters the filename. When the OK button is clicked the report gets exported to the file. There is nothing for you as a programmer to do.

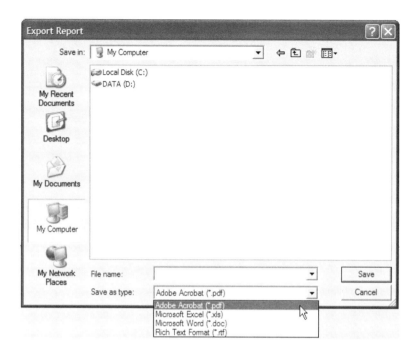

Figure 19-2. The Export Report dialog box.

The Export button does not let you export to HTML.

Exporting with Programming Code

Using the built-in export feature of the Windows viewer is nice, but as in most things related to programming, what you get in ease of use you give up in functionality. To get the most functionality for exporting a report, you have to write the programming code yourself.

It is common to export a report and find out that either the parameters or login information is lost. This is because these parameters were set using the viewer object and the ReportDocument object is used to do the exporting. These objects are exclusive of each other. When exporting, set all properties with the ReportDocument object.

Before exporting a report, you have to answer two questions. The first question is what is the destination type. There are four destination types to choose from: Disk file, Exchange folder, Email attachment and a Stream object. The second question is what is the format that the report should be exported to. There are 6 formats that reports can be converted to: PDF files, RTF, MS Word, MS Excel, HTML 3.2 and HTML 4.0. These two questions are independent of each other and are programmed differently. Figure 19-3 shows how this all fits together.

ExportOptions
-DestinationOptions : DiskFileDestinationOptions
-DestinationOptions : ExchangeFolderDestinationOptions
-DestinationOptions : MicrosoftMailDestinationOptions
-ExportDestinationType : ExportDestinationType
-ExportFormatType : ExportFormatType
-FormatOptions : ExcelFormatOptions
-FormatOptions : HTMLFormatOptions
-FormatOptions : PdfRtfWordFormatOptions

DiskFileDestinationOptions
-DiskFileName : String

ExchangeFolderDestinationOptions
-DestinationType
-FolderPath : String
-Password : String
-Profile : String

«enumeration» ExportDestinationType
-DiskFile
-ExchangeFolder
-MicrosoftMail
-NoDestination

MicrosoftMailDestinationOptions
-MailCCList : String
-MailMessage : String
-MailSubject : String
-MailToList : String
-Password : String
-UserName : String

«enumeration» ExportFormatType
-Excel
-HTML32
-HTML40
-NoFormat
-PortableDocFormat
-RichText
-WordForWindows

ExcelFormatOptions
-ExcelAreaGroupNumber : Integer
-ExcelAreaType : AreaSectionKind
-ExcelConstantColumnWidth : Double
-ExcelTabHasColumnHeadings : Boolean
-ExcelUseConstantColumnWidth : Boolean

HTMLFormatOptions
-FirstPageNumber : Integer
-HTMLEnableSeperatedPages : Boolean
-HTMLFileName : String
-HTMLHasPageNavigator : Boolean
-LastPageNumber : Integer
-UsePageRange : Boolean

«enumeration» ExchangeDestinationType
-ExchangePostDocMessage

PdfRtfWordFormatOptions
-FirstPageNumber : Integer
-LastPageNumber : Integer
-UsePageRange : Boolean

Figure 19-3. The Export object model.

The ReportDocument class has various methods and properties that are used to implement the export functionality of Crystal Reports. Table 19-1 lists each method available.

Table 19-1. Export methods of the ReportDocument class.

Method	Description
Export()	Exports a report to any of the available export formats using the properties of the ExportOptions object.
ExportToDisk(FormatType, Filename)	Exports a report to a disk file with no additional coding.
ExportToStream(FormatType)	Exports a report to a stream and returns the stream to the caller.

Easy Exporting To Disk

There is one method that makes exporting easy: ExportToDisk(). Without a doubt, the ExportToDisk() method is the most popular way of exporting a report because you are only required to specify the format type and the filename. The following code shows an example or saving a report as a PDF file. You can see that only one line of code is required to export the report to a PDF formatted file.

```
ExportToDisk(CrystalDecisions.Shared.ExportFormatType.PortableDocFormat, "C:\Report.PDF")
```

The drawback to using the ExportToDisk() method is that it doesn't have any parameters for customizing the export format. For example, there is no way to specify the page range. To customize the report format that gets exported, you have to use the more advanced Export() method. Table 19-2 shows the enumerations used with the ExportToDisk() method. Each of these enumeration constants listed in the table is within the namespace CrystalDecisions.Shared.ExportFormatType.

Table 19-2. Enumeration constants for the export format.

Format	File Extension	Enumeration Constant
Adobe Acrobat	.PDF	PortableDocFormat
Rich Text Format	.RTF	RichText
HTML 3.2	.HTM / .HTML	HTML32
HTML 4.0	.HTM / .HTML	HTML40
MS Word	.DOC	WordForWindows
MS Excel	.XLS	Excel

Advanced Exporting

When you want to do more than a simple export to disk, use the Export() method. It has many classes and properties for customizing the export process. Consequently, having additional classes and properties makes this method more complicated to learn and use. This chapter shows plenty of examples so that it is easy to copy and paste the code into your application needs.

Even though the Export() method gives you the most flexibility for exporting reports, it doesn't let you export to a stream object. Only the ExportToStream() method lets you do that. The ironic part is that the ExportToStream() method is simplistic like the ExportToDisk() method and it doesn't give you any the formatting options.

Prior to calling the Export() method, you have to create the proper objects that specify what the destination and format are. Assign these objects to properties of the report object. The two properties you have to set are called ExportDesinationType and ExportFormatType. Table 19-3 shows the enumerations for the ExportDestinationType property. Each is in the namespace CrystalDecisions.Shared.ExportDestinationType. Using these properties in your code is illustrated in the code samples that follow.

Table 19-3. Enumeration constants for ExportDestinationType.

Destination	Enumeration Constant
Disk File	DiskFile
Exchange Folder	ExchangeFolder
Email (MAPI)	MicrosoftMail

Table 19-4. Enumeration constants for the ExportFormatType property.

Format	Enumeration Constant
Disk File	DiskFile
Exchange Folder	ExchangeFolder
Email (MAPI)	MicrosoftMail

Exporting a report consists of five steps. First create the export objects and set their properties. Lastly, call the Export() method.

1. Set the ExportDestinationType property.
2. Create a destination options object and assign it to the Export-DestinationOptions property.
3. Set the ExportFormatType property to the format.

4. Create a format options object and assign it to the ExportFormatOptions property.
5. Call the Export() method of the report object.

To make these steps easy to learn, each one is described for every possible option and the complete code is shown. Listing 19-1 shows sample code of how you can set these properties in your application. This code serves as the foundation for your own application. You have to modify this code to call the procedures you need. For example, rather than calling the method to export to PDF, you might want to call the method that exports to HTML. Each of the different export methods is discussed in the following sections.

Listing 19-1. Export to a PDF disk file

```
Dim myReport As New CrystalReport1
'Export the report as destination type disk
SetDiskFileDestination(myReport, "C:\ReportExport.PDF")
'Set the format to be PDF and export all pages
SetFormatPdfRtfWord(myReport, False, 1, 1)
'Perform the export
myReport.Export()
```

In this listing, a report object is instantiated by creating a new instance of the report you are working with. In your application, you don't have to load the report into memory this way. This is strictly for showing a simple example. You have the option to load a report using whatever way is most appropriate for your project (e.g. loading an external report file).

After the report is loaded in memory, call the SetDestinationxxx() method that you need. This example uses the SetDestinationDisk() method to export the report to a disk file. You can replace this with the method call you need.

Call the SetFormatxxx() method to set the properties for how the report should be formatted. Again, you can use any formatting method that you need. They are shown in later section.

The last step calls the Export() method of the report object. This exports the report and the user can go back to previewing the report or you can dispose of the report object if you no longer need it.

Exporting to a Disk

Setting the destination type to disk is simple because there are only a couple properties. You have to instantiate a DiskFileDestinationOptions object and assign the filename to it. As you can see in Table 19-4, this is the only property available.

Table 19-4. DiskFileDestinationOptions Properties.

Property	Description
DiskFileName	The filename used for saving the report

The following code takes a report object and sets it to use a file as the destination.

Listing 19-2. Setting the destination to a disk file

```
Public Sub SetDiskFileDestination(ByRef MyReport As
CrystalDecisions.CrystalReports.Engine.ReportDocument, ByVal FileName As String)
    'Set the destination type to DiskFile
    MyReport.ExportOptions.ExportDestinationType = _
    CrystalDecisions.Shared.ExportDestinationType.DiskFile
    'Instantiate a DiskFileDestinationOptions object and set the
    'FileName property
    Dim Options As CrystalDecisions.Shared.DiskFileDestinationOptions = _
    New CrystalDecisions.Shared.DiskFileDestinationOptions
    Options.DiskFileName = FileName
    'Assign the object to the report
    MyReport.ExportOptions.DestinationOptions = Options
End Sub
```

Pass this procedure a report object and a filename. It first sets the destination type to be DiskFile. Then it instantiates an options variable and sets its DiskFileName property to be the Filename string that was passed to the procedure. The last step assigns this destination object to the report object.

Exporting to Email

Exporting a report to an email creates the report as a separate file and attaches it to an email message. This email message is automatically sent out to the recipient. Table 19-5 shows the properties for exporting to email. Each of these properties relates to the typical settings you find when sending an email message.

Table 19-5. MicrosoftMailDestinationOptions Properties.

Property	Description
MailCCList	The list of emails to send a carbon copy to
MailMessage	The text portion of the email message
MailSubject	The text subject heading of the email message
MailToList	The email(s) of those receiving the report
Password	The password used when logging on to the email account

UserName	The user name used when logging on to the email account

Listing 19-3. Send a report as an attachment of an email.

```
Public Sub SetEmailDestination(ByVal MyReport As CrystalDecisions.CrystalReports.Engine.ReportDocument,
ByVal MailTo As String, ByVal CCList As String, ByVal Subject As String, ByVal Message As String, ByVal
UserName As String, ByVal Password As String)
    'Set the destination type to EMail
    MyReport.ExportOptions.ExportDestinationType = _
    CrystalDecisions.Shared.ExportDestinationType.MicrosoftMail
    'Instantiate an Email options object and set its properties
    Dim Options As CrystalDecisions.Shared.MicrosoftMailDestinationOptions = _
    New CrystalDecisions.Shared.MicrosoftMailDestinationOptions
    Options.UserName = UserName
    Options.Password = Password
    Options.MailSubject = Subject
    Options.MailMessage = Message
    Options.MailToList = MailTo
    Options.MailCCList = CCList
    'Assign the options object to the report
    MyReport.ExportOptions.DestinationOptions = Options
End Sub
```

This procedure first sets the report object's destination type to be MicrosoftMail. Then it creates a new options variable and assigns the parameters to the appropriate properties. The last step assigns the options object to the DestinationOptions property of the report object.

> **Caution**
>
> Note: The attachment's filename is created automatically and it is in the format of "Temp_" followed by a series of random numbers (similar to a GUID). You can't specify the filename that the report gets exported to. Since email is a common method of sending viruses, this could cause the receiver to be initially alarmed or a spam filter might delete the email before it ever gets to their Inbox. Make sure the recipient knows about this anomaly prior to sending it to them.

Exporting to Exchange Folder Destination

Crystal Reports lets you export a report to an Exchange folder. Table 19-6 shows the properties that need to be set for this to work.

Table 19-6. ExchangeFolderDestinationOptions Properties.

Property	Description
DestinationType	The export destination type
FolderPath	The path of the Exchange folder
Password	The Exchange password
Profile	The user profile for accessing the Exchange folder

Listing 19-4. Export a report to an Exchange folder.

```
Public Sub SetDestinationExchangeFolder(ByVal MyReport As
CrystalDecisions.CrystalReports.Engine.ReportDocument, ByVal FolderPath As _
String, ByVal Password As String, ByVal Profile As String)
    'Set the destination type to ExchangeFolder
    MyReport.ExportOptions.ExportDestinationType = _
    CrystalDecisions.Shared.ExportDestinationType.ExchangeFolder
    'Instantiate an ExchangeFolder options object and set its properties
    Dim Options As CrystalDecisions.Shared.ExchangeFolderDestinationOptions = _
    New CrystalDecisions.Shared.ExchangeFolderDestinationOptions
    Options.DestinationType = _
    CrystalDecisions.Shared.ExchangeDestinationType.ExchangePostDocMessage
    Options.FolderPath = FolderPath
    Options.Password = Password
    Options.Profile = Profile
    MyReport.ExportOptions.DestinationOptions = Options
End Sub
```

This procedure first sets the report object's destination type to be ExchangeFolder. Then it creates a new options object and assigns the parameters to the appropriate properties. The last step assigns the options object to the DestinationOptions property of the report object.

Formatting for PDF, RTF, and Word Documents

Exporting a report to PDF, RTF or Word gives you the option to specify the page range. You can set the starting and ending page or simply print out the entire report. Note that all pages must be consecutively numbered. For example, you can't export the first few pages of a report and the last few pages of a report. Table 19-7 shows the properties used for setting the page range.

Table 19-7. PdfRtfWordFormatOptions Properties.

Property	Description
FirstPageNumber	The first page number to export
LastPageNumber	The last page number to export
UsePageRange	Boolean that enables/disables the use of page ranges

Caution

When exporting to Word, the process automatically inserts a footer at the bottom of each page that shows "Powered by Crystal" and the Crystal Decisions logo. If you want a continuous flow of data and you don't want these page footers appearing in your spreadsheet, you have to open the document afterwards and clean it up manually. There is no way to keep this from happening prior to the export. See Figure 19-4 for an example.

Figure 19-4. An exported Word document with the Crystal icon.

Listing 19-5. Set the export formatting to PDF

```
Public Sub SetFormatPdfRtfWord(ByRef MyReport As
CrystalDecisions.CrystalReports.Engine.ReportDocument, ByVal UsePageRange As Boolean, ByVal
FirstPageNumber As Integer, ByVal LastPageNumber As Integer)
    'Change the next line if you want the format to be RTF or Word
    MyReport.ExportOptions.ExportFormatType = _
    CrystalDecisions.[Shared].ExportFormatType.PortableDocFormat
    'The following lines stay the same regardless of formatting
    Dim Options As New CrystalDecisions.Shared.PdfRtfWordFormatOptions
    Options.UsePageRange = UsePageRange
    If UsePageRange Then
        Options.FirstPageNumber = FirstPageNumber
        Options.LastPageNumber = LastPageNumber
    End If
    MyReport.ExportOptions.FormatOptions = Options
End Sub
```

The listing first sets the format type to PDF. If you want to export to RTF or Word, then change this line to be the appropriate enumeration needed. After setting the format type, create an options object and set the page range. If all the pages are going to be exported, then set the UsePageRange property to False. Otherwise, to print page ranges set it to True and also set the FirstPageNumber and LastPageNumber properties.

Formatting for Excel

Exporting a report to an Excel spreadsheet gives you options to work with the report areas and how the columns are formatted. The columns can be formatted so that they have headers and that they are all the same width. Table 19-8 shows the properties used for setting the Excel formatting.

Table 19-8. ExcelFormatOptions Properties.

Property	Description
ExcelAreaGroupNumber	The base area group number if the area type is group area.
ExcelAreaType	The area type if you aren't using constant column width.
ExcelConstantColumnWidth	The width of each column (if using constant column width).
ExcelTabHasColumnHeadings	Boolean that determines if the columns have headings listed.
ExcelUseConstantColumnWidth	Boolean that determines if the columns are the same width.

Caution

Exporting to Excel is similar to Word. The export process automatically inserts a footer at the bottom of each page that shows "Powered by Crystal" and the Crystal Decisions logo. If you want a continuous flow of data and you don't want these page footers appearing in your spreadsheet, you have to open the spreadsheet afterwards and clean it up manually. There is no way to keep this from happening prior to the export.

Listing 19-6. Setting the format to be an Excel spreadsheet.

```
Public Sub SetFormatExcel(ByVal MyReport As CrystalDecisions.CrystalReports.Engine.ReportDocument,
ByVal UseConstantColumnWidth As Boolean, ByVal ColumnWidth As Integer, ByVal UseColumnHeadings As
Boolean)
    MyReport.ExportOptions.ExportFormatType = _
    CrystalDecisions.[Shared].ExportFormatType.Excel
    Dim Options As CrystalDecisions.Shared.ExcelFormatOptions = _
    New CrystalDecisions.Shared.ExcelFormatOptions
    Options.ExcelUseConstantColumnWidth = UseConstantColumnWidth
    Options.ExcelConstantColumnWidth = ColumnWidth
    Options.ExcelTabHasColumnHeadings = UseColumnHeadings
    MyReport.ExportOptions.FormatOptions = Options
End Sub
```

The listing first sets the format type to Excel. After setting the format type, create an options object and set the properties that determine how to format the columns. This procedure sets the properties for the column width and whether the columns should have headings.

Formatting for HTML

HTML output is inherently different from exporting to the other file formats. HTML files are meant to be viewed in a web browser and this can impose certain requirements on how you present the data to the user. You have the option of displaying the entire report in a single browser window or breaking it up into separate web pages. If you display the report on a single page, the user can view all the data at one time. But this requires a lot of scrolling to see everything. If you decide to break up the report into separate pages, you have to decide whether you will provide your own interface for navigating between the pages or whether you want page navigation links to be automatically added to the bottom of each page. Of course, doing it automatically is a much easier solution to implement, but you have to consider whether this fits in with the design of your entire web site. Luckily, each of these options is easy to set and you can quickly play around with each one and decide what works best for each project.

Note

HTML export isn't listed as an option when exporting from the Windows Viewer.

Table 19-9. HTMLFormatOptions Properties.

Property	Description
FirstPageNumber	The first page number to export.
HTMLEnableSeparatedPages	Boolean that sets whether the HTML output will put each report page on its own web page.
HTMLFileName	The filename used for saving the HTML output.
HTMLHasPageNavigator	Boolean that sets whether the bottom of each page should have navigation links.
LastPageNumber	The last page number to export.
UsePageRange	Boolean that enables/disables the use of page ranges.

Listing 19-7. Setting the format options for HTML.

```
Public Sub SetFormatHtml(ByVal MyReport As CrystalDecisions.CrystalReports.Engine.ReportDocument,
ByVal EnableSeparatedPages As Boolean, ByVal HasPageNavigator As Boolean, ByVal
HTMLBaseFolderName As String, ByVal HTMLFileName As String, ByVal UsePageRange As Boolean, ByVal
FirstPageNumber As Integer, ByVal LastPageNumber As Integer)
    MyReport.ExportOptions.ExportFormatType = _
    CrystalDecisions.[Shared].ExportFormatType.HTML40
    'Set the destination type to HTML
    Dim Options As New CrystalDecisions.Shared.HTMLFormatOptions
    Options.HTMLEnableSeparatedPages = EnableSeparatedPages
    Options.HTMLHasPageNavigator = HasPageNavigator
    Options.HTMLFileName = HTMLFileName
    Options.HTMLBaseFolderName = HTMLBaseFolderName
    Options.UsePageRange = UsePageRange
    If UsePageRange Then
        Options.FirstPageNumber = FirstPageNumber
        Options.LastPageNumber = LastPageNumber
    End If
    MyReport.ExportOptions.FormatOptions = Options
End Sub
```

The listing first sets the format type to HTML. After setting the format type, create an options object and set page formatting properties. The last step this code performs is setting the page range (as discussed in the PDF format).

There are two properties that deal with the filename that should be mentioned. The HTMLBaseFolderName property sets the folder that the HTML output is saved in. However, this is a little deceiving because the export process creates another folder within the BaseFolder and puts the HTML files in this sub-folder. Unfortunately, you don't have any control over the name of this sub-folder and it is named in the format "TEMP_" followed random characters similar to a GUID.

You also have to be aware of how the HTML files are named. If the property HTMLUseSeperatedPages is True, the pages will be named according to the following rules:

First page is the filename you specified (e.g. Report.html).

The next pages will have a number concatenated at the end (e.g. Report1.html, Report2.html…)

The last page will have the word "Last" concatenated to the end (e.g. ReportLast.html).

If you print a page range, the numbers will not match the actual page number. The second page printed will always be numbered with "1" regardless of its actual page number on the report. As an example, if you print pages 5 through 10, then the page 5 would be named Report.HTML; page 6 is named Report1.HTML; and page 10 is named ReportLast.HTML.

When looking at the files as a whole, the first page doesn't have a number, the second page is numbered with "1" and the last page has the word "Last".

As an example of how confusing the folder names are, Figure 19-5 shows a snapshot or an HTML report that used a base folder name of "ExportExample" and a file name of "Report".

Figure 19-5. The folder/file naming convention for exporting HTML.

The naming convention is different if you are exporting a report that was loaded from an external file. The export process inserts an additional folder that is the name of the report. It is appended to the BaseFolderName. If you are exporting the report EmployeeList to a file and path of C:\Temp\Report.HTML, then it will be saved to C:\Temp\Employee List\Report.HTML.

Deploying Reports

Have you written a .NET application and deployed it successfully? If so, there is a good chance that you found out it wasn't as easy as you expected. Microsoft advertises that .NET installations are simple "XCOPY" deployments. That sounds good in advertisements, but it doesn't always work that way. Some of the problems you can run into are determining how to install the mammoth .NET framework on machines that don't have it, how to install COM components that the application needs, and what happens when the .NET framework won't install properly? As .NET matures and it is installed on more machines via service packs and via new installations these problems will decrease. But that doesn't help us today. These are issues we have to worry about now.

In addition to the issues you have to worry about when installing a standard application, you'll find that deploying applications that use Crystal Reports has even more requirements. By default, the components that are needed to view and print reports are not included in the .NET Framework. They have to be installed along with your application. To do this you have to know which components are necessary for all reports and which components are only necessary for certain types of reports. This section covers how to create an installation package for deploying reports.

Create a Crystal Reports Deployment Package

Crystal Reports is not part of the .NET Framework. It is a tool added to the Visual Studio IDE. Consequently, an application that uses Crystal Reports can't be copied to a computer that has the .NET Framework installed. You have to manually add the Crystal Reports components to the deployment package for the application to run. Fortunately, this is a simple process because there are merge modules that have all these components included in them. Just add the appropriate merge modules to your deployment package. The merge modules are listed in Table 19-10.

Table 19-10. Crystal Reports Merge Modules.

Merge Module	Purpose
Crystal_RegWiz2003.msm	Holds the license key that registers Crystal Reports on the target computer. If you forget to set the license key property, then your reports won't run on the target computer.
Crystal_Managed2003.msm	Installs the primary components for running reports. It has the CrystalDecisions.* namespaces.
Crystal_Database_Access2003.msm	Installs database drivers for connecting reports to various data sources, components for exporting reports, and non-managed runtime components.
Crystal_Database_Access2003_enu.msm	Installs language specific components.
VC_User_CRT71_RTL_X86_---.msm	This merge module includes components for handling ADO.NET data sources. If you don't use ADO.NET in your reports (you only use ODBC or OLE DB), then you do not need to include this merge module.
VC_User_STL71_RTL_X86_-s--.msm	This merge module also includes components for handling ADO.NET data sources. If you don't use ADO.NET in your reports (i.e. you use ODBC or OLE DB), then you do not need to include this merge module.

Including these merge modules in the deployment package is very simple. Right-click on the project name and select Add | Merge Module. Select the ones you want to add (which is all of them with the exception of the VC_ modules which are only necessary if use ADO.NET data sources). To see how easy this is, the next examples walk you through creating a deployment package for a Windows application and a Web application.

Deploying a Windows Application

Create a new project with the Visual Studio IDE and select Setup and Deployment Projects. Click on the template Setup Project and enter a name for the project. Click the OK button.

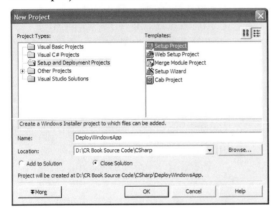

Figure 19-6. New Windows deployment project.

In the Solutions Explorer window, right click on the deployment project and select Add | File.

Browse through the directory to find the Windows application that you want to deploy. Click the Open button to add it to the Applications Folder.

In the Solutions Explorer, right-click on the project name and select Add | Merge Module. In this example, I add all the Crystal_* modules, but none of the VC_* modules because I didn't use ADO.NET in my reports.[45]

---

[45] If you recall from Chapter 14, ADO.NET datasets are the slowest way of connecting reports to a database.

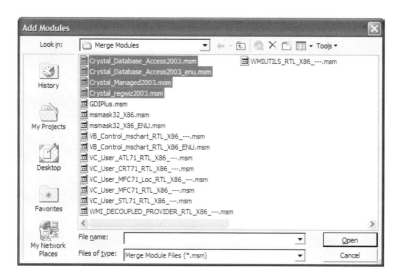

This next step is the most important: set the License Key property of the Crystal_regwiz2003.msm module. Click on the module name in the Solution Explorer window so that its properties are displayed in the Properties window.

Click on the plus sign next to (MergeModuleProperties) to expand it. Below it there is the License Key property. Enter the license key that was assigned to you when you originally registered your version of .NET with Crystal Decisions. The easiest way to find this is to click on the Help | About menu items in the IDE. It displays a list of the installed Visual Studio products and their assigned license keys.

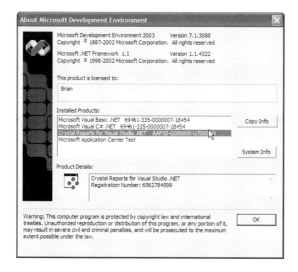

Select the Crystal Reports product and click on the Copy button. This copies the entire string to the clipboard.

Right-click on the License Key property and select Paste. This puts the string into the property field. Unfortunately, it also puts the product name. Delete all text prior to the license key numbers at the end of the string. Be careful that you don't delete too many characters or that you don't accidentally leave a leading space. The license key is nineteen characters long and you should count them to make sure you have exactly that number.

are also problems if you install CR 9/10 on your computer because there will be multiple assemblies on the computer. If possible, try building the installation on a different machine or uninstall and reinstall the Visual Studio tools to make sure all the libraries and registry keys are written correctly.

This is all that is required to deploy Crystal Reports applications. Just select Build from the Visual Studio menu and the setup files that you need to deploy your application will be created.

Deploying an ASP.NET Application

Deploying a web application is very similar to deploying a Windows application. As far as Crystal Reports is concerned, there is no difference in which merge modules you have to add. To show a different way to create a deployment project, this example walks you through the steps of adding a deployment project to an existing ASP.NET web application.

Open the project you want to deploy. Add the deployment project to it by selecting File | Add Project | New Project. Select Setup and Deployment Projects. Click on the template Web Setup Project and enter a name for the project. Click OK.

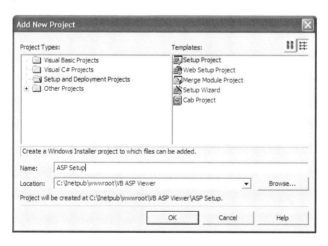

In the Solutions Explorer window, right click on the deployment project and select Add | Project Output.

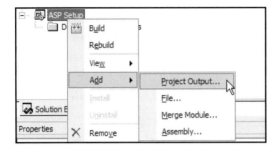

In the Add Project Group dialog box, select the Primary Output and Content Files items. Click OK.

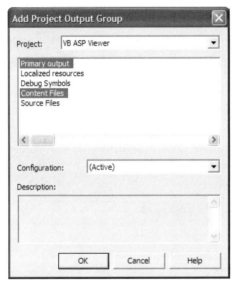

In the Solutions Explorer, right-click on the project name and select Add | Merge Module. In this example I add all the Crystal_* modules, but none of the VC_* modules because I didn't use ADO.NET in my reports.

This next step is the most important: set the license key property of the Crystal_regwiz2003.msm module. Click on the module name in the Solution Explorer window so that its properties are displayed in the Properties window.

Click on the plus sign next to MergeModuleProperties to expand it. Below it there is the License Key property. Enter the license key that was assigned to you when you originally registered your version of .NET with Crystal Decisions. The easiest way to find this is to click on the Help | About menu items in the IDE. It displays a list of the installed Visual Studio products and their assigned license keys.

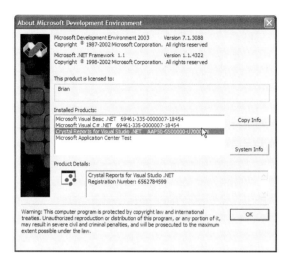

Select the Crystal Reports product and click on the Copy button. This copies the entire string to the clipboard.

Right-click on the License Key property and select Paste. This puts the string into the property field. Unfortunately, it also pastes the product name. So delete all text prior to the license key numbers at the end of the string. Be careful that you don't delete too many characters or that you don't accidentally leave a leading space. The license key is nineteen characters long and you should count them to make sure you have exactly that quantity.

As mentioned in the last section, even if you add the license key to your project correctly, you may still get an "Invalid Keycode" error when you run your project on the deployment machine. If you run into problems, search their support site and try everything possible.

This is all that is required to deploy Crystal Reports applications. Just select Build from the Visual Studio menu and the setup files that you need to deploy your application will be created.

Tip

If your ASP.NET report doesn't properly display either the toolbar buttons or the group tree images, you need to add a folder to the IIS Localhost. Create a new folder CrystalReportViewer2 and copy the \Images\Viewer and \Images\Toolbar folders to it. These folders are in the Crystal Reports folder within the Visual Studio 2003 program folder. This is where the icons needed to display the toolbar and group tree are located.

Printing with ASP.NET

Printing a report from a browser gives you a less than professional report. The browser can't differentiate between what is part of the report and the other HTML objects shown on the web page (e.g. the navigation buttons). It prints everything. Unfortunately, the web version of the viewer control doesn't have a print button that can be displayed on your form. The workaround for this problem is to export the report to a PDF file and then load the PDF file into the browser.

Caution

The normal method of viewing an ASP.NET report is very efficient because pages are generated as they are displayed and this conserves resources. This isn't the case when exporting to a PDF file. The entire report has to be generated to create the file and then it has to be sent to the user's browser to be displayed. For large reports, your users might have a longer than normal delay.

Listing 19-8 shows a generic method for printing reports. Pass it a report object (you have to declare and instantiate the report object prior to calling this method) and a filename to export the PDF file to.

Listing 19-8. Print from ASP.NET using a PDF file.

```
Public Sub PrintToPdfWithFile(ByVal MyReport As CrystalDecisions.CrystalReports.Engine.ReportDocument,
```

```
        ByVal FileName As String)
            'Instantiate the object that controls where the file is exported to
            Dim DestOptions As New CrystalDecisions.Shared.DiskFileDestinationOptions
            FileName = Request.PhysicalApplicationPath & Session.SessionID & "_" & _
            FileName
            DestOptions.DiskFileName = FileName
            'Set the Export Options
            MyReport.ExportOptions.ExportFormatType = _
            CrystalDecisions.Shared.ExportFormatType.PortableDocFormat
            MyReport.ExportOptions.ExportDestinationType = _
            CrystalDecisions.Shared.ExportDestinationType.DiskFile
            MyReport.ExportOptions.DestinationOptions = DestOptions
            MyReport.Export()
            'Display the PDF file in the current browser window
            Response.ClearContent()
            Response.ClearHeaders()
            Response.ContentType = "application/pdf"
            Response.WriteFile(FileName)
            Response.Flush()
            Response.Close()
            System.IO.File.Delete(FileName)
        End Sub
```

The first step instantiates a DiskFileDestinationOptions object that stores the destination PDF file's fully qualified file path. Notice that the FileName was modified so that it points to the local folder and also concatenates the Session ID with the name. This insures that the same report can be exported for different users without overwriting each other.

The second step sets the export options of the ReportDocument object. This tells it to use the PDF format and that it is a disk file. It also assigns the DestinationOption property so that it knows where to save the file.

Call the Export() method to save the report to the PDF file.

After the file is exported, you have to display it to the user. The last set of steps uses the Response object to load the PDF file and stream it to the browser window.

Once the file has been exported and streamed to the browser, the temporary output file is deleted.

Tip

It is very common for you to get an error stating that the temporary report file is not accessible. This is a confusing error message because it is written to make you think that you can't load the actual report file. But this isn't the case.

Exporting and Deploying   415

What the error message should have said is that you do not have write permissions to the directory where you are storing the export file. You need to make sure that the ASPNET user has proper permissions to the folder it is storing the PDF file to. Many times people insist this isn't the problem only to find out that it is. A simple way to test if this is your problem is to write the PDF file to the folder C:\Windows\Temp. The ASPNET user has full access to this folder by default. If you make this change and your report exports with no errors, then you know that you need to set the proper permissions on the output folder.

If you don't want to deal with the overhead of creating temporary export files and deleting them afterwards, export the report to a binary stream that is sent directly to the browser. This skips the intermediate step of writing the file to disk and later deleting it. Listing 19-9 shows the code for this.

Listing 19-9. Export to PDF using a binary stream.

```
Public Sub PrintToPdfWithStream(ByVal MyReport As _
    CrystalDecisions.CrystalReports.Engine.ReportDocument)
    Dim MyExportOptions As New CrystalDecisions.Shared.ExportOptions
    MyExportOptions.ExportFormatType = _
    CrystalDecisions.[Shared].ExportFormatType.PortableDocFormat
    Dim MyExportRequestContext As _
    New CrystalDecisions.Shared.ExportRequestContext
    MyExportRequestContext.ExportInfo = MyExportOptions
    Dim MyStream As System.IO.Stream
    MyStream = MyReport.FormatEngine.ExportToStream(MyExportRequestContext)
    Response.ClearHeaders()
    Response.ClearContent()
    Response.ContentType = "application/pdf"
    Dim MyBuffer(MyStream.Length) As Byte
    MyStream.Read(MyBuffer, 0, CType(MyStream.Length, Integer))
    Response.BinaryWrite(MyBuffer)
    Response.End()
End Sub
```

The previous two code samples exported to a PDF document. This is because Adobe Acrobat PDF files have become the defacto standard for displaying documents on the internet. But that doesn't mean that don't have any other options. You can export to a variety of formats. Change the ExportFormatType property and the Response.ContentType property. Table 19-11 shows the constants for setting the Response.ContentType property.

Table 19-11. String constants for the Response.ContentType property

Export Type	String Constant
Rich Text Format (.RTF)	"application/msword"
Adobe Acrobat (.PDF)	"application/pdf"
MS Word (.DOC)	"application/msword"
MS Excel (.XLS)	"application/vnd.ms-excel"
Crystal Report (.RPT)	"application/x-rpt"

C# Code Listings

The C# code listings are equivalent to the VB.NET code listings.

Listing 19-1. Export to a PDF disk file

```
Dim myReport As New CrystalReport1()
'Export the report to the destination type ReportExport.PDF
SetDestinationDisk(myReport, "C:\ReportExport.PDF")
'Set the format to be PDF and only export pages 1-3
SetFormatPdfRtfWord(myReport, False, 1, 3)
'Perform the export
myReport.Export()
```

Listing 19-2. Setting the destination to a disk file

```
public void SetDiskFileDestination(
CrystalDecisions.CrystalReports.Engine.ReportDocument Report, string FileName)
{
    //Set the destination type to DiskFile
    Report.ExportOptions.ExportDestinationType =
    CrystalDecisions.Shared.ExportDestinationType.DiskFile;
    //Instantiate a DiskFileDestinationOptions object and set its
    //FileName property
    CrystalDecisions.Shared.DiskFileDestinationOptions Options =
    new CrystalDecisions.Shared.DiskFileDestinationOptions();
    Options.DiskFileName = FileName;
    //Assign the object to the report
    Report.ExportOptions.DestinationOptions = Options;
}
```

Listing 19-3. Send a report as an attachment of an email.

```
public void SetEmailDestination(CrystalDecisions.CrystalReports.Engine.ReportDocument Report, string
MailTo, string CCList, string Subject, string Message, string UserName,string Password)
{
    //Set the destination type to EMail
    Report.ExportOptions.ExportDestinationType =
    CrystalDecisions.Shared.ExportDestinationType.MicrosoftMail;
    //Instantiate an Email options object and set its properties
    CrystalDecisions.Shared.MicrosoftMailDestinationOptions Options =
    new CrystalDecisions.Shared.MicrosoftMailDestinationOptions();
    Options.UserName = UserName;
    Options.Password = Password;
    Options.MailSubject = Subject;
    Options.MailMessage = Message;
    Options.MailToList = MailTo;
    Options.MailCCList = CCList;
    //Assign the options object to the report
    Report.ExportOptions.DestinationOptions = Options;
```

}

Listing 19-4. Export a report to an Exchange folder.

```
public void SetDestinationExchangeFolder(CrystalDecisions.CrystalReports.Engine.
ReportDocument Report, string FolderPath, string Password, string Profile)
{
    //Set the destination type to ExchangeFolder
    Report.ExportOptions.ExportDestinationType =
    CrystalDecisions.Shared.ExportDestinationType.ExchangeFolder;
    //Instantiate an ExchangeFolder options object and set its properties
    CrystalDecisions.Shared.ExchangeFolderDestinationOptions Options =
    new CrystalDecisions.Shared.ExchangeFolderDestinationOptions();
    Options.DestinationType =
    CrystalDecisions.Shared.ExchangeDestinationType.ExchangePostDocMessage;
    Options.FolderPath = FolderPath;
    Options.Password = Password;
    Options.Profile = Profile;
    Report.ExportOptions.DestinationOptions = Options;
}
```

Listing 19-5. Set the export formatting to PDF

```
public void SetFormatPdfRtfWord(CrystalDecisions.CrystalReports.Engine.ReportDocument Report, Boolean
UsePageRange, int FirstPageNumber, int LastPageNumber)
{
    //Change the next line if you want the format to be RTF or Word
    Report.ExportOptions.ExportFormatType =
    CrystalDecisions.Shared.ExportFormatType.PortableDocFormat;
    //The following lines stay the same regardless of formatting
      //for PDF, RTF or Word
    CrystalDecisions.Shared.PdfRtfWordFormatOptions Options =
    new CrystalDecisions.Shared.PdfRtfWordFormatOptions ();
    Options.UsePageRange = UsePageRange;
    if (Options.UsePageRange) {
      Options.FirstPageNumber = FirstPageNumber;
      Options.LastPageNumber = LastPageNumber;
    }
    Report.ExportOptions.FormatOptions = Options;
}
```

Listing 19-6. Setting the format to be an Excel spreadsheet.

```
public void SetFormatExcel(CrystalDecisions.CrystalReports.Engine.ReportDocument Report, Boolean
UseConstantColumnWidth, int ColumnWidth, Boolean UseColumnHeadings )
{
    Report.ExportOptions.ExportFormatType =
    CrystalDecisions.Shared.ExportFormatType.Excel;
    CrystalDecisions.Shared.ExcelFormatOptions Options =
    new CrystalDecisions.Shared.ExcelFormatOptions ();
    Options.ExcelUseConstantColumnWidth = UseConstantColumnWidth;
```

```
Options.ExcelConstantColumnWidth = ColumnWidth;
Options.ExcelTabHasColumnHeadings = UseColumnHeadings;
Report.ExportOptions.FormatOptions = Options;
}
```

Listing 19-7. Setting the format options for HTML.

```
public void SetFormatHTML(CrystalDecisions.CrystalReports.Engine.ReportDocument Report, Boolean
EnableSeparatedPages, Boolean HasPageNavigator, string HTMLBaseFolderName, string HTMLFilename,
Boolean UsePageRange, int FirstPageNumber, int LastPageNumber)
{
    //Set the destination type to HTML
    Report.ExportOptions.ExportFormatType =
    CrystalDecisions.Shared.ExportFormatType.HTML40;
    //Instantiate an options object and set its properties
    CrystalDecisions.Shared.HTMLFormatOptions Options =
    new CrystalDecisions.Shared.HTMLFormatOptions ();
    Options.HTMLEnableSeparatedPages = EnableSeparatedPages;
    Options.HTMLHasPageNavigator = HasPageNavigator;
    Options.HTMLFileName = HTMLFilename;
    Options.HTMLBaseFolderName = HTMLBaseFolderName;
    Options.UsePageRange = UsePageRange;
    if (Options.UsePageRange) {
        Options.FirstPageNumber = FirstPageNumber;
        Options.LastPageNumber = LastPageNumber;
    }
    Report.ExportOptions.FormatOptions = Options;
}
```

Listing 19-8. Print from ASP.NET using a PDF file.

```
public void PrintToPdfWithFile(
CrystalDecisions.CrystalReports.Engine.ReportDocument MyReport, string FileName)
{
    FileName = Request.PhysicalApplicationPath + Session.SessionID
    + "_" + FileName;
    //Instantiate the object that controls where the file is exported to
    CrystalDecisions.Shared.DiskFileDestinationOptions DestOptions =
    new CrystalDecisions.Shared.DiskFileDestinationOptions();
    DestOptions.DiskFileName = FileName;
    //Set the Export Options
    MyReport.ExportOptions.ExportFormatType =
    CrystalDecisions.Shared.ExportFormatType.PortableDocFormat;
    MyReport.ExportOptions.ExportDestinationType =
    CrystalDecisions.Shared.ExportDestinationType.DiskFile;
    MyReport.ExportOptions.DestinationOptions = DestOptions;
    MyReport.Export();
    //Display the PDF in the current browser window
    Response.ClearContent();
    Response.ClearHeaders();
```

```
Response.ContentType = @"application/pdf";
Response.WriteFile(FileName);
Response.Flush();
Response.Close();
System.IO.File.Delete(FileName);
}
```

Listing 19-9. Export to PDF using a binary stream.

```
public void PrintToPdfWithStream(
CrystalDecisions.CrystalReports.Engine.ReportDocument MyReport)
{
    CrystalDecisions.Shared.ExportOptions MyExportOptions =
    new CrystalDecisions.Shared.ExportOptions();
    MyExportOptions.ExportFormatType =
    CrystalDecisions.Shared.ExportFormatType.PortableDocFormat;
    CrystalDecisions.Shared.ExportRequestContext MyExportRequestContext =
    new CrystalDecisions.Shared.ExportRequestContext();
    MyExportRequestContext.ExportInfo = MyExportOptions;
    System.IO.Stream MyStream = null;
    MyStream = MyReport.FormatEngine.ExportToStream(MyExportRequestContext);
    Response.ClearContent();
    Response.ClearHeaders();
    Response.ContentType = @"application/pdf";
    Byte[] MyBuffer = new Byte[MyStream.Length];
    MyStream.Read(MyBuffer,0, (int)MyStream.Length);
    Response.BinaryWrite(MyBuffer);
    Response.End();
}
```

This page intentionally left blank

Chapter 19

Upgrading to the RDC and RAS

If you've gotten this far in the book, then you are very familiar with all the ins and outs of using Crystal Reports .NET. You also know that although Crystal Reports .NET can create powerful reporting solutions, it has features removed from it that users of the standalone Crystal Reports product expect. This includes robust reporting components and an object model that gives you unlimited runtime customization. When you find that you are trying to build reporting solutions that Crystal Reports .NET won't allow, it is time to look at upgrading to one of the developer editions of Crystal Reports.

> ### Note
>
> The examples in this chapter were written and tested using Crystal Reports 9. Version 10 was released just as the book was going to the printer. Consequently I haven't had time to learn about the new features of version 10. I do know that not much has changed with regards .NET. The improvements are focused on writing reports with the standalone application. The one major improvement for .NET is that you can now have a .NET application integrate with the RAS using only a few lines of code. This is very exciting news and I can't wait to try it out. Fortunately, version 10 is 100% backwards compatible with version 9. All the .NET examples in this chapter will work with version 10. I will post updates about Crystal Reports 10 as I learn more about it. See the book's website at www.CrystalReportsBook.com.

The Crystal Reports developer editions are a powerful reporting solution for all types of developers. Developers with prior experience programming Crystal Reports with other development tools (VB6, VC++, Delphi, etc.) are familiar with integrating the Report Designer Component (RDC) with their application. The RDC gives you complete access to the report object model and allows you to modify hundreds of properties during runtime. Many developers have been spoiled by this and feel that using Crystal Reports .NET is a step in the wrong direction. They want more options for writing .NET reporting solutions.

Here is a quick rundown of the options available to you.

Stick with CR.NET. If you are on a limited budget, then you don't have a choice but to stick with the tools you are given. You have to make the best of the situation and really convince your boss that some features just can't be implemented.

Use Crystal Reports 8.5. Millions of developers already own a copy of version 8.5 and will want to save money by using it with .NET. In one respect you are lucky because the 8.5 RDC is a COM object and it can be called from .NET using the object model you are familiar with. Unfortunately, Crystal Decisions states that although you can use the 8.5 RDC with .NET, they haven't tested it and don't support it. In other words, you will probably have some problems and there won't be any way to fix them. According to what I've seen posted to the newsgroups, there are definitely compatibility problems. It is up to you to test each individual report and decide whether the 8.5 components will function with your application.

Upgrade to Crystal Report Developer. Upgrading to the latest version of Crystal Reports is the Crystal Decisions official recommendation for adding advanced reporting functionality to .NET. It has been tested with .NET and is supported by Crystal Decisions. This upgrade gives you many new features and options to choose from.

This chapter only focuses on the using the stand-alone version of Crystal Reports with .NET. The first option has already been covered by this book and the consequences of staying with version 8.5 will vary for each application.

Upgrading to Crystal Reports 9/10

Before looking at the different upgrade options with Crystal Reports, you first have to install it on your computer. This is easy to do, but you have to be careful. There are a few things that you need to be aware of to make the process go smoothly. This includes making sure you have the correct version of Crystal Reports and making sure you install the tools in the correct order.

Installing and Uninstalling Crystal Reports

For Crystal Reports to work with .NET, you have to install the tools in the proper order. Failing to do so results in duplicate menu items and other strange behaviors. The stand-alone version of Crystal Reports must be installed AFTER Visual Studio .NET has been installed. When the stand-alone version of Crystal Reports is installed, it looks for an existing copy of Visual Studio .NET on your computer. If it finds Visual Studio .NET, it overwrites the default .NET components with upgraded versions. These upgraded components give you new features and more functionality.

If you unknowingly installed .NET after installing Crystal Reports, then you have to reinstall Crystal Reports again. .NET doesn't look for an existing copy of Crystal Reports on your computer. Even if it did, there is nothing that it could do differently because the upgraded components are included on the Crystal Reports installation CD. There is no way for .NET to install them.

If you later decide not to use Crystal Reports on your computer anymore, uninstalling it will corrupt the .NET reporting components. Uninstalling removes the upgraded components from your computer, but doesn't replace them with the original .NET components. The only way to get them back is to reinstall Visual Studio .NET and select Repair. This restores the reporting components to their original state prior to installing the stand-alone version of Crystal Reports.

Upgrade Alternatives

Installing Crystal Reports on your development machine gives you a wide range of upgrade options. Each option has its own benefits and drawbacks and this must be considered before deciding which path to pursue.

The first option is to keep using Crystal Reports .NET and only use the upgraded components. This makes it easy to work with because the way that reports are designed and integrated into an application doesn't change. Right after installing Crystal Reports you are immediately productive. The upgraded report objects give you greater control and customization than before. The following objects have more properties for you to work with: the Web viewer, Exporting options, the Graph component, Area, Section, OLEObject, Picture and BlobFieldObject. The biggest drawback to using the .NET upgraded components is that runtime customization hasn't been upgraded. If you do a lot of runtime customization and this is the primary reason for installing Crystal Reports, then you should consider one of the next two options.

The second option is to use the Report Designer Component (RDC) within a .NET application. The primary reason for doing this is to maximize the amount of control you have for runtime customization. The RDC has over 850 methods and properties to work with. The RDC also has additional events that your application can respond to. The two events that will make most programmers rejoice are the Format() and NoData() events. These events will be used in many applications. The drawback to using the RDC is that it is totally different from .NET. Since the RDC isn't a native .NET control, the method of integrating reports has changed. Modifying existing applications requires your existing code to be replaced with new code. Nonetheless, the benefits of upgrading to the RDC are so great that it justifies making the necessary code changes.

Note
Using the RDC is the Crystal Decisions recommended solution for developing Windows applications. It is not recommended for developing ASP.NET apps.

The third option is to use the Report Application Server (RAS). The RAS was designed for the sole purpose of running reports for access via the Web. All of its features have been optimized creating Web applications that are fast and scalable. Although RAS supports Windows thick-client development, it carries a huge footprint and isn't practical for distributing to client machines. If you write Windows applications and Web applications, you should learn both the RDC and the RAS.

Note
Using the RAS is the Crystal Decisions recommended solution for developing Web thin-client applications.

Scalability Concerns

Some applications and web sites are originally designed for a small number of users at the beginning with the hope that the software/site becomes successful and grows to support a larger number of users. If your application falls into this category, then you have to carefully consider your options in advance. Each of the three reporting options available with Crystal Reports require totally different programming techniques.

When you start programming with Visual Studio .NET, you will probably write reports using the Crystal Reports .NET object model. This can be used with both Windows Forms and ASP.NET. As your reporting requirements become more sophisticated, you will upgrade to the developer versions or Crystal Reports and use either the RDC or the RAS. Unfortunately, both of these upgrade paths are incompatible with the .NET object model.[46] You will have to rewrite your reporting code so that it is compatible with either the RDC or the RAS. In addition to that, if you have a Windows application that also makes the reports available via the internet, then you will have to write two different sets of reporting components for each model. The report files can be

---

[46] As mentioned at the beginning of the chapter, Crystal Reports 10 is supposed to make it easy to upgrade your .NET applications to the RAS. If this is true, upgrading to the RAS will be very simple.

used interchangeably between each type of application, but the programming code that works with the reports is different.

Remember to carefully consider your long-term reporting goals when deciding the best way to implement the reporting solution.

Recommended Upgrade Paths

Here is a summary of when you should use each of the upgrade paths.

If you want to improve the look and feel of your reports without rewriting any code, use the upgraded Crystal Reports .NET components in your reports.

If you have a Windows thick-client application and you want to maximize the ability to perform runtime customization, use the RDC.

If you have a Web application and you want to maximize its performance and scalability, use the RAS.

Upgrading Crystal Reports .NET Components

Using the upgraded .NET components is by far the simplest option. After installing Crystal Reports, the existing report objects are immediately upgraded and the menu options have been revised. The following sections give you an overview of what to expect.

Report Wizard

The report wizard had cosmetic changes to it that make it work a little differently, but this hasn't affected the functionality. The report templates that were used to create a variety of new reports have been significantly reduced. The following templates are no longer listed: Form Letter, Form, Subreport, and Drill Down. In one respect, this isn't a huge problem because each of these report types are easy enough for you to create on your own. However, having the wizard build them for you was certainly a nice bonus. You also can't build a new report from an existing report. This is a feature that I have personally used a lot because it makes it easier to create new reports that are similar to an existing report. I'm very disappointed by the decision to remove this feature.

The Data Sources Listbox has been reorganized so that all the ways to create a new connection are listed under the Create New Connection tree node. In the original .NET, most of these menu options were all listed at the same top level of the tree. Choosing data sources that already exist in the project or have been selected previously are listed individually in the tree. There are also new data sources that weren't available before. These are Crystal Queries, Dictionary/Infoview, and Olap.

A big improvement to this dialog box is that it gives you a multitude of new data sources to connect to. Previously, you could only connect to ADO.NET, Access/Excel, and a Field Definition File. Now you can connect to ACT! 3.0, Btrieve, Exchange Folders, Lotus Domino and many more. See Figure 20-1 for a screen shot that shows some of these data sources. Review the list yourself to see every type available.

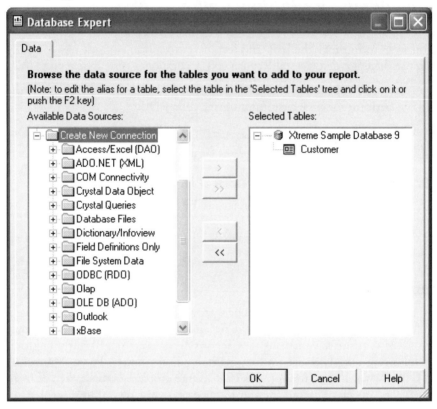

Figure 20-1. Available data sources.

After selecting the tables, the Links dialog is shown. This has changed because now it shows icons next to each type of link. For example, the color coded icons show the first index, second index and onto multiple indexes.

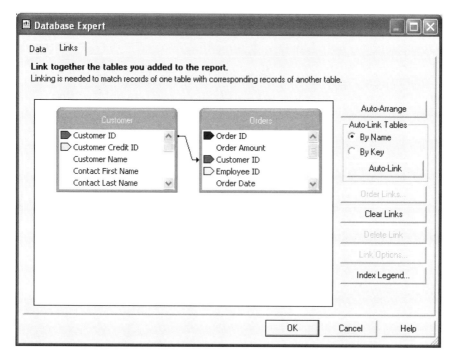

Figure 20-2. New Links dialog box.

The rest of the wizard hasn't changed much. The way the information is displayed is different, but each dialog box still has the same options to choose from. There is one minor change that is interesting. The Styles tab of the report wizard no longer lists the Report Title as an option. Previously, you entered the report title here and it would be put in the report header. Now you have to manually add the report title after the wizard has built the initial report and you are in design mode. This isn't a big deal, but I would be interested in finding out why they decided to remove it.

Exporting Reports

Exporting reports has a new option to export the raw data to an Excel spreadsheet. It lists each record as raw data only and doesn't attempt to do any formatting. This is available in every export area: the Windows viewer, the Web viewer and during runtime with programming code. The Windows viewer and Web viewer have this listed as an additional item listed under the formatting options. You don't have to do anything to implement it.

If you want to export the raw data to an Excel Record format during runtime, use the same programming code that was used to export to an Excel spreadsheet (see Chapter 19). But this time set the ExportFormatType property to be ExcelRecord.

Chart Component

The menu options for building and formatting a chart are the same, but they have been reorganized. For example, previously the Format Chart menu item had sub-menu items of Template, General, Titles and Grid. These sub-menu items have been moved under the Chart Options menu item. These are trivial changes that you will quickly adjust to.

The Chart Expert dialog box gives you two new chart types to work with: The Gauge chart and the Gantt chart.

The Gauge chart displays data as a semi-circle gauge.

The Gantt chart is typically used for project management reports. It shows a list of tasks and their start data and end date. By looking at projects tasks on a single report, you can see which tasks overlap and which ones haven't been completed yet.

Web Viewer

The Web viewer has been dramatically improved with the addition of two simple buttons: Export and Print. If you recall from previous chapters, the .NET web viewer didn't have the ability to either export or print reports. This required you to write a lot of code and add the appropriate menu buttons to your web page. Now that the upgraded Web viewer has this built-in, you can save yourself a lot of additional work. If you write a lot of reports for the internet, then this single feature alone could justify the purchase of Crystal Reports.

When previewing a report on a web page, you'll immediately notice that the menu bar looks different. Rather than using a solid row of square menu buttons, the buttons are now individual circular buttons. This is purely a cosmetic difference and doesn't have any effect on the functionality.

Figure 20-3. The viewer's toolbar in a browser.

Upon closer inspection you will notice that the first three buttons are new. The first button, Show/Hide Group Tree lets you toggle the group tree on and off. This is a convenient button to have.

The second button, Export, lets you export the report to an external file. When clicking on this button, a new page opens that lets the user select the format to export to and which pages to be exported. This page is shown in Figure 20-4.

Figure 20-4. The Export page.

You are given the standard file formats of Crystal Reports (RPT), Acrobat Format (PDF), MS Word, MS Excel, MS Excel (Data Only), and Rich Text Format. As mentioned earlier, the option to do a data only export to MS Excel is a new feature of Crystal Reports.

The Web viewer also lets you print directly from the Web page. If you recall from earlier in the book, this wasn't possible with the .NET viewer. You had to write code to export the report to PDF format and stream this PDF file to a new web page. This allowed it to be viewed by the Adobe Acrobat reader. The upgraded viewer actually prints using the same technique. It creates a PDF file and streams it to a new browser window. The benefit to you is that this code is now built-in and you don't have to do any programming.

Programming with the RDC

The default installation of Visual Studio .NET gives you a version of Crystal Reports that has had features removed from the stand-alone version. Although the .NET version has everything you need to create professional reporting solutions, the limited functionality will cause advanced programmers to run into a wall as they try to write increasingly complex applications. This is where the Report Designer Component, commonly referred to as the RDC, comes into play.

The RDC is the answer to the question, "How do I get more runtime customization from my .NET reporting application?" The RDC is a COM component that gives almost complete access to all the properties and methods of the report objects. Although certain things are restricted, there are over 850 properties and methods that will give you most everything you need.

As a developer writing reporting solutions, there are two areas of reporting that you have to be concerned with: report design and report integration. Report design hasn't changed because you still build reports in .NET just as you did previously. Report integration is a different story. Since the RDC is a COM object, it wasn't written using managed code. .NET uses a COM Interop to communicate with the RDC. This changes everything.

This chapter tells you what you need to know to do the most common reporting tasks. However, the RDC is a large and complex beast and to give you a complete tutorial on how to use it would require writing another book. Considering that I had to self-publish this book because no publisher wanted it, I doubt if I'll be writing any more Crystal Reports books in the future.

The code samples in this chapter are essential for learning how to modify your current applications to use the RDC and to become productive as quickly as possible. These samples include opening a report, performing runtime customization and exporting reports.

Note

I'm proud to say this book gives you the most comprehensive coverage of using the RDC with .NET. But after reading this chapter you might be hungry for more. Unfortunately, there aren't any other resources available. As of the time of this book's publication, the Crystal Decisions website has almost no information on using the RDC with .NET. There are a lot of code samples for using the RDC with VB6. But none of the VB6 code can be converted to .NET because the VB6 viewer classes are much more robust than the .NET viewer.

Previewing and Printing Reports

With the default installation of Crystal Reports .NET, the easiest way of printing a report is to use a strongly-typed report and create an instance of it in your application. You either assign this report object to the ReportSource property of the viewer or call the PrintToPrinter() method to send it directly to the printer. This doesn't work when using the RDC.

Note

There are two ways to view and print reports with the RDC. The first is to use the Windows Forms Viewer to display the report to the user prior to printing it. The viewer also has built-in functionality that performs common tasks such as exporting and changing the zoom level that saves you from having to write the code yourself. However, by itself the viewer doesn't justify using the RDC as part of your reporting solution. So it will only be covered in this chapter when necessary and ignored otherwise.

The RDC isn't managed code and it can't be directly referenced by any of the classes within your application. This immediately rules out the possibility of using strongly-typed reports since this treats a report as a class. Instead, you have to load the report as a stand-alone file using a fully-qualified filename. After you get a reference to the stand-alone report file, you can either assign it to the report viewer or call the PrintOut() method to send it directly to the printer. Both of these options are illustrated next.

Tip
Since the RDC can't reference reports as a class within your application, you don't need to include the reports as part of your application. Doing so will result in it being compiled as part of your application (even though it never gets used as a Strongly-Typed report). All reports are treated as Untyped reports. Either create them using the Crystal Reports stand-alone application, or create the reports inside the Visual Studio IDE but not associate them as part of the project solution you are developing.

Referencing the Crystal Report Libraries

Before you can print or preview any reports with a .NET application, the proper libraries have to be added to the project. Since the RDC consists of COM objects, a reference has to be added for them. After opening the project, select Project | Add Reference. Click on the COM tab and find Crystal Report Viewer Control 9. Double click on it to select it. This adds the viewer to the toolbox.

Find the listing for Crystal Reports 9 Active X Designer Run Time Library. Double click on it to select it. This adds a reference to the Report Designer Object Model so that you can create an instance of a report class and use its methods.

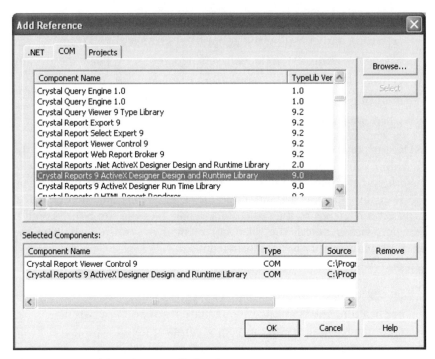

Figure 20-5. Add Reference dialog box.

The upgraded windows viewer is added to the bottom of the Toolbox window. If you scroll to the bottom of this window you will see that there are now two viewers listed. The first being the original viewer install with .NET and the second one being version 9.

Figure 20-6. RDC Viewer in Toolbox

All examples in this section assume that you already added the COM references to your project.

Previewing a Report

Crystal Reports comes with an upgraded version of the viewer controls (both Windows and ASP.NET). It gives you additional functionality over the .NET viewer.

The steps to preview a report with the upgraded report viewer are as follows:

Add the viewer to a form and resize it.

Create an instance of the Application object.

Call the Application.Load() method to load the report into memory and assign it to a report object.

Assign the report object to the viewer's ReportSource property.

Open the Toolbox and double click on the version 9 viewer to add it to the form. Change its size as necessary. My preference is to set the Dock property to Fill so that the viewer uses the entire form.

Open the code window for the Form and declare an Application object and a Report object. Although this example doesn't use any of the events of the Report class that are discussed later, I declare the object using the WithEvents keyword so that I have the option in the future.

```
Dim myApp As CRAXDRT.Application
Dim WithEvents myReport As CRAXDRT.Report
```

In the Form_Load() event create an instance of the Application object.

```
myApp = New CRAXDRT.Application
```

Call the Application.OpenReport() method and pass a fully qualified filename to it. This should be assigned to the report object that was already declared.

```
myReport = myApp.OpenReport("C:\TestReport.rpt")
```

Assign the report object to the ReportSource property of the viewer and call the ViewReport() method.

```
AxCRViewer91.ReportSource = myReport
```

The complete code listing that puts all this together is in Listing 20-1 below.

Listing 20-1. Previewing a report with the RDC viewer control.
```
Private Sub Form1_Load(ByVal sender As System.Object, ByVal e As System.EventArgs) Handles
MyBase.Load
    Dim CrApplication As CRAXDRT.Application
    CrApplication = New CRAXDRT.Application
    myReport = CrApplication.OpenReport("CrystalReport1.rpt")
    AxCRViewer91.ReportSource = myReport
End Sub
```

Run the application and it will immediately display the report using the report viewer.

Printing a Report Directly without Previewing It

Directly printing reports without using the viewer control is performed in almost the same way as using the viewer. The only changes are that you don't have to add the viewer to the Toolbox and you have to call the PrintOut() method of the Report object to send the report to the printer. The PrintOut() method takes 4 optional parameters. If you are programming with C# then all the parameters are required. These parameters are listed in Table 20-1.

Table 20-1. Parameters of the PrintOut() method.

Parameter	Description
PromptUser	A Boolean constant stating whether the user should be prompted with the Print dialog box.
NumberOfCopy	An Integer specifying how many copies to print.
Collated	A Boolean constant. If multiple copies are being printed then this determines whether they should be collated.
StartPageN	An Integer specifying the page to start printing.
StopPageN	An Integer specifying the ending page to print.

The steps to preview a report with the upgraded report viewer are as follows:

Create an instance of the Application object.

Call the Application.Load() method to load the report into memory and assign it to a report object.

Call the PrintOut() method of the report object.

Open the code window for the Form and declare an Application object and a Report object. Although this example doesn't use any of the events of the Report class that are discussed later, I declare the object using the WithEvents keyword so that I have the option in the future.

```
Dim myApp As CRAXDRT.Application
Dim WithEvents myReport As CRAXDRT.Report
```

In the Form_Load() event create an instance of the Application object.

```
myApp = New CRAXDRT.Application
```

Call the Application.OpenReport() method and pass a fully qualified filename to it. This should be assigned to the report object that was already declared.

```
myReport = myApp.OpenReport("CrystalReport1.rpt")
```

Call the PrintOut() method of the report object. Pass the appropriate properties to set the printing options.

```
'Prompt the user with the Print dia'log box
```

```
myReport.PrintOut(True)
```

The complete code listing that puts all this together is in Listing 20-2 below.

Listing 20-2. Printing a report.

```
Private Sub Form1_Load(ByVal sender As System.Object, ByVal e As System.EventArgs) Handles
MyBase.Load
    Dim CrApplication As CRAXDRT.Application
    CrApplication = New CRAXDRT.Application
    myReport = CrApplication.OpenReport("CrystalReport1.rpt")
    'Prompt the user with the Print dialog box
    myReport.PrintOut(True)
End Sub
```

Run the application and the Print dialog box will appear. Click OK to send the report to the printer.

Modifying Report Parameters and Formulas

If you recall from earlier in the book, modifying parameters during runtime was a complex undertaking. You had to get a reference to the appropriate parameter objects, create value objects and add them to the appropriate collection and assign this collection back to the parameter. This was a lot of steps with a lot of room for error. If you found yourself pulling your hair out trying to understand parameters, you are in luck. The RDC makes modifying parameters easy! Parameters can be changed with a single method call. If you work with parameters a lot, then upgrading to Crystal Reports is justified by this one improvement. Let's look at how easy it is.

There are three methods that are important for modifying a parameter: GetItemByName(), AddCurrentValue(), and AddCurrentRange(). These are discussed next.

There are a few ways to reference a parameter. The first way is to loop through each parameter object until you find the one you need. This takes a lot of unnecessary coding. The second way is to reference it by the index number. This requires you to know the index number beforehand which isn't usually known. The third, and easiest, way is to use the GetItemByName() method. Pass it the name of the parameter and it returns a reference to the appropriate parameter.

```
Dim myParameter As CRAXDRT.ParameterFieldDefinition
MyParameter = myReport.GetItemByName("myParameter")
```

After getting a reference to the parameter object, you can either assign a discrete value or a range value to it.

The method AddCurrentValue()_assigns a discrete value to the parameter. It has a single parameter, the value, which can be any data type as long as it is compatible with the parameter's data type. The example that follows uses the AddCurrentValue() method along with the GetItemByName() method to assign a value to the parameter with just one line of code. This sure beats .NET!

```
myReport.GetItemByName("myParameter").AddCurrentValue(myValue)
```

The method AddCurrentRange() assigns a range value to the parameter. The first two parameters are the beginning and ending range values. The value can be of any data type as long as it is compatible with the data type that the parameter expects. The third parameter, called RangeInfo, gives you the option of whether you want to include or exclude the values as part of the range. For example, you could specify the range of a full year by passing the values 1/1/2003 and 1/1/2004 and telling it not to include the last value. This results in the range using 12/31/2003 as the final value. Table 20-2 lists the possible options for the third parameter.

Table 20-2. RangeInfo Parameter values.

RangeInfo Parameter	Description
crRangeIncludeLowerBound	Include the lower bound as part of the range.
crRangeIncludeUpperBound	Include the upper bound as part of the range.
crRangeNoLowerBound	Ignore the lower bound value. This has the effect of not having a lower bound and printing all values up to the upper bound.
crRangeNotIncludeUpperLowerBound	Don't include both the lower bound and upper bound values. Use all numbers inside that range.
crRangeNoUpperBound	Ignore the upper bound. This has the effect of not having an upper bound and printing all values after the lower bound.

The AddCurrentRange() method doesn't allow optional parameters. Each of the three parameters must be specified. So you can't just pass it two values and assume that will be included as part of the range. You have to tell it exactly what to do with each value. The parameter is a bit mapped value. So you can specify more than one by adding them together.

You should also be aware that if you don't specify whether a value should be included or not, then by default it won't be. This is the same as passing the parameter crRangeNotIncludeUpperLowerBound. However, just because this is the default doesn't mean you don't have to pass it to the method. Since each parameter is required then you have to specify something here.

Look at the next example and see if you can determine the effective range.

```
myReport.GetItemByName("DateRange").AddCurrentRange(#1/1/2003#, #1/1/2004#,
crRangeIncludeLowerBound)
```

To figure this out, remember that by default, each value is assumed to be excluded from the range. For now, if we ignore the RangeInfo parameter, then we know that the effective range would be from 1/2/2003 to 12/31/2003. Then we look at the RangeInfo parameter to see what effect it has. This parameter says to include the lower bound. This changes the lower bound to make it 1/1/2003. Thus, the effective range is 1/1/2003 to 12/31/2003 (i.e. the full 2003 calendar year).

The best way to see how the RangeInfo works is by looking at examples. Table 20-3 shows some examples to illustrate how each parameter effects the effective range that the report uses to filter records.

Table 20-3. Examples of using the RangeInfo property.

RangeInfo Parameter Values	Effective Range
100, 200, crRangeIncludeLowerBound	100 through 199
100, 200, crRangeIncludeUpperBound	101 through 200
100, 200, crRangeNoLowerBound	Smallest value through 199
100,200, crRangeNotIncludeUpperLowerBound	101 through 199
100, 200, crRangeNoUpperBound	101 through largest value
100, 200, crRangeIncludeLowerBound + crRangeIncludeUpperBound	100 through 200
100, 200 crRangeNoLowerBound + crRangeNoUpperBound	Smallest value through largest value. This has the effect of ignoring both range values and printing all records.

Modifying formulas is even easier than modifying parameters. When modifying a formula, you only have to set the Text property to be the value of the new formula. The following formula demonstrates concatenating the employee's first name with their last name.

```
myReport.FormulaFields.GetItemByName("FullName") =
"{Customer.Contact First Name} + ' ' + {Customer.Contact Last Name}"
```

Recall that when changing the formula text during runtime you have to use Crystal Syntax. Even if the original formula was written with Basic Syntax when the report was designed, you still have to use Crystal Syntax. The runtime interpreter parser doesn't understand Basic Syntax.

Dynamic Images

One of the biggest complaints for Crystal Reports .NET programmers is that it is very difficult to dynamically change an image while a report is printing. Expert users of Crystal Reports will put a static image inside the detail section of a report and add programming code so that the image dynamically changes based upon data that is in the current record. This was easy when programming with VB6, but almost impossible when programming with .NET. The RDC now makes it possible to have a report with dynamic images in a .NET application.

The critical difference between .NET and the RDC is that the RDC has a Format() event for the Section object. Every time a section is about to be printed, the Format() event is fired. You can hook into it and modify the report objects within that section. This gives you the ability to load a new image for each record in the report. This wasn't possible with .NET because the Format() event was removed from its object model.

Images on a report are stored as OleObjects. You have to get a reference to the OleObject and call the SetOleLocation() method. Pass it a fully qualified filename for the new image to load. It loads the image onto the report and displays it. That's all there is to it!

The steps to dynamically changing images on a report are as follows:

Make sure you have a report that displays an image. If not, then create one.

Write the code as you normally would to preview/print the report.

Declare an additional object variable for the section that has the image. This variable must be declared using the WithEvents keyword so that you can hook into the Format() event.

Within the Format() event, declare an OleObject variable and set it equal to the image object in the section.

Call the SetOleLocation() method and pass it the name of a new image.

Let's walk through an example of dynamically changing an image on a report.

The first step is to use an existing report that displays an image or create one. I'll create a very simple report which just shows an employees name and displays a random image below it. Of course, in a real-world example you would want to display something much more relevant such as the person's picture.

To make sure I have some pictures to load into the report, I copied some BMP files into my project folder and renamed them in ascending order as "Image1.bmp", "Image2.bmp" up through "Image5.bmp".

<table>
<tr><td>**Note**</td></tr>
</table>

If you want to display JPG images, you need to have a JPG OLE Server application on the computer. Crystal Reports won't display JPG images natively.

After creating a sample report and making sure that the image files are ready, write the code to preview the report. This code was already shown in previous sections. In addition to this code, declare a Section object variable and use the WithEvents keyword. Since the WithEvents keyword is being used, the variable has to be declared in the Declarations section of the form class. I put it right after declaring the Application object.

```
Dim WithEvents crSection As CRAXDRT.Section
```

Assign the section variable to the report section that has the image in it. I do this right after loading the report with the Application object. In this example, Section3 has the image.

```
crSection = MyReport.Sections.Item("Section3")
```

Inside the section's format event, declare an OleObject object variable and assign it to the image control. Then call the SetOleLocation() method and pass it the name of the new image to load.

```
Dim pic As CRAXDRT.OleObject
pic = crSection.ReportObjects.Item("Picture1")
pic.SetOleLocation("NewImage.bmp")
```

Run the report and you'll see the new image loaded and displayed for each employee record. To make all this easier to understand, Listing 20-3 shows the complete code listing for using dynamic images. This lets you see the overall picture of where all the code belongs and how the pieces fit together.

Listing 20-3. Printing dynamic images.

```
Public Class ViewDynamicImages
    Inherits System.Windows.Forms.Form
    Dim crApp As New CRAXDRT.Application
    'The counter is used for naming the dynamic images
    Dim WithEvents crSection As CRAXDRT.Section
```

```
    Dim Counter As Integer = 1
#Region " Windows Form Designer generated code "
    Private Sub ViewDynamicImages_Load(ByVal sender As System.Object, _
    ByVal e As System.EventArgs) Handles MyBase.Load
        Dim MyReport As CRAXDRT.Report
        'Open the report
        MyReport = crApp.OpenReport("..\DynamicImages.rpt")
        AxCRViewer91.ReportSource = MyReport
        'Section 3 is where the image is printed
        crSection = MyReport.Sections.Item("Section3")
        'Preview the report
        AxCRViewer91.ViewReport()
    End Sub
    Private Sub crSection_format(ByVal pFormattingInfo As Object) _
    Handles crSection.format
        Dim pic As CRAXDRT.OleObject
        'Get a reference to the image object
        pic = crSection.ReportObjects.Item("Picture1")
        'Load the dynamic image into the report
        pic.SetOleLocation(Application.StartupPath & "\Image" & _
        Counter.ToString & ".bmp")
        Counter += 1
        If Counter = 5 Then Counter = 1
    End Sub
End Class
```

Notice in this listing that I made one additional change that wasn't shown earlier. I added a counter variable that gets incremented for each record. In the Format() event I use this variable to determine the filename of the image to load. Once the counter gets to 5, I reset it back to 1.

Mapping the Report Objects

As you know from previous chapters, I consider being able to map the report objects to be essential for understanding how to work with the object model. Once you have an understanding of how to navigate through every object on a report, then you can quickly get a reference to the exact report object you need and either examine its properties or change them. This section shows you how to map out all the report objects and print their properties.

Note
Navigating through the Report Designer Object Model is very similar to what has been discussed in other chapters. If you've gotten this far in the book then you are a fairly advanced programmer and there is no need for me to re-hash already discussed topics. This section will give a quick

overview of how the object model is designed and then show you the code for navigating it.

The parent object for the entire hierarchy is the Application object. As you've seen in the programming examples in this section, you have to instantiate the Application object to be able to open a report. Once the report is opened and you have a reference to it, you can navigate through the rest of the object hierarchy.

Access to all the report objects is controlled by the area and section that they are located in. The outermost collection is the Areas collection. The Areas collection stores each Area object. Each Area object has a Sections collection which stores a group of Section objects. In simple reports there is usually only one section for each area. But in more complex reports there could be many sections within an area. Navigating through the Areas and Sections collections is very simple and is done using standard For Each loops.

Each section has a ReportObjects collection where all the individual report objects are stored. Navigating through this collection is the most complex part of the code because you have to identify what the object is and call the method specific to mapping that type of report object. Each method is unique in that it has to identify the specific characteristics for that report object.

There is one big difference between the Areas/Sections collection and the ReportObjects collection. You can use a For Each loop to navigate through the Areas/Sections collection, but you have to use a For Next loop to navigate through the ReportObjects collection. Both the Areas and Sections collection have a corresponding Area and Section object. But the ReportObjects collection doesn't have an associated ReportObject class.

This sample pseudo-code loops through the Areas collection and calls a generic method called MapArea().

```
Dim myArea as CRAXDRT.Area
For Each myArea in Areas
    MapArea(myArea)
Next
```

This sample pseudo-code loops through the ReportObjects collection and calls a generic method called MapReportObject(). Notice that the index is Base 1.

```
Dim Counter as Integer
For Counter=1 To ReportObjects.Count
    MapReportObject(ReportObjects.Item(Counter))
Next
```

As you loop through each report object, the Kind property tells you what type of report object it is. This property will be one of the values in the CRObjectKind enumeration. This enumeration is listed in Table 20-4.

Table 20-4. Enumeration values for CRObjectKind.

CRObjectKind

crBlobFieldObject
crBoxObject
crCrossTabObject
crFieldObject
crGraphObject
crLineObject
crMapObject
crOlapGridObject
crOleObject
crSubReportObject

After determining the type of report object you have a reference to, it's simply a matter of getting or setting the properties of the object. This varies for each type of object and the easiest way to see a list of available properties is to use Intellisense and let it display a pop-up of all the properties.

The one report object that differs from the others is the crFieldObject. All the other objects are simplistic because they only map one type of object. For example, the crLineObject will only represent a line on the report. The field object, on the other hand, is a generic object used to represent a variety of other report objects. For example, it could be a database field, formula field, a special field (report date, page number, etc.) and other types of fields.

To determine what type of object the field object represents, you have to reference the Field.Field.Kind property. For example, this line of code displays the name of the object. It gets the name from the CRFieldKind enumeration.

```
MessageBox.Show([Enum].GetName(GetType(CRAXDRT.CRFieldKind), Field.Field.kind))
```

To find out what data the field object has in it, use the Field.Field.Name property. This is different for each type of object. For example, a database field object will show which field is going to be displayed and a formula field will show the formula's text. There are too many field types to list them all here. Experiment with the field types that concern you to see what gets displayed.

```
MessageBox.Show(Field.Field.Name)
```

Mapping subreports is easy because you use the same code for mapping reports. Once you determine that a report object is a subreport, create an instance of the subreport as a report object. Then pass the new report object to the same methods you used for mapping the parent report. The OpenSubreport() method enables you to open a subreport as a report object.

> ### Note
> You don't have to worry about recursion problems when opening subreports because a subreport can't have other subreports. Subreports only go one level deep.

```
Dim SubReport As CRAXDRT.SubreportObject
Dim NewReport As CRAXDRT.Report
SubReport = Section.ReportObjects(ObjectCounter)
NewReport = Report.OpenSubreport(SubReport.SubreportName)
MapReport(NewReport)
```

Mapping parameters and formulas is very easy because both collections are a direct child of the Report class. The ParameterFields collection stores ParameterFieldDefinition objects. The FormulaFields collection stores FormulaFieldDefinition objects. Use a For Each loop to navigate through each collection and print each object's properties.

Connecting to Data Sources

Using the RDC to connect to data sources is a pretty simple task. The RDC's object model for tables is similar to that of the .NET object model. The report object has a Database collection that stores Table objects. Each table in a report has a corresponding table object in the Database collection. But that is where their similarities end.

When referencing a table, you have to do so with its index number in the Tables collection. Be careful, because this collection is Base 1. If you use 0 to reference the first table you will get a runtime error.

Each table has a collection of name-value pairs for identifying each table property. For example, there is an item in the collection with the name "UserID" and its associated value is the ID of the user logging in. Each type of data connection has a different set of name-value pairs that get set. Listing 20-4 shows sample code that opens an OLE DB MS Access database and logs in as the Admin user.

> ### Note
> The Names in the ConnectionProperties collection are case sensitive.

Listing 20-4. Open a report using a MS Access database.

```
Dim CrApplication As CRAXDRT.Application = New CRAXDRT.Application
Dim MyReport as CRAXDRT.Report
```

```
MyReport = CrApplication.OpenReport("CrystalReport1.rpt")
Dim ConnectionInfo As CRAXDRT.ConnectionProperties
ConnectionInfo = Report.Database.Tables(1).ConnectionProperties
ConnectionInfo.Delete("Provider")
ConnectionInfo.Add("Provider", "Microsoft.Jet.OLEDB.4.0")
ConnectionInfo.Delete("Data Source")
ConnectionInfo.Add("Data Source", "C:\xtreme.mdb")
ConnectionInfo.Delete("User ID")
ConnectionInfo.Add("User Id", "Admin")
AxCRViewer91.ReportSource = MyReport
```

Notice that the code first deletes the existing property prior to adding it to the collection. This is because there isn't a way to overwrite an existing property's value with a new value. You have to first delete the existing property from the collection and then add it back with the new value. However, you can't assume that every property is already in the collection. If you try to delete a property that doesn't exist in the collection then an error is raised. Most notably is the Password property which is never saved with a report. Rather than trying to figure out in advance which properties are already in the collection and which aren't, Listing 20-4 simplifies this process with a method called AddConnectionInfo(). It demonstrates adding the Password property.

Listing 20-5. Adding name-value properties to the table.

```
Dim myReport As New CrystalReport1
Dim ConnectionNames as String
myReport.DiscardSavedData()
ConnectionNames = String.Join(",", ConnectionInfo.NameIDs)
AddConnectionInfo(myReport.Database.Tables(1).ConnectionProperties, "Password",_
"pw", ConnectionNames)
AxCRViewer91.ReportSource = MyReport
...
Private Sub AddConnectionProperty(ByRef ConnectionInfo As CRAXDRT.ConnectionPropertiesClass, ByVal
Name As String, ByVal Value As String,_
ByVal ConnectionNames As String)
    If Value <> "" Then
        If ConnectionNames.IndexOf(Name) > -1 Then
            ConnectionInfo.Delete(Name)
        End If
        ConnectionInfo.Add(Name, Value)
    End If
End Sub
```

The AddConnectionProperty() method takes three parameters: the property name, its value, and a comma-delimited string of all the connection properties. If the property name is already in the comma-delimited list then it deletes the property from the collection. The property is then added to the collection without problems.

The hard part of setting the table properties is knowing the names of each name-value pair for every type of data connection. The following sections show each type of data connection and list associated name-value pairs used.

SQL Server Using ODBC DSNs

- DSN
- User ID
- Password
- Database
- Trusted_Connection (1 for true, 0 for false)

MS Access Using ODBC DSNs

- DSN
- Password

SQL Server Using OLE DB

- Provider (set to "SQLOLEDB")
- Data Source
- Initial Catalog
- User ID
- Password
- Integrated Security (1 for true, 0 for false)

MS Access Using OLE DB

- Provider (set to "Microsoft.Jet.OLEDB.4.0")
- Data Source
- User ID
- Jet System Database (file path of the System.mdw file)
- Jet Database Password

Using ADO.NET

Reports written with an ADO.NET data source can be opened with the RDC. However, the programming code is completely different than what you've seen so far. All the data connections previously discussed use the Pull Model. The Pull Model is when the report does all the work to open the data connection and load the data into the report. But ADO.NET uses the Push Model. This means that you have to write the programming code to instantiate the data connection and load the data into the DataSet object. Since the report object doesn't need connection information for retrieving the data, the RDC doesn't use name-value pairs for ADO.NET.

The steps for working using the RDC with ADO.NET are pretty simple. You have to first populate a DataTable object with the records to be printed. There are numerous ways to get data into an ADO.NET datatable and how you do it is your choice. This chapter will show you one way of loading data into a datatable, but remember that you can use any method that is appropriate for your application.

> **Note**
>
> The RDC is designed to work with the DataTable object only. It doesn't work with the DataSet, DataView or the DataReader objects.

Once the DataTable object is ready, pass it to the report by calling the SetDataSource() method of the report object. There are three parameters that are passed to the SetDataSource() method. They are listed in Table 20-5.

Table 20-5. The SetDataSource() parameters.

Parameter Name	Description
Data Object	The DataTable object.
Data Type	The type of data object being passed. Use the constant 3 to specify a DataTable.
Table Number	The report's table number that is getting assigned the datasource. This is Base 1.

The first parameter is the DataTable object that has the data to print. It has to be fully populated with the data prior to calling the SetDataSource() method. The second parameter is an enumerator that states the type of data being passed. Use the numeric constant 3 for DataTable objects. The third parameter is the table number. This corresponds to the order that the tables were added to the report when the report was being designed. For example, the first table uses a constant of 1. Listing 20-6 shows how to open a report and pass two tables to the report.

Listing 20-6. Opening a report using ADO.NET.

```
Dim myConnection As OleDb.OleDbConnection
Dim myDataAdapter As OleDb.OleDbDataAdapter
Dim myDataSet As DataSet = New DataSet
Dim myReport As CRAXDRT.Report
crApp = New CRAXDRT.Application
myReport = crApp.OpenReport("CrystalReport1.rpt")
'Fill the dataset object with the two tables
myConnection = New OleDb.OleDbConnection(Globals.ConnectionString)
myDataAdapter = New OleDb.OleDbDataAdapter("SELECT * FROM Customers", myConnection)
myDataAdapter.Fill(myDataSet, "Customers")
myDataAdapter = New OleDb.OleDbDataAdapter("SELECT * FROM Orders", myConnection)
myDataAdapter.Fill(myDataSet, "Orders")
'Assign the tables to the report
myReport.Database.SetDataSource(myDataSet.Tables("Customers"), 3, 1)
myReport.Database.SetDataSource(myDataSet.Tables("Orders"), 3, 2)
'Preview the report
AxCRViewer91.ReportSource = MyReport
```

Programming with the RAS

The Report Application Server (RAS) is the Crystal Decisions' recommended tool for developing web-based reporting solutions for the enterprise. It is designed to be used in a high performance, high scalability environment. This section gives you an overview of the RAS and shows you sample code for creating and implementing RAS enabled applications within the .NET environment. Due to the complexity and broad reach of the RAS software, it is beyond the scope of this chapter to give a thorough analysis and tutorial of how to use the RAS components. Instead, the goal is to show you how to create a new RAS application and demonstrate common coding solutions such as changing parameters and mapping new data sources. If you want more information, the RAS software installs ample help files to study and the Crystal Decisions website has great information on it. In fact, Crystal Decisions has done such a great job that you almost don't even need to read this section of the chapter. However, I still think it's a good idea to read this chapter for a couple of reasons. First of all, there isn't any information on setting up an application to use RAS. This is not very intuitive and could take you a while to figure out the first time. Secondly, I think this chapter does an excellect job of showing you how to quickly get started with the most important parts of integrating .NET with the RAS.

The RAS software is included as a separate CD with the Developer and Advanced editions of Crystal Reports.

RAS Overview

The RAS software is a set of components designed to be installed on a web server running on Microsoft's IIS. The RAS enables report creation, processing and manipulation in a client-server environment. It consists of two separate components: the RAS server and the Software Development Kit (SDK). The server performs the work of designing, processing and customizing the reports. The SDK component is an interface to the server. It gives your application the ability to communicate with the server and make reporting requests.

Although the RAS tools can be used as part of a thick-client application, it isn't designed for this purpose. It has a large footprint and poor installation tools that prohibit it from being the best solution for Windows development. Crystal Decisions recommends using the RDC for a Windows thick-client application.

Using the RAS components gives you increased functionality over the other available .NET reporting options. Some of the new features are as follows:

Increased Performance. Each component runs independently of the other and can be installed on a separate server. This lets you balance the load on each server.

Runtime Report Creation. Only the RAS components let you create a new report during runtime. An example of how to use this would be to add a report wizard to your application. The wizard can prompt the user with questions about their reporting needs and the application can generate a custom report based upon their answers. The RAS also lets you take an existing report and add or delete report objects during runtime. If you wanted to do this with the RDC, you would have to purchase additional licenses.

Object Repository. You can store commonly used report objects (images, SQL commands, custom functions, etc.) in the object repository and share these objects across reports. If objects in the repository changed, the RAS can automatically update each report to use the new objects.

Data Extraction. You can extract raw data from a report as XML and use it in other applications.

Report Caching. Requesting the same report by multiple users is handled more efficiently by the RAS because it automatically caches the report data.

Load Balancing. The RAS server can be installed on its own server to distribute the load processing more efficiently. It can also be configured to use multiple processors on a server.

No Session Variables. Unlike the RDC, the RAS doesn't use session variables to maintain report data.

Client Printing: Reports can be automatically generated in a PDF format and sent to the client's browser.

Licensing

Disclaimer: The licensing contract that Crystal Decisions provides with RAS is complex and subject to change at the discretion of Crystal Decisions. This section is intended to give you a general understanding of the license as of the time of publication (January 2004) and how it might impact you. I am not a lawyer and this is not meant to be a legal interpretation of how your company can use the software. You need to have legal council review the contract in relation to your company's needs. If you are unsure of whether your reporting solution conforms to the Crystal Decisions license, then contact Crystal Decisions directly. They are happy to help you.

The RAS components are meant to be used for highly scalable web development. But the license that comes with a single RAS installation limits the amount of report processing that can be performed. The RAS software license gives you the rights to run three simultaneous reporting requests per server. A few examples of what qualifies as a request are initializing a report, generating report data, or loading a sub-report. Any request in excess of the available three processes are put into a queue and processed as soon as a new thread is available. Managing the print queue is completely handled by the RAS components and doesn't require any additional coding on your part.

Although you might feel that three simultaneous processes aren't sufficient for your needs, you need to perform load testing to determine whether this assumption is correct. The RAS components are designed to be very efficient at processing and caching report requests. Since additional requests are automatically added to the queue, you will find that the RAS components can process a high number of requests very quickly and your users will not notice a measurable delay.

If your usability tests show that the default RAS licensing doesn't provide the scalability that your site needs, you have two options. The first option is to buy more licenses. This increases the number of simultaneous requests that the RAS components can process. The second option is to upgrade to Crystal

Enterprise. Both options are easy to implement. Purchasing more RAS licenses only requires you to install the licenses to your server. No additional coding is required. Purchasing Crystal Enterprise requires only minimal code changes because the RAS components are designed to be compatible with Crystal Enterprise and easily upgradeable.

The limitation of three simultaneous requests is for each application, not for each server. In other words, you can't avoid purchasing more licenses by building a server farm and having a copy of the RAS installed on each server. You have to purchase the proper number of licenses for the application as a whole. Whether you use one server or a hundred servers is irrelevant.

The RAS software can only be installed on one server. Each server must be used by a separate reporting solution.

Creating a RAS Application

Let's look at how to use the RAS components by creating a simple web application that previews a report. After this example is complete, you will learn how to add additional code to this example to perform more sophisticated runtime report modification.

To implement the RAS examples, the following is assumed:

You have read the RAS setup instructions and properly installed the RAS components on your computer.

You have a sample report already built and tested. In my examples, I refer to this report as "MyReport.rpt". You need to substitute this report name with the filename of the report you want to print.

The sample report has been copied to the RAS report directory. You can see the current report directory location by running the RAS Configuration Manager. If there is a '*' in the directory location then RAS will use 'C:\' as the report folder.

To create a RAS application, first open Visual Studio .NET and create a new ASP.NET application.

Add a reference to the appropriate RAS libraries. Select Project | Add Reference and scroll through the list to find the libraries you need. Table 20-6 shows a couple of the possible libraries and what they are needed for. Both are in the namespace CrystalDecisions.ReportAppServer.

Table 20-6. RAS libraries.

Library Name	Purpose
ClientDoc	Used for getting a reference to the report object.
DataDefModel	Used for referencing objects relating to data connectivity, parameters, and formulas.

Click on the library named CrystalDecisions.ReportAppServer.ClientDoc and click on the Select button. Then click on the OK button to close the dialog box.

Open the web form in design view and double-click the CrystalReportViewer component to the form.

Add code to the Page_Load() event to preview the report.

Listing 20-7. Previewing a RAS report.

```
Private Sub Page_Load(ByVal sender As System.Object,
ByVal e As System.EventArgs) Handles MyBase.Load
    'Put user code to initialize the page here
    Dim myReport As _
    New CrystalDecisions.ReportAppServer.ClientDoc.ReportClientDocument
    'Enter the IP Number of the server
    myReport.ReportAppServer = "127.0.0.1"
    'Use the filename of the report
    myReport.Open("MyReport.rpt")
    'Perform custom report modifications here. The following commented code
    'is just an example of a possible method that would modify the report.
    'Replace it with your own method.
    'ModifyReport(myReport)
    'Preview the report
    CrystalReportViewer1.ReportSource = myReport
End Sub
```

The listing shows that a new variable, myReport, is declared and instantiated from the ReportClientDocument class. Next, set the ReportAppServer property to the IP address of the server. In this example I use "127.0.0.1" so that the LocalHost is used. Load the report into memory by calling the Open() method. For your own application, use the filename of the report that you want to preview. This report file must be stored in the RAS report directory. Finally, assign the report object to the report viewer using the ReportSource property. Run the application and the page will immediately open the report for previewing.

This is all you need to do to preview a report with the RAS. The remaining sections of this chapter show you how to modify specific aspects of a report prior to previewing it.

Modifying Report Parameters and Formulas

Parameters in RAS components use a totally different architecture than parameters in either .NET or the RDC. The RAS uses a ParameterFieldController to manage a report's parameters. The ParameterFieldController is found in the DataDefController namespace. Modifying a parameter requires you getting a copy of the existing parameter object. Make changes to this copy and then tell the controller to use the copy to update the actual parameter in the report.

Before looking at the details of how to modify parameters, you need to understand how to work with the two types of parameters: discrete value and ranged value. Each type requires using a different report object and each works slightly different than the other.

Discrete parameters use the ParameterFieldDiscreteValue class. They are the easiest to change. Simply assign a value to the parameter using the Value property.

Range parameters use the ParameterFieldRangeValue class. You have to set both the beginning and ending values (the boundary) of the range. This is done using two properties: BeginValue and EndValue. Each of these values can either be inclusive or exclusive. Each range boundary is set using the properties LowerBoundType and UpperBoundType. There are three possible settings for determining whether a value is included in the range or not. These settings are listed in Table 20-7.

Table 20-7. Possible values for the bounds type.

Value	Description
crRangeValueBoundTypeNoBound	There are no bounds for this value. For lower bounds, the smallest possible value will be included in the range. For upper bounds, the largest value will be part of the range.
crRangeValueBoundTypeExclusive	The value is not included in the range. The next possible value that is either higher or lower will be used.
crRangeValueBoundTypeInclusive	The value is included in the range.

The only part of the table that might need clarifying is the value crRangeValueBoundTypeNoBound. This setting isn't available in .NET or the RDC. It is used for ignoring either the lower or upper bounds. For example, if used for the lower bound, then there will be no lower bound and the range will only be limited to the upper bound.

Now that you've seen how to work with the different types of parameters, let's build upon this information and look at the steps for modifying parameters during runtime. The RAS object model doesn't let you modify a parameter directly. You have to temporarily build a new parameter field and set its properties. Pass this new parameter to the ParameterFieldController object and it updates the exiting parameter to have the new values. The detailed steps of how to implement this follows.

Declare two parameter field objects. One is for the existing report parameter and the other is for creating the new parameter. Each object variable is of type ParameterField.

Get a reference to the existing parameter from the ParameterFields collection. The ParameterFields collection is found in the report's DataDefinition class. The following line of code passes the value 0 so that the first parameter in the collection is retrieved.

```
OldParameter = myReport.DataDefinition.ParameterFields.Item(0)
```

This line of code requires that you know the field's index number in the collection.[47] If you don't know the index number, you can get it by calling the collection's Find() method. The Find() method is passed a string that is used for identifying the parameter you want. It returns an integer that is the index number of where that parameter is within the ParameterField collection.

The string that is used to find a parameter can actually be different things. A few examples of what the string could represent is the parameter name, its header, or its formula. Since the string could represent a variety of things, you also have to pass an enumerator that states how to use the string. The following line of code finds a parameter field with the name "EmpId". The first parameter is the string name and the second parameter is the enumerator.

```
Dim ParameterIndex as Integer
ParameterIndex = myReport.DataDefinition.ParameterFields.Find("EmpId", _
CrystalDecisions.ReportAppServer.DataDefModel.CrFieldDisplayNameTypeEnum.
crFieldDisplayNameName)
```

---

[47] The ParameterFields collection is zero based.

Due to the dynamic nature of reports as they are developed, it isn't practical to track the index number of each parameter object. To make your application easier to read and maintain, you should always use the Find() method.

After getting a reference to the existing parameter object, copy it to the new parameter object. This is done by instantiating the new parameter field and calling the CopyTo() method of the existing parameter. The CopyTo() method copies all the properties of the existing parameter into the new parameter.

```
OldParameter.CopyTo(NewParameter)
```

Modify the new parameter object so that it stores the new value(s). To do this you have to instantiate a new value object based upon the type of parameter and then assign a value to it. As mentioned earlier, since a parameter can store either discrete values or range values, this code to update the parameter value(s) is different for each type.

Programming the discrete value only requires setting the Value property. The following code creates a discrete value object and assigns it a value from the generic variable myValue.

```
myParameterValue = New CrystalDecisions.ReportAppServer.DataDefModel.ParameterFieldDiscreteValue
myParameterValue.Value = myValue
```

Programming the range value requires setting the BeginValue and EndValue properties. You also have to specify whether the bounds are inclusive or exclusive using the LowerBoundType and UpperBoundType properties. The following code creates a range value object and assigns it the generic variables myBeginValue and myEndValue. Both the lower and upper bounds are set to be inclusive.

```
myParameterValue = New CrystalDecisions.ReportAppServer.DataDefModel.ParameterFieldRangeValue
myParameterValue.BeginValue = myBeginValue
myParameterValue.LowerBoundType = _
CrystalDecisions.ReportAppServer.DataDefModel.CrRangeValueBoundTypeEnum.
crRangeValueBoundTypeInclusive
myParameterValue.EndValue = myEndValue
myParameterValue.UpperBoundType = _
CrystalDecisions.ReportAppServer.DataDefModel.CrRangeValueBoundTypeEnum.
crRangeValueBoundTypeInclusive
```

After creating either the discrete value or range value, you have to assign it to the values collection of the new parameter object.

```
NewParameter.CurrentValues.Add(myParameterValue)
```

At this point, the new parameter has been created and assigned the new values. Now you have to copy this parameter back into existing parameter and overwrite the existing parameters's values. The report object has a ParameterFieldController object which manages the parameters. Call the Modify() method and pass it both the existing parameter object and the new parameter object.

```
myReport.DataDefController.ParameterFieldController.Modify(OldParameter, NewParameter)
```

After calling the Modify() method, the parameter will have the current value(s) that the report needs to run. If there are more parameters in the report, then you have to call this code again for each parameter.

The following examples tie all the code samples into a single listing so that it is easier for you to see how all the objects work together.

Listing 20-8 is a generic method for modifying a discrete parameter in a report. Pass it the parameter name, the parameter value, and the report object that you are working with.

If you remember from the description of Listing 20-7 which shows how to load and preview a report, prior to setting the ReportSource property you should call any code that performs runtime modification on the report object. This is where you would call this procedure.

Listing 20-8. Modifying a discrete parameter.

```
Private Sub SetDiscreteParameter(ByVal myParamName As String,
ByVal myValue As Object, ByVal myReport As
CrystalDecisions.ReportAppServer.ClientDoc.ReportClientDocument)
    Dim OldParameter, NewParameter As _
    CrystalDecisions.ReportAppServer.DataDefModel.ParameterField
    Dim myParameterValue As _
    CrystalDecisions.ReportAppServer.DataDefModel.ParameterFieldDiscreteValue
    'Get a reference to the existing parameter
    Dim ParameterIndex As Integer
    ParameterIndex = myReport.DataDefinition.ParameterFields.Find(myParamName, _
    CrystalDecisions.ReportAppServer.DataDefModel.CrFieldDisplayNameTypeEnum.
    crFieldDisplayNameName)
    OldParameter = myReport.DataDefinition.ParameterFields.Item(ParameterIndex)
    'Create the new parameter and base it off the existing parameter
    NewParameter = New
    CrystalDecisions.ReportAppServer.DataDefModel.ParameterField
    OldParameter.CopyTo(NewParameter)
    'Create the value object that will go in the parameter object
    myParameterValue = New
    CrystalDecisions.ReportAppServer.DataDefModel.ParameterFieldDiscreteValue
    myParameterValue.Value = myValue
    'Save the value with the parameter
    NewParameter.CurrentValues.Add(myParameterValue)
```

```
myReport.DataDefController.ParameterFieldController.Modify( _
    OldParameter, NewParameter)
End Sub
```

Listing 20-9 shows a generic method for modifying a range parameter in a report. Pass it the parameter name, the beginning and ending values and the report object that you are working with. To make this example easier, it is assumed that each value uses inclusive bounds. It would be easy for you to modify it so that this is also passed as a parameter.

Listing 20-9. Modifying a range parameter.

```
Private Sub SetRangeParameter(ByVal ParamName As String,
ByVal myBeginValue As Object, ByVal myEndValue As Object, ByVal myReport As
CrystalDecisions.ReportAppServer.ClientDoc.ReportClientDocument)
    Dim OldParameter, NewParameter As _
    CrystalDecisions.ReportAppServer.DataDefModel.ParameterField
    Dim myParameterValue As _
    CrystalDecisions.ReportAppServer.DataDefModel.ParameterFieldRangeValue
    'Get a reference to the existing parameter
    Dim ParameterIndex As Integer
    ParameterIndex = myReport.DataDefinition.ParameterFields.Find(ParamName, _
    CrystalDecisions.ReportAppServer.DataDefModel.CrFieldDisplayNameTypeEnum.
    crFieldDisplayNameName)
    OldParameter = myReport.DataDefinition.ParameterFields.Item(ParameterIndex)
    'Create the new parameter and base it off the existing parameter
    NewParameter = New _
    CrystalDecisions.ReportAppServer.DataDefModel.ParameterField
    OldParameter.CopyTo(NewParameter)
    'Create the value object that will go in the parameter object
    myParameterValue = New _
    CrystalDecisions.ReportAppServer.DataDefModel.ParameterFieldRangeValue
    myParameterValue.BeginValue = myBeginValue
    myParameterValue.LowerBoundType = _
    CrystalDecisions.ReportAppServer.DataDefModel.CrRangeValueBoundTypeEnum.
    crRangeValueBoundTypeInclusive
    myParameterValue.EndValue = myEndValue
    myParameterValue.UpperBoundType = _
    CrystalDecisions.ReportAppServer.DataDefModel.CrRangeValueBoundTypeEnum.
    crRangeValueBoundTypeInclusive
    'Save the value with the parameter
    NewParameter.CurrentValues.Add(myParameterValue)
    myReport.DataDefController.ParameterFieldController.Modify(OldParameter, _
    NewParameter)
End Sub
```

Logging on to a Data Source

Setting the user credentials in a report is very simple with the RAS components. The DatabaseController object has a Logon() method which sets the user credentials for each table in the report.

```
myReport.DatabaseController.Logon("Admin","PW")
```

Changing Data Sources During Runtime

RAS components give you complete functionality for modifying a report's data source during runtime. You can switch between different ODBC and OLE DB data sources with ease.

As you might expect from reading the previous section, the data connectivity object model for RAS components is completely different from both the.NET and the RDC. RAS manages database connections using a collection of properties called the PropertyBag. Changing the data source is a simple matter of changing the appropriate properties in the PropertyBag. Each table in a report has its own PropertyBag collection. You have to loop through all the tables and set the properties for each table.

The names of the items in the PropertyBag haven't documented very well because they are different for each type of connection you create. For example, the property names for a SQL Server connection are not the same as the property names for a MS Access connection. To determine the name of each property, you have to create a test report, stop your code in debug mode and examine and document all the available properties. If you want to document every possible property, this can be quite tedious. Luckily, to change a data source during runtime only requires changing a couple of properties. Table 20-9 shows you the names of each property and its purpose. Keep in mind that you won't use each property for every type of report. Only use the ones appropriate to the type of database connection your report uses.

Table 20-8. PropertyBag item names for changing data sources.

Name	Connection Type	Description
Data Source	OLE DB – SQL Server	Server name
Initial Catalog	OLE DB – SQL Server	Database name
Database Name	OLE DB – MS Access	File location of the MDB
DSN	ODBC	The DSN name

Listing 20-10 is the code for changing the data source of each table in a report. Call this procedure from the code in Listing 20-7. If you remember from the description of Listing 20-7, prior to setting the ReportSource property, you should call any code that performs runtime modification.

Listing 20-10. Changing a report's data source

```
Private Sub ChangeReportTable(ByVal myReport As
CrystalDecisions.ReportAppServer.ClientDoc.ReportClientDocument)
    Dim DBConnection As _
    CrystalDecisions.ReportAppServer.DataDefModel.ConnectionInfo
    Dim Attributes As CrystalDecisions.ReportAppServer.DataDefModel.PropertyBag
    Dim LogonInfo As CrystalDecisions.ReportAppServer.DataDefModel.PropertyBag
    Dim OldTable, NewTable As _
    CrystalDecisions.ReportAppServer.DataDefModel.Table
    Dim TableCount As Integer
    'Login to the database
    myReport.DatabaseController.Logon("Admin","PW")
    'Modify the connection properties for each table
    For TableCount = 0 To _
    myReport.DatabaseController.GetConnectionInfos(Nothing).Count - 1
        DBConnection = _
        myReport.DatabaseController.GetConnectionInfos(Nothing).
        Item(TableCount).Clone(True)
        Attributes = DBConnection.Attributes
        LogonInfo = Attributes("QE_LogonProperties")
        'The next two lines are only used for OLEDB Sql Server
        LogonInfo("Data Source") = "myServer"
        LogonInfo("Initial Catalog") = "myDatabase"
        'Uncomment the next line for OLE DB MS Access connections
        'LogonInfo("Database Name") = Server.MapPath(myMdbFilePath)
        'Uncomment the next line for ODBC DSN connections
        'LogonInfo("Dsn") = "myDSN"
        OldTable = myReport.Database.Tables(TableCount)
        NewTable = New CrystalDecisions.ReportAppServer.DataDefModel.TableClass
        NewTable.Name = OldTable.Name
        NewTable.ConnectionInfo = DBConnection
        myReport.DatabaseController.SetTableLocation(OldTable, NewTable)
    Next
End Sub
```

The source code for changing a data source during runtime is simple to implement. First, login to the database to establish a connection. Then loop through each table in the report and get a reference to the current table's ConnectionInfo object. This object contains the PropertyBag collection called Attributes. Within the Attributes collection is another PropertyBag collection called "QE_LogonProperties". Essentially, this is a collection within a collection. The "QE_LogonProperties" collection is the one that has the properties you need to modify for changing the data source.

After setting the properties for the new data source, you have to create two table objects. The first table object references the existing table in the report. It has all the existing properties necessary to connect to the data source. The second table object is for the new data connection. You have to set the new properties of this table so that it points to the new data connection. This consists of setting the properties in the "QE_LogonProperties" (see Table 20-8) and setting the Name property. The Name property is just the table name. The code also shows the names if you were connecting to MS Access or ODBC. Remove the comments for the type of connection you are using.

After instantiating the two table objects and setting the properties of the new table object, overwrite the old table properties with the properties of the new table by calling the SetTableLocation() method of the DatabaseController object. After the SetTableLocation() method has been called, repeat the steps for each table.

Caution

Version 10 of Crystal Reports has a documented bug where some properties of the ReportDocument class were changed to be read only (e.g. ConditionField). If you are upgrading and application to version 10, this can introduce errors. The trick for getting around this is to assign the read-only property equal to a formula. Change your programming code so that rather than trying to modify the property directly, it modifies the formula instead. See page 318 for how to modify formulas.

C# Code Listings

The C# code listings are equivalent to the VB.NET code listings.

Listing 20-1. Previewing a report with the RDC viewer control.

```
private void Form1_Load(object sender, System.EventArgs e)
{
    CRAXDRT.Application CrApplication = new CRAXDRT.ApplicationClass();
    CRAXDRT.Report myReport;
    myReport = CrApplication.OpenReport(@"../../CrystalReport1.rpt",
    CRAXDRT.CROpenReportMethod.crOpenReportByDefault);
    axCRViewer91.ReportSource = myReport;
}
```

Listing 20-2. Printing a report.

```
private void Form1_Load(object sender, System.EventArgs e)
{
    CRAXDRT.Application CrApplication = new CRAXDRT.ApplicationClass();
    CRAXDRT.Report myReport;
    myReport = CrApplication.OpenReport(@"../../CrystalReport1.rpt",
    CRAXDRT.CROpenReportMethod.crOpenReportByDefault);
    MyReport.PrintOut(true,1,false,1,99);
}
```

Listing 20-3. Printing dynamic images.

```
public class Form1 : System.Windows.Forms.Form
{
    private CRAXDRT.Section MySection;
    private CRAXDRT.Report MyReport;
    private AxCRVIEWER9Lib.AxCRViewer9 axCRViewer91;
    private int Counter = 1;
    #region Windows Form Designer generated code
    private void Form1_Load(object sender, System.EventArgs e)
    {
        CRAXDRT.Application CrApplication = new CRAXDRT.ApplicationClass();
        myReport = CrApplication.OpenReport(@"../../CrystalReport1.rpt",
        CRAXDRT.CROpenReportMethod.crOpenReportByDefault);
        MySection = MyReport.Sections["Section3"];
        MySection.format += new
        CRAXDRT.ISectionEvent_formatEventHandler(this.SectionFormat);
        axCRViewer91.ReportSource = MyReport;
    }
    private void SectionFormat(object sender)
    {
        CRAXDRT.OleObject MyPic;
        MyPic = (CRAXDRT.OleObject)MySection.ReportObjects["Picture1"];
        MyPic.SetOleLocation(Application.StartupPath + "Image" +
```

```
      Counter.ToString() + ".bmp");
      if (Counter++ == 4)
      {
        Counter = 1;
      }
    }
  }
}
```

Listing 20-4. Open a report using a MS Access database.

```
CRAXDRT.Application CrApplication = new CRAXDRT.ApplicationClass();
myReport = CrApplication.OpenReport(@"../../CrystalReport1.rpt",
CRAXDRT.CROpenReportMethod.crOpenReportByDefault);
CRAXDRT.ConnectionProperties ConnectionInfo;
ConnectionInfo = MyReport.Database.Tables[1].ConnectionProperties;
ConnectionInfo.Delete("Provider");
ConnectionInfo.Add("Provider", "Microsoft.Jet.OLEDB.4.0");
ConnectionInfo.Delete("Data Source");
ConnectionInfo.Add("Data Source", "C:\\xtreme.mdb");
ConnectionInfo.Delete("User Id");
ConnectionInfo.Add("User Id", "Admin");
axCRViewer91.ReportSource = MyReport;
```

Listing 20-5. Adding name-value properties to the collection.

```
CRAXDRT.Application CrApplication = new CRAXDRT.ApplicationClass();
myReport = CrApplication.OpenReport(@"../../CrystalReport1.rpt",
CRAXDRT.CROpenReportMethod.crOpenReportByDefault);
CRAXDRT.ConnectionProperties ConnectionInfo;
ConnectionInfo = MyReport.Database.Tables[1].ConnectionProperties;
string ConnectionNames = string.Join(",", (string[])ConnectionInfo.NameIDs);
ConnectionInfo = MyReport.Database.Tables[1].ConnectionProperties;
AddConnectionProperty(ConnectionInfo, "Password", "pw", ConnectionNames);
axCRViewer91.ReportSource = MyReport;
…
private void AddConnectionProperty(CRAXDRT.ConnectionProperties ConnectionInfo, string Name, string
Value, string ConnectionNames)
{
  if (ConnectionNames.IndexOf(Name) >= 0)
  {
    ConnectionInfo.Delete(Name);
  }
  ConnectionInfo.Add(Name, Value);
}
```

Listing 20-6. Opening a report using ADO.NET.

```
OleDbConnection MyConnection;
OleDbDataAdapter MyDataAdapter;
DataSet MyDataSet = new DataSet();
CRAXDRT.Application CrApplication = new CRAXDRT.ApplicationClass();
```

```
//myReport = CrApplication.OpenReport(@"../../CrystalReport1.rpt",
CRAXDRT.CROpenReportMethod.crOpenReportByDefault);
MyReport = CrApplication.OpenReport(@"../../Push - ADONET.rpt",
CRAXDRT.CROpenReportMethod.crOpenReportByDefault);
//Fill the dataset object with two tables
MyConnection = new OleDbConnection(Globals.ConnectionString);
MyDataAdapter = new OleDbDataAdapter("SELECT * FROM Customers", MyConnection);
MyDataAdapter.Fill(MyDataSet, "Customers");
MyDataAdapter = new OleDbDataAdapter("SELECT * FROM Orders", MyConnection);
MyDataAdapter.Fill(MyDataSet, "Orders");
//Assign the tables to the report
MyReport.Database.SetDataSource(MyDataSet.Tables["Customers"], 3, 1);
MyReport.Database.SetDataSource(MyDataSet.Tables["Orders"], 3, 2);
//Preview the report
axCRViewer91.ReportSource = MyReport;
```

Listing 20-7. Previewing a RAS report.

```
private void Page_Load(object sender, System.EventArgs e)
{
    // Put user code to initialize the page here
    CrystalDecisions.ReportAppServer.ClientDoc.ReportClientDocument MyReport =
    new CrystalDecisions.ReportAppServer.ClientDoc.ReportClientDocumentClass();
    //Enter the IP Number of the server
    MyReport.ReportAppServer = "127.0.0.1";
    //Create an object to hold the report filename
    object ReportPath = "MyReport.rpt";
    MyReport.Open(ref ReportPath,0);
    //Preview the report
    CrystalReportViewer1.ReportSource = MyReport;
}
```

Listing 20-8. Modifying a discrete parameter.

```
public void SetDiscreteParameter(string ParamName, object MyValue,
CrystalDecisions.ReportAppServer.ClientDoc.ReportClientDocument MyReport)
{
    CrystalDecisions.ReportAppServer.DataDefModel.ParameterField
    OldParameter, NewParameter;
    CrystalDecisions.ReportAppServer.DataDefModel.ParameterFieldDiscreteValue
    MyParameterValue;
    //Get a reference to the existing parameter
    int ParameterIndex;
    ParameterIndex = MyReport.DataDefinition.ParameterFields.Find(ParamName,
    CrystalDecisions.ReportAppServer.DataDefModel.CrFieldDisplayNameTypeEnum.
    crFieldDisplayNameName,CrystalDecisions.ReportAppServer.DataDefModel.
    CeLocale.ceLocaleUserDefault);
    OldParameter=CrystalDecisions.ReportAppServer.DataDefModel.ParameterField)
    MyReport.DataDefinition.ParameterFields[ParameterIndex];
    //Create the new parameter and base if off the existing parameter
```

```
    NewParameter = new
    CrystalDecisions.ReportAppServer.DataDefModel.ParameterFieldClass();
    OldParameter.CopyTo(NewParameter, true);
    //Create the value object that will go in the parameter object
    MyParameterValue = new CrystalDecisions.ReportAppServer.DataDefModel.
    ParameterFieldDiscreteValueClass();
    MyParameterValue.Value = MyValue;
    //Save the parameter
    NewParameter.CurrentValues.Add(MyParameterValue);
    MyReport.DataDefController.ParameterFieldController.Modify(
    OldParameter, NewParameter);
}
```

Listing 20-9. Modifying a range parameter.

```
public void SetRangeParameter(string ParamName, object MyBeginValue, object MyEndValue,
CrystalDecisions.ReportAppServer.ClientDoc.ReportClientDocument MyReport)
{
    CrystalDecisions.ReportAppServer.DataDefModel.ParameterField
    OldParameter, NewParameter;
    CrystalDecisions.ReportAppServer.DataDefModel.ParameterFieldRangeValue
    MyParameterValue;
    //Get a reference to the existing parameter
    int ParameterIndex;
    ParameterIndex = MyReport.DataDefinition.ParameterFields.Find(ParamName,
    CrystalDecisions.ReportAppServer.DataDefModel.CrFieldDisplayNameTypeEnum.
    crFieldDisplayNameName,CrystalDecisions.ReportAppServer.DataDefModel.
    CeLocale.ceLocaleUserDefault);
    OldParameter=(CrystalDecisions.ReportAppServer.DataDefModel.ParameterField)
    MyReport.DataDefinition.ParameterFields[ParameterIndex];
    //Create the new parameter and base if off the existing parameter
    NewParameter = new
    CrystalDecisions.ReportAppServer.DataDefModel.ParameterFieldClass();
    OldParameter.CopyTo(NewParameter, true);
    //Create the value object that will go in the parameter object
    MyParameterValue = new CrystalDecisions.ReportAppServer.DataDefModel.
    ParameterFieldRangeValueClass();
    MyParameterValue.BeginValue = MyBeginValue;
    MyParameterValue.EndValue = MyEndValue;
    MyParameterValue.LowerBoundType =
    CrystalDecisions.ReportAppServer.DataDefModel.CrRangeValueBoundTypeEnum.
    crRangeValueBoundTypeInclusive;
    MyParameterValue.UpperBoundType =
    CrystalDecisions.ReportAppServer.DataDefModel.CrRangeValueBoundTypeEnum.
    crRangeValueBoundTypeInclusive;
    //Save the parameter
    NewParameter.CurrentValues.Add(MyParameterValue);
    MyReport.DataDefController.ParameterFieldController.Modify(
    OldParameter, NewParameter);
```

}

Listing 20-10. Changing a report's data source

```
public void ChangeReportTable(CrystalDecisions.ReportAppServer.ClientDoc.
ReportClientDocument MyReport)
{
    CrystalDecisions.ReportAppServer.DataDefModel.ConnectionInfo DBConnection;
    CrystalDecisions.ReportAppServer.DataDefModel.PropertyBag LogonInfo,
    Attributes;
    CrystalDecisions.ReportAppServer.DataDefModel.Table OldTable, NewTable;
    int TableCount;
    //Login to the database
    MyReport.DatabaseController.logon("sa","pw");
    //Set the connection properties for each table
    for (TableCount=0; TableCount<MyReport.DatabaseController.
    GetConnectionInfos(null).Count; TableCount++)
    {
        DBConnection = MyReport.DatabaseController.GetConnectionInfos(null)
        [TableCount].Clone(true);
        Attributes = DBConnection.Attributes;
        LogonInfo = (CrystalDecisions.ReportAppServer.DataDefModel.PropertyBag)
        Attributes["QE_LogonProperties"];
        //The next two lines are only used for OLE DB Sql Server
        LogonInfo["Data Source"] = "(local)";
        LogonInfo["Initial Catalog"] = "Northwind";
        //Uncomment the next line if you are using MS Access
        //LogonInfo("Database Name") = Server.MapPath("mdb filename");
        //Uncomment the next line for ODBC DSN connections
        //LogonInfo("DSN") = "dsn name";
        OldTable = (CrystalDecisions.ReportAppServer.DataDefModel.Table)
        MyReport.Database.Tables[TableCount];
        NewTable = new
        CrystalDecisions.ReportAppServer.DataDefModel.TableClass();
        NewTable.Name = OldTable.Name;
        NewTable.ConnectionInfo = DBConnection;
        MyReport.DatabaseController.SetTableLocation(OldTable, NewTable);
    }
}
```

Comprehensive Examples

During all the previous chapters, you've seen small examples of how to do everything, but there was never one big example to pull everything together. Since writing a report is a combination of so many different tasks, you can't get an idea of how they all fit into the big picture by only showing small examples of how to do a single task. You need a larger scale example to see how everything ties together.

This chapter walks you through the steps of designing and creating a report from scratch. It starts with a sample report spec that outlines the task at hand. As a software developer there are times you have to be creative and flexible. So the example gets changes made to it and you will also see how to modify it during runtime to make it fit different circumstances.

After we finish writing the report and getting it ready for production, we will create a form that serves as a customized report viewer. It shows you how to turn the different properties of the CrystalReportViewer control on and off as well as how to manually implement those properties. This gives you the ability to customize the look and feel of the viewer control so that it blends in better with your application.

> **Note**
>
> Since this chapter just summarizes what has already been taught, the C# code will not be shown for the code listings. Refer back to the applicable chapter for the C# code.

Creating the Sales History Report

Figure 21-1 shows the specs of the report project. This is a sales history report for a client. Of course, you were only given a mock-up of the report and it's your job to clean it up and make it look professional.

Customer Name ORDER HISTORY BY MONTH date
Customer Address

Order Date	Order	Product ID	Product Name	Price	Qty	Cost
Month – Year						
mm/dd/yy	xx	xx	xxxx	xx	xx	xx

			Total cost for Month – Year			xxx

Figure 21-1. The reports specs.

The page header shows the client's name, their address and the report title, "Order History by Month". There is also a note that says this will be distributed to the client. So I assume that the pages are going to be separated and mailed to the client. This will probably only be printed on a monthly basis or perhaps every six months. The report is first grouped by client and the details are grouped by month. The detail section lists the order date, order ID, product information and total cost. The group footer gives a sub-total of the costs and the page footer gives a grand-total.

There are a few things we should make note of. Since the pages are going to be distributed to clients, then there needs to be a page break after each group footer. That forces the client information to always start at the top of the page. We should also reset the page number before each group header so that the first page of a client's report is always numbered as page 1.

Creating the First Draft

Start the project by opening a new VB .NET project called Order History.

Create a new Crystal Report object called "rptOrderHistory".

When the Report Expert opens, choose the Standard option.

On the Data tab select the OLE DB category and choose the Jet 4.0 OLE DB provider.

Click the Next button and browse to where the Xtreme.mdb file is located. By default it is under the Microsoft .NET folder at Crystal Reports/Samples/Database.

Once the database is opened, select the tables Customers, Orders, Order Detail, and Product.

Click on the Links tab and you'll see that the tables are already linked properly.

Click on the Fields tab. Add the fields that will appear in the Detail Section These are Order Date, Order ID, Product Name, Product ID, Unit Price and Quantity.

The last field in the Detail section is the Total Cost. This doesn't exist in any of the tables, so it needs to have a formula created for it. Create a new formula called TotalCost and enter the following code for it.

```
Formula = {Orders.Order.Quantity} * {Orders.Unit Price}
```

At this point all the basic fields that need to be on the report are listed and we are almost ready to move to the Group tab.

Notice that only the fields showing up in the Detail section were selected with the Report Wizard. This is because the Standard report layout only puts fields in the Details section. It doesn't give you a way to specify which ones should go in the other sections. You have to wait until after the Report Expert generates the first draft of the report and then add these fields in manually.

Before exiting this tab and moving to the Group tab, we need to add a formula that is used as the second grouping field. The second group is being grouped by month, so we want to add the Order Date field. However, this would group the items by every day of the month and we only want the month to be grouped. We need to add a formula that extracts the month from the Order Date field.

Click on the formula button and name the new formula GroupMonth. It formats the date so that the year is listed first and then the month. Including the year in the formula insures that it is sorted properly.

```
Formula = CStr({Orders.Order Date},"yyyy/MM")
```

Go to the Group tab. There are two groups: one for the Customer ID field and one for the @GroupMonth formula. Add each of these fields to the Group By window with the Customer ID field being listed first.

Go to the Total tab. By default, many fields are already listed in the Summarized Fields window. The only one we need is the @TotalCost formula. Remove all fields from this list except @TotalCost.

Nothing in the specs suggests that we have to enter anything for the tabs called Top N, Chart, and Select, so skip these tabs and go directly to the Style tab. On the Style tab enter the report title "Orders History by Month" and select the Standard style.

That finishes creating a rough draft of the report. It should look like Figure 21-2. Let's preview a copy to see how close the Report Expert came to generating the proper results.

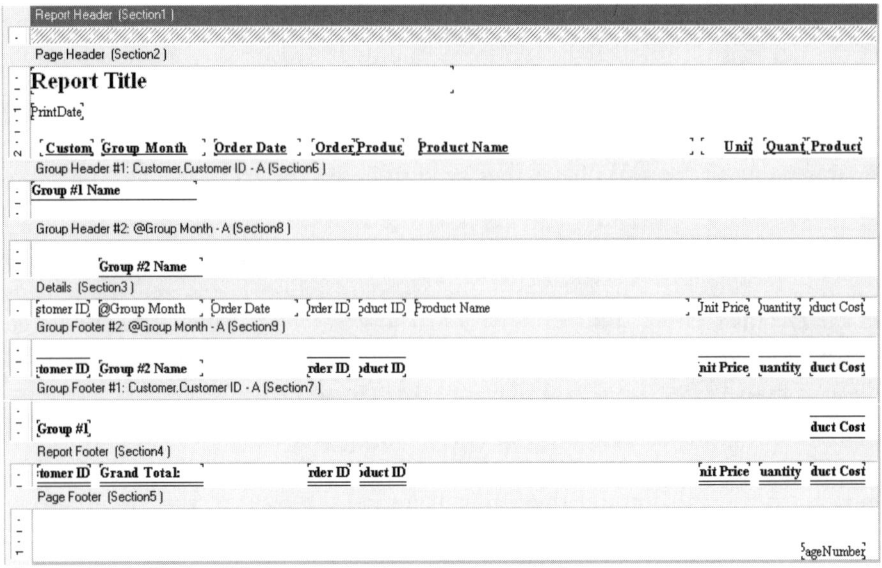

Figure 21-2. Order History report in design mode.

Creating the Preview Form

Before previewing the report, you have to add a form that has the CrystalReportViewer control on it. Right-click on the project name in the Solution Explorer and select Add New Item.

Add a new Windows Form and call it frmPreviewReport. Then click the Open button to create it.

Set the form's WindowState property to Maximized so that it is large enough to display the entire report.

Go to the Toolbox and drag a CrystalReportViewer control onto the form.

Set the control's Dock property to Fill by opening the drop-down box and clicking the box that is displayed in the middle.

The form is designed so that you can pass it any report and it will display it. To make this possible, we need to create a method that can be called from another form and pass a report object to it as a parameter. The viewer takes this report object and displays it.

Open the code editor and find the form's instantiation method. Modify it so that it has a ReportDocument parameter passed to it and it assigns this to the viewer object.

Listing 21-1. Modifying the initialization method.

```
Public Sub New(ByVal myReport As CrystalDecisions.CrystalReports.Engine.ReportDocument)
```

```
MyBase.New()
'This call is required by the Windows Form Designer.
InitializeComponent()
'Add any initialization after the InitializeComponent() call
    crystalReportViewer1.ReportSource = myReport
End Sub
```

Next we have to add a form to the project that creates the report object and prints it. Since Visual Studio automatically creates a default form called Form1 when we created the project, use that. This serves as the form where we later add options and user input for customizing the report.

Right-click on the report's name in the Solution Explorer and rename it to frmOrderHistory.

Drag a button from the toolbox to the form and change its name to btnReport.

The button needs code added to it so that it can preview the report. Double-click on the button to open the editor and enter the following code.

Listing 21-2. Previewing the rough draft.

```
Private Sub btnReport_Click(ByVal sender As Object, ByVal e As System.EventArgs)
    Handles btnPreview.Click
    Dim myReport As New rptOrderHistory
    Dim OrdersPreview As New frmPreview(myReport)
    OrdersPreview.ShowDialog()
End Sub
```

The code creates a new report object called myReport based on the rptOrderHistory report class. Then it creates a new instance of the frmPreview form and passes it the report object. The preview form is displayed by calling the ShowDialog() method.

Run the application and you should see a report that looks like Figure 21-3.

Order History by Month
10/16/20

Custom	Group Month	Order Date	Order	Produc	Product Name	Unit	Quant	Product
1								
	1996/02							
1	1996/02	2/27/1996 12:	1,366	301,201	SlickRock	$764.85	1	$764.85
1.00	**1996/02**		**366.00**	**,201.00**		**$764.85**	**1.00**	**$764.85**
	1996/12							
1	1996/12	12/24/1996 12	1,092	1,111	Active Outdoors Lycra Glove	$16.50	2	$33.00
1	1996/12	12/8/1996 12:	1,033	102,181	Mozzie	,739.85	2	3,479.70
1	1996/12	12/11/1996 12	1,041	301,201	SlickRock	$764.85	1	$764.85
1	1996/12	12/8/1996 12:	1,033	1,105	Active Outdoors Crochet Glove	$13.05	2	$26.10
1	1996/12	12/2/1996 12:	1	2,201	Triumph Pro Helmet	$41.90	1	$41.90
1	1996/12	12/8/1996 12:	1,033	1,101	Active Outdoors Crochet Glove	$14.50	1	$14.50
1	1996/12	12/24/1996 12	1,092	3,301	Guardian Chain Lock	$4.50	2	$9.00
7.00	**1996/12**		**325.00**	**,201.00**		**,595.15**	**11.00**	**4,369.05**
	1997/01							
1	1997/01	1/30/1997 12:	1,246	103,151	Endorphin	$899.85	1	$899.85
1	1997/01	1/6/1997 12:0	1,143	1,107	Active Outdoors Lycra Glove	$16.50	3	$49.50
1	1997/01	1/30/1997 12:	1,246	101,152	Descent	,939.85	1	2,939.85

Figure 21-3. Preview of the original report generated by the Report Expert.

Fixing the First Draft

You can see that the Report Expert did a decent attempt at building the first draft of the report. Of course, there are a few additional things we need to do to get into its final form. The first thing is that the top of the page doesn't have any client information. It should have the client's name and address. The report title and date also need to be moved to the right so that there is room to put the client data.

Moving the report title and date is just a matter of dragging them to the proper place. But there is one larger problem with where they are located. As you saw in Figure 21-2, they are positioned in the Page Header section. It will get printed at the top of every page. According to the specs, this should only be printed on the first page of each report

Fixing this involves two steps. The first step is to use conditional formatting so that the page header only prints on the first page. Right-click on the page header and select Format Section. For the Suppress property, click on the formula button, enter the following formula (make sure Basic syntax is selected), and then click the Save and Close button.

```
Formula = PageNumber > 1
```

If the current page number is greater than one, the group is suppressed.

The second step is to reset that page number back to 1 for each new client. Since the page number is reset for each group, go to the Group Footer section and set the ResetPageNumberAfter property to True.

Now that the page header is only printing for the first page, a new situation arises. Unlike the report title, the captions for the detail fields need to be printed at the top of every page. However, since they are also in the Page Header section they will only get printed for the first page. The captions need to be modified so that on the first page they print under the report title, but on the remaining pages they print by themselves at the top of the page. This is fixed by inserting a new Page Header section below the current one. The second Page Header section has formatting that is independent of the first Page Header and it will print on every page.

Right-click on the Page Header bar and select Insert Section Below. Drag the captions down to this second section. Since this section will print on every page, no conditional formatting formulas need to be added. Just leave it the way it is and it will always be printed.

Now that the page header has been cleaned up, we can add the customer name and address information. Drag the Group #1 Name field from the group header section into the page header and position it in the top left-hand corner.

The group name is printing the Customer ID and we want it to print the Customer Name instead. Right-click on the group header section and select Change Group. Click on Options to open the Change Group Options dialog box.

At the bottom of the dialog box, click the Customize Group Name Field option and the Choose From Existing Field option.

Select the Customer Name field from the drop down box. Instead of printing the Customer ID, it will print the Customer Name.

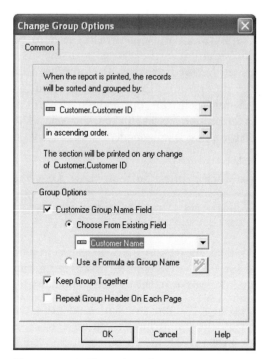

Figure 21-4. Changing the customer group name field.

Rather than go through all the trouble of changing the group's printable name, a possible option is to just put the Customer Name field in the Group Header section and delete the ID field. However, that will cause another problem. The Group Tree that is displayed within the viewer also shows the Group Name field. This idea will still show the Customer ID in the Group Tree and not the Customer Name.

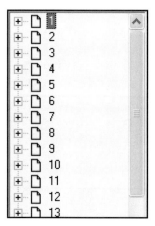

Figure 21-5. The Group Tree using Customer ID.

Unless you've memorized all the company ID's, this group tree doesn't make a lot of sense. Figure 21-6 shows the group tree using Customer Name.

Figure 21-6. The Group Tree using Customer Name.

This is much easier for a user to understand. Now let's add the customer information to the page header. The customer information lists the Customer Name, Address 1, Address 2, City, State, Zip Code and Country data. These are easy enough to display, but we want to make sure they look professional. To do that we use formulas.

One formula needs to display the city-state fields. Each field is displayed adjacent to each other and there has to be a comma between the city and state. The city-state formula concatenates all the fields together using the & operator. Create a new formula called CityStateZip and assign it the following code.

```
Formula = {Customer.City} & ", " & {Customer.Region} & " " & {Customer.Postal Code}
```

A common problem with printing addresses is that the second address line isn't always used. This leaves a blank line between the first address and the city-state information. To prevent this, use a formula that tests when the second address line is present and either display it or display the city-state information instead. If there is no second address line, then only the CityStateZip formula is displayed.

The first formula uses the IIF() function to display either the second address or the CityStateZip formula. Create a new formula called AddressLine2 and assign it this code.

```
Formula = IIF({Customer.Address2}<>"", {Customer.Address2}, {@CityStateZip})
```

The second formula only displays the CityStateZip formula if the second address line was printed. If there isn't a second address line then nothing is printed because we don't want the CityStateZip formula to be duplicated. Create a new formula called AddressLine3 and assign it this code.

Formula = IIF({Customer.Address2}="", "", {@CityStateZip})

This finishes all the formulas we need. Add all the customer fields to the Page Header section. It should look like Figure 21-7.

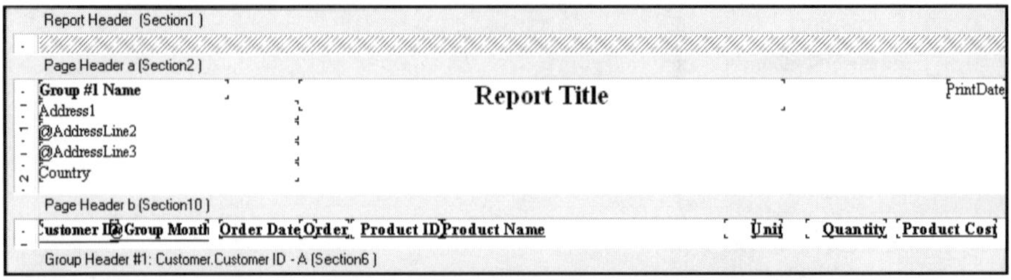

Figure 21-7. The Page Header with the customer information.

The report is pretty close to being finished, but there are still a few miscellaneous tasks to do.

The first problem is that the Report Expert gave us more information than we need. Since we are grouping on the Customer ID and the @GroupMonth formula, it added these two fields to the details. We already have that information being printed in the appropriate header sections so we don't need it here.

Delete the Customer ID and @GroupMonth formula from the Detail Section. Also delete their respective text field headers.

Shift all remaining fields and their headers over to the left and space them out appropriately.

The field captions need to have a top and bottom border added. Open the toolbox and click on the Line Object. This turns the cursor into a pencil icon. Click on the report to start drawing a line and hold down the mouse button until the line is finished. Do this for both the top line and bottom line.

The Report Expert turned on the underline option for each of the field captions. Since we added a border around these fields, they don't need to be underlined. Select all the fields and click the underline button in the toolbar to turn it off.

Move the @GroupMonth field in the group header to the far left and take off the bottom border.

Since the group name for the Customer ID group has been moved to the Page Header section, there is nothing to print in that group header section. Right-click on it and select Fit Section. This resizes it so that no space is wasted.

The last step is to add captions to the group footers so that they display the sub-totals properly. In Group Footer #2, add a text field from the Toolbox and enter the text "Total cost for". Then open the Field Explorer and drag the

Group Footer #2 field onto that text field. When the cursor is positioned on the text field, it turns the field into a cursor and you can move the cursor to the end of the line before releasing the mouse button. This appends the field at the end of the text.

Make the text bold and right-aligned.

In Group Footer #1, make the group name bold and a font size of 12.

Make it wider so that there is room to display the entire field.

Make the sub-total field a font size of 12.

Add a text field to Group Footer #1 and enter the text "We appreciate your business."

Center the text.

The report designer should now look like Figure 21-8.

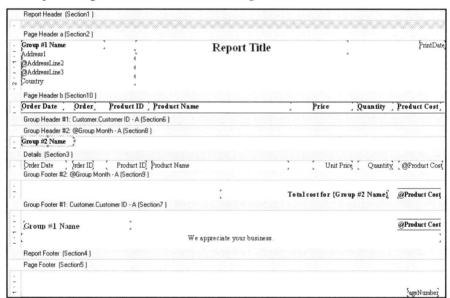

Figure 21-8. The report designer.

When you run the report it should look similar to Figure 21-9.

City Cyclist 7464 South Kingsway Suite 2006 Sterling Heights, MI 48358 USA		Order History by Month				10/17/2002

Order Date	Order	Product ID	Product Name	Price	Quantity	Product Cost
1996/02						
2/27/1996 12:1	1,366	301,201	SlickRock	$764.85	1	$764.85
				Total cost for 1996/02		**$764.85**
1996/12						
12/24/1996 12	1,092	1,111	Active Outdoors Lycra Glove	$16.50	2	$33.00
12/24/1996 12	1,092	3,301	Guardian Chain Lock	$4.50	2	$9.00
12/8/1996 12:1	1,033	102,181	Mozzie	$1,739.85	2	$3,479.70
12/11/1996 12	1,041	301,201	SlickRock	$764.85	1	$764.85
12/8/1996 12:1	1,033	1,105	Active Outdoors Crochet Glove	$13.05	2	$26.10
12/2/1996 12:1	1	2,201	Triumph Pro Helmet	$41.90	1	$41.90
12/8/1996 12:1	1,033	1,101	Active Outdoors Crochet Glove	$14.50	1	$14.50
				Total cost for 1996/12		**$4,369.05**

Figure 21-9. The preview of the report.

Finalizing the Report

So far the report is looking pretty good. But there are a few more things that need to be corrected. First off, the detail records aren't being sorted by date, and the date shows the time and it's being cut-off. We need to get rid of the time so that it doesn't get displayed with the date. The Order ID and Product ID should not have any formatting, but they are using commas. The group name for the month should have the full name spelled out and then list the year. And the last thing that needs to be corrected is that the formatting of the dollar amounts should check which country the customer is from and switch the commas and periods when they are from North America.

Formatting the price and cost according to whether the customer is in North America requires creating a formula that returns True when this is the case. Testing the Country field to see if it is either "USA" or "Canada" does this. Create a new formula called InNorthAmerica and enter the following code.

```
Formula = {Customer.Country} in Array("USA", "Canada")
```

The price and cost fields need to be modified so that they look at what the InNorthAmerica formula returns and adjust the formatting accordingly. If InNorthAmerica returns True, then the decimal place is represented by a period and the thousands separator is represented by a comma. If InNorthAmerica returns False, then the formatting is reversed.

Right-click on the price field and select Format.

Go to the Number tab and click the Customize button. This opens the Format Editor.

Click on the Formula button for the Decimal Separator and enter the following formula.

```
formula = IIF({@InNorthAmerica}, ".", ",")
```

Do the same for the Thousands Separator and enter the following formula.

```
formula = IIF({@InNorthAmerica}, ",", ".")
```

Repeat this for the cost field and its sub-totals.

Fixing how the group name for the month is displayed also requires using a formula because there are no existing fields that display the Order Date in the specified format. This time we'll see how to add the formula directly to the group formatting options.

Right-click the group header and select Change Group.

When the Change Group dialog box opens, click on the Group Month selection and choose Options.

At the bottom, click on Group Options and select Use a Formula as Group Name.

Click on the formula button.

The **CStr()** function is perfect for formatting a date field. Enter the following code.

```
formula = CStr({Orders.Order Date}, "MMMM - yyyy")
```

This displays the full month name followed by the year in four-digit format.

Changing the sort order of the detail records requires opening the Record Sort Order dialog box. Right-click on the report and select Report | Sort Records.

The right side of the dialog box already has the two group fields listed. Add the Order Date field to the list by double clicking on it. This adds it to the bottom of the list.

Click on the OK button to save the change.

Formatting the last two fields is very easy. Right-click on each one and select Format. The date field should be formatted with a four-digit year.

The Order ID and Product ID are formatted with no thousand separators. On the Number tab of the Format Editor, select the number that doesn't display a thousand's separator.

Now the report should be finished and look like Figure 21-10.

City Cyclist
7464 South Kingsway
Suite 2006
Sterling Heights, MI 48358
USA

Order History by Month

10/19/2002

Order Date	Order	Product ID	Product Name	Price	Quantity	Product Cost
February - 1996						
02/27/1996	1366	301201	SlickRock	$764.85	1	$764.85
				Total cost for February - 1996		$764.85
December - 1996						
12/02/1996	1	2201	Triumph Pro Helmet	$41.90	1	$41.90
12/08/1996	1033	102181	Mozzie	$1,739.85	2	$3,479.70
12/08/1996	1033	1105	Active Outdoors Crochet Glove	$13.05	2	$26.10
12/08/1996	1033	1101	Active Outdoors Crochet Glove	$14.50	1	$14.50
12/11/1996	1041	301201	SlickRock	$764.85	1	$764.85
12/24/1996	1092	1111	Active Outdoors Lycra Glove	$16.50	2	$33.00
12/24/1996	1092	3301	Guardian Chain Lock	$4.50	2	$9.00
				Total cost for December - 1996		$4,369.05

Figure 21-10. The preview of the report.

Customizing the User Interface

Let's add some functionality that allows the user to customize how the report prints. Let's modify the user interface so that the user can enter all the relevant information on one form and then run the report without getting prompted again.

As of right now, the form only has a single button for previewing the report. We want to add an option that lets the user set a date range for which records will be printed.

Open the form and add one checkbox and two text boxes to it. Put a label next to the checkbox that says "Use Date Range". Put the two textboxes to the right of the label and stack one on top of each other. The top textbox is the beginning date and the bottom checkbox is the ending date.

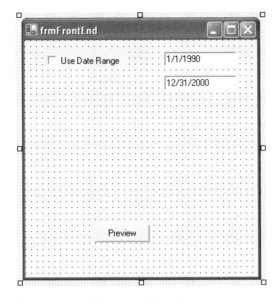

Figure 21-11. The new form layout.

Setting the date range from the Visual Studio application can be done in two ways. The first is to create two formulas in the report and set a record selection formula that includes all records that were printed within those two dates. I don't like this method because if the user wants to print all the records, then you have to fill in two dummy dates that have a large enough range to include every record. This has the potential to cause errors if you aren't careful. The other way is to create the record selection formula within the application and have the dates hard-coded within the string. I prefer this method because if the user doesn't use the date range, then you don't have to build the record selection formula.

When the user clicks on the preview button, the program looks at the date range checkbox to see if it is checked. If so, it builds the record selection formula using the values entered into the two textboxes.

Listing 21-3. Setting the date range for a report.

```
Private Sub SetDateRange(ByVal myReport As _
    CrystalDecisions.CrystalReports.Engine.ReportDocument)
    If chkUseDates.Checked Then
        Dim DateRange As String
        DateRange = "{Orders.Order Date} IN #" & txtStartDate.Text & "# TO #" & _
            txtEndDate.Text & "#"
        myReport.DataDefinition.RecordSelectionFormula = DateRange
    End If
End Sub
```

The code creates a new string for the record selection formula. It uses the IN and TO operators to test the date range. The TO operator creates a date range between the values txtStartDate and txtEndDate. The IN operator checks if the Order Date falls within this range. When using dates within the record selection formula, each date is surrounded by a matching pair of # characters.

The new string is assigned to the RecordSelectionFormula property of the reports DataDefinition class. When the report runs, it uses this string to select the records that are displayed.

Printing by Order ID

Let's build on this example by creating another report. It's similar to the sales history report, but it groups by Order ID. Figure 21-12 shows the spec for it.

Customer Name		ORDER HISTORY BY ORDER ID					date
Customer Address							
Order Date	Order	Product ID	Product Name		Price	Qty	Cost
Order ID							
mm/dd/yy	xx	xx	xxxx		xx	xx	xx

			Total cost for Order ID				xxx

Figure 21-12. Report specs for printing sales history by order ID.

Let's start by identifying the changes that need to be made. First, group on the Order ID field, not the Order Date field. Have the ability to summarize the report. The detail records won't get printed. The report title needs to be dynamic so that it properly reflects how the report is being grouped. Since the Order ID field is being displayed in the group header, it doesn't need to be displayed in the Detail Section.

Since this report is so similar, one option is to create a new report and use the sales history report as the template. Then make the necessary changes for modifying the sort order. Another option is to use the same report and perform runtime customization to modify the sort order before the report runs. The first option is useful if you think that the format of the two reports will eventually be changed and therefore having two separate copies is a good idea. The second option is useful if the reports will always have the same format but only differ by the sorting order. In this example, we will perform runtime customization to illustrate how .NET works with the report object model.

Writing the First Draft

Changing the group field from the Order Date field to the Order ID field is probably going to be the most complex change. This requires getting a reference to the proper group section and changing the field that it uses for grouping.

Listing 21-4. Modifying the group field from Order Date to Order ID.

```
Private Sub SetGroupField(ByVal myReport As _
    CrystalDecisions.CrystalReports.Engine.ReportDocument)
    Dim myGroups As CrystalDecisions.CrystalReports.Engine.Groups
    Dim myField As CrystalDecisions.CrystalReports.Engine.FieldDefinition
    'Modify the group to use Order ID rather than Order Date
    'Get the field to base the group on
    myField = myReport.Database.Tables("Orders").Fields("Order ID")
    'Access the group by traversing the groups collection
    myGroups = myReport.DataDefinition.Groups
    Dim myGroup As CrystalDecisions.CrystalReports.Engine.Group
    For Each myGroup In myGroups
        If myGroup.ConditionField.Name = "GroupMonth" Then
            myGroup.ConditionField = myField
        End If
    Next myGroup
    myReport.DataDefinition.FormulaFields("GroupMonthText").Text = _
    "CStr({Orders.Order Id},'####')"
End Sub
```

After declaring the variables, the code gets a reference to the Order ID field and assigns it to the myField variable. It does this by referencing the Fields collection of the report's Database object. The next step is to traverse the Groups collection and find the group that needs to change. The only way to uniquely identify each group is to examine the ConditionField.Name property. This property stores the name of the field that the group is based on. There is no property to get the actual group's name, so we have to use this roundabout method instead. We know that the group is based on the formula GroupMonth, so that is what we are looking for.

> ### Note
> When you normally reference a report formula field, it is prefaced with the @ character. But when referencing a formula in the ConditionField.Name property, the @ character is not included in the name.

When the correct group is found, assign the myField variable to the ConditionField property. This overrides the GroupMonth formula and uses the Order ID field instead.

Add a call to the SetGroupField() method from the Preview button's click event and see the results in Figure 21-13.

December - 1996						
12/11/1996	1,041	301,201	SlickRock	$764.85	1	$764.85
				Total cost for December - 1996		$764.85
December - 1996						
12/24/1996	1,092	3,301	Guardian Chain Lock	$4.50	2	$9.00
12/24/1996	1,092	1,111	Active Outdoors Lycra Glove	$16.50	2	$33.00
				Total cost for December - 1996		$42.00
January - 1997						
01/06/1997	1,143	4,102	InFlux Crochet Glove	$12.83	1	$12.83
01/06/1997	1,143	1,107	Active Outdoors Lycra Glove	$16.50	3	$49.50
				Total cost for January - 1997		$62.33

Figure 21-13. The report preview after changing the grouping to Order ID.

Writing the Second Draft

At this point, the report looks a little funny. The report is grouping by Order ID, but the group heading still shows the month formula that the original report showed. This is due to how we set the group options. If you recall from before, when this group was created we went to the Change Group Options dialog box and set the option for Customize Group Name Field. Rather than use the field's value for the group name, a formula was used instead. What is happening is that even though the programming code changes the field that the group is based on, the group name still uses the same formula that was entered in the Change Group Options dialog box.

To fix this, we need to directly modify the formula that the group name is based on. Unfortunately, Crystal Reports only lets you change this property when designing the report because the report object model doesn't expose this as a property that can be modified. The alternative solution is to create a new report formula that has the same information and make the group name point to this new report formula. Since we can change report formulas during runtime, then this has the same effect as changing the group name.

Tip

A lot of report properties aren't exposed via the report object model. So there isn't a direct way to modify them during runtime. But there is a trick that lets you get around this: replace the value with a formula. Since all report formulas can be modified during runtime, modifying the formula results in modifying the property value. Create a report formula that holds this value and then use the Formula Editor to set the property equal to that formula. When the report runs, instead of trying to modify the actual property, modify the formula that the property references.

The first thing to do is take the custom formula used for the group name and put it into a new report formula. Go to the Fields Explorer, right-click on Formulas and select New.

Give the formula the name GroupNameText and enter the following formula.

```
formula = CStr({Orders.Order Date}, "MMMM - yyyy")
```

After you save the formula and are back at the report designer, right-click on the group header and select Change Group.

Select @GroupMonth and click the Options button. This opens the Change Group Options dialog box.

At the bottom of the dialog box, click on the formula button for the Use Formula as Group Name. In the Formula Editor, change the formula to the following. This sets the group name to display the @GroupMonthText formula.

```
formula = {@GroupMonthText}
```

Now that the group name is pointing to the new formula, we can change the formula during runtime to display the Order ID. Add this code to the end of the SetGroupField() method.

myReport.DataDefinition.FormulaFields["GroupMonthText"].Text = "CStr({Orders.Order Id},'####')";

This line of code uses the FormulaFields collection to access the formula GroupMonthText and change its formula. The new formula is the Order ID converted to a string and formatted so that it doesn't display any commas or decimals. Now when the report is run, it should look like Figure 21-14.

1041						
12/11/1996	1041	301,201	SlickRock	$764.85	1	$764.85
				Total cost for 1041		$764.85
1092						
12/24/1996	1092	3,301	Guardian Chain Lock	$4.50	2	$9.00
12/24/1996	1092	1,111	Active Outdoors Lycra Glove	$16.50	2	$33.00
				Total cost for 1092		$42.00
1143						
01/06/1997	1143	4,102	InFlux Crochet Glove	$12.83	1	$12.83
01/06/1997	1143	1,107	Active Outdoors Lycra Glove	$16.50	3	$49.50
				Total cost for 1143		$62.33

Figure 21-14. The report preview after fixing the group name formula.

Now let's take care of the other changes that need to be made. Changing the report to a summary report only requires setting the Suppress property to True. First add a checkbox to the form called chkSuppress. Label it with "Summarize Data".

Changing the Suppress property of the Details Section requires getting a reference to it from the object model. The easiest way to do this is to use the Sections collection and pass it the name of the section. Right now, the Details

Section name is called Section3. This is the name that was automatically assigned to it by default. Since the name Section3 isn't intuitive, change the name to Details. Click on the detail section header and go to the Properties Window to change the name.

Now that the section has a better name, let's write the runtime code which turns the Suppress property on or off.

Listing 21-5. Suppressing the Details section.

```
Pulbllic Sub SuppressDetails(myReport as CrystalDecisions.CrystalReports.Engine.ReportDocument)
    If chkSuppress.Checked Then
        myReport.ReportDefinition.Sections["Details"].SectionFormat.EnableSuppress = True
    End If
End Sub
```

When the Summarize Data checkbox is checked, the EnableSuppress property is set to True for the Details section.

Order Date	Order	Product ID	Product Name	Price	Quantity	Product Cost

City Cyclist
7464 South Kingsway
Suite 2006
Sterling Heights, MI 48358
USA

Order History by Month   10/19/2002

February - 1996

                                        Total cost for February - 1996 $764.85
December - 1996

                                        Total cost for December - 1996 $4,369.05
January - 1997

Figure 21-15. The report preview when the detail records are suppressed.

There are two more changes that need to be made. The first is to modify the report header so that it says that the report is grouped by Order ID. This is simple enough. Just change the ReportTitle property of the SummaryInfo object.

The second change is to take the Order ID field out of the Details Section. Since the Order ID is being displayed in the group header, it doesn't need to be repeated in the Detail Section. This involves suppressing the data field and its associated caption. Since we are changing the properties of report objects, let's rename them to something more descriptive than their default names. Click on the Order ID field in the Detail Section and rename it to fldOrderId. Click on the associated caption in the Group Header section above it and rename it to txtOrderId. Suppress these two fields by setting the EnableSuppress property to True.

Listing 21-6. Suppressing the Order ID and changing the report title.

```
Private Sub UpdateForOrderId(ByVal myReport As _
    CrystalDecisions.CrystalReports.Engine.ReportDocument)
    'Suppress the Order Id field and it's caption
    Dim myObject As CrystalDecisions.CrystalReports.Engine.ReportObject
```

```
myObject = myReport.ReportDefinition.ReportObjects("txtOrderId")
myObject.ObjectFormat.EnableSuppress = True
myReport.ReportDefinition.ReportObjects("fldOrderId").ObjectFormat.EnableSuppress = True
'Change the title of the report
myReport.SummaryInfo.ReportTitle = "Sales History by Order Id"
End Sub
```

All the changes that need to be made are finished, but before running the report, let's clean up the user interface. Since there are now two reports, we need to give the user the option to choose which report should run.

Let's use two radio buttons to specify whether the user wants to print the report that groups by month or the report that groups by Order ID. We should also put the options in a GroupBox control so that they don't conflict with any radio buttons that might get added in a future revision of the program.

Add a GroupBox control to the form and title it "Report Selection".

Add two radio buttons inside the GroupBox control and call one optByMonth and the other optByOrderId. Label them appropriately.

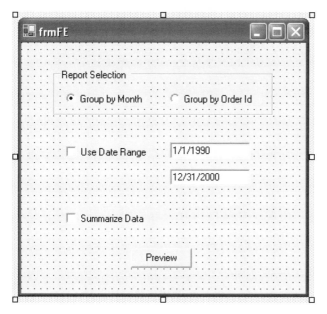

Figure 21-16. The report selection form.

Finally, the code needs to be added that determines which report to print based upon these option buttons. Not only that, but it should also take into account all the procedures that have been written for this chapter and call them as well. Listing 21-7 shows the final code for clicking on the Preview button.

Listing 21-7. The Preview button's Click event.

```
Private Sub btnReport_Click(ByVal sender As Object, ByVal e As System.EventArgs) _
    Handles btnPreview.Click
    Dim myReport As New rptOrderHistory
    Dim OrdersPreview As New frmPreview(myReport)
    'If printing by Order ID, make the necessary changes
    If optByOrderId.Checked Then
        SetGroupField(myReport)
        UpdateForOrderId(myReport)
    End If
    'Both reports can use the other features
    SetDateRange(myReport)
    SuppressDetails(myReport)
    'Preview the report
    OrdersPreview.ShowDialog()
End Sub
```

When the program is run and a standard report is printed by Order ID, it should look like Figure 21-17.

City Cyclist 7464 South Kingsway Suite 2006 Sterling Heights, MI 48358 USA	Sales History by Order Id				10/19/2002
Order Date	**Product ID**	**Product Name**	**Price**	**Quantity**	**Product Cost**
1					
12/02/1996	2201	Triumph Pro Helmet	$41.90	1	$41.90
			Total cost for 1		$41.90
1033					
12/08/1996	102181	Mozzie	$1,739.85	2	$3,479.70
12/08/1996	1101	Active Outdoors Crochet Glove	$14.50	1	$14.50
12/08/1996	1105	Active Outdoors Crochet Glove	$13.05	2	$26.10
			Total cost for 1033		$3,520.30

Figure 21-17. The final report printed by Order ID.

Customizing the Report Viewer

Another example that can build upon what we've done so far in this chapter is to customize the report viewer. We're going to build a preview form which gives you the ability to turn every option on or off. It will also let you override every option with your own functionality. Although it's unlikely anyone will ever need all the functionality that this example provides, it will make a good reference for the future.

There are three primary areas of the viewer that can be worked with: hiding the toolbar's buttons, changing the viewer's layout, and manually implementing the same functionality. Hiding the toolbar's buttons consists of setting certain properties to True or False. Changing the viewer's layout consists of enabling/disabling the group window, the status bar and the toolbar. The viewer's functionality can be manually implemented within your application by calling the methods of the viewer control.

Adding General Features

Before jumping into how to make a lot of changes using the viewer, let's start by taking care of the basic form management features first. Most applications have a way to open a document, close the document and exit the program. The same applies to this example except that we are going to want to open and close reports.

Since frmPreview has the viewer control on it, we'll modify it. All the changes to this form are going to be implemented with a menu control. Menus are very easy to work with and they don't take any additional room on the form. This lets us continue to allocate the entire form for displaying the viewer control.

Go to design mode for frmPreview and double-click the MainMenu control in the Toolbox. This adds a menu to the form.

Add the main menu option File and below it add the items Open, Close and Exit.

Add the OpenFileDialog control to the form by going to the Toolbox and double-clicking on the control.

The Open menu option displays the OpenFile dialog box and prompts the user to select a report file. When the OK button is clicked, the filename is passed to the Load() method of the ReportDocument object. This loads the report into memory and it is then passed to the viewer object.

Listing 21-8. Opening and previewing a report file.

```
Private Sub mnuOpen_Click(ByVal sender As Object, ByVal e As System.EventArgs) _
    Handles mnuOpen.Click
    'Set the file filter to only show reports
    openFileDialog1.Filter = "Crystal Reports|*.rpt"
    If openFileDialog1.ShowDialog() = DialogResult.OK Then
        'Load the report into memory and preview it
        Dim myReport As New CrystalDecisions.CrystalReports.Engine.ReportDocument
        myReport.Load(openFileDialog1.FileName)
        crystalReportViewer1.ReportSource = myReport
    End If
End Sub
```

Closing the report is done by setting the ReportSource property to Nothing (null for C#).

Listing 21-9. Closing the report.

```
Private Sub mnuCloseFile_Click(ByVal sender As Object, _
    ByVal e As System.EventArgs) Handles mnuCloseFile.Click
```

```
crystalReportViewer1.ReportSource = Nothing
End Sub
```

Exiting the form is done by calling the Close() method of the Me object (this for
C#).

Listing 21-10. Closing the form.

```
Private Sub menuItem1_Click_1(ByVal sender As Object, _
    ByVal e As System.EventArgs) Handles menuItem1.Click
    Me.Close()
End Sub
```

The standard tasks of managing the form are finished. Let's start customizing
the different features of the viewer control.

Hiding the Toolbar Buttons

Enabling and disabling the toolbar buttons is pretty simple because each button
has a corresponding property that hides it. Set the property to true and the
button will not be shown. Figure 21-18 shows the Properties Window for the
toolbar control. You can see that there is a property listed for each button.

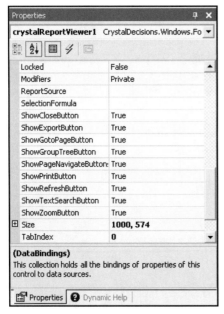

Figure 21-18. The Properties Window for the viewer toolbar.

Create a new menu item titled "Toolbar" and add an item for each button on
the viewer's toolbar. It should look like Figure 21-19.

Figure 21-19. The menu options for manipulating the toolbar.

Notice that each menu item is checked by default. This is because we want each button on the toolbar to be displayed when the form opens. Hiding the button is done by clicking on the menu option. The checkmark goes away and the corresponding button is hidden. The code for hiding the Zoom button is shown in Listing 21-11.

Listing 21-11. Implementing the Zoom menu option.

```
Private Sub mnuZoom_Click(ByVal sender As Object, ByVal e As System.EventArgs) _
    Handles mnuZoom.Click
    mnuZoom.Checked = Not mnuZoom.Checked
    crystalReportViewer1.ShowZoomButton = mnuZoom.Checked
End Sub
```

When the user clicks on the menu item it immediately reverses the value of the Checked property. If the option is checked, then this will uncheck it. If it is already unchecked, then this will check it. The button's Checked property is set to the Checked property of the menu item. If the menu item is checked, then the button is displayed. Otherwise it is hidden.

The rest of the toolbar's buttons use the same code. The only things that change are the property names and the associated menu items.

Replacing the ToolBar Functionality

After hiding all the buttons on the toolbar, you need to replace their functionality within your application. The viewer has a method for each button on the toolbar. We are going to add menu options that correspond with every button on the toolbar and implement the code to call the appropriate methods.

The methods that implement this functionality are well named, but not completely intuitive. Table 21-1 is provided as a reference that lists each method for you.

Table 21-1. Method reference for the viewer control.

Method Name	Method Description
CloseView()	Close current tab.
ExportReport()	Export the report.
ShowNthPage()	Go to a page.
ShowFirstPage()	Navigate to first page.
ShowNextPage()	Navigate to next page.
ShowPreviousPage()	Navigate to previous page.
ShowLastPage()	Navigate to last page.
PrintReport()	Print the report.
RefreshReport()	Refresh the report.
SearchText()	Search for text.
Zoom()	Zoom.

Add a menu item for each method available. The menu items should look like Figure 21-20.

Figure 21-20. The menu options for manipulating the toolbar.

Most of the menu options are trivial to implement. For example, the go to the last page of a report, call the ShowLastPage() method. This is implemented in Listing 21-12.

Listing 21-12. Calling the ShowLastPage() method.

```
Private Sub mnuManualLastPage_Click(ByVal sender As Object,  ByVal e As System.EventArgs) _
Handles mnuManualLastPage.Click
    crystalReportViewer1.ShowLastPage()
End Sub
```

Other methods only require the addition of prompting the user for input. For example, the SearchText() method takes a single string as its input. The following code uses the VB6 InputBox() to prompt the user for the text to search for.[48] Then it calls the SearchText() method.

Listing 21-13. Searching for text in a report.

```
Private Sub mnuManualSearch_Click(ByVal sender As Object, _
    ByVal e As System.EventArgs) Handles mnuManualSearch.Click
    Dim SearchText As String
    SearchText = Microsoft.VisualBasic.Interaction.InputBox("Search Text", "", "0", 50, 50)
    crystalReportViewer1.SearchForText(SearchText)
End Sub
```

The methods ShowNthPage() and Zoom() require passing an Integer parameter. The Close() method either takes a string representing the name of the tab to close, or Nothing to close the currently selected tab.

Customizing the Viewer Layout

This application also has the options to change the viewer layout. There are three controls that can be hidden: the GroupTree, the ToolBar, and the StatusBar. The first two can be turned on or off by setting a single property to True or False. For example, the following line of code hides the group tree.

```
CrystalReportViewer1.DisplayGroupTree = False
```

Hiding the toolbar is done by setting the DisplayToolbar property to False.

Hiding the StatusBar is more complicated. The viewer doesn't have a property to hide the StatusBar because it is always displayed. A way around this is to increase the viewer's height. This has the effect of hiding the StatusBar below the visible region of the form.

This idea works really well, but you have to be careful if the viewer has its Dock property set to Fill. When this is the case, you have to set it to None so that you can change the viewer's height. But when you set this property to None, it automatically resizes the viewer to its original size when in design mode. This has the potential to make the width of the viewer too small. To get around this problem, you have to save the values of the height and width properties prior to setting the Dock property to None, and then restore these values afterwards. Listing 21-14 shows the complete code for the StatusBar menu option.

Listing 21-14. The menu option to hide the StatusBar control.

```
Private Sub mnuStatusBar_Click(ByVal sender As Object, _
```

---

[48] The InputBox is included by default with VB.NET for compatability purposes. If you are using C#, click on Project | Add References and add a reference to Microsoft Visual Basic .NET Runtime.

```
ByVal e As System.EventArgs) Handles mnuStatusBar.Click
    Dim NewHeight, NewWidth As Integer
    mnuStatusBar.Checked = Not mnuStatusBar.Checked
    If Not mnuStatusBar.Checked Then
        'Increase the height by 20 to hide the status bar
        NewHeight = crystalReportViewer1.Height + 20
        'Keep the current width the same
        NewWidth = crystalReportViewer1.Width
        crystalReportViewer1.Dock = DockStyle.None
        'Set the size to what it needs to be
        crystalReportViewer1.Height = NewHeight
        crystalReportViewer1.Width = NewWidth
    Else
        'Display the statusbar by setting it back to Fill
        crystalReportViewer1.Dock = DockStyle.Fill
    End If
End Sub
```

Another feature that we can add to the viewer is to display all the events that are triggered as the user navigates through the report. Having every event documented as it gets fired would be very educational for seeing how much information can be derived about what the user is doing. Certain events can be used to add a custom StatusBar to the viewer. For example, you can display the current zoom level of the report by handling the ViewZoom() event.

Since the viewer is a control, it inherits from the UserControl class. This means that it has dozens of events that are fired continuously. Since these are standard events that aren't specific to displaying reports with the viewer class, we will ignore them in this application. Instead, the program will only handle the events that are unique to report writing. The events that are being used here are Navigate(), ReportRefresh(), Search() and ViewZoom().

To create the event viewer, first add a ListBox control to the form that has the viewer control and call it lstEvents.

Change the Dock property to Right. This will list all the events on the right side of the screen.

Displaying the information as each event is fired is pretty simple. An event uses two parameters to pass information. The first is an object that represents the sender and the second is an object with properties specific to the event. We use the second object parameter to display the important properties in the ListBox. The properties are different for each event and you should consult the MSDN help file for a complete reference.

For each of the report specific events, enter code that updates the ListBox with the relevant information. Listing 21-15 shows the code for the Search() event.

Listing 21-15. Displaying information relating to the Search() event.

```
Private Sub crystalReportViewer1_Search(ByVal [source] As Object, _
    ByVal e As CrystalDecisions.Windows.Forms.SearchEventArgs) Handles _
    crystalReportViewer1.Search
    lstEvents.Items.Add(("Search: " & e.TextToSearch))
    lstEvents.Items.Add(("Found on Page: " & _
        crystalReportViewer1.GetCurrentPageNumber().ToString()))
End Sub
```

When the application runs, these events get fired in response to the user's actions. But this is really a tool that we as programmers are going to use to learn more about how Crystal Reports works. It isn't a feature that you want a user to see by default. To keep the events hidden, set the Visible property of the ListBox control to False.

Once the program starts running, we want to be able to view the events when necessary. Add another menu item under the Viewer option called Show Events. When this menu option is clicked, it sets the Visible property to True.

Showing the ListBox causes a problem with the viewer control because the two overlap each other. This results in a portion of the report being hidden. Fixing this problem requires resizing the viewer control so that its right edge is adjacent to the left edge of the ListBox. This is done in a manner similar to hiding the StatusBar control. You have to save the viewer's location properties, set the Dock property to None, and then resize the viewer using the saved properties. Listing 21-16 shows the code for handling the Show Events menu item.

Listing 21-16. The menu option to show the events.

```
Private Sub mnuShowEvents_Click(ByVal sender As Object, ByVal e As System.EventArgs) _
Handles mnuShowEvents.Click
    mnuShowEvents.Checked = Not mnuShowEvents.Checked
    If mnuShowEvents.Checked Then
        Dim NewHeight, NewWidth As Integer
        lstEvents.Visible = True
        'Keep the same height
        NewHeight = crystalReportViewer1.Height
        'Subtract the left edge of the listbox to get the new width
        NewWidth = lstEvents.Left - crystalReportViewer1.Left
        crystalReportViewer1.Dock = DockStyle.None
        'Resize the viewer
        crystalReportViewer1.Height = NewHeight
        crystalReportViewer1.Width = NewWidth
    Else
        'Hide the listbox and set the viewer back to full screen
        crystalReportViewer1.Dock = DockStyle.Fill
        lstEvents.Visible = False
```

```
    End If
  End Sub
```

When the program is run and the ListBox is shown, it should look similar to Figure 21-21.

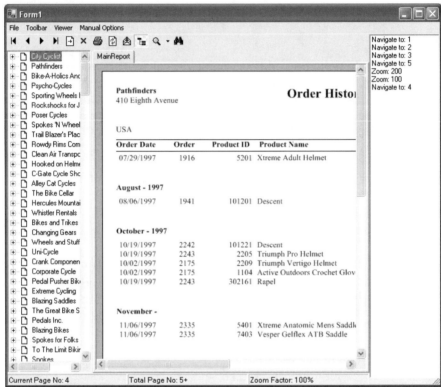

Figure 21-21. Displaying the event viewer ListBox.

APPENDIX A
Crystal Syntax Reference

Chapter 8 taught programming using Basic syntax as the primary language. This appendix builds on that chapter by showing you the Crystal syntax. It should be used as a companion tutorial with Chapter 8. It strictly shows what is unique about Crystal syntax compared to Basic syntax. It doesn't try to teach you programming all over again. The best way to use this appendix is to read through Chapter 8 first and become familiar with all the concepts. Then come back and read this appendix to see what the differences are with Crystal syntax.

The end of this appendix has conversion tables from Basic syntax to Crystal syntax. You'll notice that most of the functions are identical and there are only a few differences. The tables list the function names only. If you need more information about how the functions work, look at the table captions to get their reference number and flip back to Chapter 8 or 9 to see the details.

Writing Comments

Crystal syntax uses // within a line to comment out the remaining characters.

```
//This is a comment
```

Line Terminators

Crystal syntax uses the semicolon to mark the end of a line. A programming statement can use multiple lines with no special characters. If there are multiple statements within a formula, then use the semicolon to separate the lines. If a formula only has one line of code, no semicolon is needed (but you can put it there if you wish).

```
X := 5;  \\ This is a single line
Y := "This is also "
& "a single line";
```

Returning a Value

To return a value with Crystal syntax, put the value on a line by itself. Nothing else should appear on the line. The following code returns True if the employee received a bonus. If not then False is returned.

```
If {Employee.Bonus} > 0 Then
    True
```

```
Else
    False
```

Declaring Variables

Crystal syntax lists the variable scope and data type before the variable name.

```
Local datatype var
```

A variable's scope determines which formulas have access to that variable. There are three operators that you use to declare scope:

1. Local (Dim for Basic syntax): The variable can only be seen within the current formula. In a sense, a variable declared using the Dim keyword effectively defaults to Local scope.
2. Global: The variable can be seen within any formula inside the same report. Sub-reports do not have access to the variable.
3. Shared: Similar to Global, but the variable can also be seen within sub-reports.

```
Local HireDate As Date
Shared AffiliateCities() As String
```

In Crystal syntax the default scope is Global, not Local. This is the exact opposite of how Basic syntax handles the default scope.

Variable Assignment

Crystal syntax uses the := for assignment.

```
X := 5
```

Array Data Types

Crystal syntax uses square parentheses to specify the array bounds.

```
X[1] = 5
```

To declare an array with Crystal syntax, use the Array keyword after the data type.

```
Local NumberVar Array X
Local NumberVar Array Y[10]
```

Assigning values to an array is done in different ways. If you know what the values of an array are during the development process, you can initialize the array with these values using the MakeArray() function. Pass the MakeArray() function all the elements as a comma delimited list and it returns an array that is fully populated with these elements. When using the MakeArray() function you don't have to specify the array size. The compiler figures that out for you.

Range Data Types

Crystal syntax puts the Range keyword after the data type.

```
Local datatype Range var
```

Conditional Structures

Crystal syntax does not have an End If statement. It also considers the entire If block a single statement. Put the line terminator after the Else block to terminate it. The Else If keyword is actually two words. If there is more than one statement within a code block, then enclose the statements within parentheses and use the semicolon to terminate each statement.

```
If condition1 Then
    ...code...
Else If condition2 Then
    (
    ...code...;
    ...code...;
    )
Else
    ...code;
```

Crystal syntax Select statements are slightly different than Basic syntax. The Case keyword is only used for testing the conditions. Put a colon at the end of the condition. If no conditions match the value being tested, the program executes the Default case. There is no End keyword.

```
Select var
    Case condition1:
        ...code...
    Case condition1, condition2:
        ...code...
    Default:
        ...code...
```

For Next Loop

Crystal syntax uses := to assign the loop range and it has the Do keyword at the end of the line. Rather than terminating the loop with the Next keyword, it requires parentheses to surround the code block.

```
For var := start To end Step increment Do
(
    ...code...
```

```
If condition Then
    Exit For
End If
)
```

While and Do Loops

Crystal syntax has few looping structures to choose from. It has the While..Do loop and the Do..While loop. It uses parentheses to define the code block.

Code template for While ... Do:

```
While true_condition Do
(
    ...code...
)
```

Code template for Do..While:

```
Do
(
    ...code...
) While true_condition
```

Table 8-1. Data Type Default Values

Basic Data Type	Crystal Data Type	Default Value
Number	NumberVar	0
Currency	CurrencyVar	$0
Boolean	BooleanVar	False
String	StringVar	""
Date	DateVar	Date(0,0,0) – The Null Date value00/00/00
Time	TimeVar	No default valueNull
DateTime	DateTimeVar	No default valueNull

Table 9-1. String Analysis Functions

Basic Syntax	Crystal Syntax
Asc(str)	Asc(str)
Chr(val)	Chr(val)
Len(str)	Length(str)
IsNumeric(str)	N/A
InStr(start, str1, str2, compare)	InStr(start, str1, str2, compare)
InStrRev(start, str1, str2, compare)	InStrRev(start, str1, str2, compare)
StrCmp(str1, str2, compare)	StrCmp(str1, str2, compare)
Val(str)	Val(str)

Table 9-3. String Parsing Functions

Basic Syntax	Crystal Syntax
Trim(str)	Trim(str)
LTrim(str)	TrimLeft(str)
RTrim(str)	TrimRight(str)
Mid(str, start, length)	Mid(str, start, length)
Left(str, length)	Left(str, length)
Right(str, length)	Right(str, length)

Table 9-4. String Manipulation Functions

Basic Syntax	Crystal Syntax
Filter(str, find, include, compare)	Filter(str, find, include, compare)
Replace(str, find, replace, start, count, compare)	Replace(str, find, replace, start, count, compare)
StrReverse(str)	StrReverse(str)
ReplicateString(str, copies)	ReplicateString(str, copies)
Space(val)	Space(val)
Join(list, delimiter)	Join(list, delimiter)
Split(str, delimiter, count, compare)	Split(str, delimiter, count, compare)
Picture(str, template)	Picture(str, template)

Table 9-5. Conversion Functions

Basic Syntax	Crystal Syntax
CBool(number), CBool(currency)	CBool(number), CBool(currency)
CCur(number), CCur(string)	CCur(number), CCur(string)
CDbl(currency), CDbl(string), CDbl(boolean)	CDbl(currency), CDbl(string), CDbl(boolean)
CStr()	CStr()
CDate(string), CDate(year, month, day), CDate(DateTime)	CDate(string), CDate(year, month, day), CDate(DateTime)
CTime(string), CTime(hour, min, sec), CDate(DateTime)	CTime(string), CTime(hour, min, sec), CDate(DateTime)
CDateTime(string), CDateTime(date), CDateTime(date, time), CDateTime(year, month, day)	CDateTime(string), CDateTime(date), CDateTime(date, time), CDateTime(year, month, day)
CDateTime(year, month, day, hour, min, sec)	CDateTime(year, month, day, hour, min, sec)
ToNumber(string), ToNumber(boolean)	ToNumber(string), ToNumber(boolean)
ToText()	ToText()
IsDate(string), IsTIme(), IsDateTime()	IsDate(string), IsTIme(), IsDateTime()
IsNumber(string)	N/A
ToWords(number), ToWords(number, decimals)	ToWords(number), ToWords(number, decimals)

Table 9-8. Math Functions

Basic Syntax	Crystal Syntax
Abs(number)	Abs(number)
Fix(number, decimals)	Truncate(number, decimals)
Int(number), numerator \ denominator	Int(number), numerator \ denominator
Pi	Pi
Remainder(numerator, denominator), numerator Mod denominator	Remainder(numerator, denominator), numerator Mod denominator
Round(number, decimals)	Round(number, decimals)
Sgn(number)	Sgn(number)
Sqr(number), Exp(number), Log(number)	Sqr(number), Exp(number), Log(number)
Cos(number), Sin(number), Tan(number), Atn(number)	Cos(number), Sin(number), Tan(number), Atn(number)

Table 9-10. Date and Time Functions

Basic Syntax	Crystal Syntax
CurrentDate, CurrentTime, CurrentDateTime	CurrentDate, CurrentTime, CurrentDateTime
DateSerial(year, month, day), DateTime(hour, minute, second)	DateSerial(year, month, day), DateTime(hour, minute, second)
DateAdd(interval, number, date)	DateAdd(interval, number, date)
DateDiff(interval, startdate, enddate, firstdayofweek)	DateDiff(interval, startdate, enddate, firstdayofweek)
DatePart(interval, date, firstdayofweek, firstweekofyear)	DatePart(interval, date, firstdayofweek, firstweekofyear)
MonthName(date, abbreviate)	MonthName(date, abbreviate)
Timer	Timer
WeekDay(date, firstdayofweek)	DayOfWeek(date, firstdayofweek)
WeekdayName(weekday, abbreviate, firstdayofweek)	WeekdayName(weekday, abbreviate, firstdayofweek)

Appendix B

APPENDIX B
Report Object Model Diagrams

The reporting classes are mapped throughout the book in various chapters. This appendix shows the diagrams in a single location to make it easier for you to visualize their relationship. Each one is labeled with the original caption that was used in the chapter so that it is easy to go back and read more about it.

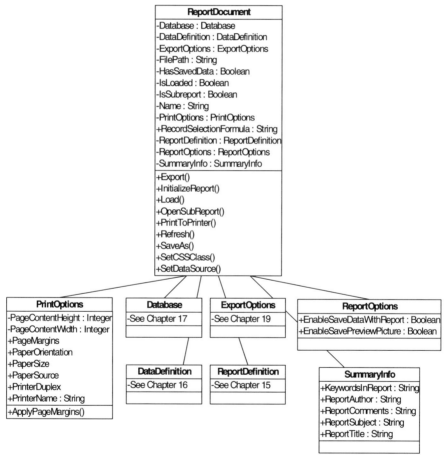

ReportDocument
- -Database : Database
- -DataDefinition : DataDefinition
- -ExportOptions : ExportOptions
- -FilePath : String
- -HasSavedData : Boolean
- -IsLoaded : Boolean
- -IsSubreport : Boolean
- -Name : String
- -PrintOptions : PrintOptions
- +RecordSelectionFormula : String
- -ReportDefinition : ReportDefinition
- -ReportOptions : ReportOptions
- -SummaryInfo : SummaryInfo

- +Export()
- +InitializeReport()
- +Load()
- +OpenSubReport()
- +PrintToPrinter()
- +Refresh()
- +SaveAs()
- +SetCSSClass()
- +SetDataSource()

PrintOptions
- -PageContentHeight : Integer
- -PageContentWidth : Integer
- +PageMargins
- +PaperOrientation
- +PaperSize
- +PaperSource
- +PrinterDuplex
- +PrinterName : String
- +ApplyPageMargins()

Database
- -See Chapter 17

ExportOptions
- -See Chapter 19

ReportOptions
- +EnableSaveDataWithReport : Boolean
- +EnableSavePreviewPicture : Boolean

DataDefinition
- -See Chapter 16

ReportDefinition
- -See Chapter 15

SummaryInfo
- +KeywordsInReport : String
- +ReportAuthor : String
- +ReportComments : String
- +ReportSubject : String
- +ReportTitle : String

Figure 14-2. The ReportDocument object model.

CrystalReportViewer
+DisplayBackgroundEdge : boolean
+DisplayGroupTree : boolean
+DisplayToolbar : boolean
+EnableDrillDown : boolean
-LogOnInfo : TableLogonInfos
-ParameterFieldInfo : ParameterFields
+ReportSource
+RightToLeft
+SelectionFormula : String
+ShowCloseButton : boolean
+ShowExportButton : boolean
+ShowGotoPageButton : boolean
+ShowGroupTreeButton : boolean
+ShowPrintButton : boolean
+ShowRefreshButton : Border
+ShowTextSearchButton : boolean
+ShowZoomButton : boolean
-ViewCount : Integer
+CloseViews()
+DrillDownOnGroup()
+ExportReport()
+GetCurrentPageNumber()
+PrintReport()
+RefreshReport()
+SearchForText()
+ShowFirstPage()
+ShowGroupTree()
+ShowLastPage()
+ShowNthPage()
+ShowPreviousPage()
+Zoom()

Figure 14-3. The CrystalReportViewer object model.

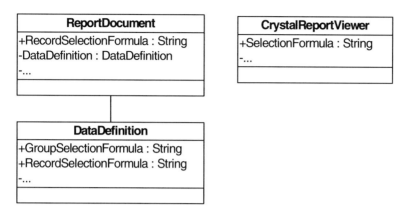

Figure 15-1. Properties used in selecting records.

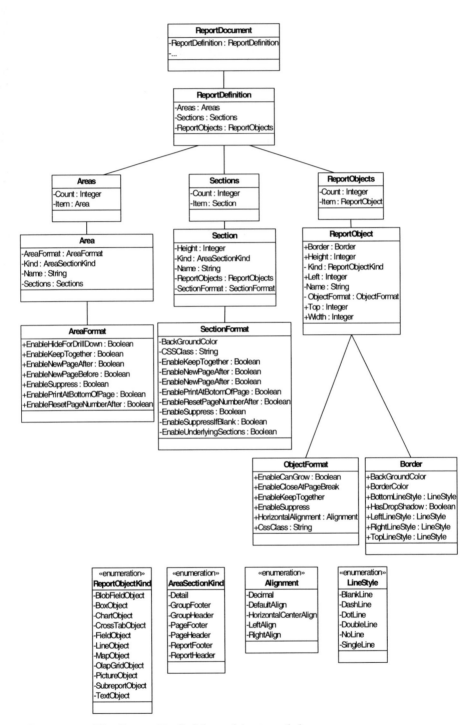

Figure 15-2. The ReportDefinition object model

FieldObject
+Border
+Color
-DataSource : FieldDefinition
-FieldFormat
+Font
+Height : Integer
-Kind : ReportObjectKind
+Left : Integer
-Name : String
+ObjectFormat : ObjectFormat
+Top : Integer
+Width : Integer
+ApplyFont()

FieldDefinition
-FormulaName : String
-Kind : FieldKind
-Name : String
-ValueType : FieldValueType

BlobFieldObject
+Border
-DataSource : FieldDefinition
+Height : Integer
-Kind : ReportObjectKind
+Left : Integer
-Name : String
+ObjectFormat : ObjectFormat
+Top : Integer
+Width : Integer

TextObject
+Border
+Color
- Font
+Height : Integer
- Kind : ReportObjectKind
+Left : Integer
-Name : String
+ObjectFormat : ObjectFormat
+Top : Integer
+Width : Integer
+Text : String
+ApplyFont()

SubreportObject
+Border
+EnableOnDemand : Boolean
+Height : Integer
-Kind : ReportObjectKind
+Left : Integer
-Name : String
+ObjectFormat : ObjectFormat
+Top : Integer
+Width : Integer
+OpenSubreport()

LineObject
+Border
+EnableExtendToBottomOfSection : Boolean
+EndSectionName : String
+Height : Integer
-Kind : ReportObjectKind
+Left : Integer
+LineColor
+LineStyle : LineStyle
+LineThickness : Integer
-Name : String
+ObjectFormat : ObjectFormat
+Top : Integer
+Width : Integer

PictureObject / ChartObject / CrossTabObject
+Border
+Height : Integer
-Kind : ReportObjectKind
+Left : Integer
-Name : String
+ObjectFormat : ObjectFormat
+Top : Integer
+Width : Integer

BoxObject
+Border
+EnableExtendToBottomOfSection : Boolean
+EndSectionName : String
+FillColor
+Height : Integer
-Kind : ReportObjectKind
+Left : Integer
+LineColor
+LineStyle : LineStyle
+LineThickness : Integer
-Name : String
+ObjectFormat : ObjectFormat
+Top : Integer
+Width : Integer

Figure 15-3. The report classes that inherit from the ReportObject class.

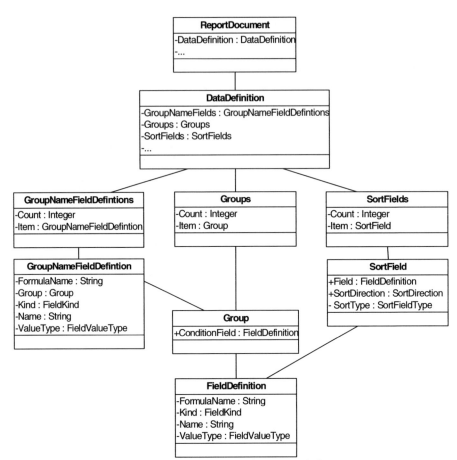

Figure 15-6. The Sorting and Grouping object model.

«enumeration» **FieldKind**	«enumeration» **FieldValueType**	«enumeration» **SortFieldType**	«enumeration» **SortDirection**
-DatabaseField -FormulaField -GroupFieldName -ParameterField -RunningTotalField -SpecialVarField -SQLExpressionField -SummaryField	-BitmapField -BlobField -BooleanField -ChartField -CurrencyField -DataField -DateTimeField -IconField -Int32Field -NumberField -OleField -StringField -TimeField	-GroupSortField -RecordSortField	-AscendingOrder -BottomNOrder -DescendingOrder -TopNOrder

Figure 15-7. Sorting and Grouping enumeration constants.

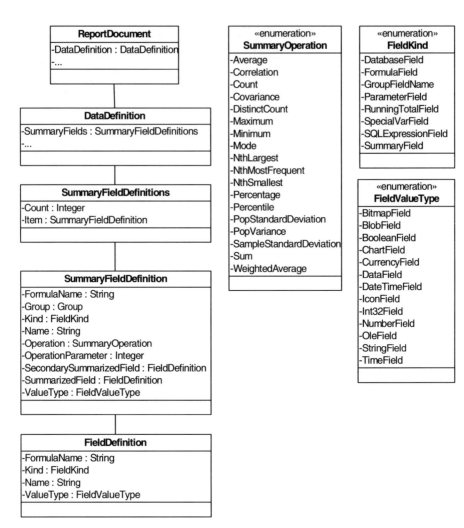

Figure 15-13. The Summary Field classes.

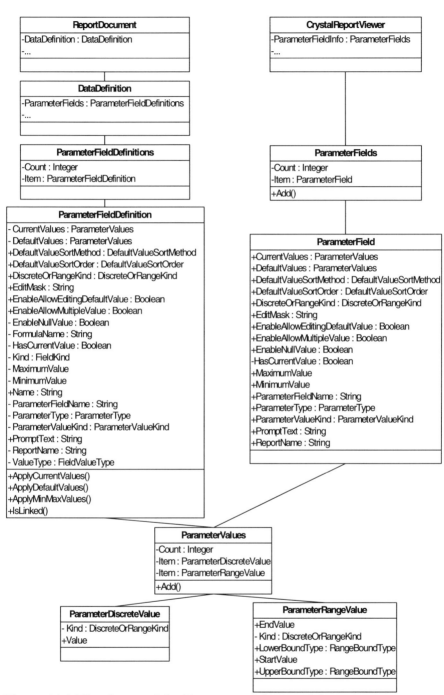

Figure 16-1. The classes of the Parameter object model.

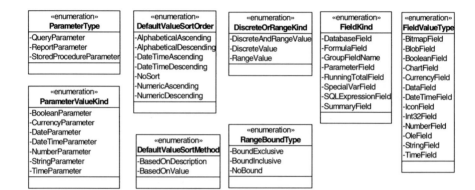

Figure 16-2. The enumeration constants of the Parameter object model.

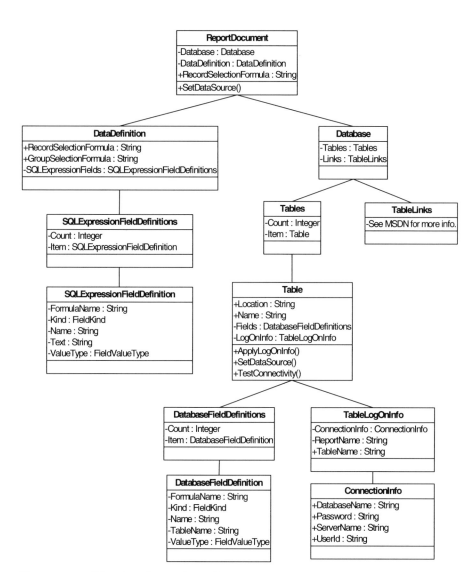

Figure 17-5. The Database class diagram.

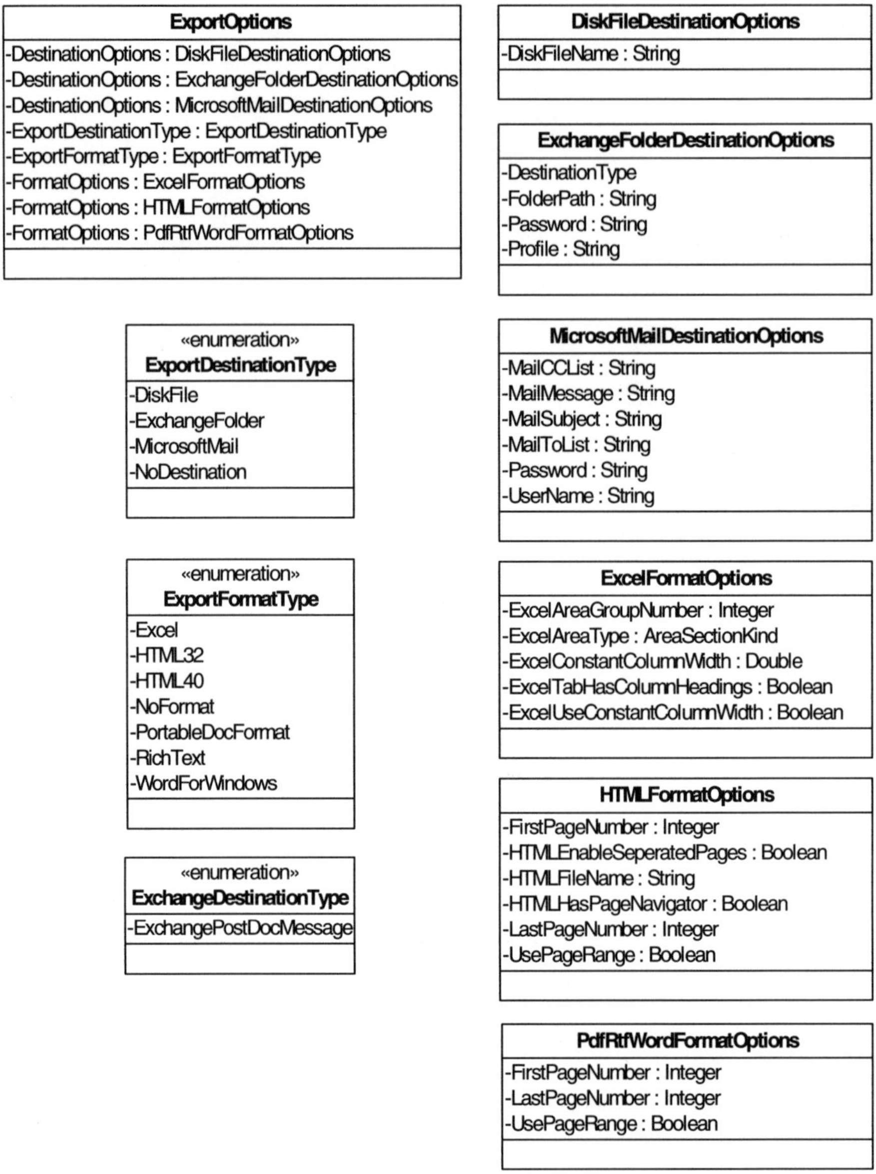

ExportOptions
-DestinationOptions : DiskFileDestinationOptions
-DestinationOptions : ExchangeFolderDestinationOptions
-DestinationOptions : MicrosoftMailDestinationOptions
-ExportDestinationType : ExportDestinationType
-ExportFormatType : ExportFormatType
-FormatOptions : ExcelFormatOptions
-FormatOptions : HTMLFormatOptions
-FormatOptions : PdfRtfWordFormatOptions

DiskFileDestinationOptions
-DiskFileName : String

ExchangeFolderDestinationOptions
-DestinationType
-FolderPath : String
-Password : String
-Profile : String

«enumeration» ExportDestinationType
-DiskFile
-ExchangeFolder
-MicrosoftMail
-NoDestination

MicrosoftMailDestinationOptions
-MailCCList : String
-MailMessage : String
-MailSubject : String
-MailToList : String
-Password : String
-UserName : String

«enumeration» ExportFormatType
-Excel
-HTML32
-HTML40
-NoFormat
-PortableDocFormat
-RichText
-WordForWindows

ExcelFormatOptions
-ExcelAreaGroupNumber : Integer
-ExcelAreaType : AreaSectionKind
-ExcelConstantColumnWidth : Double
-ExcelTabHasColumnHeadings : Boolean
-ExcelUseConstantColumnWidth : Boolean

HTMLFormatOptions
-FirstPageNumber : Integer
-HTMLEnableSeperatedPages : Boolean
-HTMLFileName : String
-HTMLHasPageNavigator : Boolean
-LastPageNumber : Integer
-UsePageRange : Boolean

«enumeration» ExchangeDestinationType
-ExchangePostDocMessage

PdfRtfWordFormatOptions
-FirstPageNumber : Integer
-LastPageNumber : Integer
-UsePageRange : Boolean

Figure 19-3. The Export object model.

APPENDIX C
Crystal Reports Resources

Finding information about Crystal Reports for .NET isn't always easy. Here is a list of resources that you can use.

http://support.CrystalDecsions.com – Find technical articles, a .NET forum for posting questions, and the latest service packs.

Microsoft.Public.vb.Crystal newsgroup – Originally created for VB6 programmers, it is now frequented by .NET programmers as well (both VB.NET and C#). I often browse the questions when I have free time. Please put ".NET" in the header then I will know (as well as others in the group) that it is a .NET specific question. Otherwise I will probably not even bother reading it.

http://www.tek-tips.com – There are four sections dedicated to Crystal Reports.

http://groups.yahoo.com/group/CrystalReportsDotNet – This is a public forum dedicated to Crystal Reports .NET. There is a decent amount of activity and knowledgeable members.

INDEX

The .NET Languages: A Quick Translation Guide

If you are looking for a quick way to translate code between VB.NET and C#, this book is just what you need. Reviewers have praised "The .NET Languages" for its no-nonsense writing style that is so uncommon in today's computer books. Concise and to the point so you can take programming code and convert it to either .NET language without wasting time. The jewel of this book is the translation tables found at the beginning of each chapter. Every syntax keyword is clearly listed with a one-to-one mapping between languages. You'll keep this book close to your computer for these tables alone. The remainder of each chapter follows up with explanations for avoiding the programming traps you can fall into if you aren't careful. As a bonus, VB6 programmers will find that the entire VB6 syntax is included so that you can upgrade your skills to .NET in record time.

Buy "The .NET Languages" at bookstores worldwide and on Amazon.com (ISBN 1-893115-48-8). Also available in Italian and French.